A Force Profonde

Pennsylvania Studies in Human Rights

Bert B. Lockwood, Jr., Series Editor

A complete list of books in the series is available from the publisher.

A Force Profonde

The Power, Politics, and Promise of
Human Rights

Edited by Edward A. Kolodziej

PENN

University of Pennsylvania Press

Philadelphia

51898694

10 9 8 7 6 5 4 3 2 1

Published by
University of Pennsylvania Press
Philadelphia, Pennsylvania 19104-4011

Library of Congress Cataloging-in-Publication Data

A force profonde : the power, politics, and promise of human rights / edited by
Edward A. Kolodziej.
    p. cm.—(Pennsylvania studies in human rights)
Includes bibliographical references and index.
ISBN 0-8122-3727-7 (cloth : alk. paper)
1. Human rights. 2. Political science. I. Kolodziej, Edward A. II. Series.

JC571.F628 2003
323—dc21

2003047384

Contents

Part III: Retrospect and Prospects

Chapter 1
A *Force Profonde*: The Power, Politics, and Promise of Human Rights

Edward A. Kolodziej

Whither Human Rights?

Chou En-lai was allegedly asked what he thought were the results of the French Revolution. He supposedly replied: "It's too early to tell." Adam Hochschild's prize-winning study of King Leopold's plundering of the Belgian Congo's rubber and ivory at the cost of countless native lives makes the same point. In tracing the careers of the long-forgotten reformers who exposed Leopold's depredations, Hochschild (1999, 306) linked their moral lineage as revolutionaries to the tradition of "the French Revolution and beyond." They selflessly dedicated their lives and fortunes to the human rights of people they scarcely knew. Their example continues to be emulated today in more ways than can be told. Evidencing his own revolutionary credentials, Hochschild concludes: "At the time of the Congo controversy a hundred years ago, the idea of human rights, political, social, and economic, was a profound threat to the established order of most countries on earth. It still is today."

Building on these insights, this volume takes stock of the vitality and impact of the force of human rights today—a *force profonde*, working through time and space, shaping and shoving human societies. Given space constraints, this study provides a selective set of up-to-date photographs of how well or ill this force is faring in key regions around the world. These snapshots reveal strategies pursued by key regional actors and the resources they dispose either to foster or to frustrate the realization of human rights. A regional, worm's eye view has been adopted to get clearer and sharper pictures of what is actually happening on the ground in the many ongoing struggles for human rights around the globe, to place into relief a bird's eye view—the photo album as a whole—which projects the global scale of this *force profonde*.

Human rights assume many forms, shaped by the historical, socioeconomic, political, and cultural conditions through which this revolutionary force works its will. Like photos of any complex process, the pictures displayed in the chapters below will hardly capture the full impact of its protean power. Nor do they—nor can they—freeze the rapidly changing circumstances under which human rights are fostered or frustrated. The immediate aim of this exhibition of regional photos is more modest. It attempts to contribute to a better understanding and explanation than we have now of how and why human rights advance in one region of the globe and are resisted or in retreat elsewhere. By that token, it highlights policy paths that might be taken to circumvent the many roadblocks barring progress.

This study is also down payment on a more long-term, ambitious goal. Regional descriptions of human rights struggles, like those in this volume, lay the groundwork for a theory of human rights—what we lack today, but need, to guide public policy. Much like the ancients who could recognize and even measure the impact of tides on their daily lives without being able to explain them, humans today are also quite capable of charting the force of human rights on their thinking, choices, and actions and those of their agents without being able to explain why this force arose, how it actually impels their responses to the socioeconomic and political imperatives they mutually confront, and the forms it assumes under these varying social conditions. It would be reassuring to be able to tell where rights are heading or at least to be able to identify the conditions for their protection and promotion. A theory of human rights, based on experience and observation and validated by systematic testing, would in principle be able to provide such guidance.

Given the complexity of human rights and the deep and presently intractable discord over their meaning, content, and exercise, a fully reliable theory of human rights is likely to exceed our grasp for some time to come. Given, too, the freedom of intelligent and creative humans to redefine the animating ideals of their societies and their own identities and worth—capacities consciously understood by enlarging numbers of people across cultures—there is little reason to believe that human rights represent some fixed point of convergence toward which its partisans are moving in lockstep. Yet no less evident is the crystallization of a moving consensus about what is permitted or not to be done to individuals and groups relative to those with power to abuse or abrogate their rights. This volume attempts to provide a sounding board capable of authentically rendering the dominant chord of a progressively enlarging consensus on human rights, while faithfully recording the dissonant voices at odds with this evolving accord.

Human Rights: A Contested Notion as a *Force Profonde*

This chapter briefly outlines the assumptions on which this volume is organized. It assumes that good theory begins with careful description of the thinking, decisions, and actions of relevant actors (King 1994). These descriptions should be viewed through a shared conceptual lens by all of the observers. Otherwise, they will be talking about different things and talking past each other.

This raises the first problem confronting the editor and contributors to this volume. Agreeing on a single lens through which to view the rival and conflicting notions of human rights across regions has not been easy. As the discerning reader will readily discover, the contributors do not always agree on the size, dimensions, or number of lenses to be used or where they should be focused. So it seems sensible in the interests of full disclosure to alert the reader to these differences.

For purposes of this discussion, however, the agreements are more important. We agree that the volume should pivot on the assumption that power—power in the broadest sense of the term—is indispensable for the realization of human rights—a point elaborated in more detail below. A theory of human rights, both empirical and normative, must be built on this foundational assumption. That beginning point sobers expectations about the daunting task before us. The volume's textured, in-depth discussions of the multiple and contrasting human rights struggles raging around the globe show human rights to be a protean force. No simple or single perspective can fully reveal the complex social networks within which human rights are embedded and pursued across states and regions.

The first two chapters, which (heroically) attempt to summarize conflicting Western and Islamic conceptions of human rights, were invited to underline the point that human rights are fundamentally contested notions over deeply held, genuinely affirmed values of central concern to millions of people. As the regional chapters further confirm, humans and their institutional and organizational agents disagree, not seldom violently, over their meaning as well as their social content and exercise. For example, consider the rights of women either between or within Western and Islamic societies. Contrast two Islamic societies—Turkey and Afghanistan. The secular Turkish state, ruling over a predominantly Muslim society, stands in stark contrast to recent Taliban rule in Afghanistan. The differences in social status, economic roles, and legal standing of women in these two Northern Tier states could not be greater. Turkey treats women as equal to men under the law; the Taliban systematically suppressed women's rights in applying their singular interpretation of Islamic law. Similarly, the place of women in Western societies has radically changed from that of a servile status, bereft of rights to property or voting, to that of growing equality with men across all comparative dimensions from income to child care, service in the military, and venues for competitive sports.

Disputes over human rights and their practice are not static. They are as dynamic and changing as the socioeconomic and political systems in which they are nurtured or negated. Human rights evolve in meaning and social impact as these systems change—an evolutionary process accelerated by the globalization of human exchanges sweeping relentlessly across states and peoples. Thomas Jefferson, revered for his proclamation of humankind's endowed right to "life, liberty, and the pursuit of happiness," now comes under scrutiny because of his ownership of slaves and his intimate relations with Sally Hemings. However liberal and farsighted Jefferson may have been for his era, his actions fell short of his words and well below today's standards. One can well wonder what future generations will think of those who today appear as human rights visionaries and reformers as ideas about human rights change.

The chapters on contrasting and clashing Western and Islamic views about human rights dampen expectations that human rights will submit to a simple set of universally acknowledged meanings and norms once and for all—now or ever. Valerie Hoffman argues persuasively that there may be more room for agreement between these traditions than meets the casual eye, but there is little doubt by her own accounting that the gulf between them remains wide. A closer look within these traditions also reveals internecine conflicts between conservatives and reformers in both camps. These conflicts, as Marvin Weinbaum's chapter on the Northern Tier describes, have reached a fever pitch of incipient civil war in Iran. As Taliban rule in Afghanistan revealed, Muslim extremists are no less prone than their homologues among other great religions to impose their constrictive social practices on the co-religious and to commit widespread criminal acts against humanity in attacking those whose beliefs they deplore. Ironically, Islam, viewed as a social process and historical product, more divides than unites Muslim countries and their domestic populations.

Those for or against the prevailing cultural canons and values within different cultures are relentless in their quest to put their stamp on what is authentically Western or Muslim. Which faction will become ascendant, if any, cannot be predicted with any degree of certainty. It is useful to remember that a century of two world wars and a Cold War arose from profound divisions over ideology *within* the Western camp. These internal culture clashes are no less true of other traditions. One is reminded, for example, of militant and passively contemplative forms of Buddhism and how these contrasting orientations clash in South Asia. As Stanley Kochanek's chapter suggests, the intractable conflict over Kashmir between Pakistan and India raises into question the very legitimacy of both states—built respectively on the rival principles of a theocratic and secular state. What is clear from these examples is that there is no single Western or Islamic model to which one can authoritatively repair—a dilemma confronting any attempt to reduce rich, historically determined, and heavily encumbered cultural heritages to a few principles or aphorisms.

It would be misleading, too, as the chapters on regional patterns of conflict over human rights detail, to believe that culture and religion are the only challenges to human rights. The deep splits, delineated in the chapters on South and Southeast Asia, the Northern Tier, and Africa, revolve as elsewhere around differences of nationality, ethnic and tribal origins, language, social status, gender, or class. The former Soviet republics and Eastern Europe, including the Balkans, split principally along ethnic and national lines. The decision of David Ben Gurion and early Israeli settlers to establish an ethnocentric popular regime rather than a liberal democratic polity along the lines of the United States inevitably worked to discriminate against the Arab minority, as Ilan Peleg contends. The violations of human rights committed by both the Algerian regime and its militant Muslim opponents have more to do with clashes over class, social status, economic privilege, and personal power than religious differences. The violence unleashed in Indonesia in the wake of the implosion of the Suharto regime was largely driven by ethnic and local tribal divisions as well as by fierce battles over competing economic interests among desperately impoverished peoples, as Clark Neher describes.

The West has not been spared these conflicts over identity. If they appear less violent today than at the dawn of the Protestant revolution, five centuries later their effects are still acutely apparent in Northern Ireland (not to say Canada and the United States). The splits within the West between rival Christian sects or between religious adherents and partisans of secularization are no less profound than those in other cultures, although the propensity to use violence to impose one's beliefs on others has dissipated since the religious wars of the seventeenth century. Howard Wiarda's chapter on Latin America traces the evolution of Catholic, hierarchical conceptions of rights and the recent challenge that Anglo-Saxon notions of equality and freedom pose to them. Yet both are clearly Western. Similarly, Michael Newman contrasts the radically different views of the European Union and the United States over the death penalty. Europeans have raised freedom from the death penalty, the ultimate state sanction, to a human right, while most Americans deny that such a right is justified.

Distinguishing Among Contesting Rights

Procedural or Substantive Rights?

In reading the chapters below, three key distinctions might be kept in mind as points of departure and comparison. First, are we talking about procedural or substantive rights (Donnelly 1984, 1989)? This is well-traveled ground. Under procedural rights are included political liberties guaranteeing humans rights to free speech, assembly, and petition. These protections extend to individuals and groups to shape and legitimate the rules and institutions governing them and to hold accountable elected officials in the exercise of their authority. They cover rights to organize politically, to compete for office, and to vote for candidates and policies without fear of coercion or intimidation. They also rest on the assumption of a uniform and equitably applied rule of law and freedom from torture, capricious arrest, or incarceration without cause.

This brief sketch skims only the surface of the claims made under the heading of procedural rights as human rights. Cited simply are the key rules, norms, and social processes in whose absence individual freedoms would otherwise be threatened and invaded. Procedural rights are also dedicated to ensuring a level playing field in the struggle for power and for freedom from unlawful coercive constraint, whether perpetrated by the state or civil society. They imply a rule of law applied equally and equitably to all parties. These procedural rights are no less important in defining how state power is to be acquired, legitimated, used, and constrained in protecting human rights. These larger social and political processes address not only human rights claims and their normative justification but all matters of paramount interest to individuals, including property, personal security, and quality of life concerns.

Substantive rights are similarly disputed notions and values. Partisans of substantive human rights insist that the deprived and destitute can scarcely be expected to worry much about procedural human rights if they lack the material means to exercise them. Or, if they can exercise such rights to some degree, it is not always clear whether they have equal access to centers of power to ensure that their concerns are heard and equitably addressed. Those in poverty are also typically exposed to greater threats to their security than those who have more wealth. The latter can more easily command state power in their service or rely on their private resources—what economists call clubs—to exercise their rights or, worse, to limit the free exercise of these rights by those who are less materially advantaged.

As Jack Donnelly observes, the West privileges the material welfare of its populations over foreign peoples. Moreover, it links Western and global material welfare to the adoption of market rules defined by an economically and technologically endowed West. Beyond these self-help formulae, there is little popular or elite sentiment to broaden the notion of human rights to establish an irrevocable right of all humans to some defined level of material subsistence or comfort and a corresponding obligation to create the conditions for its realization. That would imply enormous transfers of economic wealth, technological knowhow, and assistance—policy goals whose support would appear to be actually receding at this writing among the ascendant Western coalition of democratic market states in the post-Cold War era.

This broader conception of human rights, extending to the material welfare of populations, raises even more complex and challenging issues than those associated with procedural guarantees. They are not easily resolved since they imply considerations that go beyond the ideational and psychological claims of individuals and groups. Raised is the practical question of how to allocate scare resources and limited wealth over the enlarging demands of an expanding world population. Central to responding effectively to substantive human rights claims is how to decide between conflicting prescriptions to sustain economic growth. These encompass demands for the provision by the state and other agencies of minimal levels of food, shelter, health, education, and social welfare for national populations. As the Soviet experiment reveals, the state and its bureaucracies in control over all aspects of economic life can become more predators than providers of wealth and welfare (Kornai 1992). Neoclassical economists argue (Olson 1982), moreover, that there is no necessary relation between voting for greater equality in the distribution of wealth and the actual enjoyment of greater personal or national welfare, if the incentives to produce wealth are frustrated and refracted. The pie must first get bigger before the slices are passed around. The discipline of market rules—Thomas Friedman's (2000) "Golden Straitjacket"—and the privatization of investment are now, in the post-Cold War era, the prevailing formulae for the wealth of nations.

Conversely, if market rules are allowed to work unconstrained, it is certain that personal wealth and welfare will be unequally divided. The gap between haves and have-nots promises to widen, not narrow. There is also no assurance that adequate social safety nets will be constructed to meet the educational and welfare needs of populations exposed to the rigors of global markets (Hurrell 1995). Free markets are not designed to meet an equity test. Markets, unless qualified by human rights claims to offset inequitable outcomes, decide the relative power of actors in the market, the distribution of wealth among them, and their differential capacity to determine future economic priorities and investments.

Individual or Group Rights?

A second level of conflict is that between individual and group rights. The legacies of history conspire with the multiplication of diverse human societies and identities to preclude easy reconciliation any time soon between these two competing sets of rights. Yet both can be properly understood as falling within the larger set of fundamental human rights. The tensions between these rival claims are profound. From a moral and legal perspective, Western thought privileges individual human rights, precluding their invasion by investing the individual with moral and legal autonomy. National, ethnic, and cultural definitions of citizenship, as Jack Donnelly notes, increasingly cede to a juridical and potentially universal conception of human rights. These are enshrined in the French Declaration of the Rights of Man and in the U.S. Declaration of Independence as "certain inalienable rights; that among these are life, liberty, and the pursuit of happiness." These rights have come to be understood to be insulated from limitation by individuals, by groups within national and international civil societies, or—and especially—by states and their governing regimes. Governments, "deriving their just powers from the consent of the governed" are "instituted among men," as the signers of the Declaration of Independence instruct, "to secure these rights." Indeed, governments have a proactive obligation to extend these rights.

On the other hand, those animated by strong cultural, national, ethnic, or religious identities conceive human rights in collective or group terms. This is clearly the position taken by conservative and reformist Islamic theorists, as Valerie Hoffman describes. However much Muslims may disagree, and sometimes quite violently if the real and incipient civil wars, respectively, in Afghanistan and Iran are any indication, religiously defined group rights are in principle privileged over the claims of individuals. Many Christians assume the same divided stances. Take the struggles over abortion between the partisans of right to life and pro-choice or those for and against the death penalty. Those who assert a collective, religious identity as paramount, putatively dictated by an omnipotent creator, derive their conceptions of human rights from a stipulated divinely designed human nature. Rejected is the assumption of an autonomous individual whose personal choices and conduct are free of these moral constraints. Yet both camps claim devout Christian adherents among their partisans. This does not mean that those peoples who privilege group rights extend no rights to individuals, nor that individual rights enjoy little support or sanction. The contrasting attitudes of the Northern Tier states toward women say otherwise. The distinction between individual and group rights shifts in focus as one moves across regions. These categories mean different things to different people. Within each state the line between them shifts in impact and weight in how human rights are exercised, qualified, or prohibited. As Pascal suggested, rights change with geography.

Take, for example, the conflict between two social rights: self-determination and popular sovereignty (Bendix 1978). While self-determination is one of the few universally acknowledged principles of international governance today, there is, as James Mayall (1990, 1992) demonstrates, no agreed upon set of norms about how it should be applied or how the rival claims of self-determination and state sovereignty should be adjudicated. Self-determination has been successfully used against foreign rule. It was the single most important normative challenge to the legitimacy of European imperialism. As William Zartman's chapter also shows, it has been used, ironically, by self-appointed elites in Africa to arrest popular rule and human rights. Even so, self-determination remains a powerful force for mobilizing subject populations against oppressive states. National self-determination undermined the Soviet experiment calculated to surmount it (Kaiser 1994). To impose a socialist model on the Soviet Union's disparate ethnic and cultural groups, the regime, unwittingly, fostered and created national identities as a transition to a unified Soviet citizenry, principally among Central

Asian populations hitherto inured to national sentiment.[1] When the Russian national challenge to Communist rule was joined by the election of a Russian president for the first time in a millennium by the Russian people versus the legitimacy claims of the Communist regime under Mikhail Gorbachev, the Soviet Union was irreversibly pushed and pulled to its own dismemberment along national, not ideological, lines. There appears to be no clear end in sight for the working out of the principle of self-determination in global politics once it is set in train. Witness the Middle East (Palestinians), Africa (non-Muslims in Sudan), the Northern Tier (Kurds), Northeast, South and Southeast Asia (respectively Tibetans, Kashmiris, and East Timorese), and central Europe (the Balkan peoples), where this principle continues to play out in multiple forms in the struggles by otherwise vastly different peoples either for greater autonomy within a state—socioeconomic, cultural, or political—or for their own state and regime.

The *force profonde* of human rights is forged in these local and regional crucibles. What human rights relevant populations enjoy are fired in these local struggles. Pure or real conceptions of human rights, however heuristically useful as tools of analysis on which this volume draws, should not obscure the larger point, central to this volume, that these "pure" or "ideal" forms of human rights crystallize as historical products out of these forging processes. These historical products, impurities and all, are the real and true measures of human rights progress or regression. It bears repeating that social power counts—and counts decisively in determining whether human rights are, or can be, exercised. Explaining these power sources and supports for human rights goes far to explain variances in practices across states and regions.

Universal or Relative Rights?

A third set of distinctions to keep in mind is between the conceptions of human rights as universal or as relative. If universal, they apply to all human beings irrespective of social conditions and circumstances of time and place or of the cultural or particular social origins of human rights claims. History and local traditions have, putatively, little or no claim to limit the protection and exercise of these rights. The initial formulation of these rights in Western thought conceived them as universal and applicable to all humans, however much local or historical circumstances might have shaped their socioeconomic and political expression or however much the history of the Western imperial expansion testifies to their violation. Social contract theorists, their profound differences notwithstanding, agree on the notion of universal human rights. On this point, social contract theorists and their partisans stipulate these rights, although theorists like Hobbes, Locke, and Rousseau begin from different vantage points in addressing human rights and are focused on different moral and practical concerns (Laberge 1995; Rawls 1971).

The Kantian categorical imperative is also rooted in the presumed universality of humankind through reason and the sharing of a common human nature from which universal rules of ethical conduct can be deduced. If Kantian qualifications are introduced to account for and to justify different historical, cultural, and linguistic paths for democratization and civil and human rights across the globe (Kant 1970), these variances do not vitiate the stipulated universality of some set of human rights yet to be definitively defined and effectively accorded to all humans. It should be kept in mind that all the great religions—notably Christian, Muslim, Hindu, and Buddhist—preach a universal mankind and a divinely revealed code binding all humans, whether the latter acknowledge their particular interpretation of this revelation or not. These competing universal claims complicate enormously the problem of defining human rights coherently and cogently. This complexity does not necessarily lead to the presumption that human rights are inherently historical, contingent, and relative. That question remains open.

These ideational supports for a universal conception of human rights, however variously defined, run counter to the perspective of many contemporary theorists in the West. This philosophical position accords, curiously enough, with the interests of governing elites, principally in the developing world. For different but converging reasons, many contemporary Western social theorists subscribe to the proposition that all human values are relative. From this perspective, human rights are conventional, the products of prevailing social forces, and the relative power of individuals and groups to impose their preferences on others. As such, they have no foundation in nature or revelation. Socially defined and determined, they necessarily vary from one society to another over time and space. At one extreme of this position, the claims of human rights are put on the same plane with all other claims of power and depicted as in the service of oppressive state or capitalist interests (Foucault 1977). For their own particular interests, most if not all of the leaders of states outside the West are keen to stress the relativity of human rights—human rights with a Chinese character, as Beijing's apologists like to say. This line of defense is hardly new. Edmund Burke's (1909) philippic against the excesses of the French Revolution contrasted the historic rights of Englishmen against the claims of universal human rights for all mankind. This volume does not resolve this debate. It would have it both ways. It traces human rights as a universal force and normative ideal through key regions of the globe, but it is equally sensitive to the varying meaning, forms, and practices, which this *force profonde* assumes. The stance is neither to dismiss out of hand the possibility of discovering universal, existential claims for these rights as attributes of human life and its social expression, nor to discount the contending power and ideational contexts within which they are currently delineated.

Rights as Social Power

This background discussion brings us finally to the principal assumptions on which this volume rests. For purposes of analysis and comparison in the chapters below, human rights, whether viewed as a value or ideal or as the actual exercise of these values or ideals, are conceived as fundamentally social. Their realization depends on social and political supports. They cannot be enacted in a social power vacuum. Their existence in the consciousness of individuals and in their ability to enjoy a right—say freedom from torture or discrimination—implies a social context, power structures, and a process of decision and action by which these rights are understood and made available to humans if they choose to fight to attain them (Goertz 1994). Roy Bashkar (1998, 34) states this assumption succinctly in observing, "the social cannot be reduced to (and is not the product of) the individual. It is equally clear that society is a necessary condition for any intentional human acts at all." The volume identifies both key social power supports for the enjoyment by groups and individuals of human rights and, through feedback, the impact of human rights and their exercise as social facts on power structures across states, peoples, and cultures. Together this dialectical process of social ideals and power form the evolving contexts for local and global expression.

Consider, for example, the right to privacy as a limiting case. The notion of privacy immediately raises the question of private toward what? It implies the preexistence of a set of social relations that individuals wish to be excluded from in exercising their rights of privacy. Invasion could not come from any other source than from other humans, whether individuals or social agents, like states or corporations. Privacy thus depends on the cooperation of other actors—the state and members of civil society—for its exercise. These social and political arrangements and the collective support and inter-subjectively shared values in which those arrangements are embedded make privacy possible in some measure. This volume identifies some of these key institutional arrangements working at regional levels. They are the preconditions for the realization of human rights by individuals; they are the evidentiary grist for a mill grinding out a theory of human rights.

While the social composition of human rights, empirical and normative, is stipulated, the principal touchstone used in this volume to assess whether human rights are advancing or receding is the individual. For example, applied by this volume as a measure of human rights progress is a limit on the state's authority to invade group rights—say religious freedom—or the state's obligation to enlarge group rights—the end of racial segregation ordered by the U.S. Supreme Court. It is assumed that these group rights will be benefits extended to each and every member of the discriminated or oppressed group. Following this "pure" conception of human rights,[2] the group right, if honored by a state and civil society, is assumed to be consistent with all other claimed human rights attached to the individual. In other words, the awarding of a group right is not viewed here as a license to limit the human rights accorded an individual within the group. This perspective is also consistent with the view taken by several contributors—a point stressed in Edward Friedman's chapter on China—that one of the principal mechanisms for the advancement of human rights is the acquisition of those rights by a group. The English religious toleration acts, the U.S. civil rights laws, and the protections extended to untouchables in India illustrate how a group right translates into expanded individual human rights. Also implied is the corollary principle that enlarging group freedoms—say greater inter-ethnic tolerance—advances human rights if individuals within the group not only enjoy greater freedom, but also are also equally free of group constraints to which they have not given their consent.

The reader is advised to use the individual person or human being as the standard to assess the status of human rights across states and regions. This pivot point for comparison is obviously not without its problems. It does not solve the issue of the moving and changing notions of what a human right is, notably for those states and peoples who insist on the primacy of the group over the individual and the definition of human rights as derivative of that identity. It does at least identify a point of departure for the evaluation of human rights across states and regions as a product of social power. The Western bias of this move is acknowledged, but this does not imply that because rights were defined initially within a Western cultural setting that they could not also reflect universal aspirations. Edward Friedman's probing of ancient Chinese culture suggests that there is more room for overlap between Western and Asian conceptions of human rights than the Beijing regime will allow in its drive to suppress all real or imagined opponents to its rule. Valerie Hoffman is also convinced, editorial and some contributor skepticism aside, that there is not an unbridgeable gap between some reformist interpretations of the Prophet's message and the universal possession of human rights by believers and nonbelievers.

While the enjoyment of human rights, however conceived, resides in individuals, wherever they may be situated in a particular state or region, the existence of that right and the scope of its real or potential exercise is stipulated to depend on the social power mobilized to support or deny its realization. If a theory of human rights is to be advanced and confidently relied upon to guide public policy, it is important to recognize, as Thomas Risse-Kappen (1994) reminds us, that ideas (values really) do not "float freely." They are embedded in social power networks and institutions. These have positive or negative valences that determine whether human rights will survive and thrive in one region of the globe over another. These networks act as power grids. They supply rules, norms, and principles of social behavior that either sustain and protect human rights or impede or short-circuit the

possibility for their expression. Human rights as social constructs are activated when sustained by other humans and their agents—actors, disposing
varying resources, influence, and power to make human rights effective or
not. These actors pursue diverse and conflicting strategies either to support
or to resist the possession, expansion, and exercise of human rights. This
volume attempts to describe how these power grids work and how they work
for or against human rights.

Points of Comparison

The authors have been asked to sketch the human rights power grids or
networks working in their respective regions. Specifically, they address three
questions to enable comparisons and generalizations across these cases.
While they have not been uniformly attentive to each question—evidence
of the editor's limited persuasive skills—these questions and parallel author
responses still provide an epoxy binding the chapters together to provide a
montage of human rights that transcends the individual regional photos
comprising it.

What Are the Human Rights Agendas Across Regions?

First, what does the human rights agenda look like in the region under examination? This refers to those rights that regional actors believe are most
important to them (not just to the analyst or observer) either as claims to
be honored or as threats to the existing order if realized.

Not surprising is the diversity of the agendas of each state and region covered in this survey. In Europe, for example, the human rights agenda currently focuses on the rights of women and immigrants. Europe has passed
well beyond the primordial concerns of establishing a rule of law and institutions to ensure an open society. The European Union and its liberal democracies set a standard for other states, however much that those suffering a
denial of their rights might dispute progress. The European Union has
also gone farther than any other state in insisting that candidate states for
admission to its ranks meet rigorous democratic and human rights tests to
be considered as fully competent states. In effect, de facto and de jure principles of recognition are being applied to a state before it will be adjudged
by the member states of the European Union to be the legitimate representative of its population and to possess the properties of a state consistent with
the European ideal. Even member states like Austria, as Michael Newman
relates, are subject to review and sanctions if they condone political parties
or leaders who advocate ethnic and religious discrimination or who promote group hatred.

On the other hand, the European Union, like the United States, has
largely resisted raising substantive economic rights to the same privileged

level as procedural and political human rights. What can be said in its favor is that in absorbing the weak economies of Ireland, the Mediterranean states, and the German Democratic Republic, and in opening the European Union to East European state membership, the European Union has implicitly laid the groundwork for such a right to be recognized in principle as a consequence of its gradual realization in practice. Practices can eventually create new values, norms, and human rights where they did not exist before. The European Union's announced public agenda may unduly veil the degree to which it is actually promoting substantive human rights, even more than Michael Newman's analysis would seem to admit. If the expansion process eventually incorporates the states of Eastern Europe, the Balkans, and even Muslim Turkey, admission implies a compromise on welfare rules among member states to harmonize community economic policies. That is tantamount to honoring the claim that human rights include both procedural and substantive rights.

What is particularly striking between the Western democracies and most of the developing, non-Western world, including the states of the former Soviet Union, is the priority assigned to substantive socioeconomic over procedural rights by the latter. This is understandable, given the disparity between the developed West and developing states. Eighty percent of the world's wealth continues to be owned and disposed by 20 percent of the world's population, a division that continues despite the overall accumulation of wealth by the states of the world since World War II. Whatever the differences in the human rights agendas across developing states, and they all are scenario specific, there is a clear and discernible convergence that the West's control of the economic and technological resources of the world poses serious impediments for the sustained and expanding economic growth of four-fifths of the world's populations. This imbalance of power also raises serious human rights issues for these peoples. That the world now claps with one hand in having adopted world capitalistic markets as the principal solution to global welfare does in no way dilute the significance of this North-South split and economic inequality and the so-called digital divide as human rights concerns.[3] Measured by what is done, not just proclaimed, majority sentiment within the Western coalition resists stipulating substantive rights as universal with an accompanying obligation to ensure their realization. That is not true of most people and elites in the developing world, as the chapters covering these states affirm. The West currently has the material power to speed or slow the extension of human rights to welfare. What is beyond its power is stanching this claim of developing peoples, braking its accelerating thrust, or diminishing its power to work its will on the demands of populations everywhere for "more now."

Human rights can also be viewed from the narrow perspective of power politics, not just as a force placing constraints on a state or on actors in civil society or in enlisting them to expand the scope of human rights. Human rights can be used as a tool of foreign policy and, paradoxically, as a mechanism to suppress those human rights articulated by subjugated peoples from the perspectives of their cherished values and norms. Developing states almost universally condemn what they charge is Western, notably United States, use of human rights as a tool of domination and covert imperialism. Except for a few states—for example, South Africa, where Western pressures helped bring about Black majority rule—most of the regimes of the states discussed below have tried to turn their human rights agenda on its head. The ploy has proved useful in deflecting attention from the dismal human rights record of many states and the predatory practices of their regimes. In some instances, such as Beijing's conflict with the United States over Taiwan, the Communist regime has been able to mobilize sentiment against the United States by linking human rights to what Edward Friedman terms a "potent form of chauvinism" to keep dissidents in line. Like Malaysia and Singapore, which also have authoritarian governments, the Beijing regime has until now been able to strike an implicit bargain with potentially unruly populations by trading economic growth and welfare policies for political obedience and loyalty. So far this strategy has worked. The West has resisted using its economic power to pressure these regimes to liberalize. Successive European states and America rationalize that globalizing economic exchange and open market practices, which place resources in the hands of individuals and widen their potential leverage over the state, will eventually promote political liberalization and greater scope for human rights. The jury is still out on these claims.

The use of human rights as a strategic tool or instrument of foreign policy also cuts in another way. The oppressive Algerian regime, as Badredine Arfi exposes, manipulates Western fears of Muslim radicalism. It fends off human rights pressures from the West by playing the human rights card, while annulling elections and majority rule. This poses, of course, the well recognized problem that democratization does not automatically increase human rights protections. Democratization can, as the Balkan crisis indicates, be the occasion for members of a majority ethnic group to commit crimes against humanity and unspeakable atrocities against minorities in the name of popular rule. On the other hand, the post-Cold War era has opened new choices in Central and Latin America for the United States. During the Cold War, as Howard Wiarda recounts, the ruling coalition in the United States across party lines hindered left-wing forces throughout the region from gaining ascendancy as they had in Cuba. As a result, human rights as a policy goal was subordinated to strategic power concerns. Right-wing and military regimes can, presumably, no longer play the Communist card to hold onto power at the cost of the civil and human rights of their citizens in the region. The end of the Cold War may, as Wiarda suggests, create the conditions for the advancement of Anglo-Saxon notions of human rights in Central and Latin America. The region's integration into global capitalist markets increases pressures on regimes to democratize. On the other hand, as Wiarda and Arfi also show, history serves up multiple and conflicting legacies. Reforms designed to advance human rights, whether responsive to pressures within or from outside the state, risk failure, if they are applied to societies faster and go farther than recipients are ready to accept or to absorb them.

Who Are the Principal Actors with Power to Foster or Frustrate Human Rights?

The contributors to this volume also identify the principal actors engaged in advancing or retarding human rights in a region. What emerges from these several discussions are clear pictures of the localization of the human rights process against the background of a global politics of human rights. This finding reflects those of other observers who study global cultural exchange and religious interaction as hybrid processes (Robertson 1992). Human rights, whether individual or group, are principally mediated through the states and the nation-state system. This is true for the West, as Jack Donnelly observes, and it is confirmed in all of the regional chapters.[4] These observations reinforce the view that key human rights struggles will continue to move along channels carved by a diverse and decentralized state system. The progress of the European states in harmonizing divergent conceptions of human rights, as Michael Newman relates, indicates some notable limits on state sovereignty and the strengthening of the right of individuals and groups to avail themselves of the European Convention on Human Rights (ECHR) under the Council of Europe. The European Union is also making strides in this direction as one of its principal pillars of union under the Maastricht treaty. Similarly, the United States and other Western states have recognized limits on state sovereignty in supporting special UN-sponsored courts for Yugoslavia and Rwanda to try those accused of crimes against humanity or have attached conditions to aid to these states contingent on their cooperation with these courts. Officials, like Slobodan Milosevic in Yugoslavia or Augusto Pinochet in Chile, are no longer immune from prosecution when they commit crimes against humanity against their own citizens and neighbors. On the other hand, the EU states and the United States remain deeply split over the treaty to create a permanent International Criminal Court—the European Union for, the United States against.

The normative theory of the liberal state predicts that the state will use its coercive power to arbitrate civil conflicts in the pursuit of human rights claims. It is also expected to protect those who might have their rights invaded by actors inside and outside the state. The liberal state is also limited in the scope of its power to ensure that it will not threaten or trample on civil liberties or human rights. These expectations can hardly be confidently applied to most of the states of this study. This is not to say that the West's record on human rights is without serious blemish. Continued gender, racial, ethnic, and religious discrimination persist—practices at serious odds with the proclaimed liberal model. Western states, however, confront an array of actors that can mobilize countervailing power to contain and contest violations of human rights. Open civil societies support civil rights and human rights advocates, who can freely participate in the political process to make their voice and influence felt. A free press can expose state abuses by elected officials, bureaucrats, the police, and armed forces. To address human rights wrongs, aggrieved parties can avail themselves of courts that are partially insulated from state and civil societal pressures. Even foreign governments and transnational actors, like Amnesty International or Catholic and Protestant churches, may apply pressures to check governmental action.

Among the West European states, as Michael Newman sketches, there are highly developed institutions to protect human rights at an interstate level. The Council of Europe, the institutions of the European Union and its growing body of community law under the guidance of the European Court of Justice, and the Conference on Security and Cooperation in Europe—all of these institutions and organizational mechanisms evidence substantial and reliable supports for a large and growing body of human rights claims. Indeed, one generalization that emerges from this discussion is the indispensability of these institutions, notably an independent judiciary, a free press, and active and well-financed human rights groups—domestic and transnational actors—if progress in human rights is to be assured. They are key nodes in the power grids energizing the exercise of human rights within states and regions.

This panoply of active human rights actors and their impressive assets are not readily available to most individuals or groups outside of the Western camp. Only selected elements are at their disposal. Some states, like Iran and Turkey, have lively and growing civil societies. They are capable of supporting domestic groups dedicated to human rights. In league with outside actors, like the United Nations or the European Union, these states and their enlarging civil societies have made notable human rights progress, although their records are still marred by many violations of human rights norms. Other states, like Burma, North Korea, and China, have successfully blocked the efforts of outside actors to constrain state power. Opposition groups are marginalized or kept under tight regime control, as in Burma, or directly attacked and suppressed as in China's relentless campaign against the Falun Gong. Yet, as the experience of South Africa and Latin and Central America suggests, outside pressures to liberalize authoritarian regimes should not be discounted as human rights, as a force, works its way through world society.

The role of the military and the police as the coercive arms of the state is particularly crucial in determining the progress of human rights. In states divided by deep and intractable conflicts between enduring rivals, loyal to clashing group identities, a strong state is indispensable to maintain order and peace. The Turkish military are self-appointed guarantors of the secular state. Turkey is also one of the principal violators of human rights, evidenced in its aggressive suppression of Kurdish secessionists. The military are no less counted upon to ensure order between warring groups in Israel, India, Indonesia, Sri Lanka, Pakistan, and Nigeria. And in all of these cases, as the discussion below recounts, the military and the police are, as often as not, more the principal source of the problem of human rights than a provisional solution to ensure their protection.

Yet, as noted earlier, there has been discernible progress in some regions. South Africa offers some evidence that the police and military can be disciplined to democratic controls. The same cannot be said of the civil wars in Central Africa and the Hobbesian end games engulfing them. There is some hope, as William Zartman suggests, that Nigeria may now be back on the road to democratization and that its progress will spill over into neighboring states. The military have also been gradually restrained and confined to their barracks in Latin America. These gains are threatened, however, by the drug war and by chronic civil strife in Colombia with the highest rate of kidnapping per capita in the world. They are also under siege as a consequence of mounting class conflict in Venezuela, fueled by the Chavez regime, bent on imposing plebiscitarian rule over the deep class divisions in Venezuelan society.

What Strategies Are Pursued by Actors to Get Their Way?

The third question addressed by the regional chapters concerns the strategies pursued by actors and how they use their power resources to advance or resist the march of human rights. The distinctive agendas and differing actors engaged in these struggles across regions paint so complex a picture that the moves of each actor would have to be plotted separately to fully appreciate the tangled exchanges that comprise the politics of human rights in each region. The Chinese case is illustrative. The Tiananmen Square crisis underscores Beijing's vulnerability. That it has survived without significant reform of its political institutions appears partially the result, as Edward Friedman shows, of a favorable conjuncture of regional politics, Western priorities in weighting economic over human rights priorities, and the relentless and ruthless suppression of regime opponents, real or imagined. A democratic India is restrained as a critic of Chinese practices, given its flawed record of human rights in Kashmir (a tradeoff with Tibet), its domestic violations of human rights, as Stanley Kochanek relates, and its historical legacy of castes and institutionalized social discrimination. The states of ASEAN also recoil from interfering in each other's domestic affairs and offer no succor to groups and individuals under siege by a member state. ASEAN turns a blind eye to Burma and Vietnam and places no discernible constraints on its member states for their violations of civil and human rights. Beijing is accorded, as a result, a free hand to intimidate human rights advocates and suppress the claims of citizens for greater personal and group freedom.

On the other hand, nongovernmental bodies and actors have had a positive effect on some states. Foreign investors pulled the plug on crony capitalism in Indonesia and precipitated the collapse of the Suharto regime. As Mattes and Leysens recount, foreign investors and multinational corporations, applying the Sullivan rule against investing in a state guilty of racial discrimination, and human rights groups in and out of South Africa played key roles in ending apartheid in South Africa. Once the end of the Cold War abruptly discounted the perceived strategic value of a White South Africa, the Western liberal democracies were freed to increase pressure on the apartheid regime to bring about Black majority rule. These same economic and political forces would also seem to be partly responsible for the widening democratization of Central American politics, most prominently in Mexico where the ruling party was finally overturned after having governed Mexico since its social revolution in the early decades of the twentieth century.

As Carol Leff suggests, non-state actors have helped keep the Russian regime open to democracy. They have assisted embattled groups against the punitive strikes of the state. These buffers have had little or no effect, however, on the Chechnyan conflict. Russia continues to ignore Council of Europe standards in this civil war. The loud silence of the European states in failing to condemn Russian atrocities marks a regression in the movement towards human rights protections in the republics of the former Soviet Union. It would not appear that simple size and power, as in the case of the Russian Federation and China, explain the capacity of states in the developing world to resist outside pressures. The global war on terrorism, launched by the United States, may well have improved the human rights lot of Afghans with the overthrow of the Taliban regime, but the "coalition of the willing" formed by Washington to overthrow the Iraqi regime of Saddam Hussein and the hollowing out of the United Nations and NATO as the frameworks within which American security policy is fashioned fundamentally weaken these international organizations as vehicles for the effective promotion of human rights and democratization. Progress will depend on the unilateral exercise of power by Washington in cooperation with willing allies of the moment. The opposition of the members of the UN Security Council to Iraq war, notably France, Russia, and China as permanent members wielding veto power, bodes ill for the reliance on multilateral cooperation in moving human rights agendas across the globe.

Toward a Theory of Human Rights as a *Force Profonde*

So far the discussion has tried to establish several points. First, good description of actor behavior centered on human rights concerns is a prerequisite for developing theory. These descriptions should identify outcomes that result in the extension, contraction, or elimination of human rights in the thought, decisions, and actions of relevant actors. The initial chapters on Western and Islamic conceptions of human rights help set the stage for the regional chapters to follow by sketching in broad strokes what actors in each tradition mean by human rights in terms of the values they care about and what they are willing to fight for. These meanings establish criteria, however conflicting, that define human rights as complex sets of social values and practices. The regional chapters attempt to define how human rights are supported or opposed by actors and how they use their resources and pursue strategies to advance their conflicting preferences. The latter are crystallized in the form of social power. These result in rules, norms, and systems of law—institutional patterns—as well as organizations dedicated to protect or preclude the exercise of human rights by the populations of the globe. This volume makes no claim of providing a theory of human rights. Rather, it charts human rights as social phenomena, linking their power and ideational value, to lay the groundwork for such a theory and to jog research agendas to give more attention to the power-ideational fusion that drives human rights. It contributes to the yet uncompleted and complex task of disentangling analytically the causal and transformational force of human rights on human societies and their governance, the power supports, principally their material components, on which the fostering or frustration of human rights depend, and the perverse and aberrant uses of human rights to deny, paradoxically, their realization.

Second, in describing the actors engaged in human rights struggles as well as the resources and strategies pursued by them, this volume implicitly provides evidence for the existence of what Emile Durkheim would have termed a "collective conscience" in support of human rights. Durkheim recognized that social outcomes—say suicide or the privileged status accorded by liberal societies to individuals—could be partially, if not conclusively, explained by the shared and contesting values binding (or alienating) members of a group. These values are sources of social power, whether fusing or fracturing social ties. What we are witnessing today, as the product of several centuries of social evolution, is the gradual recognition by increasingly larger numbers of peoples from diverse national, ethnic, and cultural backgrounds that they are also members of a human race to which rights can be ascribed simply by their being human (Searle 1995). The multiplying exchanges of humans at global levels in number, scope, accumulating density, and real-time impact create the material, psychological, and ideational networks and shared experience to create and ascribe rights to humans simply by virtue of their membership in the species. This social evolution-ary process parallels but by no means matches the advances already made in the life sciences, which have conclusively established the biological unity of the human species regardless of race or social conditions (Cavalli-Sforza 1995, 1994; J. Diamond 1992).

The crazy-quilt human rights patterns this volume depicts caution against optimism that this ascriptive process of a shared humanity will be realized sometime soon. Nor, given the differentiated historical baggage with which particular peoples are laden, can one reasonably expect any kind of con-vergence that discards the weight of the past on present and future social choices concerning human rights. The "shadow of the future," posited by some theorists as a systemic force moving even egoists to choose coopera-tion over conflict as a consequence of their continuing social exchanges, has to be seriously qualified in light of the findings of this volume (Axelrod 1984). Social identities that mutually exclude each other, as "shadows of the past" rooted in enduring rivalries or clashing cultural values, are formida-ble barriers to cooperation. Presupposed by positing the causal force of the "shadow of the future" is the existence of a particular Western-defined notion of a shared humanity, that is, the standardization of all humans as rational actors. But rationality in the pursuit of human rights assumes mul-tiple forms across regions. It cannot be assumed as a free good subject to the whim and will of the analyst. The eminent historian William McNeill, ironically, offers a more prudent and reliable guide to the "shadow of the future." He notes that "consciousness of the human species as a whole is potential rather than actual. But just as most of the nations of the earth were created by political events, and then, with the help of historians, achieved a common consciousness, so, it seems to me, real human consciousness can only be expected to arise after political and economic processes have cre-ated such a tight-knit community that every people and polity is forced to recognize its subordination to and participation in a global system."[5]

From the evidence afforded by this volume, human rights have a long way to go before they can be said to depend for their protection on a shared conception of a common humanity. The "shadow of the future" has first to be deliberately created by human intervention rather than left as the prod-uct of blind chance or of the evolution of an infinite number of iterated game plays. A pure or ideal end point for human rights is not likely ever to be reached, nor would that endpoint be necessarily desirable, since human freedom would in principle have reached the extremities of its possibilities. Recognition of a common humanity and of collective membership in the human species admits, paradoxically, by the very creativity of the species itself, to multiple expressions for that humanity and its realization in human rights. The conclusive DNA evidence of a biologically uniform human spe-cies certainly fuels the possibility of a socially defined universal species, although social differentiation has been the dominant characteristic of this evolutionary process. The possibility of at least a "thin," if not thick, notion of a shared humanity scarcely implies that social evolution will move toward a single, homogenized, and banalized end point and, accordingly, that human rights will be codified once and for all, as some have suggested (Waters 1995).

The important point to remember is the globalization of the human rights project. That convergence is not likely any time soon is less important than recognizing that each *particular* representation of human rights—Western, Islamic, Chinese, et al.—must now be justified in universal terms, although its multiple local expressions may well be at odds with each other. The process is global, but the results will be hybrids as a consequence of differential historical evolution and diverse and divided societies, something Kant recognized two centuries ago in rejecting a cosmopolitan solution for perpetual peace.

No less than military or market forces, human rights as a social force can shove and shape other actors to adapt to its power. Humans can be expected to adapt to these competing environmental constraints, or be selected out for survival. Note the implosion of the Soviet Union or the emergence of a European Union whose members less than sixty years ago were locked in a fatal global conflict, resulting in over fifty million deaths and untold misery and hardship to scores of millions more. Neither of these contrasting outcomes of disintegration and integration can be reasonably and fully explained in the absence of stipulating some notion of a collective conscience or, simply, a social force driving these events. As Durkheim put the matter: "Whenever certain elements combine and thereby produce, by the fact of their combination, new phenomena, it is plain that the new phenomena reside not in the original elements but in the totality formed by their union" (Ruggie 1998, 858). The force of human rights is ultimately rooted in the individual choices of individuals who identify themselves as members of a larger community. The actor of this shared identity embeds these choices in the implied stipulation. This implied affirmation of membership in a global system infuses meaning and value into these choices and, from the perspective of the analyst, renders them sensible and explicable.

The findings of this volume also extend Durkheim's (1915, 1984, 1993) notion of "collective conscience." What we are witnessing is not one collective conscience labeled "human rights." Viewed from the vantage points of the principal regions of the globe, the force of human rights appears as complex webs of "collective consciences." While these webs of human exchange can be usefully viewed as social facts arising from a shared collective conscience, the force of human rights as a driver of social exchanges is necessarily expressed through the pre-existing socioeconomic, political, and material social structures or "facts" already in place on which its future prospects depend. The claims of human rights certainly foreshadow the future and raise the expectation of a converging conception of human rights, as Robert Axelrod suggests, but the "shadow of the future" is inconceivable unless viewed as emerging from the "shadows of the past," cast by the many histories and contending identities composing the emerging world society.[6]

As Chou En-lai and Hochschild remind us, human rights, while possessed and exercised only by individuals, whether viewed as autonomous actors or members of a group, become more fully comprehensible when viewed as the outcomes of a collective, if not converging force. That force depends on individuals who internalize its attractive pull, however perceived or mediated through the historical, psychological, and ideational processes of thought animating them. In the absence of such a force, the adaptation of individuals and groups to a new global social environment and emerging society, directed by human rights concerns, would not make fully rational sense. In the absence of stipulating this force and the collective conscience (or consciences) propelling it, why else should one expect self-selected individuals from different countries and circumstances to band together, risking their lives and treasure, to help anonymous millions in faraway places to unsettle and unseat a powerful Belgian king? How else to fully explain the fundamental transformation of the sovereign and imperial state into limited liberal states? The state's coercive powers have been gradually constrained and its authority circumscribed to check the threat they pose to human rights. Its authority and monopoly of legitimate force are now invoked to protect and promote these rights against attack within and outside its territory. That the ideals embedded in human rights claims have scarcely been achieved, even among the advanced liberal market democracies, is not evidence that this force does not exist as a social fact and as a challenge to actors to adapt to its prescriptions and proscriptions.

The difficulties of developing a satisfactory theory of human rights should not be underestimated. First, prevailing theories of global politics, specifically those associated with neoclassical economics, realism, and liberal institutionalism, are primarily based on utilitarian assumptions about the composition of human actors—what is real or ontologically unique about them. They have little or no room for notions of collective conscience or a shared humanity as the basis for human rights claims and as a causal force to explain behavior. Realism, and its neorealist progeny (K. Waltz 1979), and neoclassical economic theorists confine their explanations of social conduct—of individuals and states—largely to the material conditions of choice, notably the incentives respectively induced by violence or economic goods, by which actors adapt to their environments.[7] Liberal institutionalist theory tries to cope with the seeming dilemma of explaining cooperation between selfish egoists, whether individuals or states, which is the starting point for neoclassical economic theory and realism. For institutionalist theorists, social exchange and cooperation is possible through institutions. They furnish crucial "information, reduce transaction costs, make commitments more credible, establish focal points for coordination, and in general facilitate the operation of reciprocity" (Keohane 1995, 42; Baldwin 1993). Through learning actors can cooperate to their mutual benefit without defecting from shared norms and without imposing costs on their partners for their temporary and short-run advantage.

While subjective human rights claims and their impact on social practices and values challenge neoclassical economic or realist theory, it does not follow that order and material welfare are not relevant to human rights. As long as human preferences cannot be assumed to converge, some form or order, resting on coercion—currently embodied in the nation-state—will be necessary. This seemingly paradoxical limitation holds, however much human rights partisans view them as absolutes and, by that token, as self-executing and eventually converging once their universality is recognized (Mansbridge 1996). Nor can human rights, notably in their substantive form, be realized, as the discussion has already signaled, in the absence of a theory of the wealth of nations, as Adam Smith might have insisted. The assumption that most humans, most of the time, will choose more goods rather than less at the same cost has powerful explanatory power.

Conceding these material determinants of human rights does not require either the diminution or the denial of the *force profonde* of human rights as a limit on prevailing political and economic theory. Putting that collective force back into play is an important aim of this volume. Realism, liberal institutionalism, and neoclassical economic theory agree on a common unit of analysis—rational egoists (whether individuals or states) that seek to maximize security, wealth, or both, as well as the material capabilities or power associated with these interests. This commitment to an individualist methodology in the pursuit of a positivist social science rules out or marginalizes the existence of a collective conscience or social force to explain human rights outcomes.[8] The notion of shared values and social bonds, whether defined by human rights or by their denial in the form of ethnic, racial class, national and religious opposition, does not easily square with the utilitarian assumptions of prevailing theory.

Utilitarian biases are not the only obstacles to an integrated theory of human behavior. The prevailing methods, epistemological assumptions, and evidentiary criteria of the social sciences must also be expanded and cooperation across disciplinary lines deepened to extend the boundaries of relevant theory to cover the behavior of actors working for or against human rights. That would require that the search for an integrated theory take account not only of the external, material forces directing and guiding actor choices and behavior, but also Max Weber's (1949, 81) insistence that humans alone possess the capacity, will, and determination "to take a deliberate attitude towards the world and to lend it *significance*." It is this social fact—that humans always and everywhere approach their physical and social environments with an "attitude"—that impelled Weber (1958b), not without many critics, to trace the impact of the Protestant Revolution on the rise and spread of capitalism. This volume follows in these big footsteps by attempting to trace the force of human rights in the conflicts over their meaning, content, and social expression around the globe, but in light of their specific historical representations and power supports. There is no necessary contradiction in asserting the existence of human rights as a collective force, while expecting that it will be socially realized in a bewildering number of varying and conflicting forms.

Social science theory has to make room for humans and human rights. Certainly, as Marx recognized, humans "do not make [history] just as they please; they do not make it under circumstances chosen by themselves, but under circumstances directly found" (Ruggie 1998, 876). States and political regimes are quite capable of choking aspirations for democratic rule and of stifling stirrings of human rights demands. These material "circumstances" have much to say about whether, why, and how human rights arise, survive, thrive, and spread across the world society. They are the evidentiary basis for prevailing realist, liberal economic, and liberal institutionalist theories of state and social behavior. But no less an outcome of human will is the obvious social fact that those material circumstances are subject to transformation over time if humans do not continually reaffirm them.[9] These changes, as in Great Britain, may be slow in developing as the evolution of civil liberties and the implantation of the notion of a rule of law, binding ruler and ruled, were only gradually raised to the level of universal human rights, not just as historically determined and unique liberties enjoyed by Englishmen alone. Or group and individual rights may be abrupt in their origins, as they burst to the surface in the French Revolution, but varying in their impact on other human societies or halting and discontinuous in their realization as the civil and human rights movement in the United States illustrates.

Such a social science is obviously a challenge. It would require a theory of global politics in the broadest sense of that term to include material constraints as well as ideas, values, and psychological states of mind as data. That would require more, not less, cooperation among theorists, researchers, and informed observers than exists today. More important, social science theory would have to widen its focus, presently concentrated narrowly on particular disciplinary concerns, to embrace the factors and actors determining human rights. The reduction of human behavior to a ceteris paribus clause for the sake of rigorous and parsimonious analysis would have to be relaxed in much the same way that the model of physical chemistry had to be reformulated and expanded to encompass the wider scope and greater complexity of chemical activity associated with environmental chemistry and biochemical behavior.

In enlarging the vision and scope of social science inquiry, the difficulty of verifying what are the true subjective and inter-subjective states of mind of humans as data for scientific investigation should not be minimized. Strides have certainly been made in developing social theories by simplifying assumptions about the make-up of "humans"—what is real about them—by using the tools of science and rigorous observation to describe, explain, and predict their behavior. But current theory falls short of what actors think, decide, and do or their capacity to re-invent themselves. This is pointedly the case with respect to the globalization of popular sovereignty, democratization, and human rights. It is the behavior of humans and their agents, not that of theorists, that is to be finally understood and explained. If humans still challenge established order, then their persistent determination to assign meaning and significance to the universe and to their necessary and inescapable social exchanges and mutual dependencies challenges the present limits of social inquiry and practice. Barring such an opening will almost certainly lead to more surprises. Illustrative are the Cultural Revolution in China, its surprise shift to a market economy in the late 1970s, the Tiananmen Square explosion, the implosion of the Soviet Union, or the destruction of the World Trade Center on September 11, 2001. Legitimacy, authority, and human rights—these subjective values, however defined or however relied on to infuse meaning into their material conditions—count, and count decisively, in human affairs, assuring their perfection or perdition.[10]

The enlargement of social inquiry and theory to embrace human volition and creativity, as preconditions for social reconstruction, does not imply that the prospects of change and reform are ever easy or that they will necessarily be successful. The many impediments to human rights recounted in the chapters below should throw cold water on assertions that social arrangements of social power are infinitely malleable and ultimately disciplined to ideational or psychological determinants. They do not sustain the expectation that just because humans have the capacity—arguably the need—"to take a deliberate attitude to the world and to lend it significance"—that saying so will be enough to transform prevailing social conditions and powerful socioeconomic and political power structures. Given that human preferences do not converge, as Hobbes compellingly argues, and given that the bioeconomic needs of humans are permanently tied to providing for their material survival, as Marx (1970) makes clear, it is presumptuous to assert that the assumed anarchy underlying human exchanges (itself a problematical statement) is anything humans want to make it (Wendt 1992).

Recognizing these still real if imprecise limits does not suggest that humans passively submit and mindlessly adapt to their physical and biological environments and social conditions. Rather it sobers expectations that they will rapidly surmount countervailing coercive or economic constraints, social taboos, psychological blockages, and political intimidation to expand their freedoms. These formidable, humanly created barriers and the powerful interests castellating around them are compelling forces of nature. They cannot be simply willed away, however much the *force profonde* of human rights may be said to possess its own autonomous power resources.

Finally, this volume offers countervailing evidence as antidotes to the proclivity either to reduce the globalization of human exchanges to a dichotomized set of finite and inevitable choices or to posit a linear projection of the globalization process. On the one hand, there are those, following in the footsteps of Ferdinand Tönnies (1957), who contend that humankind will move either toward "Jihad vs. McWorld" (Barber 1995) or, metaphorically, toward a choice between Lexus and the Olive Tree (T. Friedman 2000). On the other hand, there are others who prophesy unavoidable culture clashes (Huntington 1996), coming chaos (Kaplan 2000), the triumph of liberalism and market capitalism (Fukuyama 1992), or eventual cultural convergence (Waters 1995). The contributors to this volume, while agreed that human rights is a social fact and globalizing force, are too informed by the complexities of power associated with their regions of expertise to support such sweeping generalizations. Human rights come in many forms. As the authors of this volume remind us, human rights cut paths in many ways, some skewed, others at cross purposes. As a social force it is mediated through the power structures of a bewildering array of "material circumstances"; yet, as Weber insists, human rights are "social facts" infusing significance into material circumstances, even transforming them. The challenge to existing order, posed by human rights as a *force profonde*, has scarcely begun if the many battles being fought today around the world in its name are any indication.

Whither human rights? It's too early to tell.

Part I
Contending
Legitimacies

Chapter 2
Western Perspectives

Jack Donnelly

To talk intelligently about something as vast and varied as "the West" is virtually impossible, even on the relatively narrow topic of the place of human rights in dominant conceptions of political legitimacy. Politically, the West has been classically embodied in Sparta, Athens, and Rome, both the Republic and the Empire; the France of Louis IX, Francis I, Louis XIV, Robespierre, Napoleon, Louis Napoleon, the Third Republic, the Popular Front, Petain, and de Gaulle; the Germany of Emperor Frederick III, the Great Elector Frederick William, Frederick the Great, Kaiser Wilhelm II, Adolf Hitler, Willy Brandt, and Helmut Kohl; the England of Henry VIII, Elizabeth I, Oliver Cromwell, George III, Gladstone, Disraeli, Lloyd George, Chamberlain, Churchill, Thatcher, and Lady/Princess Diana; and the United States of Washington, Jefferson, Jackson, Lincoln, Grant, Wilson, two Roosevelts, two Johnsons, several Kennedys, and various Bushes—not to mention Nixon, Carter, Reagan, and Clinton. The "Western tradition" includes both Caligula and Marcus Aurelius, Francis of Assisi and Torquemada, Leopold II of Belgium and Albert Schweitzer, Jesus of Nazareth and the Holocaust—and just about everything in between.

With such diversity—at which the preceding paragraph only hints—any account of the West must be highly selective. Declining the invitation to write this chapter probably would have been the sensible course. Having accepted, what I can offer are caricature highlights of a few widely shared features commonly encountered in contemporary discussions of legitimate governance.

Linking the West and Human Rights

My starting point is the orienting premise of this volume, namely, that the practices of human rights are embedded in complex and varied political processes. Human rights, rather than a timeless system of essential moral principles, are a set of social practices that regulate relations between, and help constitute citizens and states, in "modern" societies. As a matter of historical fact, these practices, and the underlying idea of equal and in-alienable rights held by all human beings, emerged first in the modern West.[1]

The West is also historically associated with the Atlantic slave trade, often-savage colonialism, religious persecution, virulent racism, absolute monarchy, predatory capitalism, global warfare of almost unthinkable de-structiveness, fascism, Naziism, communist totalitarianism, the Holocaust, and a host of other evils and social ills. Many countries, groups, and indi-viduals, both Western and non-Western, suffered, and continue to suffer, under burdens directly or indirectly attributable to such reprehensible Western practices. Nonetheless the association of the West with interna-tionally recognized human rights is not only common but also essential to discussions of governance in contemporary international society.

The West is the only region of the world in which political practice over the past half century has been largely consonant with, and in significant measure guided by, the extensive set of civil and political and economic, social, and cultural rights laid out in the 1948 Universal Declaration of Human Rights and the 1966 International Human Rights Covenants.[2] The West has also begun to come to grips with some of its more unsavory *anti*-human rights legacy. And, over the past decade, the Western vision of polit-ical legitimacy has come to dominate international discussions—because of the collapse of the leading alternatives; because of Western military, political, and economic power; but also because of the normative power of the idea of human rights as reflected in Western practice. This (initially Western) vision has become close to internationally hegemonic in the Gramscian sense of the term, which sees rule as based not simply on mate-rial power/force but also on control over ideas and at least quasi-voluntary acceptance of ruling norms and values. This chapter offers an ideal type account of the Western model of legitimate governance: the liberal demo-cratic welfare state, as represented by the United States and the countries of the European Union that link the West and human rights unusually closely.[3]

My discussion is arranged around the concepts of order, welfare, and legitimacy. By "order" I mean dominant forms of constitutional organiza-tion, or structures of law and coercion; by "welfare," the dominant eco-nomic model, or structures of production and distribution; by "legitimacy," the dominant structure of legal and political norms.[4] Table 1 summarizes my account. The following sections move through the two columns in the table. Although I happen to endorse much of the substance of the Western

TABLE 1. The Western Model of Governance

	National	*International*
Order	Nation-state/Rechtstaat	(Society of) states
Welfare	Welfare state	Global markets
Legitimacy	Liberal democracy	Sovereignty

model, especially in its national dimensions, I try to treat this chapter as an exercise in empirical analysis rather than advocacy.

To avoid misunderstanding, let me repeat that this is an ideal type model presented at a very high level of abstraction. Although neither "complete" nor "neutral," it is widely accepted internally and projected externally by leading Western individuals, organizations, and states. Whatever one's views of its substance, the fact that it is endorsed by the world's leading powers makes it centrally relevant to contemporary discussions of governance.

States and Citizens

Dominant Western political forms have ranged from the polis and feudal fiefs to empires. Modern Western politics, however, has been organized around the state. As dynastic states and multiethnic empires gave way to parliamentary and popular governments, nineteenth- and twentieth-century Western states increasingly came to be (re-)organized in nationalist terms. Although the aspiration for "nation-states," terminal political entities in which peoples and political boundaries coincide, has always been problematic, it was a powerful ideal in much of the West for a century or more, expressed, for example, in understandings of France as the state of the French and Germany as the state of the Germans.

This nationalist model has undergone substantial revision in recent decades. Although the state remains the primary organizing principle of political action and loyalty, citizens are increasingly seen in juridical rather than national/ethnic/cultural terms. Consider, for example, the rise of the language of multiculturalism, diversity, and inclusion. "The people" are coming to be seen more as those who share a common political life under the jurisdiction of the state rather than those who share a culture, past, or blood. For example Germany's new citizenship laws move substantially in the direction of the territorial *jus soli*, in sharp contrast to the traditional German adherence to a genealogical *jus sanguinis* doctrine.

In redefining the people increasing emphasis has been placed on the rule of law or the related idea of a Rechtstaat. Political authority, rather than grounded in charisma, divine donation, custom, inheritance, or even the will of the people, is increasingly seen to reside in impartial law. The state thus appears as a juridical entity in which the people are bound together by common participation in and subordination to (democratic) law.

The growing separation of citizenship from traditional ethnic, cultural, or historical ties—the transition from nationalist to territorial and juridical conceptions of political community—has been closely associated with an ideology of human rights. One's human rights depend not on who one is—for example, a well-born English Protestant male property owner—but simply on the fact that one is a human being. In a world of states, this has taken the form of an emphasis on equal rights for all citizens.

At minimum, a citizenship-based conception of political membership and order, as it has come to be understood in the West, involves tolerance for diversity. Historically, this began with religious tolerance, which made very slow and uneven but nonetheless steady progress following the Thirty Years' War. Intense, often violent, struggles in the nineteenth and twentieth centuries have also eliminated (at least the formal) links between basic rights and class, gender, race, and ethnicity. More recently, factors such as age, sexual orientation, and disability have been challenged, with some success, as bases for assigning rights.

No less important, mere toleration has given way to more active policies of nondiscrimination, equal protection, and inclusiveness. For example, the multicultural ideal is making significant progress in Western countries such as Canada, the United States, Britain, and the Netherlands. Throughout the West, nondiscrimination has become a central focus of legal and political action and is championed by all mainstream political parties.

The roots of this approach lie in the social contract tradition that runs from Locke, through Paine and Kant, to Rawls. The state is seen as an institution to realize the rights of its citizens, making political authority largely a function of the extent to which a government gives practical effect to the morally prior rights of its citizens. Politics thus has come to be seen as a matter not of the state and its subjects but rather of a state that is subordinate to the people.

The Welfare State

A prominent myth in the human rights literature of the Cold War era was that the Western approach to human rights rested on a near-exclusive commitment to civil and political rights, plus the right to private property. "In Western capitalist states economic and social rights are perceived as not within the purview of state responsibility" (Pollis and Schwab 1979, xiii).[5] Such claims bear little connection to reality. Quite the contrary, during the Cold War the West was the only region that in practice took seriously the often repeated assertion of the indivisibility of all internationally recognized human rights.

Locke's list of rights was indeed restricted to "life, liberty, and estates." Private property was the only economic right that received extensive state protection in the nineteenth century—and in the United States in particular, well into the twentieth century. But it boggles the mind that anyone with even a passing acquaintance with the American welfare state, let alone post-World War II Western Europe, could claim that this has been true of the West over the past half century. In fact, political debate in all Western countries has concerned not whether the state should recognize and protect economic and social rights but how massive the commitment of resources should be, to which particular rights.

There have certainly been both controversy and considerable diversity within the West over the relative balance between state and market provision, as well as other strategic issues. In a fine recent study that combines careful conceptual analysis with innovative empirical work, Goodin and others (1999) identify liberal, social democratic, and corporatist welfare regimes, represented by the United States, the Netherlands, and Germany that involve different strategies for reducing poverty while promoting efficiency, equity, integration, stability, and autonomy. The thirty or forty million Americans who are largely excluded from access to most of the health care system illustrate the human consequence of such differences. But in broad comparative terms the similarities between different Western welfare regimes are much more striking, not only in contrast to the other leading approaches of the Cold War era, but also in comparison to the nineteenth-century West.

The Western approach to welfare emphasizes individual rights; that is, guaranteeing every citizen certain minimum goods, services, and opportunities. This is in sharp contrast to more collectivist visions that dominated in the Third World and Soviet bloc during the Cold War era, where the focus was more national than individual and more on development than on rights.

The Western approach (with the partial exception of the United States) is also distinguished by an emphasis on state provision, in contrast to the greater reliance on families and firms in Asian countries such as Japan, Korea, and Singapore. Welfare rights seek to protect those who are severely disadvantaged in the primary system of production and distribution; that is, capitalist markets in the West (and many other countries). State provision seeks to assure that those without the necessary connections to employers and kin—the socially marginalized—are able to enjoy their rights.

Liberal Democratic Legitimacy

Westerners typically call their form of government "democracy." But democracy, understood as popular empowerment or rule by the people, need not protect human rights: "the people" often want to do extraordinarily nasty things to their fellow citizens. The hegemonic form of government in the West is better described as liberal democracy, a regime in which the morally and politically prior rights of citizens, and the requirement of the rule of law, limit the range of democratic decision-making. Legitimacy in the West rests on a particular fusion of individual human rights and popular sovereignty.

In liberal democracies, some rights-abusive choices are denied to the people ("Congress shall make no law . . .") and some rights-protective choices are mandated ("Everyone has the right . . ."). The democratic logic of popular rule operates only within the constraints set by individual human rights. The adjective "liberal"[6] rather than the noun "democracy" does most of the human rights work.

Although my focus here is on the national dimensions of the Western model, this point has important foreign policy implication. "Democracy promotion" programs, especially those sponsored by the United States, often place inordinate emphasis on elections—and thus popular rather than rights-protective rule. The struggle for liberal democracy is a struggle for human rights (only) because human rights have been built into the definition through the adjective. The link between electoral democracy and human rights is much more tenuous. Establishing secure electoral democracy in, say, Indonesia or Nigeria will be only a small (if valuable) step toward establishing rights-protective regimes.

Liberal democracy is a tempered or constrained democracy, not a matured or fully developed form of electoral democracy. Electoral democracies need not develop into liberal democracies; certainly we cannot expect them to do so automatically or inevitably. Liberal democracies must meet substantive, not merely procedural standards that require a difficult balancing of democratic and human rights principles. Only those governments able to strike this balance are, according to liberal democratic standards, legitimate.

To return to the language of social contract theory, a state is legitimate to the extent that it recognizes, implements, enforces, and protects the human rights of its citizens. Those rights include, centrally, rights of political participation, including a right of democratic control through free, fair, and open elections. But democracy is more an instrument than an end. The legitimacy of even a "democratic" government is to be judged by its commitment to individual human rights.

Inside and Outside

Human rights have an inherently universalizing logic: because all human beings have the same human rights, they ought to be treated equally in so far as those rights are involved. One might expect, therefore, that Western internal human rights commitments would be linked to advocacy of cosmopolitan international politics. In fact, however, the state remains the central organizing principle in Western conceptions of international order and legitimacy. The result is a vision of legitimate governance that at the national level is individualistic but internationally is largely communitarian (statist).

This disjunction has at least three sources. First, it reflects accommodation to, even unthinking acceptance of, a world of sovereign states. Second, it helps to protect the privileged position of Western states and societies. Third, it is rooted in a social contract vision of political society that authorizes, perhaps even encourages, the "choice" of individuals to form political associations that are not global in extent.

The balance among these three explanations will largely determine how one evaluates this disjunction. Is it a matter of necessity? Is it a manifestation of unjustifiable self-interest? Or is it the legitimate expression of national autonomy and community integrity? In any case, the process of growing inclusiveness that I emphasized above is largely limited by state boundaries in contemporary Western theory and practice.

The Society of States

The "English School" of international studies distinguishes three traditions of international theory (Bull 1977, ch. 2; Wight 1992). The "realist" tradition sees the society of states as extraordinarily thin and not very far removed from the constant threat of war. The "revolutionary" tradition envisions something much more like a cosmopolitan world society. The "internationalist" tradition envisions and advocates a society of states that is relatively thick but still a pluralist society of states, rather than a single world society. The contemporary Western approach is, in these terms, internationalist. To return to contractarian language, individuals form societies and states that then interact politically with one another.

Kant's three definitive articles of perpetual peace (1983, 112–19) provide a classic theoretical expression of this vision. States should be "republican," or roughly what I have called liberal democratic. "International right" should be based on a federation for peace rather than even a federal world government, leaving international relations largely the province of sovereign states (operating in a relatively thick society of states). And "cosmopolitan right," Kant argues, should be limited to freedom of movement and trade, again emphasizing the centrality of states.

The essential statism of the Western approach to international order is clearly reflected in the national implementation of international human rights norms. Most states have undertaken a considerable array of international human rights treaty obligations.[7] Implementation of those obligations, however, has been left almost entirely to states. There is no judicial enforcement at the global level. Treaty supervisory bodies such as the Human Rights Committee handle only a very small number of individual cases and their decisions lack the force of law. Most of the international machinery is devoted to encouraging state implementation through relatively impartial non-intrusive international monitoring.[8]

The principal exception is the system of regional judicial enforcement within the Council of Europe.[9] But even among the states of the European Union there is no evidence of any enthusiasm for a truly cosmopolitan system of human rights implementation.

Nonetheless, in the West as in most other regions, there is a growing emphasis on transnational nongovernmental organizations and advocacy networks (Keck and Sikkink 1998), and even increasing talk of "global civil society."[10] Such developments, along with the increasing importance of regional and global organizations, suggest that the simple equation of international society with the society of states is becoming increasingly problematic. States remain the central feature of international (and national) order. But they certainly are no longer the only important actors, especially on issues of human rights. Although this would seem to pose no serious short- or medium-run challenge to the central ordering role of states, it does indicate that international society is becoming thicker and more complex.

Global Markets

The Western approach to international welfare is built almost exclusively around global markets rather than even a very thin global welfare state. Although clearly a reflection of the self-interest of states that are relatively well positioned to compete in international markets, self-interest is not the entire explanation.

There is no central political authority in international society and most states, both Western and non-Western, are profoundly disinterested in creating one. Self-determination, which provides the most obvious moral justification for sovereignty, is an extremely important value for most peoples. And the leaders of states, large and small, in all regions of the world, tend to be very sensitive to their sovereign rights and privileges.

Most Third World and Eastern European governments would, of course, like to see increased flows of resources from the West to their states, preferably without political, economic, or human rights conditions attached. But as was the case during the discussions over the New International Economic Order in the 1970s, their approach to welfare remains as statist as that of the West. They show no interest in allowing their citizens to establish direct links with foreign states or existing international organizations, let alone the stronger organizations suggested by a cosmopolitan approach to welfare.

But once we reject a cosmopolitan welfare state, no overwhelmingly obvious model presents itself for organizing the international economy. In an international society in which power and authority are decentralized—that is, a system of sovereign states—we can expect dominant international norms and institutions to reflect the preferences of leading powers. That is largely what we see in the neoliberal[11] "Washington consensus," which revolves around open international markets.

Western power and self-interest preclude serious discussion of radically redistributive schemes. But the picture is not simply one of raw power. The terms of economic liberalization and structural adjustment are in large measure imposed, especially the insistence that most costs be borne by the adjusting countries. The need for adjustment, however, is increasingly, if reluctantly, accepted.

During the Cold War, resistance to the West was the norm. Most non-Western countries argued that development not only could be achieved by relying on state direction but that this was the best and most efficient route to realizing economic and social rights. Such projects, however, usually proved unsustainable, when they were not failures from the outset. And the leading *dirigiste* development successes (excluding the special case of oil exporting countries) were states such as Taiwan, Korea, and post-Mao China that relied heavily on the economic discipline of international markets.

Today, however, there is a grudging but growing recognition that realizing economic and social rights requires a complex combination of efficiency in production and equity in distribution. Given the continued exclusion of the possibility of radical structural reform, substantial reliance on national and international markets is becoming closer to a hegemonic, rather than simply an imposed, principle. Although there is little enthusiasm for neo-liberal international economic regimes even in the West (outside of the United States), there is no serious challenger, at least at the level of inter-state elite debate. The range of mainstream debate thus seems to be settling into questions of how far to push neoliberal principles and what sorts of national variations are acceptable in what circumstances.

Although my orientation in this chapter is descriptive and explanatory, I find it impossible not to draw critical attention to the disjunction between Western internal and international approaches to welfare. Even giving full weight to the moral and political justifications for a statist rather than a cosmopolitan approach to welfare issues in international society, the Washington consensus—which "conveniently" overlooks the well-known fact that free markets create, perpetuate, and intensify social and economic inequality—smacks of willful ignorance, even pathological denial, rooted in narrow self-interest.

Markets alone have never produced growth with equity. Typically, inequitable growth has been followed by redistribution. In rare cases such as Korea and Taiwan, market-led growth has been accompanied by a relatively egalitarian social ethic and a state that intervened regularly to constrain capitalist predation and support the rural and urban poor and middle classes. Even at their abstract textbook best, markets are institutions geared to efficiency, maximizing output while minimizing costs, not distributing goods, services, and opportunities to realize economic and social rights.

At home, all Western states, including the United States, have thoroughly institutionalized comprehensive redistributive mechanisms to cope with the negative human externalities of markets. Abroad, however, Western states act as if the failures of non-market mechanisms obviate the need to consider the (different but no less real) failures of markets in the struggle to improve human welfare. Perhaps this will begin to change as Western states begin to grapple more seriously with the "adjustment costs" of greater international openness. But an ideological commitment to international markets—with some rather crude, self-interested interventions to protect national labor and firms—is clearly the dominant model of international welfare in the West today.

Sovereignty and International Legitimacy

Without denying the argument of the preceding paragraphs, we can discern a deeper consistency in the Western approach to the institutions of international society. For both order and welfare—that is, for all internationally recognized human rights—the Western approach is radically statist. States are seen as responsible for implementing the human rights of their own citizens, whether this involves developing political and legal practices that respect civil and political rights or marshaling the resources and administrative skills needed to deliver education, health care, and other economic and social rights.

Self-help is the norm. International institutions may moderate conflict and facilitate cooperation among states. They are not mechanisms to realize a broader substantive vision of a collective good. The Western society of states is more a practical than a purposive association (Nardin 1983, ch. 1). Its rules seek more to facilitate states' realization of their own purposes, both individually and collectively, than to realize any particular shared substantive purposes. To use a distinction that has become popular within the English School, the underlying conception of international society is "pluralist" rather than "solidarist" (Bull 1977, 148–49, 156–58, 238–40; Wheeler 2000, 27–51).

Sovereignty has been at the heart of the Western approach to international legitimacy over the past two centuries. In the decades following World War II, the tradition of sovereign legitimacy was strongly reinforced by the rise of the principle of self-determination for colonized people, whose post-independence governments typically embraced a rigid, statist understanding of sovereignty and non-intervention with even more enthusiasm than their colleagues in the West.

More recently however, there have been signs of Western rethinking of the boundaries and scope of sovereign rights and prerogatives. The economic and technological logic of globalization have driven much of this reconsideration. I want to focus here, however, on the ways in which conceptions of international legitimacy are being reshaped by human rights ideas.

Although states often talk as if their sovereignty were a matter of natural right or an inescapable logical feature of their existence, it in fact rests on mutual recognition. Those who are sovereign are those who are recognized as sovereign by other sovereigns. And that recognition need not be unconditional. The classic example was the nineteenth-century legal doctrine and practice that extended full recognition only to those states that met minimum criteria of "civilized" treatment of both native and foreign populations.

As opposed to the contemporaneous practice of colonial rule, Western states recognized rather than denied or extinguished the sovereignty of China, Japan, the Ottoman Empire, and Siam. These "uncivilized" states enjoyed a restricted set of international legal rights. Their sovereignty, however, was treated as real, if impaired (Gong 1984; Roling 1960, ch. 4; Schwarzenberger 1955). The Holy Alliance was a more short-lived and purely regional example of an attempt to impose substantive standards of recognition. Consider also the substantive standards of recognition imposed on revolutionary regimes by the United States throughout the twentieth century.

I would suggest that human rights—or, more precisely, the avoidance of genocide—is emerging as something like a new standard of civilization.[12] For all the recent failings of international humanitarian action, especially in Rwanda, the comfortable assurance of genocidal regimes during the Cold War that they need not worry about multilateral international action— consider, for example, Pol Pot and Idi Amin, who were toppled by unilateral action by neighbors for largely geopolitical reasons—has been shattered. The emergence of a doctrine of international criminal responsibility, reflected in the creation of the International Criminal Court and in the surprisingly successful attempt to prosecute General Pinochet, points in the same direction. Perhaps the most interesting case is the NATO intervention in Kosovo.

Humanitarian Intervention

Full recognition as part of European international society has long required more than just control over one's territory and people. The Council of Europe and the European Union insist on democracy and protection of human rights as conditions of membership, as reflected in the exclusion of Franco's Spain and Salazar's Portugal, the sanctions against Greece under the generals, and dealings over the past decade with former Soviet bloc states. Kosovo can be read as extending this policy to regional resistance to genocide.

Let us, for the sake of argument, grant that the NATO action was in large part humanitarian. Let us also grant that the Kosovo intervention—however badly executed, and whatever else it was about—reflected learning from Bosnia and Rwanda: rather than wait until the bodies had piled up, there is a right (although not an obligation) to intervene when genocide is imminent. But whether genocide was in fact imminent is questionable. And the claim that regional groups are authorized to act for the international community is extraordinarily contentious. Therefore, let us talk about Kosovo, an idealized construct of heuristic value however problematic it may be historically.[13] Kosovo, read as the culmination and extension of post-Cold War humanitarian interventions going back to Somalia, suggests an emerging redefinition of the bounds of sovereign prerogative.

In the aftermath of Bosnia, all Western states continued to recognize Kosovo as subject to Serbian/Yugoslav sovereignty. The sovereignty of Yugoslavia/Serbia, however, increasingly came to be seen as imperfect or impaired. When a determination was made that genocide in Kosovo was likely, perhaps even imminent, the United States and NATO acted as if the sovereign rights of the authorities in Belgrade did not extend to that sort of action within what still was legally recognized as "their" territory.[14]

Genocide is becoming conceptualized more like aggression. States guilty of aggression forfeit their right to non-intervention, as the case of Iraq illustrates. They remain sovereign. But their aggression authorizes international action that infringes their territorial integrity and political independence. Kosovo suggests that states guilty of (or about to embark on) genocide likewise forfeit the standard protection of the international legal obligation of non-intervention.

The development of international humanitarian and human rights law over the past half-century, going back to Nuremberg and the Universal Declaration of Human Rights (UDHR), created the normative foundations for an extension of minimal international legal guarantees to nationals against their own governments. Kosovo represents the first (relatively) unambiguous coercive international action[15] to enforce such standards.

It has long been established that massacring foreign nationals in one's own territory is not a right possessed by sovereign states. Kosovo suggests the emergence of comparable protections for citizens against their own state. Read in this way, the Kosovo intervention implies a new international division of responsibility for implementing internationally recognized human rights, at least in cases of genocide (committed by states that are not great powers). We are, I think, seeing the beginnings of a (very limited) practice of national responsibility to the international community for at least certain human rights practices (International Commission 2001). International society—or at least European international society—is refusing to accept as full members states that do not meet very minimal human rights standards in the treatment of their subjects.

We should not over-estimate the depth or significance of these changes. Regimes guilty of human rights violations other than genocide, and perhaps systematic torture and disappearances, still are treated as unsavory but legitimate. Nonetheless, the old, strictly statist, legal positivist conception of international legitimacy has had its armor at least dented, especially in post-Maastricht Europe, but also in post-Cold War international society, where the West is playing a leading role in setting the pace of change.

Conclusion: Thinking About the Future

I am painfully aware of numerous glaring omissions and controversial readings in the above account. I only hope that, like any good caricature, it has drawn attention to a few important features in order to sketch a distinctive vision of the subject. That vision, as I indicated at the outset, is of a Western approach to legitimate governance that is closely associated, especially in its national dimensions, with internationally recognized human rights.

The Western approach, even in my ideal type presentation, is neither entirely coherent nor static. Quite the contrary, it is constantly, if slowly, changing, in response to varied internal and external forces. Were I to speculate on future developments, I would focus on the problematic nature of a vision of governance that relies so heavily on national boundaries.

Western states are no less threatened by globalization than their non-Western counterparts. The liberal democratic welfare state seems to have "fit" the post-World War II world rather well. Boundaries were substantially less porous to goods, capital, people, and information alike, and the scale of production had not yet so obviously outgrown territorial states. Despite titles in the scholarly literature such as *Beyond the Nation State* (Haas 1964) and *Sovereignty at Bay* (Vernon 1971), a state-centered approach to governance was still at least workable. The state, as realists constantly remind us, remains surprisingly robust and certainly is not yet clearly obsolete. I do, however, think the possibility is worth seriously considering that the state is becoming obsolescent.

Were this the case, I think it would be extremely problematic for human rights, which do not protect or implement themselves. If states do not have responsibility for human rights, who or what will? The progress of human rights has been inescapably tied to states. Can these achievements be sustained in a world no longer organized around sovereign territorial states?

With firms increasingly operating globally, will states (or their successors) be able to continue to extract the resources necessary to fund their welfare programs? The European Union appears to be working to avoid a race to the bottom, but regionalism would seem to be at best a stopgap measure if we really are moving towards a single global economy. Whatever the poetic justice in the Western welfare state being destroyed by global neo-liberalism, it seems unlikely that the result would be better enjoyment of economic and social rights.

Consider also the fragmentation of identities and loyalties often presented as a hallmark of our postmodern era. To the extent that loyalty has become instrumental—one identifies with those institutions, individuals, and groups that enable one to enjoy one's rights or with whom one has elective affinities—the special links between citizens and states that are at the heart of the Western contractarian approach may be undermined, especially if Western states are unable to continue to restrict the flow of migrants.

The resulting systems of multiple cross cutting linkages and loyalties that would result are often labeled "neo-medieval" (Bull 1977, 254–55, 264–76). Although such scenarios come in benign as well as malign versions, I worry about large numbers of individuals and groups ending up marginalized.

The decline of central political institutions aggressively committed to active inclusion of all citizens in the equal enjoyment of basic rights seems to me more ominous than liberating. The liberal democratic state, for all its shortcomings, aspires to treat all citizens as "self" rather than "other" when it comes to human rights, and has had considerable success in realizing these aspirations. Will smaller, more fragmented, less powerful (although perhaps more focused) institutions prove as successful?

In any case, the Western vision of legitimate governance over the past half century has been dominated by the liberal democratic welfare state. It remains hegemonic today. And no attractive alternative has yet appeared on the horizon.

Chapter 3
Muslim Perspectives

Valerie J. Hoffman

There is no single Muslim perspective on the topic of human rights. Although virtually all Muslims believe that Islam guarantees human rights, there is a great deal of disagreement on specifics. Many Muslims believe that there is no incompatibility between Western notions of human rights and Islam; some even argue for an Islamic derivation of Western human rights concepts. Islam has also often provided the idiom in which Muslims have expressed their demands for human rights in the face of government oppression. On the other hand, Islamization programs instituted by governments have often involved human rights violations that have been justified in the name of Islam. Any discussion of contending legitimacies must take into account the struggle taking place within the Muslim world itself before focusing on the compatibility of Muslim concepts of human rights with international norms. There is broad divergence on the definition of Islam itself and on the extent to which Islam contains within itself a comprehensive and unchangeable blueprint for society. We may wish to acknowledge the legitimacy of religiously based conceptions of human rights that vary from Western models, but situating the authoritative definition of Islamic human rights is virtually impossible.

The Nature of Islamic Law

Muslims often claim that Islam is distinct from Christianity in that it is not only a religion but also a complete way of life. This claim is based on the fact that the massive volumes of Islamic jurisprudence have something to say on *all* aspects of life: not only religious obligations, but also social, economic, and political relationships. Islamic jurisprudence is concerned not only with commands and prohibitions, but also with an ethical analysis of *all* acts. These are classified according to one of five categories: obligatory, recommended, permitted-neutral, reprehensible-disliked, or prohibited. Of these categories, only the first and last would concern government, as only these would entail punishment for omission or commission. However punishments were rarely prescribed, unless such were already mentioned in the Qur'an for a similar or analogous situation. Even in cases where the jurisprudents have prescribed penalties—for example for neglect of obligatory prayer—governments have rarely enforced these punishments. So despite the theoretical inclusion of all aspects of life in a publicly mandated system, from the beginning large segments of life have been relegated de facto to the private sphere.

Furthermore, Muslim jurisconsults have rarely agreed on the details of law. The famous twelfth-century philosopher of Spain, Ibn Rushd (known in the West as Averroes), was not only an important commentator on the works of Aristotle, but also chief *qadi* (judge) of Cordova. His masterpiece on jurisprudence, *Bidayat al-mujtahid wa nihayat al-muqtalid* (Promoting Reasoning in Law and Putting an End to Reliance on Established Legal Opinions), examines Islamic law with respect to the divergences that exist among the four Sunni legal schools. These regard each other as valid interpretations of the law (Shi'i and Ibadi legal schools are not even considered). Nearly every new topic is introduced with the words, "The jurisprudents disagree . . ." Most disagreements are based on divergent *hadiths* (accounts of what the Prophet Muhammad said and did). In other words, divergence of purportedly authentic textual sources and divergence of jurisprudential opinion are accepted within Islam. There is even a hadith to reassure Muslims concerning this: The Prophet allegedly said, "Disagreement among the jurisprudents of my community is a blessing." According to another hadith, individuals who do *ijtihad* (systematic individual reasoning on matters of law) are guaranteed a divine reward for their efforts, even if their conclusions are incorrect, whereas those who come to a correct conclusion will receive a tenfold reward. Therefore one European scholar of Islam said that Islamic law is not a code of law, but rather a discussion on the duties of Muslims (Gibb 1953, 68). The first attempt to codify Islamic law occurred in the eighteenth-century Ottoman Empire. But such attempts have always been problematic.

Despite slogans issued by Islamist groups like the Muslim Brotherhood or the Saudi regime proclaiming, "The Qur'an is our constitution," the legal content of the Qur'an is minimal; it nowhere approaches the comprehensiveness of Islamic law. Islamic law is based not only on the Qur'an, which Muslims believe to be God's word, but also on Hadith, the huge body of literature that organizes under topical headings the various and often conflicting accounts of what the Prophet said and did. Concerning new issues that were not discussed in these two sources, qualified scholars exercised their individual judgment (ijtihad) by analogical reasoning based on a common motive or element existing between the new issue and precedents contained in the Qur'an and Hadith. Finally the law is based on the consensus of scholars, such as it might exist. Sunni Muslims revere the earliest generation of Muslims as closest to the Prophet and best able to make judgments on all issues. In the tenth century a general consensus emerged among Sunni Muslims that the "gate of ijtihad" should be closed, as earlier Muslims had dealt with all problems adequately; all Sunni Muslims were now obliged to follow the opinions of earlier scholars. Of course there have been Muslims who continued to exercise ijtihad, and the title of Ibn Rushd's book indicates his desire to promote its practice. In the eighteenth and nineteenth centuries, Muslim reformers of various persuasions began to insist on the necessity of reopening the gate of ijtihad. Modernists in particular insisted on this, in order to modernize Islamic law.

We have established, then, that Islamic law is not monolithic, and that there are divergences in its interpretation. We also see the high priority given to the Prophet Muhammad's example as the basis for articulation of the law. What this means is that the norms of a rudimentary seventh-century society, as reported and interpreted by Muslim scholars of the ninth century, became the basis of Islamic law. It is this fact that has been most problematic for Muslims trying to articulate a modern Islamic identity.

Conservative, Modernist, and Islamist Muslims

In order to give some structure to this morass, we will employ broad categories and terms that necessarily camouflage the very real diversity that exists within those categories: conservative Muslims claim that the model for the present is essentially that of the past, whereas modernist or liberal Muslims distinguish the essential, unchanging theological teachings of Islam from social laws that are bound to specific sociohistorical contexts and are inappropriate or even offensive for application in modern contexts. Modernists believe that the interpretation of Islamic law requires looking at the spirit, purpose, or "moral thrust" of Qur'anic teachings rather than following the letter of the law as traditionally understood (Rahman 1982). Modernist Muslims believe that the liberal potential of Islam has been limited or stifled by concessions to human stubbornness, cruelty, and traditional culture. They believe that Islam embodies within itself the spirit of freedom, justice, and equality among people, and that all laws purporting to derive from Islam but inhibiting human rights are the result of the limitations and selfishness of the men who composed the books of Islamic law. Rather than examining the laws derived from Hadith and other ninth-century texts, modernists believe it is the responsibility of modern Muslims to examine the moral teachings of the Qur'an in a fresh light, to discern their high ethical values, and then devise laws embodying those values that are suitable for contemporary society and its aspirations. For modernists, what cannot change and evolve is stagnant and lifeless, and Islamic law as traditionally conceived is precisely such a lifeless and stifling body of tradition that choked Muslim initiative and the spirit of freedom for many centuries.

Some modernists, like Jamal al-Din al-Afghani (1838–97) and Muhammad 'Abduh (1849–1905), saw the earliest Muslim community as embodying a flexibility, intellectual vitality, and liberality of spirit that must be recovered by modern Muslims in order for them to survive and prosper in the modern world. Other modernists however, such as the Lebanese woman Nazira Zein-ed-Din (born around 1905), the Sudanese reformer Mahmud Muhammad Taha (1909 or 1911–85), and the contemporary scholar Mohamed Talbi of Tunisia, fault the early Muslim community for its inability to receive the true message of the Qur'an in its earliest, egalitarian form, necessitating the imposition of regulations in the Medinese period of Muhammad's rule (622–632) that were intended to die away in time.

Islamists are members of movements that intend to make Islam the basis for political and social life. As there have been a large number of such movements, their ideological approaches may vary, although they tend to be fundamentalist: that is, rejecting much of the accumulated tradition as inconsistent with the foundations of Islam, which lie in the Qur'an and Sunna. In reality, their positions are often quite conservative, although they are critical of conservative Muslim scholars for their tendencies to allow themselves to become the mouthpieces for governments that are (in their view) not based on Islam. However, there are exceptions. 'Ali Shari'ati, ideologue of the Islamic revolution, was quite modernist in his thinking and employed Marxist vocabulary to reinterpret basic concepts of Twelver Shi'ism and make them a basis of political action. Rashid al-Ghannoushi, leader of the Al-Nahda (Renaissance) party of Tunisia, often speaks as if he were a modernist, although some suspect this to be merely a ploy to disarm non-Islamists, not a genuine reflection of his ideas (Dunn 1992). And Hasan al-Turabi, until recently the ideologue of the Sudanese government, cunningly employs a very Western vocabulary that makes him sound like a modernist, although his party's regime in Sudan has been authoritarian and fundamentalist.

Defining Islamic Politics

Earlier we pointed out the fallacy latent in the Muslim Brotherhood slogan, "The Qur'an is our constitution." Another Brotherhood slogan, "Islam is religion and state," is also highly problematic. In fact, the historical manifestations of states claiming validity on the basis of Islam have been highly variable, even in the pre-modern period. Advocates of democracy, socialism, and totalitarianism have all been able to find justifications in Islamic principles and precedents. Even if we admit that the basic feature of an Islamic state is that it applies Islamic law, we find that "Islamic" states have been variable and highly selective in their application of this law. The questions of who has the authority to define an Islamic state, which precedents constitute genuine models for Islamic states, which interpretations and what parts of Islamic law should be applied in an Islamic state, and whether the Prophet ever even intended to establish a theocratic state, are all hotly contested and debated among Muslims today.

Authority and Political Activism

The Qur'an connects obedience to the Prophet "and those in authority among you" (4:59) with obedience to God. Although there are hadiths that recommend correcting rulers who do not follow the prescriptions of the Shari'a, with the sword if necessary, a preponderance of Sunni hadiths favor obedience to those in authority, even if they order something that contravenes the Shari'a: "he will be punished [in the afterlife], but you will be rewarded for your obedience." Another hadith says, "Seventy years of tyranny are better than a single day of civil war." Sunni scholars came to favor political quietism.

Traditional Sunni political treatises were concerned with the institution of the caliphate (*khilafa*), which literally means "vicegerency," a concept of Qur'anic derivation: God created human beings as his vicegerents on earth. Sunni Caliphs sometimes adopted the title "shadow of God on earth," but they were nonetheless subject to the Shari'a and were not authorized to define Islamic law or dogma. The Imams of the Twelver and Isma'ili Shi'a were often not political leaders at all, but were deemed by their followers to be chosen by God, heirs of a portion of divine light inherited from their ancestor, the Prophet Muhammad, by virtue of which they are immune from error and know the hidden meanings of the Qur'an, and serve, consecutively, as the only true spiritual guide for the Muslim community. The Isma'ilis have had continuous lines of Imams in several distinct sects, but the last of the Twelver Imams disappeared in 874 and is thought to be in hiding, undying, until the end of the age, when he will return as the Mahdi "to fill the world with justice, as it is now filled with iniquity." In his absence, it has often been argued that there can be no truly legitimate government. In fact, Twelver Shi'i ulama have often cooperated with various governments. Ayatollah Khomeini put an entirely new twist on traditional Twelver Shi'i politics by arguing that in the absence of the Imam, government should be placed under the guardianship of a qualified scholar of law or group of such scholars.

The Oath of Allegiance

The oath of allegiance (*bay'a*) is an institution that predates Islam, as it was used in Arabia to confirm the selection of a new tribal or clan head. In this sense the bay'a has sometimes been described by Western scholars as a type of electoral process, at least among Sunnis, Ibadis, and Zaydi Shi'a, as well as a promise of obedience to the person to whom the oath is given. In most circumstances, however, the bayʿa essentially confirms pre-established authority (Tyan 1999). During the lifetime of the Prophet, conversion to Islam was marked by offering him the bayʿa through shaking hands or dipping hands in a common bowl of water that would be passed among the group. The Qurʾan says that God's hands are over the hands of the Prophet in the bayʿa, making it a most holy institution (48:10, 18; 60:13).

Islamic jurisprudence regards the bayʿa that elects a caliph as a contractual agreement. The earliest ideal was that the electors included all "upright men of the whole empire," but this ideal rapidly eroded, especially as de facto dynastic succession became the norm, and the bayʿa was no longer voluntary. Political theorists like al-Mawardi (died 1058), trying to uphold the theory of election in the face of its utter absence, held that an election was valid even if there were only a single elector; that is, a caliph could designate his successor. The practice of having representatives from various regions come to give their oaths to new caliphs nonetheless remained. According to Sunni political theory, termination of the contract between a caliph and the people was only permitted if a change took place in the caliph's status and condition such as might threaten the rights of the community. However, there was no tribunal authorized to depose the caliph.

Consultation

The Qurʾan says, "Rule among you shall be by consultation (*shura*)" (42:38), although details regarding who was to be consulted and in what manner and how binding the advice of counselors is on the sovereign are all left unstated. Nonetheless this is the term, more than any other, which according to some thinkers indicates the essentially democratic nature of true Islamic rule, despite a history and current reality of overwhelmingly autocratic regimes. The first shura committee was officially formed by the second caliph, ʿUmar ibn al-Khattab (ruled 634–644), as he lay on his deathbed, to select the next caliph. The same procedure, with the same surviving individuals, was reactivated to select the fourth caliph. However, it is noteworthy that the conclusions of this last consultation were rejected by significant segments of the Muslim population, and the period of ʿAli ibn Abi Talib's rule was one of civil war that ended in his assassination in 661. No other instances of shura committees have been recorded. The concept of shura has never been institutionalized or elaborated in works of Islamic jurisprudence.

Theoretically, the caliph ought to consult the scholars of the law, who are often called "the people of loosing and binding," but there is nothing that requires him to follow their bidding. Rare exceptions to this rule may be found in the history of the tiny Ibadi sect of Oman (Wilkinson 1987), which is the closest to a democratic model of government, but these have been achieved rarely and usually with a great deal of bloodshed and instability.

Ottoman sultans had *diwans* or councils consisting of leading men to discuss affairs of state, but ultimately power remained solely in the hands of the sultan. Modern Muslim nation-states wishing to enhance their Islamic credibility have sometimes in the last few decades established a shura council, usually consisting of leading religious scholars, even if these states already had functioning parliaments. Other states that until recently lacked any parliament have given in to domestic and international pressures to democratize their political systems by establishing shura councils that serve the function of parliaments in other countries. In none of the Muslim nation-states, however, does the legislature have real effective power; power remains firmly concentrated in the hands of the head of state.

Are Democracy and Human Rights Compatible with Islam?

We will attempt to answer this question by comparing Islamic theory with the elements inherent in international standards of democracy, which are elaborated in Donnelly's contribution elsewhere in this volume.

Popular Sovereignty

Although some Muslims have argued that sovereignty belongs to God and not to the people, the combined thrust of the concepts of consultation and human vicegerency have often been interpreted as meaning, in practice, nothing less than popular sovereignty. In practice, however, power has usually been concentrated in the hands of a single man and his cohorts. There has never, before the creation of modern nation-states, been any tradition of popular elections. The concept of bayʿa has sometimes been discussed as an electoral process, but even when an actual selection by a group of people was taking place, the group was always limited to the leading men of the community. It has also been described as a type of contract, but, as we have seen, there are no procedures in Sunni law to remove rulers who fail to uphold their side of the contractual relationship. Throughout the Muslim world today such elections as do take place are often very flawed in their procedure.

The Rule of Law

Even the direst Western critics of Islam have had to admit that Islamic tradition certainly contains a deep respect for the rule of law. Nonetheless, despite the existence of judicial courts that could rule independently of the opinion of the caliph, we have no instances in Sunni history of these courts actually functioning in such a way as to limit the authority of the ruler or dismiss him.

The Creation of Legislative Bodies

There is no tradition of legislative bodies in Islam before the creation of modern nation-states. Such bodies as do exist are usually rubberstamp legislatures, lacking real, significant power to create laws or to limit the power of the head of state.

Another important question is the legitimacy of human legislation. Some Muslims have argued that the Shari'a is so complete that human legislation is unnecessary, and it is on such a basis that Saudi Arabia resisted the formation of any representative body for decades. Nonetheless many Islamists recognize the need to create laws that reflect both the ideals of Islam and the needs of modern societies. Some nations, like Pakistan, contented themselves with saying that the laws that are created should not be repugnant to the Shari'a. But when Zia ul-Haqq overthrew Bhutto's regime in 1977, he inaugurated an Islamization program that was designed to implement Shari'a laws directly. The question of whether Shari'a laws as traditionally understood can actually produce economic prosperity and social harmony is a matter of tremendous controversy among Muslims today.

Freedom of Thought, Conscience, Religion, and the Press

Many Muslims cite the Qur'anic verse, "There shall be no compulsion in religion" (2:256), to indicate that Islam favors freedom of thought, conscience, religion, and the press. Nonetheless, some Muslims believe that the legal weight of this passage is overridden by other verses that order Muslims to fight unbelievers, "until idolatry is no more and God's religion reigns supreme" (2:193), and to slay unbelievers wherever they may be found (2:191). The official policy of the early Muslim community was rigid harshness in dealing with polytheists, but to allow Jews, Christians, and others who could be construed as monotheists, such as Zoroastrians or even Hindus, the freedom to practice their religion, provided they did not oppose Muslim rule, paid the prescribed taxes, and did not propagate their religion or repair existing houses of worship. The Qur'an says that God will harshly punish Muslims who renounce the faith (2:217), but Islamic law as drawn up by Muslim scholars mandates capital punishment for apostates, an undeniable limitation on freedom of religion. Many modern Muslims, however, have embraced the notion of freedom of religion and believe that this is endorsed by Islam itself—that recourse to violence in the time of the Prophet was limited in scope and must be understood in that particular social context, not seen as the model for all time.

Although the press did not exist in the time of Muhammad or in the period when Islamic law was being formulated, poets often served as political satirists, and Muhammad was often the butt of the satire of poets in the period before the Muslim conquest of Mecca. When Mecca was conquered a general amnesty was declared for all Meccans who had resisted Islam, except for the poets, who were executed. One would have to conclude that the model offered by the early Muslim community and traditional Islamic law is one that places severe constraints on freedom of speech, although there are a number of contemporary Muslims who offer much more liberal interpretations. While nearly all Muslim countries constitutionally guarantee freedom of speech, provisions excepting blasphemy often curtail this freedom. Governments are able to construe the statements of their opponents as blasphemy or treason, thereby de facto prohibiting free speech.

A number of modern Muslim writers have advocated absolute freedom of religion. For Mohamed Talbi of Tunisia, faith has no meaning if there is no freedom of choice. He sees humanity as naturally and rightly fragmented and diverse in outlook, and that the refusal to deny equal validity to points of view other than one's own is against innate human nature (*fitra*) (Nettler 1998, 133–35). Mahmud Taha of Sudan, who was executed for his unusual Islamic interpretations in 1985, also proposed "absolute individual freedom" as a right enjoyed by all human beings, regardless of religion or race (Mahmoud 1998, 110). Talbi addresses the thorny issue of apostasy from Islam. "During the history of Islam," he says, "I am not aware of any historical or current application of the law condemning the apostate to death." The cases of "apostates" killed in the time of the Prophet and the early Caliphs involved defending the small, vulnerable community of Muslims against groups of people who had taken up arms against them, not individuals exercising freedom of conscience. Talbi (1998) considers the issue of real apostasy largely theoretical, for Muslim conversions to other religions are largely unknown in most of the world.

Rashid al-Ghannoushi, Islamist leader of Tunisia, likewise says that early Muslims considered apostasy a political crime. He adds that there are "examples during and after the Prophet's life, where the apostate was not executed, but was forgiven." The fact that the Hanafi school of law does not allow the execution of a female apostate, because she is not expected to carry arms, supports this perspective. Ghannoushi (1998) favors freedom of belief and prohibition of compulsion, as this is in keeping with Qur'anic injunctions not to try to compel people to believe (10:99; 50:45).

Nonetheless, calls for the application of the death penalty for apostasy have been made not only against those who have publicly disavowed Islam, but also against individuals whose views have been deemed insufficiently Islamic. While the case of Salman Rushdie is most famous in the West, the court conviction of Egyptian professor Nasr Abu Zayd of apostasy (with the intention of forcing the dissolution of his marriage), the execution of Mahmud Taha in Sudan, and the assassination of liberal journalists such as Farag Foda in Egypt and countless individuals from all walks of life in Algeria, illustrate the possible ramifications of rigidity and intolerance, even among professing Muslims.

Freedom of Peaceful Assembly and Association

This is not a topic with which Islamic law deals, but there is an incident mentioned in the Qur'an that provides a fairly disturbing precedent in this regard. A group of Muslims in Medina had built a mosque in which they could meet and pray separately from the Prophet's mosque, which was virtually an extension of the Prophet's house. This mosque is described as a rival mosque and a source of discord, and it is ordered destroyed (9:107–10). This incident would give paranoid rulers excellent precedent in denying people the right of peaceful assembly and association.

Existence of Political Parties

The Qur'an looks unfavorably on any divisions among Muslims, and the Arabic word for political party, *hizb*, is mentioned with great disfavor in the Qur'an. The unity and brotherhood of all believers is emphasized in numerous verses, and the Qur'an speaks disparagingly of those who separate themselves from "the party of God" (5:56; 30:31–32). Many contemporary heads of state also decry the "factionalism" of political parties, thereby justifying the hegemony of a single ruling party.

Freedom from Arbitrary Arrest, Detention, Exile, Torture, and Cruel or Unusual Punishment

Although these issues are not discussed as such in Islamic law, there are innumerable Qur'anic verses and prophetic sayings enjoining justice and kindness. Modernist and conservative Muslims agree that Islam accords full dignity to the individual. Islam is seen as a religion that promotes social justice among individuals, guaranteeing them the right to life and a minimal standard of living, and freedom from torture, seizure of their property, arbitrary imprisonment, or execution without just cause. They agree that the weak elements of society, such as women and ethnic or religious minorities, should be protected by the state.

Nonetheless, many non-Muslims, like many Muslims, fear the imposition of Islamic criminal law, which imposes penalties deemed harsh by contemporary standards. International Muslim reactions to the execution of Shari'a penalties may be illustrated by an exchange that came over the Muslim e-mail network of east-central Illinois in February 2000. One man wrote, "Praise be to God! Shari'a has come to Nigeria!" He proceeded to illustrate this joyous news with the description of the amputation of the hand of a notorious cattle thief before a crowd of thousands of cheering onlookers. This message prompted the following response from another local Muslim: "We're talking about ripping somebody's hand off! Is this the kind of Islam we want to see? Wouldn't it be something if Muslims came up with a

Shari'a-based law that gave greater honors and privileges to non-Muslims, so they would see that Islam is a religion of peace?"

Free Choice in Marriage

Islamic law grants fathers, grandfathers, or other guardians of minors and women the right to choose spouses and contract marriages for those in their care. Children may dissolve the marriage bond by mutual agreement once they come of age. In the case of a woman marrying for the first time, silence on her part is construed as consent, whereas a divorcee or widow must give explicit consent for marriage. The social reality of marriage is often even more coercive than these regulations from the Shari'a indicate, however, as women are frequently forced into marriages against their will, even when their aversion to the match is publicly expressed. Although there have been considerable social shifts in parts of the Muslim world on this issue, with young people in urban areas in particular postponing marriage in order to pursue careers and education and insisting on taking part in their own marriage choices, this remains a major area of contention. The cultural constraints on marriage choices extend, however, even to guardians, because Islamic law requires that a woman not marry beneath her social station. Furthermore, although Muslim men may marry Jewish or Christian women, according to Islamic law, Muslim women may only marry Muslim men. A traditional interpretation of Islamic marriage law would obviously not accord with modern notions of free choice in marriage. Nonetheless, Tunisia's modernist Personal Status Law of 1956 allows both men and women complete freedom in marriage, seeing this as consonant with the spirit of Islam.

Equality of All Citizens Before the Law

This most fundamental of all topics has been left for last, not because it is least important, but precisely because it is the most problematic and requires detailed examination. The word "equality" (*musawat*) does not exist in the Qur'an, although the verses that proclaim the brotherhood of all Muslims are sometimes taken today in the sense of equality. The Qur'an says that the only distinction among Muslims is their piety (49:13), which provided a popular movement of the 'Abbasid period known as the Shu'ubiyya (literally those belonging to the "peoples," that is, non-Arabs) the ammunition they needed to demand equal rights with Arabs under the Islamic empire. The Shu'ubiyya were sometimes known as *ahl al-taswiya* ("proponents of equalization") (Bosworth 1999). But the notion of human equality is clearly a Western import into the Muslim world. Of the three principles of the French Revolution—liberty, fraternity, and equality—the first two appealed most to westernizing Muslims. The concept of human equality is clearly problematic for a society accustomed to making distinctions between Muslim and non-Muslim, male and female, and free versus slave, of which in each category of paired opposites, those who fall into the first group are accorded significantly superior legal rights. Slavery was gradually abolished under Western pressure in the late nineteenth century. Constitutions drawn up in the newly modernizing nation-states until the last quarter of the twentieth century often granted Muslims and non-Muslims equal rights, but nations like Pakistan and Saudi Arabia whose very raison d'être is Islam found it far more difficult to allow such equality. Moreover, in most countries gender equality was never realized, even on paper, although a number of governments did work to improve women's legal status. The concept of human equality did make some headway in the early twentieth century when the ideas of the European Enlightenment and socialism became fashionable among some sections of the westernized intelligentsia.

Ann Elizabeth Mayer finds that conservative Muslims assert that Islam endorses the principle of equality and requires equal treatment of individuals under the law, regardless of race, ethnicity, or language. Conspicuously absent is inclusion of gender and religion in the list of categories among which discrimination is not allowed. Muslims are socialized to believe that the innate differences among the sexes go well beyond their reproductive roles, and that men are inherently superior (Mayer 1991, 94).

Conservative Islamic Human Rights Schemes

Rashid Ghannoushi, a leading Islamist of Tunisia living in self-exile in London, undoubtedly reflected the opinion of many in the Third World when he said, "This New World Order, from the point of view of its intellectual content, its ideology, and its religion, is not new. It is simply U.S. hegemony over the world, clothed in the ideology of human rights." Nonetheless, when asked to elaborate on this statement, Ghannoushi expressed his gratitude to human rights organizations for their fight for the rights of all people, including Islamists.

Ghannoushi's position on human rights is representative of that of many Muslims, and undoubtedly many non-Muslims, regarding the value of having an international standard of human rights, but deeply resenting the arrogation by Western nations to themselves of the prerogative of defining and enforcing those rights while maintaining and exercising a worldwide hegemony that freely tramples on the rights of others. It is not surprising that Muslims should decide to draw up their own human rights schemes with the aim of subscribing to international notions of human rights while preserving Islamic cultural particularities.

In 1981 a group of conservative Muslims from a number of countries prepared a document entitled the Universal Islamic Declaration of Human Rights (UIDHR) that was presented in Paris to the UN Educational, Scientific and Cultural Organization (UNESCO). The title of the document indicates that it is intended as an Islamic response to the UDHR. Mayer discerns "a pattern of borrowing substantive rights from international human rights documents while reducing the protections that they actually afford. This is accomplished by restricting them so that the rights can only be enjoyed within the limits of the shariʿa, which are unspecified. These emendations leave virtually unlimited discretion to states in deciding what the scope of the affected rights should be" (Mayer 1991, 76).

The fact that conservative Muslims have tried to pattern their document after the UIDHR and camouflage divergence from it indicates their sensitivity to international opinion and their desire to be recognized in the international community as preserving human rights in their domains, even as they arrogate to their governments vast areas of authority to curtail human rights in the name of Islam. Mayer sees in the writings of many conservative Muslim theorists on human rights a tendency to make individual rights subordinate to their obligations to the community (64–65).

While Islamists actively oppose governments they see as un-Islamic, they assume that it is the role of governments to take responsibility for the ethical character of the public arena (Ayubi 1991, 35). Their writings often reflect a vision of an idealized, altruistic society in which government and society will naturally cooperate to bring about God's will on earth and advance the welfare of society, despite the fact that they readily acknowledge the absence of such a government and society since the time of the Prophet and his four immediate successors. Such a perspective is in radical opposition to the notion of constitutionalism, which places limitations on the power of the government over individual freedoms and guarantees the autonomy of different branches of government. The system of checks and balances assumes that self-interest is the main operative principle at the level of both individuals and government.

What the UIDHR says is that people have equal rights under the Shariʿa, a code of law that retains discriminatory categories, making distinctions between free and slave, male and female, and Muslim and non-Muslim. Although slavery has no legal existence in the Muslim world any more and most Muslims agree that it is a retrograde institution, application of the same assessment to Shariʿa distinctions on the basis of sex and religion is much more problematic. The equality of which the UIDHR speaks is an equality of all Muslim men with each other, and of all Muslim women with each other, but not with Muslim men, and so forth.

It is not only conservative Muslims who insist on having the right to draw up a specifically Islamic formulation of human rights. Bassam Tibi, professor of international relations at the University of Gottingen, comments, "Committed as I am to the *idea* of individual human rights, I, as a liberal Muslim, ask that we seek instead, ways for us Muslims to speak the language of human rights *in our own tongues.*" Nonetheless, he insists that despite the

Western derivation of the notion of universal human rights, they do not belong exclusively to the West. He sees political Islam and all varieties of fundamentalism, including those in the West, as obstacles to the establishment of international human rights. He also objects to the tendency of Islamists to isolate Muslims from the rest of the world by their over-insistence on Muslim particularity (Tibi 1998, 205–7).

Regardless of the lack of real democracy and the reality of political oppression throughout the Muslim world, most Muslim theorists endorse the notions of democracy and free political expression. The problem is that the regimes in power simply do not allow democracy to exist. Likewise, Muslim theorists would all agree on the equality of Muslim men, regardless of ethnicity, so the actual instances of persecution of ethnic minorities such as the Kurds in Iraq have no religious justification. However, the questions of the status of religious minorities and women remain the most universally problematic theoretical issues because they come into direct conflict with Islamic law and precedent.

The Rights of Religious Minorities

Historical Perspectives

In addition to placing restrictions on religious minorities to propagate their religion and repair their houses of worship, the policy toward minorities drawn up by the second caliph, 'Umar ibn al-Khattab (reigned 634–644), was that non-Muslims were denied the right to carry arms and were required to show their subservience to Muslims by not riding horses, by showing humiliating deference to any Muslims they passed on their way, and by wearing distinctive colors and belts that would immediately let people know their inferior status. They were not to hold political office. Actual application of these rules has varied, and it is fair to say that Christians and Jews were relatively well treated under Muslim rule, especially compared to the treatment of Jews in Western Europe under many Christian regimes in the Middle Ages. Nonetheless it is obvious that the second-class status accorded to "People of the Book" and the official nontolerance of those not belonging to a recognized "heavenly" religion do not accord with modern international notions of human rights.

The social disadvantages of Jewish and Christian minorities were later reversed under colonialism or imperialism, as they were disproportionately represented in the new systems of modern education and in government bureaucracies. Minorities have often been viewed with suspicion as allies or potential allies of Islam's enemies, and such suspicions have naturally been exacerbated by the establishment of a Jewish state in Palestine. The attacks on and intimidation of Jews in Arab countries in the 1950s are now finding an echo in attacks on and intimidation of Christians, leading to the exodus of many Arab Christians from their homelands. These attacks are often linked to radical Islamist groups, who see the presence of religious minorities as an impediment to the implementation of Islamic law in their countries. The recent imposition of Shari'a law in some northern Nigerian states has prompted intense Muslim-Christian violence, and this issue also figures in the ongoing civil war in the Sudan. The treatment of minorities is clearly an area on which Islamists who favor the application of traditional Islamic law differ with liberals, who advocate complete equality of all citizens before the law.

Conservative Muslim Perspectives

It is not surprising that conservative Muslims have sought to justify and preserve traditional discriminatory practices against non-Muslims, such as disallowing marriage between Muslim women and non-Muslim men and prohibiting the election of non-Muslims to high office. Furthermore, the Iranian constitution explicitly limits recognized protected religious minorities to Iranian Zoroastrians, Jews, and Christians; the Baha'is are excluded because only those monotheistic religions that existed prior to Islam are recognized, since Muslims see Islam as the completion and perfection of earlier forms of monotheism. Baha'ism challenges the finality of Islam and seeks converts among Muslims. They have therefore met with considerable persecution in Iran, both before and since the Iranian revolution. In Pakistan another nineteenth-century sect, the Ahmadiyya, see themselves as Muslims, but are perceived as heretics by other Muslims; in 1974, bowing to pressure from Islamists, the Ahmadiyya were constitutionally declared non-Muslim. Baha'is and Ahmadis are further tainted by being formerly Muslim or of formerly Muslim ancestry. As is clear in the aforementioned Shari'a law regarding apostasy, most Muslims have not been able to tolerate the notion that a Muslim could change his religion.

In most countries the application of Islamic law is limited to family law, and recognized religious minorities are allowed to follow the personal status regulations of their own faith. In Egypt, for example, Coptic Christians cannot obtain a divorce, but Muslims can; therefore, the only option for Christians caught in an unhappy marriage is to convert to Islam. In matters of litigation involving Muslims and non-Muslims, judgment in an Islamic state (that is, a state in which all aspects of government are based on Islam) would be in an Islamic court, where non-Muslims may reasonably expect bias.

Modernist Perspectives

Liberal Muslims often emphasize the essential unity of humanity as the foundation for religious equality and freedom, in addition to quoting the Qur'anic verse, "There is no compulsion in religion" (2:256). Mohamed Talbi (1998, 164) says,

To be a true Muslim is to live in courteous dialogue with peoples of other faiths and ideologies, and ultimately to submit to God. We must show concern to our neighbors. We have duties to them, and we are not islands of loneliness. The attitude of respectful courtesy recommended by the Qur'an must be expanded to embrace all mankind, believers and unbelievers, except for those who "do wrong"—the unjust and violent, who resort deliberately to fist or argument.

Humayun Kabir (1906–69), an Indian Muslim who remained in India after the partition of 1947, was concerned with Muslim coexistence not only with Jews and Christians, but naturally with the people who form the majority of the Indian population, the Hindus (1998). He held that ethnic and religious diversity, with a balanced distribution of power among a number of different centers, is a source of strength for a nation and is the very essence of democracy. He recalled that the Qur'an itself says that all religions were initially the same (2:213), and that prophets have been sent to every country in every age, each bringing the message of God in the language of his people (14:4). He urges Muslims to recognize the truths embedded in Hinduism and Buddhism, and to recognize Hindus and Buddhists as People of the Book, like the Jews and Christians.

The Position of Women in Traditional Islamic Law

Muslims of both conservative and liberal persuasions often claim that Islam significantly improved the status of women in seventh-century Arabia. They claim that women were severely devalued in Arabia before Islam, subjected to the whims of their often brutal husbands, who regarded them as little more than chattel. Islam banned female infanticide, limited polygamy, and gave women the right to own and manage property, rights that Western women came to enjoy only recently.

There is little historical evidence to substantiate most of the claims concerning the miserable condition of women in pre-Islamic Arabia. Although the Qur'an does mention and prohibit female infanticide, examination of the genealogies of pre-Islamic Arabs raises questions concerning the frequency of polygamy. Although Muslims interpret the Qur'an as limiting the number of wives a man may take to four, the wording of the verse in question—"Marry such women as seem good to you, two, three, or four" (4:3)—could equally be seen not as limiting polygamy, but encouraging men to take more than one wife. The wording of the verse suggests imprecision in the number of wives a man may take. The claim that women did not own or inherit wealth is contradicted by the story of Muhammad's own life: he was a poor man until he married a wealthy widow who had employed him in her caravans and later proposed marriage. The stories of Khadija, Hind, and other great female personalities of Muhammad's early life hardly suggest that women were chattel. But in an attempt to defend Islam against charges of antifeminism, the advantages Islam gave to women have been

exaggerated so consistently and repeatedly that even many Western scholars have come to accept them as true. The claims that Islam radically
improved the rights of women have served the agendas of both conservatives, who are concerned to demonstrate the superiority of the Shari'a over
Western norms, and modernists, who wish to demonstrate that Muslim
jurisprudents sabotaged the originally feminist agenda of the Prophet.

Marriage

As we have seen, Islamic law provides that "marriage is in the hands of the
guardian." That is, male guardians have the right to contract marriages for
women in their care. Men have exclusive rights of polygamy and marriage
to non-Muslims. Men are obligated to provide their wives with food, clothing, and shelter ("maintenance") as befitting the social station they were in
before marriage, and in return they may demand obedience from their
wives (Haeri 1993). Husbands are not allowed to take any of their wives'
wealth without their permission. The Qur'an (4:34) allows men to take certain measures against disobedient wives, including striking them, although
Qur'an commentaries and legal scholars mitigate this somewhat by saying
that beating should be a last resort and should not produce bruising, bleeding, or broken bones. Nonetheless, the subordinate position of the wife in
marriage is clear.

Divorce

The Qur'an allows men to "replace a wife with another" (4:20) with ease,
although it encourages men to treat their wives justly and fairly. Hadith
records Muhammad's statement that of all permitted things divorce is the
most hateful to God, but the Qur'an takes the matter in stride and Islamic
law places no restrictions on a man's ability to divorce his wife by simple
verbal pronouncement. If the husband initiates the divorce, he may not take
back the dower. Divorce is only effective after a waiting period of four
months, during which the husband may reconcile with his wife. He may
divorce her and reconcile twice, but the third time the divorce is irrevocable, and he may not contract a new marriage with the same woman until she
has married and been divorced from another man. There is no alimony
in Islamic law; the husband's obligation to maintain the wife ends with the
end of the waiting period. The Qur'an urges women who are unhappy with
their marriages to seek reconciliation (4:128). It does allow women to ran-
som themselves from an unhappy marriage by returning the dower to their
husbands, if the latter agree (2:229), but no recourse is mentioned in the
Qur'an for women whose husbands do not agree to divorce. Most schools
of Islamic law (although not the Hanafi school, which was favored in the
Ottoman empire and predominates in Pakistan) grant women very limited

grounds on which they may appeal to a judge for the dissolution of an un-happy marriage: failure of the husband to maintain the wife properly, the husband's sexual impotence, the husband's terminal illness, or abandon-ment. Only the Maliki and Hanbali schools include wife abuse among the grounds for divorce through the court.

After divorce, the child continues to belong to the father and his lineage. The mother may have temporary custody of the child up to a certain age, which varies according to different schools of Islamic law and sometimes also according to the gender of the child. The variation is generally from age two to age nine. The father is responsible to maintain the child, and if the mother is breastfeeding the child (normally expected until age two), he is responsible to maintain both of them until the child is weaned.

Inheritance

The Qur'an outlines specific shares that each relative of the deceased will inherit (4:11–12). In general, children are favored more than spouses in inheritance, and women receive about half the inheritance of men in a comparable kin relationship to the deceased. This is justified by Shari'a-defenders on the basis of male financial provision for women.

Legal Testimony

According to the Qur'an, loan contracts require two male witnesses, or if two men cannot be found, one man and two women, "so that if one of them forgets, the other will remind her" (2:282). The implication that women are more forgetful than men was not lost on medieval Muslim men. In Islamic law a woman's testimony is always worth only half that of a man, and concerning crimes that would require the death penalty it is disallowed altogether.

Freedom of Movement

The Shari'a grants men authority over the movements of women, including the right to keep women secluded in the home, although Hadith allows women to go the mosque—a right that was denied women for centuries, but which they have reclaimed in recent decades.

Education

Hadith dictates the obligation of all Muslim men and women to "seek knowledge," which was traditionally limited to religious knowledge ade-quate to allow the Muslim to perform all of her religious obligations.

Competence

Muslims find in the classical Islamic literature ample justification for the notion that men are innately superior to women. Hadith has a number of antifeminist sayings attributed to the Prophet, indicating that women are morally and intellectually inferior to men, that women are dangerous to men, and that the majority of the inhabitants of hellfire are women. Although the Qur'an appears to make men and women equally responsible before the law, with equal punishments for crimes like adultery, medieval Muslim scholars seemed to feel that women's moral and intellectual weakness necessitated male guardianship and responsibility even in the moral sphere. Given that presupposition, it is not surprising that conservative Islamic human rights schemes grant women rights of dependence and maintenance by men rather than rights of autonomy and self-determination.

The right to work and the right to political participation are not discussed in traditional Islamic law.

The Rights of Women: Modern Discussions

Women's status is clearly the most controversial and visible topic in public discourse in modern Muslim societies. Islamist political movements have described the breakdown of sexual segregation and traditional patriarchy as sources of moral disintegration in their countries, and have tried to project themselves as the protectors of women and promoters of their dignity. One author, for example, says that the inevitable result of Western-style feminism is the propagation of pornography, nude beaches, sexual promiscuity, and the breakdown of the family (al-Bahi 1979). Many Islamist groups have in fact been successful in appealing to women for a broad range of sociological and psychological reasons that are beyond the scope of this chapter (Hoffman 1995, 212–16). Western observers since the nineteenth century have targeted the veiling and oppression of Muslim women as an indication of the inferiority of Islam as a religion (Ahmed 1992, 144–68), forcing Muslims into defensive postures, either in the direction of defending traditional sexual segregation as morally superior to Western gender relations, or in the direction of finding traditional sexual segregation and antifeminist biases to be antithetical to the spirit of Islam, the result of Muslims' patriarchal rigidity and poor understanding of the exalted morality and human equality propagated by authentic Islam.

Modernists would say that such Qur'anic laws as the allowance for men to take up to four wives (4:3) need to be understood within their social context, being revealed directly after a battle in which many men had been killed, leaving women and girls as widows and orphans. In fact, the Qur'anic verse that allows polygamy also tells men that if they fear they cannot treat their wives equally, they should marry only one. Another verse in the same chapter of the Qur'an (4:129) tells men that no matter how hard they try they will never be able to be impartial concerning their wives. Therefore some Muslim modernists conclude that the real intention of the Qur'an was to limit or even prohibit polygamy. The jurisprudents who formulated the law, however, placed no legal restrictions on a man's right to have four wives, deeming the Qur'anic qualifications to be nonbinding moral constraints. In many Muslim countries today, restrictions have been placed on a man's ability to contract a second marriage, ranging from the need to procure the first wife's permission to the need to prove to an administrative committee his ability financially to support two wives in separate houses. Turkey prohibited polygamy by adopting Swiss law as the basis of its civil code, but only Tunisia has prohibited it by adopting a modernist interpretation of the Qur'an.

Conservative Muslim Perspectives

The result of the intense international focus on women's rights in the Muslim world is that conservatives who oppose granting women rights they see as conflicting with Islam have become more clever at camouflaging their restrictions behind rhetoric extolling women's freedoms, a move that Ann Elizabeth Mayer (1995) has called the "new world hypocrisy."

Mayer examined various conservative Muslim documents on human rights and their compatibility with international human rights standards as articulated in the UDHR and the International Covenant on Economic, Social and Cultural Rights (ICESCR) of 1966, and the International Covenant on Civil and Political Rights (ICCPR), also of 1966. Besides the Universal Islamic Declaration of Human Rights, she examined the Iranian constitution of 1979, the Draft of the Islamic Constitution devised by the Islamic Research Academy of Cairo, affiliated with al-Azhar University, the most internationally prestigious institution of higher education in Sunni Islam, as well as publications by the Iranian Sultanhussein Tabandeh (1966) and the influential and productive Pakistani writer, Abu 'l-A'la Mawdudi (died 1979). While finding, not surprisingly, that these documents overwhelmingly uphold traditional interpretations of the Shari'a with regard to women's social roles, she finds, perhaps more fundamentally, "an absence of any willingness to recognize women as full, equal human beings who deserve the same rights and freedoms as men" (Mayer 1991, 136). All these documents speak of women only in the context of marriage, and assert the authority of men over women; the idea of an unmarried, autonomous woman is never contemplated.

Among these sources, only Tabandeh is explicit in his opposition to the concept of gender equality and his claim that the political domain is innately alien to the domain of women. He affirms the necessity that women stay at home and avoid public gatherings attended by men unless absolutely necessary, in order to preserve public morality (Mayer 1991, 116–17). Maw-dudi, on the other hand, "was a canny politician who seems to have appreciated the damage that it would do to the credibility of his human rights scheme if he admitted that it aimed at denying fundamental rights to one-half of the population," so he avoided discussion of women in his writing on human rights, although his views on the subject are amply expressed elsewhere, often in a highly polemical tone linking gender equality, female autonomy, and sexual integration with moral disintegration, promiscuity, and perversion. Mawdudi lists as one of his "basic human rights" respect for the chastity of women, but, as Mayer points out, "the need to shield women's chastity has been exploited by Muslim conservatives like Mawdudi as a justification for denying women a broad spectrum of rights and for keeping them largely restricted to the home" (Mayer 1991, 117–19).

Islamic human rights schemes like the UIDHR maintain an idealized vision of Muslim society in which all women are maintained by husbands or male relatives and have no need of financial autonomy, ignoring the hardships of indigent divorced women. Mayer also notes that one of Ayatollah Khomeini's first acts after the Iranian revolution was the abolition of the relatively liberal Iranian Family Protection Act, which had required that all divorces be pursued through a court, significantly broadened the grounds on which a woman could seek divorce, assigned custody based on the best interests of the child, and required a husband to get permission from the court before marrying a second wife. The Khomeini regime lowered the minimum marriage age from eighteen to thirteen and drastically curtailed women's activities outside the home, including educational and employment opportunities and the ability to participate in sports activities (Mayer 1991, 130–31). Mayer concludes that conservative Islamic human rights schemes violate the following provisions of the UDHR: Article 1 (guarantee of equality), Article 2 (guarantee against discriminatory treatment), Article 7 (guarantee of equal protection of the law), and Article 16 (guarantee of the freedom to marry the partner of one's choice), as well as the following provisions of the ICCPR: Article 2 (guarantee against discriminatory treatment), Article 3 (equal rights guarantee), Article 12 (guarantee of liberty of movement), and Article 26 (guarantees of equality, equal protection, and nondiscriminatory treatment).

Modernist Muslim Perspectives

Modernists since Qasim Amin (1863–1908) have argued against the notion that men and women are fundamentally different or that differences in biology surrounding reproductive functions necessitate radically different social functions. Qasim Amin's book, *Tahrir al-mar'a* (The Emancipation of Women), published in Egypt in 1899, articulated the essential early modernist position and catapulted the issue of women's rights into the forefront of Muslim consciousness, provoking a debate that has not abated to this day. Amin targeted women's veiling (meaning, at that time, the face veil) and seclusion, polygamy, divorce laws, and education as areas requiring reform. He did not advocate the adoption of Western dress for Muslim women, but felt, based on his experience as a judge in civil law court, that the face veil, which is not required by the Shariʿa, resulted in many abuses of women in the legal system, such as having them married or having their property sold without their knowledge, as well as preventing women from participating in society in a healthy manner, enabling them to gain a wholesome education and learn marketable skills. As a judge, he was too close to real-life problems to disregard the problem of indigent, unskilled women with no male relatives to support them. Like many early modernists and later Islamists, Amin did not advocate radically new gender norms. He advocated women's education mainly to enable women to be better companions for their husbands and mothers to their children, and in order to eliminate superstition among the people (that was seen as propagated mainly by women). But he argued that if women seem more infantile than men and lacking in intelligence, that is only because men have deprived them of education for so many generations; a girl, he said, has the same innate intelligence and curiosity as a boy (Hoffman-Ladd 1987, 25–27; Ahmed 1992, 142–45, 155–64).

Consistent with the tendency among modernists to regard the laws of the Qurʾan as too contextually bound to be compatible with modern society, Mohamed Abed Jabri of Morocco argues that the regulations of the Qurʾan were the result of historical conditions that gave the fully Islamic principles of freedom of faith and equal rights for women a content that is below the modern aspirations of Muslims (Filali-Ansari 1998, 160).

In her many writings, the contemporary Moroccan feminist scholar, Fatima Mernissi, takes an innovative look at the textual foundations of Muslim misogyny. She uses the criteria of traditional Islamic scholarship to examine the validity of some of the hadiths that have been most frequently quoted to justify a gender ideology that views women as tainted through impure bodily functions (menstruation, postpartum bleeding) and mental and moral limitations, as well as the famous hadith that is typically used to justify denying women participation in the political process: "The nation that is ruled by a woman will never prosper." Traditional Muslim scholarship examines the reliability of the individuals cited in the chain of authorities for each individual narrative (hadith) in order to assess its soundness. By this criterion and others, Mernissi succeeds in undermining the credibility of these allegedly "sound" hadiths, and counters them with others that she believes have been deliberately suppressed by Muslim scholars. She says:

All the monotheistic religions are shot through by the conflict between the divine and the feminine, but none more so than Islam, which has opted for the occultation of the feminine, at least symbolically, by trying to veil it, to hide it, to mask it. Islam as sexual practice unfolds with a very special theatricality because it is acted out in a scene where the hijab [veil, seclusion] occupies a central position. This almost phobic attitude toward women is all the more surprising because we have seen that the Prophet has encouraged his adherents to renounce it as representative of the jahiliyya [pre-Islamic Arabian period] and its superstitions. (Mernissi 1991, 81)

Conclusion

Muslim opinions on issues pertaining to human rights are diverse, and it would be a cruel caricature to limit them to those conservative spokesmen who arrogate for themselves the right to speak on behalf of Islam. While it is laudable to respect the rights of other cultures to formulate their own human rights programs, we need to be alert to the uses and abuses of such arguments of cultural relativity on the part of those in power. Do most Muslims endorse the restriction of their rights in the name of Islam? Concerning the question of the compatibility of Islam with democracy, for example, there are few Muslims who would publicly disavow the ideal of democracy in some form. However, Mohamed Abed Jabri notes that real democracy, the participation of the masses, is feared by both modernists and traditionalists, because neither group trusts the wisdom of the masses, and both elites tend to see themselves as entrusted with guiding the masses to political and social maturity. Nevertheless, Jabri argues, recent deep and rapid changes have imposed democracy as the only acceptable form of legitimacy in the Muslim world and enabled the silent majority to express its views. Democracy has become an aspiration and a mode of legitimization deeply entrenched in the modern consciousness (Filali-Ansari 1998, 157–58).

That Muslims today largely endorse the idea of democracy, regardless of the reluctance of elites to implement democracy in their countries, indicates that Muslims are indeed part of the international community and susceptible to international pressure to democratize, if the international community really desires to make this a major focus of international relations. In point of fact, however, democracy has rarely been a significant factor in international relations. The United States, leader of the "free world," has for decades favored alliances with autocratic strongmen more than faith in the results of democratic processes in the Third World. Sese Mobutu of Zaire, King Hassan II of Morocco, the Shah of Iran, Husni Mubarak of Egypt, and Saddam Hussein of Iraq are all twentieth-century autocratic rulers whose trammeling of human rights in their own countries has been consistently overlooked by the United States in the name of *realpolitik*. Only governments in obvious ideological opposition to the West are criticized for their human rights violations. Islamist violence has raised concerns about security, leading the United States to be silent in the face of human rights abuses committed by the governments of Egypt and Tunisia—and overlooking the fact that such abuses produce further Islamist radicalism.

Although this paper fully acknowledges and details the problems inherent in reconciling modern notions of human rights with conservative Islamic models, we need to examine the broader context in which human rights abuses are taking place. Most human rights abuses in the Muslim world are not justified on the basis of Islam; governments that lack real legitimacy perpetrate them and they are justified on the basis of the security of the state. The Western tendency to single out Islam as the problem serves the interests of totalitarian regimes very well. But the breadth of disagreement among Muslims indicates that "Islam" in and of itself is not the main issue. As in other parts of the world, repression is simply justified by those in power through appeal to traditional sources of legitimacy, the credibility of which is declining in the face of a growing internationalization of democratic consciousness.

Part II
Regional
Perspectives

Chapter 4
The Northern Tier

Marvin G. Weinbaum

There is much to distinguish among the three countries of the northern tier of the Middle East. The governments of Turkey, Iran, and Afghanistan draw on different sources for their legitimacy. Despite predominantly Muslim populations, the three societies are varied in the ideologies that guide their leaders and inspire their publics. They have distinctive problems in sustaining domestic order and providing for national security. The very different economic assets of the three also pose separate challenges in providing for the well-being and enlightenment of their citizens. Yet among the features they share is that each confronts formidable issues of human rights.

Abuses of human rights are, of course, hardly recent developments in Turkey, Iran, and Afghanistan. The histories of the three countries are replete with examples of ethnic, religious, and sectarian discrimination and violence against national minorities. Although the scale of abuses by the state against particular groups, or among groups in society, was often great, most of them went unrecorded or even unnoticed. More recently, as U.S. State Department Country Reports demonstrate, the international community has forced greater attention to a human rights agenda and to claims and evidence of violations. Above all, allegations against the state for treatment of the Kurdish minority in Turkey, Baha'is and Jews in Iran, and Hazaras (among other ethnic groups) in Afghanistan, are aired widely inside and outside these countries. The treatment of women in Muslim Iran and Afghanistan, particularly the latter, has drawn special notice.

State actions are less likely than in the past to be ignored or condoned as falling within sovereign rights and thus outside the reach of foreign criticism. The behavior of domestic groups against one another, with or without the state's imprimatur, is also subject as never before to outside scrutiny. While direct foreign intervention has thus far occurred only rarely—U.S. military action in Afghanistan being only tangentially on behalf of human rights—the legal and moral bases for external monitoring have been established, along with precedents for internationally imposed sanctions. If across the region progress on human rights issues seems evident, there have also been some setbacks.

In some cases, violations of human rights in the countries studied here result from private acts or come about because the institutions that enforce order are unable to halt them. No doubt many of the prejudicial behaviors against social minorities are not abetted by state action. But more often, they take place with the tacit approval of state authorities. In the cases of Turkey, Iran, and Afghanistan, the states themselves have been major agents of human rights abuses, often by providing a legal basis for violations and frequently by directly denying or withdrawing basic rights. More indirectly, the authorities make no effort to arbitrate differences among individual and social groups that raise human rights issues. Nor do any of the three countries give groups in civil society entirely free reign to expose human rights violations or publicize their complaints without restrictions.

Changing global attitudes about human rights reflect in no small part a diminished tolerance of cultural relativist arguments to exonerate human rights abuses. While historical and religious explanations for policies and practices are often appreciated, critics have increasingly been unwilling to accept the view that there are no applicable universal standards. Nonetheless, reproaches from abroad are still often countered with pleadings of distinctiveness based on religion, culture, and national heritage across the countries of the Middle East's northern tier.

The experiences of this region also raise the question of whether there might be an implicit hierarchy in rights, allowing for lesser observance of some protections in favor of fuller achievement of those rights with greater priority. The need to choose reflects the reality that rights may come into conflict and, however regrettably, the goal of realizing all those desired freedoms within a particular time frame may be impossible to achieve.

The focus on human rights in the region falls, as it does elsewhere, mainly on minority, sectarian, and women's rights, and the rights of the criminally accused. Child labor abuses and lack of access to educational opportunities are often frequently included. Some would further expand the definition to encompass hunger and malnutrition—if within the power of national authorities or anyone else to prevent. Allegations may, then, be raised against international actors as well as domestic ones. The issue, familiar with respect to Iraq, was raised in recent years in connection with alleged negative humanitarian consequences after UN sanctions were imposed on Afghanistan for the Taliban's refusal to surrender Osama bin Laden for trial.

A case can be made for the attainment of democracy for a country's citizenry as a universal human right. The intimate connection between human rights and democracy must take cognizance of the fact that Turkey has long functioned with a guided parliamentary system; Iran remains, despite its lively politics, a theocracy; and under the rule of the Taliban, Afghanistan offered an even more rigid religious autocracy. Plainly, these institutions shape the character of human rights politics in these countries. Advocates for human rights are usually associated with those who are also arguing for change at both the social and political levels. They seek greater freedom for individuals to pursue a wider range of societal choices, and to pick their rulers and hold them accountable. Arbitrary, despotic authority is plainly incompatible with a respect for human rights, just as it is the antithesis of democracy.

The Normative Context

The Islamic heritage and individual historical experiences have deeply influenced the human rights practices of the countries under study. The focus of debate in Iran and Afghanistan is usually over the extent to which those rights afforded by religious law, the Shari'a, provide an alternative to commonly defined, internationally recognized human rights. Put otherwise, it is asked whether Islamic human rights norms should be subjected to international human rights benchmarks (Mayer 1991, 1–21). Islamic challenge to the idea of universal human rights rests largely on the belief that these rights are artifacts of Western ideals that have evolved with Western institutions.

Conceding how commonly observed human rights receive their fullest expression in a Western democratic tradition does not disqualify their applicability for other areas and cultures. Nor does it deny that they may be reshaped to fit local conditions and temperament. Even in the Western experience, there exists wide disparity and debate on the scope of human rights protections, and there is no single body of agreed rights. In Europe and the United States, strong controversies rage over whether abortion and capital punishment are covered. Moreover, the emphasis on majoritarian democracy in many Western countries can, in fact, delay the realization of substantive rights by minorities and less popular groups.

Despite the criticism from some quarters of the rights associated with the West, large numbers of Turks, Iranians, and Afghans, notably in the educated middle classes, aspire to most of the same set of human and political values as their non-Muslim counterparts. There is more overlap in what they espouse than would appear from the rhetoric alone. This is especially true with respect to democratic ideals. While secularism, materialism, individualism, and Western morality elicit specific disapproval (Ibrahim 1996, 251), Western liberal values—when identified as democracy, civil and human rights, equality before the law, representation, and individual liberty—carry a more positive valence. Most citizens in Turkey and Iran want to vote, form parties, hold their officials accountable, and yet retain their faith in Islam (Deegan 1994, 15). It is commonly thought possible to have the fruits of modernization yet remain somehow immunized to debased Western values. Others put their faith in finding some original synthesis of what is foreign and what is indigenous.

Institutional Parameters

Across the northern tier, it is necessary to ask whether the central state uses its coercive power to increase or decrease, expand or contract human rights. Does the state provide the legal framework and build the institutions that would discourage or prevent violations of human rights? Does it, for example, offer the means for dampening ethnic or tribal rivalries, or threaten those engaged in abusive actions with heavy penalties? Or is the state, either through its own actions, its complicity with others, or its omissions, responsible for the denial of basic rights?

Identity problems and those of state building influence the quest for democracy as well as for policies respecting human rights. Efforts by governments in the Northern Tier countries to strengthen national identity and build support for the state against its perceived enemies involve fostering policies that stifle political dissent and build national unity at the expense of those individuals, institutions, and minorities that deviate from the mainstream opinion. The adoption of measures that deny these elements full exercise of their rights (often along with everyone else) is carried out in the name of ensuring security and order. Dissenting political views and also minority religious or ethnic rights are perceived as detracting from the unity of the state and the control of the authorities.

National security figures in the development of democracy and exercise of human rights. Instability and tension, whether domestic or foreign in origin, tend to work against both democratic practices and the observance of human rights. The threshold for making the judgment of whether security and order are threatened is in almost every case a very low one. Protected rights are often treated as luxuries that in times of crisis cannot be afforded, rather than as strengths on which to build a national consensus around policies that require sacrifices. Although all three countries under study are subject to internal tensions, only Afghanistan is too unstable to enforce human rights, even were they the preferred norms.

Certain political and social structures in the three countries promote or, alternatively, stand as barriers to the furtherance of democracy and human rights. Although the existence of representative institutions and popular participation can stymie or mitigate attempts to deny rights by government, these same institutions are sometimes manipulated to provide legitimacy for the actions of authorities. Although protection of human rights may in the last analysis depend on the existence of certain societal norms, constitutional provisions and legislated laws make tangible these values and facilitate their application. They can help to instill these values broadly in the public, and also provide refuge against short-term outbursts of sentiment and the whims of leaders. An absence of formal provisions or the failure to implement them is apparent, in varying degrees, in Turkey, Iran, and Afghanistan.

The responsibility for pushing for protection of human rights and the rule of law is also likely to rely on an invigorated civil society. A civil society that is vibrant and energetic can occupy an important place in mediating between the individual's assertion of rights and the state's need for order. One particular measure of the health of civil society and status of human rights is the ability of workers to organize freely and make their demands on the country's decision-makers. Civil society in the form of groups providing effective interest articulation and organizational capacity, especially if also represented in a legislative body, can also hold markets accountable. In any case, the involvement of associational interests in a critical dialogue over the contours and conceivably the details of policy requires more than a narrow procedural democracy. Turkey comes closest to this kind of civil society, but with some notable deficiencies.

Socioeconomic conditions can make a particular contribution to the exercise of democracy and respect for rights. It is often further argued that human rights receive more protection in systems where economic growth is accompanied by a high degree of economic freedom. Some contend that an intrusive government that prevents economic freedom also inhibits democracy. This conclusion arises from the fact that a state-dominated economic system, practiced on a large scale, is nowhere associated with open political systems. It follows that without democratic practices, human rights are not well protected. In turn, controversy about human rights and political instability discourage investment. A judicial system that disregards individual freedoms is also likely to cast in doubt a supportive legal climate that interested investors look for in contemplating new enterprises and the purchase of privatized ones (Canevi 1994, 188; Dogan 1997). Rather than eroding civil liberties, liberal economic reforms that in time lead to a more open society and politics create conditions as well for the observance of human rights.

Often in the name of economic justice, Turkey, Iran, and Afghanistan reserve a large role for the state. At present, Turkey is still being weaned from its statist economic past, and Iran is struggling with an economy heavily influenced by quasi-public religious foundations. However, Turkey's modern economic elite has adopted the norms of the global market and democratic ideals, while in Iran, a still powerful traditional *bazaari* community, despite its transnational connections, remains comfortable with a restrictive brand of politics. Afghanistan is poised to rebuild its state and economy with international aid—after years in which little existed outside of the drug trade and the activities of smuggler cartels. Without the revival of a viable central government in Afghanistan, however, local commanders will coopt and monopolize most economic activity.

Turkey

Liberalizing Turkey politically over the last half century has been a gradual process punctuated most dramatically by three military coups and the restoration of power to civilian governments after relatively brief intervals. While each intervention, always in the name of restoring the essential constitutional character of the republic, carried in its aftermath evidence of a maturation of democracy, the development of a politically liberal state has not proceeded in a straight line. Some periods have been more restrictive of individual and group liberties than others. With the sweeping electoral victory in November 2002 of a party with Islamic roots, Turkey does appear to have taken a major step forward. Capturing a rare parliamentary majority, the new Justice and Development Party challenges the country's long established antireligious secularism and hopes to demonstrate that Islam and democracy can live together. The party, stressing its pragmatism, speaks of fostering human rights and freedom of speech.

But, given past false starts, progress is hardly assured. Turkey's democracy has far to go to overcome its defective record in civil and human rights. More than 150 laws and regulations are currently available to limit freedom of expression; although aimed mainly at Kurds and elements of the left, they can be used against anyone in the society. The alleged menace of Islamic radicalism has often been used cynically to deny rights and suppress groups acting within a legitimate constitutional framework.

Successive Turkish governments have nevertheless stated their commitment to human rights and their willingness to give high priority to eliminating abuses. The issue with these governments has been, however, over their performance. Charges focus on extrajudicial killings, excessive use of force, and torture. Further accusations against authorities depict arbitrary arrests and detentions, denial of a fair public trial, and poor prison conditions. Where governments have undertaken investigations and trials of suspected officials and personnel, these cases have gone without resolution over many years. When on rare occasions convictions have been obtained, the sentences are light; a fact not lost on the country's police and other security forces.

Leading the list of human rights charges is the treatment of supposed "separatists" (pro-Kurdish activists). The Kurdistan Workers Party (PKK) is believed to hold sway in Turkey's southeast. It is alleged that in these areas the government's security forces, including the Turkish National Police and their "special teams," have committed the most serious abuses of the rule of law in the name of maintaining order and upholding the constitution. The PKK can be rightly accused of having engaged in terrorism against local officials and Kurdish civilians, including random acts of violence. Still, despite the enactment of legislation in August 2002, it is widely acknowledged that government policies continue to deny the Kurdish population full political, cultural, and linguistic rights.

Also at risk are leftist organizations, even those with supposedly legal status, and Islamic parties accused of being led by reactionaries. Among the latter, legal actions were taken against successful politicians widely regarded as moderate. In January 1988, Turkey's Constitutional Court banned from political activity six Islamic leaders of a party that only recently led a national government coalition. In January 2002, the highest court banned from high office the former mayor of Istanbul, leader of a newly founded and highly popular Islamic party—successor to two previous outlawed Islamic parties. Secular authorities have also harassed religiously observant Muslim businessmen. The imposition of a fifty-year-old ban on wearing religious head covering in government-owned facilities has similarly aroused complaints from human rights monitors.

Although the government appears at times to tolerate human rights groups and even work with them, it frequently shows little patience for individuals advocating changes who are close to the mainstream of Turkish life. Targeted are human rights monitors, journalists, and lawyers who publicly condemn official policies and behavior. Many have been intimidated and sometimes indicted and imprisoned, charged with support of Islamic fundamentalists and pro-PKK sympathies. Nor are these individuals and groups held in high esteem by much of the public. Often, human rights activists are seen as responsible for Turkey's poor reputation in the West and especially its problems with the European Union (EU).

Many liberal provisions of the constitution are not fully realized in practice. These include the creation of an independent judiciary, the right to a public trial in a court of law, the inviolability of a person's domicile, and freedom of speech and the press. Other provisions guarantee freedom of assembly, association, and religion. Administrative requirements like prior notification or cumbersome process can limit the exercise of presumed liberties. State Security Court prosecutors continue to confiscate issues of leftist, Kurdish nationalist, and pro-PKK periodicals. Often the enabling laws are flawed and, at other times, have the effect of overriding the very protections they were designed to realize. Other laws, including the 1982 constitution and the 1991 anti-terror law, provided justifications for limiting freedoms of expression. They have been used to close down political parties for challenging the secular nature or unity of the state and to bar politicians from seeking office.

Within the government, the state minister for human rights serves as chair of the High Council for Human Rights, which is supposed to investigate human rights abuses and establish contacts with nongovernmental organizations (NGOs). The High Council is charged with implementing legislative and administrative reforms. Representatives from several ministries sit together on the body. The Parliament in 1997 also created a Human Rights Commission that is authorized to oversee compliance with the relevant laws and international agreements. The commission makes periodic visits to prisons throughout the country. But a series of courageous and widely publicized reports issued in 2000 prompted the dismissal of its chair by then Prime Minister Bulent Ecevit, despite a public outcry. High profile prison hunger strikes in 2001 were testimony to the failure of the authorities to deal with some of the worst abuses. A repentance and amnesty law passed by the Parliament in 1999 has also fallen short of expectations that it would lead to a breakthrough in human rights protections and help resolve the Kurdish conflict.

Signs of relief from laws that encourage rights abuses come from Turkey's Constitutional Court, its highest tribunal. In 1988, it annulled a provision of the penal code that had allowed for the punishment of women found guilty of infidelity. It also ordered the government to revise a 1996 Provincial Authority Law that authorized authorities to fire on suspected terrorists without appropriate warning. More often, however, the regular court system has acted leniently toward suspects, sometimes overturning their convictions.

The country's anti-terror law allows those accused of terrorism or mistreatment of prisoners to continue to work while their cases are being investigated. Under the law, special provincial administration boards rather than regular courts determine whether enough evidence exists to prosecute cases; those suspected have their legal fees paid by the government agency that employs them. Official efforts designed to prevent human rights abuses in police stations through inspections by public prosecutors have been superseded by regulations that restrict the monitoring to a period of investigations after the likely violations would have occurred. At the same time, a 1997 law requires that for crimes that fall under the Anti-Terror Act, persons detained cannot be held beyond a specified time period, depending on the nature of the charge, or be denied access to an attorney for more than four days. However, its implementation is reportedly uneven.

A regular dialogue is maintained with the Council of Europe's Committee for the Prevention of Torture. On at least three occasions in 1999 the European Court of Human Rights, whose jurisdiction Turkey recognizes, ruled that Turkey had violated individual rights in investigations and treatment of prisoners. But when the European Court ruled against Turkey for dissolving the country's Socialist Party, the Turkish Court of Appeals upheld the party leader's 1996 conviction charging him with acting against the integrity of the state during an earlier election campaign.

Most secular-minded Turks identify themselves and link their country's future with the international community, especially Europe. In 2000, the government dropped its refusal of over 34 years to sign two UN conventions guaranteeing the social and political rights of minorities. An influential liberal-minded elite continues to hope that formal economic bonds with Europe will solidify the country's commitment to the West and provide incentives and models for economic and political reform. The exclusion of Turkey from the EU appeared to have ended in December 1999, with a Helsinki summit where Turkey was designated as a full-fledged candidate for membership—after considerable lobbying by Washington. But the refusal through 2002 of European leaders to set Turkey as a candidate for membership has deeply offended these Turks. They express concern that continued delay will drive the country toward those who would have it mainly aligned economically and politically with an Islamic East.

Turkey remains on notice that it will have to meet difficult human rights standards, including protection of the minority rights for Kurds. Although Turkish officials continue to deny that the Kurds are in fact a minority, the renunciation of violence by jailed (in February 1999) Kurdish leader Abdullah Ocalan together with a subsequent decline in violence by the PKK in the country's southeast has affected views. Many rights advocates believe that the time has come to accommodate the Kurds' nonpolitical demands, and some relaxation of language and cultural restrictions has occurred.

With more than a decade before the country can hope to actually enter the EU, heated discussions continue over the benefits. Even many pro-European Turks view the standards for admission set by the EU as offensive. The country's leaders resent human rights issues and the adherence to certain democratic norms being raised as non-economic obstacles to membership, especially when they believe that the real barriers to EU membership are in fact cultural and religious.

Despite internal debate, any associations or expressions deemed as undermining the secular nature of the state, disuniting the country, or insulting the military remain as grounds for court action and imprisonment. The most difficult challenge may be for the military to reappraise its role in Turkish government and society. The military will be obliged to permit greater responsibility to pass to Turkey's politicians and must be prepared to accept a less stringent definition of the country's Kemalist tradition. For the time being, while recent developments suggest that the military may finally be ready to accept some important changes, Turkey's willingness to cede its Kurdish or Islamic problems to democratic solutions remains to be tested.

Iran

A discussion of human rights in Iran must begin by noting that serious factional differences exist within the country. Repeatedly, conservative religious clerics and their supporters have thwarted civil liberties and cultural freedoms in Iran. No simple division of opinion can be found on most issues, and all factions pay verbal homage to the tenets of Shi'a Islam and its primacy in matters of governance. Yet the ongoing struggle between President Sayed Mohammad Khatami and the country's conservative Muslim clerics is sharply edged, much of it around the observance of civil and human rights. The February 2000 parliamentary elections seemed to tilt the political battle clearly in favor of the reformers. That election was expected to test the reformers' ability to overcome remaining conservative strongholds, particularly the un-elected Council of Guardians—a body empowered to scrutinize laws on religious grounds and screen candidates for elected office. By the end of 2002, the imprisonment of senior officials and others allied with President Khatami underscored the unyielding grip of the conservatives led by the Supreme Leader Ayatollah Ali Khamenei.

During the 1990s, some improvements in human rights were evident. With a general political relaxation after the election of Hashami Rafsanjani as president in 1988 and then the first Khatami election in 1997, those demanding greater political freedom made modest gains, while the actions of security forces and the judiciary became the subject of public debate. But arbitrary arrests and detention continued, as did harsh prison conditions. Intellectual and political rights activists disappeared and died under suspicious circumstances. During a two-month period in late 1998, prominent political activists were murdered; it was later revealed that the murders were carried out by active duty agents of the Ministry of Intelligence. Human rights groups have remained under intense pressure from the country's security forces. Complaints are also aired about academic censorship and the ideological intimidation of professors. Women, although given wider opportunity than in other conservative Islamic states in the Middle East, still face social discrimination.

Friends of the current government contend that as a reformer Khatami embraces many of the universal criteria for human rights. Supposedly, he values public opinion and has staked much on free elections. It was hoped that Khatami would give attention to individual rights and the advance of civil rights, even making progress toward a functional bill of rights for citizens—something that Iranians have never enjoyed from their governments. While most Iranians still have confidence in Khatami, as his overwhelming reelection in June 2001 indicates, his accomplishments to date are modest. Despite initial improvements in media freedom, the president and his supporters have continued to fight off a rear guard action by conservatives, who have been able to close media and publishing outlets supporting reform. Many charge that as president he has encouraged people to criticize those in authority, but has done little or nothing to defend them from the heavy hand of the conservatives. Independent-minded newspaper editors or government officials have often been left exposed, even though they were staunch supporters of the president. Trials of tens of writers and intellectual dissidents, accused by Iran's hard-line Revolutionary Court of plotting the overthrow of the Islamic system, have been conducted behind closed doors.

Although Iran's human rights record most often focuses on policies toward political dissidents, personal liberties of all Iranians are constrained, and in this theocracy religious freedoms are especially restricted. Singled out for particularly harsh treatment among religious minorities are Iran's Baha'is, a nineteenth-century offshoot of Islam, now a very distinct religion. The Baha'i faith gained a degree of toleration under the Shah, and many of its members rose to positions of political and economic influence in the country. Following the revolution, the Baha'i community was associated with the deposed monarchy and, more than ever, viewed as a serious deviation from Islamic values. The now approximately 350,000 holding the faith are not recognized as belonging to a legitimate religion. Their institutions and meetings are subject to raids and closure. Since the early 1980s, those found to be Baha'i can be dismissed from jobs. They are barred from the universities and, for a variety of reasons, subject to arrest, even to execution.

Jews, Christians, and Zoroastrians are tolerated, but they, too, feel official discrimination. Armenian Christians have fared best under the Islamic Republic. Other Christian groups are subject to greater harassment and must be especially careful to avoid giving the appearance of aiming to convert Muslims. Anti-Semitic propaganda is clearly on the rise. The intimidation of Jews—an ever-dwindling community of fewer than 35,000—gained international attention in early 1999 with the arrest of thirteen Jews from Isfahan and Shiraz, who were charged with treason for spying for Israel and the United States. That the thirteen had waited until March 2000 for their trials can be largely explained by the adverse European reaction and the Khatami government's hesitation to take on the hard-line forces controlling the judiciary. Ten of the thirteen were eventually convicted in trials largely void of due process.

Since the 1979 revolution, authorities in Iran have been explicit in rejecting the notion that their rule is subject to universal human rights. They contend that claims of rights are subject to the country's culture and its Shi'a Islamic heritage. International NGOs that monitor human rights are barred from establishing offices in the country. Even UN agencies are prohibited from conducting investigations.

Domestic human rights groups tread carefully, but are visible. They are closely monitored and their activities are restricted. Like the human rights committee of the Iranian parliament, they are considered to be lacking in independence and influence. Those who speak up for civil liberties, namely groups of writers, journalists, editors, and publishers, and some public officials, focus mostly on restrictions that pertain to freedom of expression. They often incorporate in their attacks the lack of judicial due process and—though less frequently—take up the cause of women and religious minorities. Some prominent dissidents, including religious scholars and leading members of the Shi'a clergy, have even dared to question the authority of the *velayat-e fiqih,* or rule by the supreme religious authority, thus earning them at least house arrest.

Those agencies engaged in the restrictions on political rights are the same ones that normally threaten human rights. These include the Ministry of Intelligence and Security, the Ministry of Interior, and the Revolutionary Guards. The last is a military force formed during the revolution against the Shah. As a voluntary, paramilitary group, the Basijis remain a potent weapon of conservative elements, acting as vigilantes to enforce conformity to social restrictions, often at the behest of members of the Islamic clergy.

A critical test for a strengthened reform movement would be its ability to restrain the Basijis.

The judicial and prison systems draw special condemnation for the common practices of arbitrary arrests and detention, coerced confessions, and the torture of detainees and prisoners. Rapes of female prisoners as well as intimidation of family members of detainees are also reported. The discretionary authority of the Islamic judges is often challenged, as is the limited access of defendants to counsel. In general, trials are neither open nor fair by most international standards. Because of invoked Islamic law, females are denied the same legal redress as men and are treated more harshly under the law.

Employment opportunities, legal rights, and the lifestyle of women are circumscribed. To be sure, women have access to educational institutions and are permitted to take a wide range of jobs. Moreover, the percentage of illiterate women—less than 10 percent—reflects considerable progress over the last generation. But with few exceptions, higher positions are not open to women in either the public or private sector. The segregation that is common in traditional homes applies to everyone in the public sphere. Restrictions on women are most conspicuous in a dress code and in the provision for medical care. Legal provisions most of the time buttress social discrimination, as is evident in such areas as family and spousal rights, and landlord-tenant relations.

Proponents of change in Iran argue that practices explained as conforming to Islamic civil and criminal laws in fact contradict Iran's constitution as well as international human rights conventions. These critics contend that provisions of the constitution, if implemented, would bring Iran much more into conformity with international standards. But unless Iran's hardline jurists relent on rights policy, it is unlikely that even a reform-led parliament's approach to Islamic law can make much difference any time soon. For all the popular disapproval of the conservatives for their social and economic policies, there is no stomach among Iranians for another revolution.

Afghanistan

Few regimes confronted more serious criticism of their human rights policy than did Afghanistan's Taliban. Denied international recognition by nearly all countries, the Taliban government was accused of intolerance toward the country's ethnic minorities and retrogressive policies regarding women's education, health, and employment. The ordered destruction of the country's ancient Buddhist statues in March 2001 drew worldwide condemnation. The Taliban's religious dictates required strict conformity to dress codes for men and women, and men's uncut beards were an enforced requirement. The country's few Christians, Hindus, and Sikhs were exempt, but subjected to other forms of harassment. Taliban leaders defended a system of justice viewed as overly harsh and conspicuously primitive. Yet few governments were less apologetic for practices and policies deemed abhorrent by most of the international community.

In rejecting many of the Taliban's social policies, successor governments are expected to improve human rights practices. The global attention drawn to the military campaign that effectively ended Taliban rule in November 2001 greatly enhances the possibility that more enlightened policies will emerge. The presence of foreign forces and plans for a substantial international investment in Afghan recovery makes it likely that leaders in Kabul will continue to come under considerable scrutiny, not the least for their policies toward women. But caution is in order because many of the regional and local leaders who have returned had little regard for individual and group rights when they held power prior to the Taliban's reign. It is therefore instructive for gauging hoped-for improvements under future Afghan regimes that we have a picture of human rights practices under the Taliban mullahs.

If there is anything that even the Taliban's severest detractors are willing to concede, it is that the movement brought a higher degree of societal order to Afghanistan. A state of near anarchy marked by an absence of the most basic human rights protections existed under governments formed by the mujahidin parties after the Afghan communist regime collapsed in 1992. Kidnapping and murders were common occurrences in the urban areas and banditry in the countryside. Popular anger at the widespread lawlessness contributed to successive Taliban victories across Afghanistan beginning in 1994. Taliban fighters could also capitalize on a population who were exhausted from years of war, and who were attracted to what seemed an idealistic Islamic movement promising a full peace.

On assuming power, the Taliban's strict and often aberrant interpretations of Islamic law departed widely from international norms of human rights. Most controversial was the treatment of women. Justifying their puritanical practices as a religious obligation to "protect" women, Taliban government officials sanctioned policies that permitted only limited health care and prohibited females from attending school or holding most jobs. The Taliban leadership frequently claimed to have no objection to educating girls and young women so long as their education was separate. They argued, however, that while the fighting continued and international sanctions were imposed, the lack of funds constrained the construction of adequate facilities.

The Taliban system of justice was no less offensive by international standards, and was often at variance with practices traditionally prescribed by religious doctrine and Afghan custom. For all the rationale by the Taliban focused on the implementation of Islamic codes, much of the judicial administration was highly inconsistent and arbitrary. At the local level, various interpretations of the Shari'a law were joined with those of traditional tribal codes know as Pushtunwali. Legal and judicial institutions remained weak and subject to bribes and other forms of corruption.

Outside monitors regularly denounced arbitrary detention, poor prison conditions, and summary trials that resulted in public executions, sometimes by slitting throats and, in the case of adultery, by stoning. Other punishments were describable as cruel and disproportionate such as amputations for theft. Extrajudicial killings were also observed. The use of torture against political opponents and POWs was frequently alleged, and reports spoke of children being taken hostage to compel the surrender of their fathers.

These and other rights violations, including large-scale massacres of civilians and execution of captured fighters, might be just nasty byproducts of a civil war. But they also appeared to grow out of an ideology and value system. Ethnic, sectarian, and racial prejudices in Afghanistan were served in these violations. The Hazara minority, mostly adherents of Shiite Islam and identifiable by oriental features, have traditionally suffered socially and economically. But their oppression assumed a far more deadly form under the Taliban. As Sunnite Pashtuns and adherents of the Diobandi religious school of thought, the Taliban viewed Shia Islam with particular disdain. The evidence indicates that Taliban fighters massacred noncombatant Hazara men, women, and children. Taliban-imposed blockades frequently halted shipments of food and other supplies into the group's home region of Hazarjat. Taliban forces, joined by Pakistani and Arab volunteers, were also accused of ethnic cleansing and scorched-earth practices against ethnic Tajiks. Reports of the killing of Tajik men and boys and the torching of villages were largely verified.

As a theocracy subject to the edicts of a small group of mullahs, freedoms of speech and press were denied to Afghans. Movies, television, and listening to music were all outlawed. No laws provided for the freedom of the press or speech. Foreign journalists were restricted when they tried to report on human rights, and sometimes arrested. Domestic as well as foreign NGOs operated in the country, but they were strictly limited to humanitarian, rehabilitation, education, and agricultural support activities. To continue their critical operations, these organizations tried to avoid criticism of Taliban policies.

Several Afghan-led human rights organizations were dedicated to focusing attention on abuses. Most were based in Peshawar, Pakistan, and tried—with limited success—to monitor and document developments inside Afghanistan. All these groups adopted a strategy based, above all, on drawing international attention to the plight of the Afghan people. None were part of Afghanistan's domestic political process.

Among the foreign critics of Taliban policy during the Taliban era were Amnesty International, Human Rights Watch, and the UN Special Rapporteur on Afghanistan. The International Red Cross was also active and, to the extent it could, observed prison conditions. But the U.S. government, which had declared Afghanistan to be a terrorist state, served as the major catalyst for pressure on the Taliban. The United States was also behind the UN-approved sanctions in November 1999 and January 2001. But sanctions policies, while officially exempting humanitarian relief, may have inadvertently increased the hardship on ordinary Afghan citizens. Also, the publicity given to the Taliban's dismal human rights record served as an impediment to international assistance for rehabilitation and reconstruction of the war-ravaged country. The heavy criticism by women's groups in the West and of the government's policies of "gender apartheid" quite possibly had the unintended effect of reducing outside funding for other humanitarian causes.

The framework for a future democratic government for Afghanistan as laid out under strong international guidance in December 2001 and reaffirmed at a *loya jirga* (grand council) in June 2002 took important, if largely symbolic steps toward recognizing human rights. Women have been appointed to the ministries of the interim and subsequent transitional administration, and assurances were made that women's employment and other rights would be observed. Overall, the leadership is not ethnically balanced, but the principle that future Afghan governments should be broad-based has wide appeal. Deep concern remains, however, about whether the central government will have the leverage necessary to gain cooperation from provincial and local authorities for reforms aimed at creating a more equitable and freer society.

As a legacy of the civil war, Afghans may have to address the issue of accountability. Some senior Taliban and other militia commanders have been held accountable, but less for human rights violations such as wartime atrocities than for political allegiances. Offers of reconstruction aid could be conditional on the adoption of mechanisms for accountability and reconciliation. Approaches to transitional justice may draw on models used elsewhere in recent years, but must be suitable for the Afghan context, that is, consistent with the country's traditions and core values. Also for the future, until a national army, local policing forces, and formal and informal judiciaries are restored, few rights can be guaranteed.

The Strategic Environment

In the preceding cases there are domestic movements and groups that are critical to directing attention to human rights issues. Their effectiveness is often constrained by the normative and institutional context in which they operate. No less so, strategic choices and available resources help to determine their success in pursuing a human rights agenda. The strengths and weaknesses of these groups are often determined by whether they are well integrated into the society and body politic, and to what degree they are accorded legitimacy. More detailed study can ask about the extent to which the claimants for human rights are afforded access to the leading decision makers and the media. Do they have the necessary funding, the ability to mobilize supporters, and the requisite leadership skills? Have they succeeded in making strategic alliances, both domestically and with outside players? In general, how appropriate are their strategies in confronting and overcoming formidable adversaries and other obstacles?

In Iran and in a Taliban-controlled Afghanistan, Islamic governance has been the major basis of legitimacy. The assertion of rights determined by Islamic values as opposed by Western values offered a means by which the regimes in these two countries could deny the freedoms that might challenge their grip on power. Both these states often seemed uncompromising, but Iran less so. The conservative leadership in Tehran makes allowance for greater civil and human rights for citizens in response to popular demand in elections, and under pressure by liberalizing elements in the leadership and society. In Afghanistan, in the absence of political pluralism or institutions of representation, few compromises were offered. Only in response to international aid groups and the criticism of foreign governments did the Taliban leadership on rare occasions show an inclination to modify those policies accused of violating basic human rights. Their successors are at least promising to be more observant of international norms, although the reach of their authority beyond Kabul remains to be seen.

Normally, the existence of internal pressures coincides with a tolerance for a range of political expression. Of the three countries, Turkey, the most democratic, also has the greatest number of indigenously organized groups to voice disapproval of the state of human rights. Afghanistan has had the fewest domestically based groups. By contrast to the situation in Turkey and Iran, in Afghanistan groups from outside the country were until very recently more influential. Under Taliban rule, a civil society that could embrace human rights groups was virtually nonexistent. Inside Afghanistan, complaints, particularly about women's access to education and health services, were widely but privately expressed, and no organized effort emerged to challenge the leadership on these and other rights issues. It fell most to opposition forces outside the Taliban's military control to point to the government's abusive rights policies. These elements, largely representing the country's ethnic minorities, stressed discrimination by the dominant Pashtun community and pointed to atrocities allegedly committed by Taliban fighters. But the practices of opposition militias toward noncombatants suspected of collaborating with the Taliban probably paralleled those of their adversaries. Torture of Taliban prisoners held by Northern Alliance commander Ahmed Masud was often alleged. Following the Taliban's fall, some of the most serious crimes were committed against Pashtuns and Pakistani and Arab volunteers held captive by the forces of the Uzbek commander Abdul Dostam.

For all Turkey's official policies that effectively curtail rights for Kurds and supporters of Islamic parties, its human rights advocates are able to assume the kind of legitimate role not available in Afghanistan and barely tolerated in Iran. Critics in Turkey point up the ambivalent character of ruling elements that are willing to be judged by Western standards but also to defy them where they feel that national security and integrity are challenged. While allowing Turkey's organized rights community a place in the civil society, officials regularly impede their operations. On occasion, government institutions, most notably the parliamentary committee on human rights, have managed to show independent judgment and offer protections. More often, officials seek to coopt and neutralize those who raise complaints. Rights groups find it difficult to present their case in the arena of public opinion, where they are subject to denunciation as front organizations for banned elements and as being unpatriotic in maligning the country. In Turkey, a Human Rights Association demonstrates how under adversity, a mass membership organization can persevere. It has benefited from dedicated leadership and has sought strategic partnerships. Turkey's contradictory experiences suggest that it is difficult to decide how much a formal commitment by central authorities to a broad public debate and a respect for human rights actually matter.

Because Iran's movements for a more liberal, tolerant society are attached to a wider campaign for political and economic reforms, both strengths and weaknesses are revealed. Rights advocates can draw on the popularity of leaders associated with the popular movement associated with President Khatami to criticize some of the worst examples of judicial abuse and restrictions of freedom of expression. Their strategy relies heavily on an ability to outwit their enemies in creating outlets in the press to present their views. At the same time, however, those groups concerned with attitudes toward minorities find little support among political reformers whose agenda largely ignores minority issues. If for no other reason, the bias occurs because the reform leaders as well as their conservative opponents are almost entirely from the Persian-speaking dominant Shiʿa population.

The hope has been that with their parliamentary losses in recent years, Iran's conservative elements would begin to yield their domination of the system of justice, just as they have lost control over much of the country's cultural and intellectual activities. There was also some expectation that those in ethnic and sectarian minorities who until now have been reticent to defend their rights openly would press for them more aggressively. These groups have, by and large, relied on strategies designed to find accommodation and minimize their inferior status rather than articulate their grievances publicly. Christians, Jews, and Zoroastrians have enjoyed a degree of legitimacy in being recognized within the constitution and allotted token representation in Parliament. But aside from soliciting expressions of support and some funding from abroad, these minorities have built no alliances domestically. In a more liberal state, the rights of women are most likely to see the greatest improvement, the delegitimized Baha'is least so. In sum, the power of the conservative clergy in Iran remains largely unassailable.

In the three countries under study, impelling pressures to improve human rights policies have come through links to outside actors, some of them international and government agencies, but more often nongovernmental groups. External sanctions can in some cases work; in other cases they are counterproductive. The sensitivities of the international community toward extra-constitutional or military takeovers have, in any case, changed. More-over, the level of tolerance for flawed democracies has diminished. Western countries and international loan agencies have called for progress in ending human rights abuses and denying civil liberties. Of late, creditors have also looked with disfavor on countries devoting large fractions of their GNP to national defense. While these criteria are not applied consistently and evenly across countries, and political expediency is still often overriding, liberal principles are pronounced with greater frequency.

The governments under study react in varying degrees to organizations such as Amnesty International and Human Rights Watch, and to the human rights assessments of the U.S. State Department. Ordinarily, the critics' most effective weapon is public exposure. Where criticism is more likely to be heard is when there are direct economic consequences, as with the employment of child labor. International pressures had very limited impact on the Taliban movement, which continued to the end to deny the applicability of Western standards. Winning international approval has had a greater effect on decisions reached in Tehran. Turkey takes human rights criticisms from abroad seriously, but again, often not seriously enough to change policies when these collide with long-held nationalist doctrines and deep-seated majority prejudices.

The global economic context creates incentives for gestures toward democratic practice and the observance of international rights standards that should not be underestimated. In the case of Turkey, failure to deliver satisfactorily on both accounts explicitly impedes admission to the European Union. In Iran, any hope of closing the distance in relations with Western Europe, desired mostly for economic motives, had to wait until at least a seeming reversal of the *fatwa* against Salman Rushdi was offered by Tehran. While the major international creditor institutions do not claim to set standards based on political or normative criteria, in fact, these conditions do influence member governments in providing economic relief. This is especially the case where a country in difficult economic straits, such as Afghanistan, may be perceived as defying international community norms. At the same time, the limited transnational market integration (drug trafficking aside) of Afghanistan makes it less vulnerable to formal sanctions from outside.

Conclusion: Power and Change

Notwithstanding changing international sensibilities, governments in Turkey, Iran, and Afghanistan give the highest priority to regime survival and maintenance. This is the case even if that means paying the price of offending domestic and international advocates of liberal policies and the expansion of human rights. To the extent that control and liberalizing are not seen as being in serious conflict, these governments may be willing to relax their grip on freedoms, that is, so long as their legitimizing ethos is not violated. But those freedoms are subject to withdrawal at the hands of the military in Turkey and the religious hierarchy in Iran. In Afghanistan, many of these rights have had no standing because they lacked normative sanction, constitutional restraints, and legal systems to safeguard them.

Although Turkey falls short of its own stated objectives in protecting human rights, it is relatively open to international groups that seek to monitor conditions in the country. Whereas in Iran and Afghanistan, it is Islamic norms that supposedly pose obstacles to universal ones, in Turkey it is the ideology of the unified secular state that challenges these rights. As this ideology is modified, the climate for human rights is certain to improve. Even now, the country compares well with Iran and Afghanistan.

In Turkey's bidding for incorporation into the European Union, its human rights policies are explicit criteria. Membership has opened a fervent debate, including the government, the military, and the press, over what changes are necessary, given perceived dangers to the state. With membership, adherence to rulings of the European Court of Human Rights and other legal standards would go far in assuring that the governing authorities adopt standards on a par with other EU countries. But the European states are also anxious to use the promise of eventual membership to solidify democracy in Turkey and to strengthen the hands of those seeking to promote values of tolerance and diversity. Increasingly, all these EU objectives seem interlinked.

The prospects for human rights in Iran hinge mostly on domestic developments. Should the more reformist elements prevail, rights will improve as a more open society is achieved. International linkages are also important in view of the structure of Iran's economy. But, despite the desire for trading partners and more normal relations with Europe, the adjustment of rigid Islamic policies to satisfy Western critics cannot be expected. Even without improved human rights policies, prevailing economic relationships are likely to remain. Current limited economic sanctions, imposed mostly by the United States, are unlikely to expand unless Iran were to engage in a full-fledged repression of its minorities or a reign of terror against political adversaries.

Until the Taliban's collapse under military onslaught, the best that could be expected was that, in time, they might moderate their stringent social policies, especially toward women. Feeling more secure, the Taliban might have accorded greater respect to ethnic minorities. But some of those practices in Afghanistan found objectionable by human rights monitoring groups outside Afghanistan are part of the country's customary practices, both Islamic and traditional in origin. Still, economically dependent successor governments are less likely to argue that human rights demands from outside constitute both an unwarranted interference and a desecration of Islam. Ironically, a greater danger may be that human rights watchers may lose much of their interest in Afghanistan with the conclusion of its humanitarian crises and peacekeeping.

The future of human rights in the three countries of the Northern Tier is intimately tied to far-reaching normative and political changes. In each, a revised understanding of the relevance of Islam may be necessary in order that human rights issues attract broad recognition and legitimacy. Improving group and individual rights also require institutional changes that allow for the invigoration of organized interests to serve as the instigators and guardians of rights, as well as for legal and constitutional changes to ensure the sustainability of hard-won gains. None of these changes are close at hand in Turkey, Iran, and Afghanistan. Yet there are hopeful signs in all three countries.

Chapter 5
North Africa

Badredine Arfi

All the North African states—Morocco, Algeria, Tunisia, and Libya—have been confronted since independence with a lack of popular legitimacy. In the 1980s, domestic political debates about human rights slowly became an integral part of a seemingly never-ending process of state legitimation. The agenda of human rights has thence evolved as a constitutive element of the ongoing contest about state legitimation. The politics of human rights in North Africa has assumed the character of a manipulation of history, culture, and Islam to shape the balance of social—symbolic, economic, and political-institutional—power between the state and societal actors as well as among the latter themselves.

Public debates over human rights first emerged when state leaders repressively responded to public demands for political participation and public frustration with both regime corruption and continuously worsening socioeconomic conditions. Neither subsequent ruling regimes nor the varieties of opposition and social, popular movements have rejected human rights ideals as purely Western ideas. International norms of human rights have been viewed, at least in principle, to be compatible with the predominant Islamic culture of the region. By 1978 the North African states had indeed acceded to the two principal international human rights covenants, and representatives from the region assumed leadership positions within the UN human rights bodies. However, toward the end of the 1980s new political actors forced the question of human rights on the national political agenda by effectively challenging the legitimacy of the repressive governments and attempting to redefine the official political discourse and practice on human rights. Consequently, statesmen who had been reluctant to permit groups even to operate outside state control and supervision began to "chant" the tune of human rights both in domestic politics and in the international arena. To a significant degree the human rights struggle in North Africa has been a contest over the nature of the official political discourse. At a more practical level, though, the states reluctantly began to respond to the challenges through legal measures by creating "cosmetic" government agencies purported to address the issue of human rights abuses. The states nonetheless sought in parallel to coopt nongovernmental organizations effectively so as to suppress or minimize criticisms and challenges.

The progressive legitimization of human rights concerns in official political discourse has for the most part been instrumental. In general, the practical commitment of the states in the region to human rights has remained shallow. Heads of states and governing elites saw human rights as a political device for advancing self-serving programs and enhancing their own legitimacy. By participating in the debates about human rights, the North African states (except Libya) ironically ended up sanctioning a change in the language of politics. North African states willy-nilly legitimized new actions and raised new popular expectations about the respect and importance of human rights. The credibility of states that claimed to promote human rights became increasingly dependent in part on a willingness to surrender or constrain the purview of state coercive power.

This legitimization of human rights discourse has been no easy task because of the very nature of these regimes. In Tunisia, Morocco, Algeria, and Libya, a client system secures societal interests by linking them closely to the state interests. In all four states central governments controlled sociopolitical power and economic resources and then redistributed them to the various social forces that contributed to sustain the sociopolitical order. Private investors, organized labor, and the middle class, as well as the poor, benefited from a host of state-led economic activities, subsidies, and subventions. In exchange the state extracted loyalty, compliance, and complacency, while reserving itself the right to use repression against those groups that dared to question state-controlled sociopolitical order.

The global economic recessions of 1980–82, which caused a decline in the demand for hydrocarbon and other primary exports from Algeria, Morocco, Tunisia, and Libya, shook the basis of these *rentier* states. The *rentier* institutional arrangements within North Africa, which had at first facilitated the project of state building, subsequently became a liability hindering economic development. Irrespective of the regime type—monarchist, authoritarian, or semi-authoritarian—the role of the state in economic development henceforth came under close scrutiny, consolidating and sometimes partially causing the emergence of increasingly vocal and diverse opposition groups in each country. In all four countries, various forms of opposition became agents of political debates about the source of state legitimation throughout the 1980s. Faced with an increasingly critical opposition and with acute crises of legitimacy and dire socioeconomic conditions, state rulers have attempted to partly reconstruct some of the institutions and agencies that represent the state. The initial efforts in both Algeria and Tunisia focused on creating some form of political pluralism. However, both experiments are far from consolidating effective pluralistic multi-party systems and the rule of law.[1] The Moroccan state has perpetuated the circumscribed semi-democratic system with the king reserving to himself the sacrosanct right to absolute decision on whatever matters he deems relevant to maintain and expand his authority. These regime changes have opened up and expanded a political space for debating human rights.

Constructing and playing the politics of human rights and shaping the outcomes of this game increasingly became part of, and hence shaped, a competition-collaboration between the regime and a variety of opposition groups. Indeed, in all four countries the manipulation of symbolic links among the ruler, the ruled, and the country's history and culture has been an integral part of the politics of human rights. Both the state representatives and those contesting the state brandish the powerful symbols of national identity and Islam to advance their agendas or to attempt to delegitimate the other players. For example, the symbols of Islamic solidarity, equity, equality, and Arabization invoked by Islamist leaders such as Abdessalem Yassine in Morocco, Rashid al-Ghannoushi in Tunisia, and Abassi al-Madani in Algeria, and by Libya's self-exiled Islamists are those already invoked by the first generation of North African rulers (Burgat and Dowell 1993). The latter had skillfully manipulated them in their own search for legitimacy and national unity at the wake of independence or at various turning points in post-colonial history. The symbolic contest is now much more pronounced, however, because the link to the colonial era and independence struggles invoked by subsequent regimes in power has lost much of its appeal. Significantly most of the recent confrontations with the state as well as those who claim to represent or support it in North Africa have been initiated by a younger generation. These late comers do not share for the most part the historical memories or ideological commitments that were at the heart of the symbolic link between their elders and the state and its agents.

The next section discusses the main domestic actors that have contributed to defining and shaping the politics of human rights in North Africa. These actors used a variety of strategies and diverse resources to participate in the continuous process of collectively constructing human rights. The outcome of these constructions has been a dynamic balance of social power that, when formed and stabilized, in turn shapes the debates over human rights. Although these actors are domestic and driven by specific national and local circumstances, international human rights organizations, foreign states (especially West European ones and to a lesser degree the United States) as well as "fifth columns" of North African expatriates living in Europe also contributed to shape the domestic balances of social power in Morocco, Algeria, and Tunisia. The third section of the paper addresses more specifically the nature and roles of these external actors in shaping the politics of human rights in North Africa. I conclude the chapter with a set of recommendations on what processes would reshape human rights in North Africa.

Playing the Politics of Human Rights in North Africa

Principal Actors in the Politics of Human Rights

Four distinct if somewhat overlapping categories of actors have participated in the process of constructing and shaping the politics of human rights in North Africa—political parties, human rights organizations, Islamist movements, and ruling regimes and their domestic allies and clientele. Each of these actors has shaped the discourse of human rights. The debates were a combination of confrontation and cooperation, but overall produced a whole that is larger than the sum of the individual efforts of these actors—a symbiotic combination of a variety of conceptions and practices that constructed human rights as an inseparable element of the process of state legitimation.

Political Parties

In North Africa political parties have been of two kinds: (1) those working for, affiliated with, or complacent toward the regime, and (2) those opposed to the regime either from within the official institutional framework or outside the system. The various regimes controlled, coopted, or repressed these political parties. Minor parties were simply ignored or occasionally reminded of their precarious positions. In any case, the position of the majority of these political parties on the issue of human rights remained either unclear or very close to the position of the nongovernmental human rights organizations in their respective countries. A minority of these parties demarcated itself with the Islamist parties and groups as they themselves also became victims of state repression.

In Tunisia (after 1987) and Algeria (before 1989) the ruling regime heavily relied on a single political party, respectively the Rassemblement Constitutionel Démocratique (RCD) in Tunisia and the Front de Libération Nationale (FLN) in Algeria to dominate the political space. These dominant parties were simply an extension of the regimes and thus, not surprisingly, did not have an independent role in the human rights politics. The most vocal parties had been the Islamist party al-Nahdah in Tunisia and the Berber opposition such as the Front des Forces Socialistes of Ait Ahmed and the Islamists in Algeria. In Libya, political parties were banned altogether and the Mu'ammar Qadhafi regime did not create its own political party as in Algeria and Tunisia. In Morocco, although kings Mohammed V, Hassan II, and Mohammed VI have allowed the existence of multiple legal political parties, the latter do not effectively constitute an independent political force. Thus in Morocco the issue of human rights was rather relegated for the most part to the domestic human rights groups as well as to the Islamist groups.

Human Rights Groups

The principal activists in the early human rights movements in North Africa came from the privileged classes. Virtually all the movement leaders were university educated. Either through professional status or family connections, or a mixture thereof, these leaders believed that they commanded enough respect, which could be harnessed to pursue a human rights agenda. The goals that inspired these human rights activists were however generally tempered with caution, for they understood the necessity to avoid being perceived as direct threats to the regime and its support clientele. In addition, most groups recognized the advantage of having well placed and politically unassailable members of the regime at or near the top leadership of the human rights group. Especially desirable were those high-ranking officials whose moral integrity and political conduct could not be questioned. Such a person can indeed be a credible public advocate for human rights while simultaneously not being perceived as a threat by the incumbent regime and its domestic defenders. These groups had indeed learned that they might suffer stiff penalties were they to allow principled commitments to override their pragmatic assessment of political realities irrespective of the situation.

In Morocco, human rights organizations were established in the early 1970s following the failed military coups and subsequent arrests of large numbers of officers and many of their family members. Members of the Istiqlal political party founded a human rights organization, the Ligue Marocaine pour la Défense des Droits de l'Homme (LMDDH) in 1972. At the same time student-led left-wing groups formed together the illegal Comités de Lutte Contre la Repression au Maroc (CLCRM). The Association Marocaine des Droits de l'Homme (AMDH), was founded on June 24, 1979, as a wing of the Union Socialiste de Forces Populaires (USFP). This organization was set up particularly with the aim to publicize abroad human rights violations by the Moroccan regime. In December 1988 a group of Moroccan intellectuals founded another human rights organization that proclaimed its independence of political parties, the Organization Marocaine des Droits de l'Homme (OMDH). The OMDH recruited government officials as well as persons closely connected to the government. The cooperative efforts of these various human rights groups produced a common National Charter of Human Rights in 1990. The AMDH, LMDDH, and OMDH also cooperated with the Association Marocaine des Avocats and the Association Professionelle des Avocats Marocaines. A group of lawyers, doctors, journalists, former inmates, and entertainment personalities also created a nongovernmental organization, the Observatoire National des Prisons Marocaines (ONPM), to advocate the improvement of living conditions within prisons and to call for and support penal reform efforts. These human rights organizations maintain close and officially collaborative relations with the regime. In addition, the Conseil Consultatif des Droits de l'Homme (CCDH), an advisory body to the king, counsels the palace on human rights issues, and is charged by the king to resolve cases of disappeared persons (Basri 1994; Bensbia 1996). The CCDH's agenda has been to improve the penal law system and prison conditions, establish continuous communications with human rights NGOs, work to better the inhuman conditions of refugees in Polisario-controlled camps in Tindouf, Algeria, and address various issues on economic, social, and cultural rights (Souhaili 1986).

In Tunisia, the Ligue Tunisienne des Droits de l'Homme (LTDH) was founded in 1976 as a reaction to growing state repression. One year later the Bourguiba government legalized the organization. Because there was no legal alternative voice for opposition during the Bourguiba era, the LTDH became a melting pot for political opposition for all causes. This brought ideological differences within the organization and caused many internal conflicts that could not be easily solved (Dwyer 1991, 168–81). President Bourguiba did not reject the idea of human rights and, hence, the Tunisian human rights movement seized this rhetorical commitment to put public pressure on the Tunisian government. The regime was hence forced either to deny or justify its lack of effective policy on human rights abuses. This occasional influence however remained limited and in fact ended with the change of government tactics after the 1987 coup.

The new self-appointed president, Ben Ali, adopted the human rights discourse to consolidate his power base immediately after the coup (Waltz 1995). Positive rhetoric and minor institutional measures initially created the impression that the human rights situation was improving. The government endeavored to suppress criticisms about its human rights policies and practices by putting itself in charge of defending human rights and coopting domestic human rights organizations. Consequently, the only recognized human rights organization, the LTDH, dissolved itself in 1992 following a dispute with the government. The league reemerged in 1994, but with a much more modest agenda, much of it in conformity with the government agenda.

In Algeria, the impetus for the Algerian human rights movement goes back to the early 1980s with the first eruption of popular unrest (Charef 1994). The government ban of a seminar on Berber poetry angered the Berbers in the Kabilya capital, Tizi Ouzou (Aziz 1993). Unrest over cultural issues grew steadily thereafter, only to become more complicated with clashes with a rising Islamist current. As a reaction to the harsh regime repression of these mutually clashing political currents, two politically independent human rights groups emerged almost simultaneously in the mid-1980s. The most active as well as independent human rights group has been the Ligue Algérienne pour la Défense des Droits de l'Homme (LADDH). The LADDH has not, however, been allowed much access to the authorities or to prisons beyond the normal consultations allowed between a lawyer and a client. The less active Ligue Algérienne des Droits de l'Homme (LADH) is also an independent organization, but has much better relations with the regime. The events following the cancellation of the parliamentary elections in 1992 have sharply demarcated these two groups in terms of their respective positions and actions regarding the then two main protagonists in the emerging armed conflict, the regime and various armed Islamist groups. The LADDH has unequivocally and continuously denounced abuses by the regime. Its president, Abdenour Ali Yahia, has continuously held principled postures, for example, when he assumed the legal defense of the FIS leaders arrested in 1991, Madani and Benhadj. He also persistently called for the return or civilian rule and a lifting of the emergency rule imposed by the regime after the cancellation of the 1992 elections. The LADH position has been much more mixed. The regime formed in 1992 the Observatoire National des Droits de l'Homme (ONDH) with the task of monitoring and reporting human rights violations to the authorities. Obviously such an action was a measure largely taken to rebut too much criticism on the international scene.

In contrast with Morocco, Algeria, and Tunisia, the Libyan government prohibits the establishment of independent human rights organizations. Instead, the Libyan regime created a "cosmetic" Libyan Arab Human Rights Committee in 1989.

Islamist Groups

Since the 1970s Islamism has increasingly become a major force in the sociopolitical life of North African societies (Burgat and Dowell 1993). A variety of groups have actively reasserted Islam as a source of political development, a symbol of political legitimacy, and as a source of political and social activism and popular mobilization. Islamist movements and organizations have been the driving force behind this dynamic spread of the Islamic resurgence. The North African governments have increasingly perceived them as threats to their authority and legitimacy. Nor have the populaces been spared the challenge of making choices among corrupt, inefficient, and unaccountable governments and Islamist groups who aim at reconstructing not only the states, but also these societies. For large sections of these divided populaces, Islamist movements represent either an authentic alternative to these regimes, or a destabilizing force and a tool of demagogues employing any tactics to gain power.

Islamist movements in North Africa form a continuum in terms of their diverse strategies, goals, and resources. Alongside violent radical rejectionists are organizations that espouse political liberalization and democratization. Islamist groups have won seats in parliaments, held portfolios in governments, and emerged as a significant, sometimes leading, opposition in Tunisia, Algeria, and Morocco. Most of these Islamist movements grew from small groups of like-minded professionals, students, and intellectuals. Although the Islamists had widespread appeal in the lower strata of the North African societies, the active adherents and entrepreneurs tended to be university graduates. The Islamist movements build their popular power bases by providing free medicine, distributing school equipment, cleaning neighborhoods, offering legal and administrative advice, organizing scouting groups, and providing subsidized grocery markets in poor neighborhoods during Ramadan. The Islamist groups hence discharge many social functions that the governments had once claimed as part of the state's rentier role.

A variety of specific cultural contexts, differences of political economy, histories, distinctive personalities and ambitions of individual leaders and ideologues shape the ideologies and actions of Islamist movements in North Africa. One common aspect of Islamist movements is that they have increasingly clashed with their respective national regimes. These clashes, however, are more the products of local circumstances and conditions than of any transnational organizational links or planning, doomsday chroniclers' claims to the contrary notwithstanding. The spectrum of Islamists, extending from relatively strong movements in Tunisia and Algeria to moderately weak groups in Morocco and no organization inside Libya, is illustrative.

This Islamist spectrum became manifest on the Algerian political scene after the October 1988 riots. On the one hand, the powerful Algerian Front Islamique du Salut (FIS), which in itself was an outgrowth of a variety of Islamist groups and individual activists who had been working for the most part underground since the mid-1970s, emerged in 1988 to self-appropriate the nationalist discourse. The FIS adapted to the current situation the ideals and slogans previously used by the FLN during and immediately after Algeria's war of independence (1954–62) to legitimize the state (1962–89). The FIS thus engaged the regime in a symbolic war about the ideological and moral orientation of the country. The cancellation of the 1992 parliamentary elections and immediate harsh suppression of the FIS top and middle leadership fragmented the FIS and its sympathizers, resulting in a bloody confrontation with the army. The latter banned the FIS and launched an armed campaign against a variety of Islamist groups. On the other hand, movements such as the Mouvement pour une Société de Paix (MSP) and al-Nahda party have become part of the political establishment and won many seats in the 1997 parliamentary elections as well as holding various ministerial posts in succeeding governments.

In Tunisia, the al-Nahda party (formerly Mouvement de la Tendence Islamique—MTI) has shifted between radical violent opposition such as during the pre-1987 Bourguiba regime and seeking legal political participation under the Ben Ali regime (Hamdi 1998). However, Ben Ali's continuous persecution of the Islamist tendency in Tunisia since the early 1990s has very much weakened the role and impact of the al-Nahda party, thereby forcing most of its leadership and free members into exile or underground (Toumi 1989).

In Morocco, King Hassan II's claim to be the Ameer al-Mu'mineen (commander of the faithful) has deprived the Islamist movement of most of the religious symbolism that Islamist movements in Algeria and Tunisia have used to appeal to the populace and discredit the secular-oriented regimes in power (Burgat and Dowell 1993).[2] For a somewhat similar end although using ruthless ways, Libya's Qadhafi appropriated the realm of religious symbolism to promote a reconstruction of the Libyan society according to his Green Book ideology. Consequently, most of what might be termed as an Islamist tendency in Libya is either underground and constantly pursued and persecuted by the Qadhafi regime and its allies or is in self-exile in various parts of the world.

Ruling Regimes

The Tunisian, Algerian, and Moroccan constitutions stipulate the legal separation of the executive and legislative and guarantee universal protection of human rights. However, these constitutional guarantees have yet to translate fully into active public policy and effective institutional enforcement.

Morocco is a constitutional monarchy, centrally ruled by a king who possesses extensive powers of legislation. The Moroccan king is not accountable to law. The fundamental axiom is that the king is sacrosanct. It is forbidden by law to publish an article offensive to the king and the royal family, as it is illegal to inquire about royal finances[3] (Damis 1992; Entelis 1989). The power of the Moroccan monarchy's symbols helps it to engender popular loyalty and fear (Burgat and Dowell 1993). The mass media constantly reaffirms the king's unchallengeable authority. Consequently, the largely undisputed posture of the king defines the boundaries of the political game as well as the relationship between the king and the political class. The king presides over the Council of Ministers, appoints all members of the government, and may, at his discretion, terminate the tenure of any minister, dissolve the parliament, call for new elections, and rule by decree. The Moroccan multiparty system, codified by the constitution, has been relatively flourishing since the 1960s after the king encouraged the founding of new parties. However, parliamentary opposition has somewhat effectively developed only since the early 1990s (Bensbia 1996). Most important, despite these constitutional guarantees, government and commercial perquisites actively cultivate a royal clientele and, in turn, make powerful patrons of the king's own clients. Moroccan political economy turns on such relations, and the close incorporation of political elites into the system reinforces the king's own position (El-Aoufi 1992).

Tunisia is a republic largely dominated by a single political party. President

Zine El-Abidine Ben Ali and his RCD party have controlled the government, including the legislature, since the 1987 coup (Garon 1994). Recent revisions to the constitution allowed opposition candidates to run against Ben Ali in the presidential elections. Nevertheless, the president and his immediate entourage did not genuinely relinquish any power. The president appoints the prime minister, the cabinet, and the governors. The executive branch and the president strongly influence the judiciary, particularly in sensitive political issues. The president directly controls the police forces and secret services. Any opposition from any quarter of the populace, especially if it is perceived to have an Islamist flavor, is harshly suppressed (Hamdi 1998). Even though the Tunisian government is officially structured along the lines of Western liberal democracies, democratic practices have yet to become the norm. Tunisia has instead evolved into a strong one-party police state. The repeated reelection of Ben Ali as president and his party's (RCD) stronghold on the parliament are illustrative. Although Ben Ali began his tenure with some symbolic gestures of political opening and liberalization, the regime soon became more aggressive, introducing political and legal measures to curtail the activities of the domestic human rights groups as well as limiting the freedom of press, association, and information, especially during and after the Gulf War (Garon 1994, 1995a, b). The first repressive measures were directed particularly against the Islamists, whom the regime portrays as a threat to Western values and national integrity and security.

Since its independence in 1962 Algeria has been under the strong influence of an army-led coalition made up of high-ranking military commanders, a petite bourgeoisie, a corrupt bureaucracy, and many local and national officials who have transformed state institutions and public domains into private properties (Hidouci 1995; Goumeziane 1994). Many active or retired senior army officers perceive the army because of its historic role during the war of national liberation (1954–62) as the soul and backbone of the Algerian state (Spencer 1994). To a large extent, the bonds among these factions have not been ideological, but rather exist to preserve economic interests, privileges, and power status and oppose the creation of an Islamic state.

Neither the FLN nor the army has officially ever denied a limited role to Islam within the Algerian polity—all subsequent Algerian constitutions stipulate that Islam is the state religion. However, subsequent regimes have continuously attempted to exclusively control the role of Islam in the polity since 1962 through various strategies such as the creation of a Ministry of Religious Affairs, the construction of mosques, the appointment and control of state-sponsored Imams, and the cooption of many Islamic figures. In spite of these efforts the regimes have failed to limit the symbolic-religious space. The different movements of political Islam, particularly after the mid-1980s, have been able to assume increasingly larger roles as defenders and advocates of Islamic societal and political projects, culminating in the astonishing and unexpected landslide victories of the FIS in the local elections in June 1990 and the first round of national elections in December 1991. Moreover, the incorporation of the MSP and al-Nahda parties in the parliament and governments evidence that, even though the FIS has largely disappeared from the national scene, political Islam is still an integral part of the political spectrum of Algeria that the regime has to cope with either cooperatively or coercively.

The Socialist People's Libyan Arab Jamahiriya is an absolutist dictatorship that Colonel Mu'ammar Al-Qadhafi (the "Brother Leader and Guide of the Revolution") has singlehandedly and ruthlessly ruled since the 1969 military coup against King Idris (Vandewalle 1998). Through a manipulation of many symbols and tenets of Islamic and pan-Arab cultures and histories and strongly repressive measures, Qadhafi has created a political system that rejects democracy and political parties, claiming to establish instead a "third way" superior to capitalism and communism as articulated in his "Green Book."

In theory Libya is ruled by the citizenry through a series of popular congresses, as laid out in the Constitutional Proclamation of 1969 and the Declaration on the Establishment of the Authority of the People of 1977. In practice Qadhafi and his innermost circle tightly control all aspects of political and socioeconomic life. Qadhafi maintains an extensive security apparatus, consisting of several elite military units, including his personal bodyguards, local Revolutionary Committees and People's Committees, as well as the "Purification" Committees newly formed in 1996. The government dominates the economy through complete control of the country's oil resources, which account for almost all export earnings and approximately 30 percent of the gross domestic product. Despite efforts to diversify the economy and encourage private sector participation, the economy continues to be constrained by a system of extensive controls covering prices, credit, trade, and foreign exchange. The result is a multi-layered, pervasive surveillance apparatus that monitors and controls the political, economic, and religious activities of the people (Vandewalle 1998).

In sum, various North African groups have emerged and increasingly contested the state monopoly of political space. The whole process by and large started after various symptoms and manifestations of increasingly incompetent rentier states of North Africa in time led the regimes in place to use repression as a means of self-preservation. State repression compounded with the effects of the global economic recession of the mid-1980s and a seemingly inexorable rise of Islamism in the region forced the issue of human rights on the national scene (Seddon 1989; Roberts 1995; Henry 1996). The global economic recession of the mid-1980s severely diminished and undermined the distributive role of the rentier regimes, highlighting the lack of popular support as well as an increasing frustration both within the regime and among the populace. The Islamist opposition became increasingly stronger and effectively eroded the legitimacy of the state.

By emphasizing the preeminence of law, domestic human rights organizations have directly challenged the framework of governance that does not often abide by the rule of law, especially when incumbent regimes or their clients and close supporters feel threatened. The efficacy of the groups in pursuit of these ends owes much to the fact that, for the most part, some of their members are drawn from elite classes. These members usually operate independently, but at the same time, share interests with the ruling elite who contribute to mitigate the threatening aspects of their human rights agenda. This has, however, also contributed to reducing their public appeal, for they could be perceived either as too accommodating of the regime or out of touch with the realities of societal life. Domestic human rights groups thus had to remain as firmly principled as they could short of a direct and costly confrontation with the regimes in place. Striking such a balance was not always a realistic or feasible option. This dilemma became much more difficult to resolve with the rise of the Islamist groups that engaged the regimes into symbolic wars of attrition. Nongovernmental human rights groups could not avoid risking their credibility and power position, whether they sided with one of the two protagonists or decided to remain neutral in the regime versus Islamist confrontations.

Islamist movements have thus played an important role in the political game of human rights, but their importance is country specific (Esposito and Voll 1996; Burgat and Dowell 1993). In both Morocco and Libya the Islamist movements have had less impact on human rights. In contrast, the Algerian and Tunisian Islamists have contributed to the collective construction of human rights in two different if reinforcing ways.

First, the Islamists have been for most of the time either in the opposition or the victims of state repression. In Algeria, the Islamists had to remain underground, if occasionally emerging on the political scene such as during the mid-1970s debates on Boumediene's proposals for a National Charter and a new constitution. Only after the October 1988 riots did the Islamists effectively begin openly opposing the regime as an organization (FIS). In Tunisia, the Islamist tendency attempted to acquire legal status under Ben Ali in the post-1987 era, but to no avail. During both the pre- and post-1987 eras, the MTI remained a vocal opposition. Because the political game of human rights in North Africa has been for the most part a defining and challenging aspect of state legitimation, the Islamists, being a highly committed opposition with a strong popular power base, constituted an ongoing challenge to the regime's claims about human rights. The Islamist groups simultaneously contributed to negate the government's claims and challenge the principled practice of human rights organizations.

Second, the Islamists also advanced their own notions of human rights as part of the Islamic heritage and culture. Matters were somewhat different in Tunisia and Algeria. Whereas Rashid al'Ghannovshi (the leader of the Tunisian MTI) has more or less kept a consistent and coherent vision of the Islamist discourse on human rights (Hamdi 1998), there has been a lack of coherence among the much more varied Islamist groups that have evolved in Algeria both before and after the 1988–92 period of transition (Burgat and Dowell 1993). Nevertheless these multiple and varied conceptions of Islamic human rights are all based on the precept that Islam should be the authoritative source that defines human rights. Such an unequivocal position has continuously put the Islamists and the various domestic human rights organizations on a collision course. Continuously being the victims of human rights abuses committed by the regimes made the Islamists the "perfect" case that human rights organizations would normally be expected to defend. However, advocating an Islamist version of human rights made the Islamist case not particularly appealing to most of the human rights organizations that perceived the Islamists as inherently opposed to a liberal notion of human rights.

By openly and strongly opposing the regimes in place the Islamists contributed to unveil the regimes' instrumental advocacy of human rights. By advocating Islamic human rights the Islamists forced the human rights organizations either to confront the governments or to remain silent on the abuses against the Islamists. The human rights organizations could not call for an institutionalization of human rights and the rule of law while at the same time opposing or neglecting the plight of the Islamists. Each actor sought to dominate the balance of social power—that is, to possess discretion over social and political action (Barnes 1988, 58)—to promote its political agenda not only on human rights, but also as a means to shape state legitimation and authority to its liking.

Balancing Social Power Among Principal Players

In North Africa subsequent regimes did not hesitate to use the coercive institutions of the state to ensure domination of the political space and the protection of economic interests of state officials and clientele. Because most of the legalized human rights organizations worked from within the existing institutional and legal systems in North Africa, it is the Islamist groups that for the most part engaged the incumbent regimes in direct battles for the symbolic space to define legitimacy and human rights.

The fate and scope of these tripolar confrontations—regime, human rights organizations, Islamist groups—depended on how much symbolic-social space was up for grabs. In Morocco the king has made himself the guarantor of the Islamic faith and as such self-appropriated the Islamic discourse. Similarly, after the coup in 1969 Qadhafi also appropriated the symbolic-social space that Islam provides to justify and legitimize his revolution and his regime as well as the harsh repression of any genuine opposition. Thus in both cases, the Islamist movements had to compete with the incumbent regimes for an already very limited and largely state-dominated, religious-symbolic space.

In contrast, the Tunisian and Algerian regimes have more or less ignored the symbolic-social space that was available. Although their state constitutions stipulate that Islam is the state religion, the political capital that inheres within the symbolic-social space of Islam was relegated to a secondary role and replaced instead with more secularist types of ideology and discourse. A continuous competition for symbolic-social space thus characterizes the discourse and debates on human rights in both Tunisia and Algeria. These characteristics of the political game of human rights in North Africa are born out in two particularly sensitive issues that have shaped the evolution of the balance of social power in North Africa: the rise of Islamism as a strong sociopolitical current and the 1991 Gulf War.[4]

North African human rights groups have not always been guided by clear principles. Nor have they been able to resist being drawn into issues that, while politically compelling, lay beyond their range of effective action. The rise of Islamism forced them to confront such dilemmas. In Tunisia the LTDH presented itself as a loyal opposition, but the evolution of the Islamist movement has continuously exposed and strained such a position. Although many within the LTDH saw the Islamist movement as fundamentally intolerant and anti-liberal, the league was forced, for example, in 1987 to condemn firmly regime abuses against the Islamists and to advocate the MTI's right to exist within the law. When Ben Ali acceded to power in 1987 the issue was again confused. The league president became the Minister of Education and thence adopted the forceful anti-Islamist position of the regime. In Algeria Ali Yahia (leader of the LADDH) clung steadfastly to the universality of human rights, regardless of the victim's political orientation. He denounced the 1992 coup and thereafter defended the Islamists' rights to political freedom and provided legal defense to the FIS leaders. The other Algerian league, LADH, assumed a more equivocal position on the 1992 coup and remained somewhat soft-spoken against the regime while at the same time denouncing violent Islamist groups that emerged after the 1992 coup. In Morocco the OMDH has also confronted similar issues with Islamism and was relatively slow to make public statements about cases that had for example been taken up by Amnesty International (Waltz 1995).

The Gulf War also strained the North African human rights community. The Algerian LADH and LADDH stopped short of supporting Iraqi claims, but condemned the privations imposed upon the Iraqi people. The Moroccan OMDH was more outspoken than its Algerian counterparts in condemning the West. The Tunisian LTDH position was the most complex, and most contested. At the outset of the conflict the LTDH leaders joined Tunisian political parties in expressing their solidarity with Iraq and supporting the

Tunisian government decision not to follow Egypt into an alliance with the United States.

Whereas the Gulf War provided an opportunity and a test for the Islamists to strengthen their bases of social power in both Morocco and Algeria, in Tunisia the regime launched a serious campaign of anti-Islamist repression, thereby further weakening the al-Nahdah base of social power. Because the Tunisian human rights organizations were occupied and largely torn apart internally by the Gulf War challenge to their integrity and cautious approaches, they more or less looked the other way and did not strongly condemn the human rights abuses committed against the Islamists. The Ben Ali regime was able to relegate the politics of human rights to the background while everyone else was busy with the developments in the Middle East. In Morocco, the Islamists were allowed to organize large demonstrations and rallies in support of the Iraqi people. However, the Islamist discourse did not go beyond the war issue and did not attempt to question the official posture on the crisis.

In Algeria, the Islamists condemned the Algerian regime not only for being too soft in its criticism of the "West," but also for not training or at least allowing the Islamists to organize a popular army to support the Iraqi people. The issue of state legitimation became the more acute for the Gulf War provided a "perfect" opportunity for the Islamist FIS to mobilize a large section of the populace, thereby deepening the political crisis of the state even further. The Islamists' self-appropriation of the Iraqi cause and the government's temporary incapacity to contain the FIS contributed to weakening the politics of human rights as an important determinant of the process of state legitimation. State legitimation became linked to the evolution of events in the Middle East, and the Islamists' strong posture lessened their cause as victims of human rights abuses, creating a temporary collective amnesia on the regime's violations of human rights.

Therefore, during the Gulf War the Algerian FIS was able to tilt the balances of social power to its liking, thereby antagonizing even more an already worried and somewhat fearful army. In Tunisia the Ben Ali regime was able to severely weaken the Islamist tendency. In Morocco the status quo of the balance of social power dominated by the king regime remained intact.

Internationalizing the Political Game of Human Rights

Although human rights is by and large an endogenous issue in North Africa, outside forces and actors have constantly contributed to shaping its discourse as well as the symbolic, legal, and material resources that the protagonists use in their struggle. Human rights groups have at times profited from mutual solidarity. Inter-Maghrebi relations among human rights groups were inspired primarily by the Algerian LADH, anxious to establish its legitimacy. The 1988 meeting produced a joint document (the Declaration of Nouakchott) and allowed activists across the region to become acquainted with one another and compare experiences. Since the 1970s expatriate and solidarity groups in Europe created a backdrop for the politics of human rights in North Africa. Expatriates, who were well informed about politics in their home countries, were usually among the first to call public attention to these problems. Their principal contribution was to make abuses more visible.[5] Personal and informal contacts between domestic human rights groups in North Africa and respective emigrant groups in Europe transmitted precise information about the human rights violations to European and international human rights organizations.

Three particular types of actors have also played important roles in somewhat internationalizing the political game of human rights in North Africa: (1) international human rights groups, (2) international press and public opinion, and (3) Western states and international governmental organizations.

International Human Rights Groups

International human rights groups have contributed to shape the political game of human rights in North Africa in important ways: by lending moral support to domestic nongovernmental organizations and groups, criticizing the governments' policies and practices, providing informational support for domestic activists, pressuring European states to express their concerns about North Africa to government officials, mobilizing public opinion and press opinion in Europe, and extending legal as well as institutional membership privileges to leaders of domestic nongovernmental human rights organizations and leaders of victimized groups.

For example, local Amnesty International groups in Tunisia often act to remind local authorities about their obligations to honor their commitments to international human rights conventions. Extensive mobilization against the Moroccan king during his state visits in Europe has often increased the pressure on Western states to act. The European parliament expressed serious objections against the human rights situation in Morocco when the king visited the parliament (Europa Publications 1995). The successful inter-play between outside and inside actions exposed the Moroccan regime as a human rights violating state, forcing the king to react to the accusations (Waltz 1995, 203–15). In May 1990 the king announced the creation of the CCDH and encouraged all human rights NGOs to participate. In November 1993 the government was restructured to include a Ministry for Human Rights.

International human rights organizations also extend protection to the domestic groups. The international protest over the 1986 arrest of Ali Yahia and the swift action of the Fédération Internationale des Droits de l'Homme (FIDH) to affiliate his group had a positive impact on the Algerian government. As a measure of protection for the LTDH, its president (Khemais Chemmari) was appointed an FIDH vice president. His arrest in the final months of Bourguiba's rule generated hundreds of letters and telegrams of protest. In 1990, at the FIDH recommendation, Chemmari was awarded a prize by the French government to support human rights training in Geneva. The FIDH also serves a clearinghouse function, allowing North African activists to learn from the experience of other groups. Research work done by international human rights groups helps increase the effectiveness of domestic groups. Amnesty International's 1991 questions about deaths in detention in Tunisia reinforced and amplified the LTDH position on the issue. International human rights organizations like the FIDH and Amnesty International also support local NGO initiatives to collaborate with regional organizations such as the Arab Organization of Human Rights, various medical groups and other international human rights organizations such as the Lawyers Committee for Human Rights and Middle East Watch.

International Press and Public Opinion

North African regimes are particularly sensitive to their images as portrayed in the European press and public opinion. Because of this special position the European press has been able to reflect, shape, and amplify the cause of human rights in North Africa. Throughout the 1980s the French press increasingly depended on the LTDH for reliable information about political developments in Tunisia. Wire services disseminated communiqués ignored by or censored from the domestic Tunisian press, and prestigious papers like the French national newspaper *Le Monde* reported them regularly. *Le Monde*'s 1989 story about a virtually forgotten five-year-old hunger strike in Morocco aroused interest and protest. The International Commission of Health Professionals and the Association Internationale des Juristes Démocrates sent a joint fact-finding mission that issued a lengthy report. Gilles Perrault's (1990) critical evaluation of human rights issues in Morocco contributed to a diplomatic crisis between France and Morocco. Stories in prominent news broadcasts on Radio France Internationale also help to shape public opinion in North Africa as well as in Europe.

Two factors augment the vulnerability of the North African regimes to criticisms of their policies and practices by the European public and mass media. First, all North African countries have sizable populations of expatriates in Western Europe, especially France. This large population can be influenced by the European news media and at times mobilized against their respective regimes. A mobilized immigrant population can, if well organized, influence the government policies of the host country toward the home state as well as provide moral and logistical support to domestic NGOs and opposition groups. Second, a large proportion of the North African elite reads French fluently and, hence, can go beyond their censored national news media to have access to other sources of information and criticisms of their regimes. A critical French and more generally European press is thus one more weapon that domestic NGOs and opposition groups use to voice their opinions about domestic issues such as the politics of human rights. This can pressure the respective regimes for either consultation with them or an implicit adoption of their views.

Western States and International Governmental Organizations

Because Western democracies (especially France, the European Union, and the United States) and North African states share many economic and security interests, the role of the former states in shaping the politics of human rights in North Africa has been somewhat mixed. Since the Barcelona Conference in November 1995, the allocation of development aid has in principle been tied to a commitment on behalf of Tunisia and Morocco to preserve human rights. But in practice the dismal condition of human rights in each country has never been invoked as justification for stopping the flow of development aid. Similarly, by the late 1980s U.S. congressional representatives were paying attention to human rights concerns expressed by constituents and documented in the human rights reports of the State Department. After 1990 the Moroccan government closed many long-standing human rights dossiers featured in subsequent yearly reports by the U.S. State Department, and in 1993 the regime invited an American firm to observe parliamentary elections.

All North African states are members of international organizations such as the United Nations, the Organization of African Unity, and the League of Arab States, as well as signatories of international conventions on human rights. The impact of these international organizations and conventions on the politics of human rights in North Africa has been minimal, in fact much less effective than that of international nongovernmental organizations. The North African regimes have constantly resorted to the principle of national sovereignty and noninterference in domestic affairs of sovereign states to reject or minimize the role of international critics of their human rights policies. States constantly endeavor to polish their official images in foreign capitals. For example, Tunisia distributes English language publications to various foreign governments and embassies and regularly inflates the Tunisian government commitment to human rights.

Although external actors have to some extent influenced the evolution of human rights in North Africa, the game has mainly remained a domestic affair, that is, a domestic balancing of social power among the regimes, human rights organizations, and Islamists as well as other opposition parties.

Going Beyond Human Rights as a Political Game

How can the region go beyond human rights as a political game played for the sake of shifting the balance of social power within the North African states? First, the prospects for institutionalizing human rights in North Africa will remain precarious unless two conditions are met: (1) an effective institutionalization of the process of democratization that all North African countries claim to have launched and (2) a depoliticization of the national army and judiciary system. Second, international concerns for human rights cannot be successful in positively contributing to institutionalizing human rights in North Africa if regional and domestic particularities of history, culture, and religion are not factored in. Third, international nongovernmental organizations can proactively contribute to institutionalize human rights in North Africa by shaping the policies and practices of the neighboring Western states with which North Africa has tight economic relations as well as common security interests.

Effective Institutionalization of the Process of Democratization

In three of the four North African countries—Morocco, Algeria, and Tunisia—the regimes in place claim to have launched a process of democratization toward pluralist political systems. However, this democratization process is rather superficial because it lacks two essential ingredients: generalized uncertainty on the outcomes of the electoral processes and a free press and news media.

President Ben Ali has been reelected since the 1987 coup without any serious contender. In Algeria, although two different persons have been elected president since 1992, the preferred candidate of the army has always won. Before both elections (in 1995 and 1999) it was known who the successful candidate would be despite the fanfare process of campaigning and the multiplicity of candidates. The unanimous drop out by all six opposition candidates in the 1999 elections occurred precisely because they all became certain of the outcome of the elections.

In both Algeria and Tunisia the presidential elections are also marred by a lack of genuinely free press or access to national TV stations. Nor are the parliamentary elections genuinely free. In Tunisia, the president's party (RCD) is always guaranteed a supermajority despite the best of efforts by opposition parties. In Algeria, the outcome of the parliamentary elections held in 1997 was a landslide victory for the president's party (RND) constituted just few months before the elections. Other parties received decent numbers of seats in the parliament, but could in no way rival the president's party. The situation in Algeria is not much different from Tunisia despite the differences in parliamentary elections. In both Algeria and Tunisia the president and his inner circle (in Algeria a small group of high-ranking generals) have the final say on most important state issues.

As long as democracy remains cosmetic in these two countries, the issue of human rights will still be an issue of legitimacy, which both the regime and main opposition use to tilt the balance of social power to their liking. An institutionalization of human rights cannot be effectively achieved as long as state power is capriciously used by the regime, which in turn prompts the opposition, most notably the Islamists, to aim at either transforming the state itself or at least delegitimate it. Full and effective democratization is a necessary step for the institutionalization of human rights in both Tunisia and Algeria.

In Morocco there is a pluralist democratic system. The fact that the king remains above the law and unimpeachable makes the democratic process more or less capricious. Although the regime in Morocco has taken non-negligible steps toward an institutionalization of human rights compared to the other states in the region, an effectively constitutional monarchy is the next step that would guarantee a complete institutionalization. Supreme authority should be in the hands of the law and every Moroccan should be under the law, including the king, his family and their immediate entourage.

Depoliticization of the Army and Judiciary System

In all four North African states, the army and judiciary system have been essential institutions of the political game of human rights. In Algeria, the army has remained the backbone and brain of the regime. The army is strongly politicized and its high-ranking officers almost unilaterally decide on the major issues of the country. Compared to the political power that the army has in Algeria, recently elected officials are but "technocrats" hired to implement the general guidelines of the army. Without a depoliticization of the army, the institutionalization of human rights in Algeria is impossible. To paraphrase Lord Acton, the Algerian army has absolute power in the country and thus the process of institutionalizing human rights cannot but remain absolutely corrupt.

In Tunisia the regime is built around a personality cult that Ben Ali has been developing by coopting "soft" sections of the opposition and using an iron fist against any radical ones such as the Islamists. Without the support of the secret service forces and a complacent or compliant judiciary, the Ben Ali regime would have had hard time achieving and sustaining a personality cult. In this case a truly independent judiciary system that can constrain the unlimited power of the secret services would be the best guarantee for an institutionalization of human rights as well as ensuring an effective democratization of the political system.

Sensitivity to Cultural and Religious Particularities

A lack of consensus on the meaning and purview of human rights has more or less hampered the efforts of domestic nongovernmental human rights organizations. Most of the human rights organizations in Morocco, Algeria, and Tunisia hold a Western notion of liberal human rights. In contrast, most Islamist groups strongly believe in an Islamic version of human rights (see Hoffman's chapter). Despite the fact that there is a large area of overlap on many aspects of the various notions of human rights that have been promoted in North Africa, ideological commitment has not only divided the opposition camp, but also reinforced the regime's self-serving claim that the Islamists are a threat to democracy. This has sometimes created a de facto alliance of human rights organizations with the regimes against victims of state repression.

The cause of human rights cannot be successfully advanced if domestic human rights groups and the Islamists (and others) do not attempt to compromise toward at least a minimalist definition of human rights. Short of this the regimes in place will continue to use one group against the other. Human rights organizations will be better off to refrain from downplaying the cultural sensitivity of the Islamists. Nor will the Islamists be better off if they do not reach a compromise with the human rights organizations. In any case, an institutionalization of human rights in North Africa will not succeed if the regimes keep on playing the "Islamist threat" card to cover up their lack of legitimacy and genuine concern for human rights.

The most active states and international organizations of human rights hold a liberal notion of human rights rooted in a Western historical evolution not always compatible with cultural and religious particularities of North Africa. For example the issue of women's rights is an area where most Islamists would differ with the Western counterpart notion. These dilemmas—upholding a universal notion of human rights sensitive to historical and cultural particularities—will never be resolved to the full satisfaction of all concerned parties. These dilemmas are part of the political game of human rights whether at the domestic or international level.

Role of International Actors

Two points might be made about the leverage available to Western states to advance human rights in North Africa. First, given the severe economic conditions confronting North African states, Western donor states and international economic and financial institutions, like the European Union, IMF, and World Bank, can induce these regimes, through positive and negative sanctions, to pay closer attention to human rights concerns in their countries. For example, the European states can effectively enact the provisions of the 1995 Barcelona Conference by linking the allocation of development aid to a commitment on behalf of Tunisia and Morocco to preserve human rights. This would pressure the Tunisian and Moroccan regimes to work toward improving their human rights agendas and records.

Second, domestic and international tribunals might also be more widely employed to contest these states. The international and supranational institutions of the European Union such as the European Parliament and the European Court of Justice, as well as domestic courts can be used to more or less pressure West European states to be more responsive to concerns about human rights abuses in North Africa.[6] But no one should have any illusions that progress in advancing human rights will be easy or swift for some time to come, nor assured.

Chapter 6
The Middle East: Israel

Ilan Peleg

This chapter is based on two main theoretical constructs. The first is the argument that the long-term stability of a political regime depends, to a large extent, on its ability to generate social legitimacy. The widespread acceptance of the regime's fundamental values is a key for the ability of the polity to maintain its governance patterns; the increasing rejection of those fundamental values by significant segments of the population is likely to generate revisions in those governance patterns. Put differently, erosion in social legitimacy results in increased instability.

The second theoretical claim is that in today's world human and civil rights are increasingly important as "fundamental values" of most regimes, especially democratic ones. Therefore, a democratic regime must demonstrate commitment to human and civil rights or it will face certain erosion of its social legitimacy, reflected in powerful challenges from significant segments of the population under its control.

Contemporary Israel is an example of a polity suffering from sharp decline in social legitimacy despite (or possibly because of) increasing commitment to human and civil rights on the part of many Israelis. It is a polity experiencing a multidimensional crisis of legitimacy, characterized by serious challenge to existing, entrenched political forces by new, rising political forces. The new forces typically demand the redefinition of the polity's patterns of governance, and especially the place of individual and collective rights within these patterns.

This chapter begins by offering an analysis of Israel's traditional "rights order" (or "rights regime"), emphasizing not only the overall character of the Israeli polity in the country's formative years but its specific approach to civil and human rights. The second section deals with the challenges thrown at the contemporary Israeli polity, and particularly its traditional approach to justice and rights, by various groups under its control. The historical processes leading to the evolution of these challenges will be analyzed, as will the mixed, incomplete, and hesitant response of the system

(Peleg 2001). The final section assesses how the Israeli system might eventually redefine its notions of rights, so as genuinely to integrate the challenges into a revamped rights regime. While that regime may not be able to integrate all challenges into a new "rights order," it will surely need to absorb large numbers of these in order to guarantee the survival and stability of the political system.

The "old" Israeli regime, still in evidence today in many parts of the Israeli polity, openly privileged Jews over Arabs, Israel proper (pre-1967) over the occupied territories, Ashkenazim (Israelis of European descent) over Sephardim (Israelis whose origins are in Arabic-speaking countries), secularists over religionists, military personnel over civilians, and men over women. Although the precise form and the depth of that discrimination varied dramatically from one group to the other, it existed in all these areas. The current challenge to the established order is seen most clearly in the ongoing rebellion among Arabs in the Territories and inside Israel proper, the demand for women's rights, and other phenomena.

Israel's Traditional Rights Regime

The formative period of the State of Israel, starting with the establishment of the state in 1948, is often viewed as somewhat of a political "Golden Age." Subscribing to centrist positions and building political coalitions to sustain such positions, David Ben-Gurion, Israel's founding father and first Prime Minister, is seen by those who promote this perspective as a tough but pragmatic politician. According to this common view, while Israel of the post-1967 era raises "serious questions about the maintenance of the democratic values of liberty and equality, and commitment to the rule of law" (Medding 1990, 229), the Ben-Gurionist era, ending in 1963, is characterized by positive development of a young and vibrant Israeli democracy.

From the perspective of civil and human rights, the periodization of Israeli history implicit in this approach has far-reaching implications, many of them relevant for Israel at present and in the future. This approach views pre-1967 Israel (preceding the Six-Day War) positively, emphasizing that the trend during the founding period was in the direction of greater democratization, heightened political competition, increasing autonomy of various social groups, greater media independence, and a more active role for right-protecting judiciary (Medding 1990, 226). Where discriminatory practices existed, they are perceived and described as "necessary" (for state security), "modest," or forced on Israel by a hostile environment. Even Ben-Gurion's personal deviation from his commitment to democratic principles is often explained as reflecting others' positions, not his. Thus the decision not to enact a full-fledged constitution is often blamed on Israel's religious parties. Some analysts go as far as describing Israel's formative years as "a high point of universalistic, civic, and liberal fulfillment" (Dowty 1995).

Political developments in the post-1967 era, which has witnessed Israel's long-term occupation of the West Bank and Gaza as well as an intensive settlement effort there, have made the Golden Age prism less attractive. The rise to power of the nationalist right under Menachem Begin, Yitzhak Shamir, and eventually Binyamin Netanyahu and Ariel Sharon and the widespread legitimation of their annexationist ideologies within Israeli society created an alternative view on the nature of Israel's polity.

The alternative view, also of great implications for the rights regime in today's Israel, emphasized the tension between opposing forces inherent not merely in the Israeli experience (that is, post-1948) but in Zionism itself. Horowitz and Lissak state that

There were inherent contradictions between the components of the Zionist ideology . . . [especially] between particularist Jewish values, reflected in a desire for a *national state*, and humanist-universalist values. (Horowitz and Lissak 1990, 157, emphasis added)

Some analysts have gone a step further. Thus Ezrahi maintained that

The Zionist movement (especially in its socialist and liberal segments) achieved . . . precarious but politically *effective balance* between universalism and particularism. . . . The commitment to Jewish national liberation was tempered by extranationalist commitments to Enlightenment visions of progress, individual freedom, and social justice. (Ezrahi 1993, 256–57, emphasis added)

From the perspective of democratic rights in Israel of the early statehood period, and even today, both the Medding-Dowty developmental hypothesis (the argument that young Israel was democratically on a positive developmental path) and the contradiction hypothesis of Horowitz, Lissak, and Ezrahi (the contention that while some Israelis were "nationalists," others were truly "universalists") are seriously problematic as macro explanations of the embryonic Israeli society. Neither hypothesis comes to terms with the fundamental structural flaws of Israel's rights regime from the very beginning; for that reason, neither hypothesis is helpful in terms of resolving some of Israel's *current* problems in the field of civil and human rights.

In praising Ben-Gurion's alleged commitment to democratic ideals, the "developmentalists" ignore the fact that the Ben-Gurionist republic was blatantly discriminatory toward certain segments of Israeli society and, overall, illiberal toward all its "subjects." In focusing on the various and allegedly different camps within the Zionist movement—especially the differences between particularists and universalists—the "contradictionists" fail to show that, *despite* some inconsistencies, Israel decisively chose the nationalist, ethnic route in 1948 and, as shown by Sternhell, much before (Sternhell 1995). Moreover, the "contradictionists" fail to show the grave implications for the "rights regime" of the country emanating from its fundamental choice.

In offering a new perspective on Israel's current political crisis, it is important to realize that, during Israel's formative era, contradictions between universalism and particularism—the very essence of the meaning of rights—were invariably decided in favor of particularistic forces, ideas, and policies, thus creating a flawed rights regime. While the ruling party, Mapai, was often perceived as if it were coerced into abandonment of its universal dream (in its socialist or liberal version), in fact it led Israel away from liberal democracy. Even Mamlachtiut, a Ben-Gurionist term emphasizing the centrality of the state over all other social forces (Don-Yehiya 1989; Yanai 1989), was in fact not a universalistic grand design but an instrument of ethnocentric particularity (Peleg 1998).

To understand the fundamental problems of Israel's traditional rights regime, a regime that is still dominant today, it is essential to realize that in 1948 the leadership made a conscious (albeit not public) decision to establish in the young country an ethnocentric order rather than a liberal democracy. While this decision had enormous negative consequences for the Arab minority in Israel, as an elite decision it had widespread negative implications for all Israelis. The leadership chose to establish an ethnically based Jewish republic. Between liberal and organic nationalism (Sternhell 1995, 19–22), Ben-Gurion and his associates preferred the latter as an overall design for nation building. This "architecture" destined Israel to develop a flawed "rights order" that has affected the polity ever since.

The flaws of the "rights order" of young Israel are reflected in several crucial areas. None was as important, in the long run, as the decision not to adopt a constitution for the newly born state. A formal domestic and international commitment to elect a Constituent Assembly and not a regular parliament, which would adopt a constitution, accompanied the birth of the state (Shapiro 1996a, especially ch. 2; Strum 1995). The Declaration of Independence stated that a constitution would be adopted "no later than 1 October 1948." The would-be document was to include all the principles contained in the Declaration itself, such as "complete social and political equality." Yet, a short time after the first Israeli elections in 1949, Ben-Gurion suddenly announced that there was no need for a constitution.

According to Chaim Zadok, a close aide to Ben-Gurion and later Israel's justice minister, Ben-Gurion had a "desire to govern without constitutional restrictions, taking whatever action he deemed best to put the State on a firm footing" (Strum 1995, 92). Ben-Gurion himself argued that a constitution would give too much power to minorities and would cripple governmental power. In view of what was quickly to follow—for example, the establishment of military government in areas inhabited by Arabs and the large-scale expropriation of Arab lands (Jiryis 1969; Lustick 1980)—Ben-Gurion's words were ominous.

The human and civil rights implications of not enacting a constitution were enormous. A constitution could have protected the Arab minority, crucial in view of the fact that Israel defined itself from the very beginning as a Jewish state, and the Arabs, even though citizens, needed to be defended against the majority and "its" state (Negbi 1987, 42).

But the non-adoption decision was not limited to Jewish-Arab relations. The same Declaration of Independence that promised all Israelis full equality also promised to protect their "freedom of religion and conscience." Yet such freedom was never established. Already the 1947 so-called "Status Quo Agreement," reached between the Jewish agency and the ultra-orthodox Agudat Israel, promised the latter exclusive orthodox control over large numbers of important issues, including personal status matters, the Sabbath, and so forth. Additional concessions, such as exemption from military service to religious students, quickly followed.

Rather than separating religion and state or, alternatively, creating other reasonably liberal arrangements that would guarantee all Israelis freedom of and from religion, the state became an instrument of religious coercion and illiberality. Adopting the old Ottoman tradition of defining individuals as members of religious communities (*millets*), the state transferred control over important areas of people's lives to the hands of religious establishments, mainly the Chief Rabbinate. By not adopting a liberal constitution—which would have secularized public life, privatized religion, and guaranteed religious freedom—the Ben-Gurionist system endorsed the massive violation of civil rights with which Israelis are still struggling.

But without a doubt the most flagrant set of violations of fundamental civil rights under the traditional "rights regime," violations that still exist today, were committed in the relations between Jews and Arabs (Kimmerling 1994). While the Declaration of Independence allegedly tried to "reconcile the national character of the Jewish state with universalistic civil equality" (Cohen 1991), in practice the Arabs had been the target of systematic discrimination from the very beginning. In no other area has this been so clear as in the establishment of Military Government.

Lasting for eighteen years (1948–66), the Military Government was applied to all Arabs in Galilee, the "Triangle" (along the Jordanian border), and the Bedouin of the Negev. By the time of its elimination, the Military Government covered 220,000 of the 260,000 Israeli Arabs. It controlled all aspects of Arab lives: travel, land development, business activity, employment, and so forth. While the totality of the control normally assured the good behavior of the Arab population, in some cases the authorities had to resort to severe penalties (internal exile, administrative detentions without trial, and so forth).

The domination of the Arabs, achieved by paying a huge price in civil rights violations, was part of a national effort to establish, sustain, and strengthen the newly formed ethnocentric order. The Military Government not only "marked" the Arabs as second-class citizens; it declared them an unmeltable, unintegratable minority, people of a different kind, the "ultimate other" (Peleg 1994a, b).

The regime established in Israel in 1948, and lasting substantially until quite recently—when increasing challenges have begun to emerge—had a number of *distinct characteristics*, generally problematic from the perspective of civil and human rights:

1. Although the regime was generally democratic, its notion of democracy was and to a large extent remains rather narrow. For Ben-Gurion and most of his successors "democracy" meant majority rule via periodic elections, not minority protection and individual rights (Shamir and Sullivan 1983). Israel's traditional democracy has been distinctly "illiberal" (Zakaria 1997).

2. The overall design of the regime has been ethnic. An Israeli sociologist, Sami Smooha, coined the term "ethnic democracy" in describing that regime (Smooha 1990). The meaning of ethnic democracy Israel-style has been that the state has defined itself as "Jewish," has given Jews some exclusive legal rights (for example, immigration, citizenship, land purchasing), and has discriminated against Arabs in numerous areas (Kretzmer 1990; Rouhana 1997).

3. While the fundamental democratic order has been enhanced through the years via legislation (for example, two important Basic Laws in 1992), Supreme Court rulings (on freedom of expression, religious equality, and recently even equality in land allocation) and practice, a full-fledged constitution or even a Bill of Rights have not been enacted to date.

4. In general, the Israeli system has traditionally emphasized the rights of the collective over that of the individual, the prerogative of the state over that of "private" interests and the centrality of the "core nation" (Brubaker 1996) over any other group.

5. Although Arabs have been the main victims of the overall character of the Israeli regime, others have been marginalized as well: in order to guarantee orthodox support for State action, religious circles have been accorded preferential treatment in numerous areas, thus discriminating against the nonreligious; the Israel Defense Forces were given special status within the Israeli society, resulting in unprecedented political power and unfair advantage to current and former generals; with the position of the IDF enhanced, men have been given systematic advantage over women in the country's economic and political life.

Those generally negative characteristics of Israel's traditional "rights order" were further exacerbated as a result of the all-important 1967 War. Israel's decisive victory resulted in further marginalization of the Palestinians inside Israel and in the newly occupied territories. Human rights violations on the part of the state and its military forces—now even more prestigious institutions than before—became more severe, more frequent, and a lot better known (Peleg 1995). The expansion into the biblical lands of Judea and Samaria further strengthened the power of religious elements within the Israeli regime, weakening the power of liberal circles supportive of enhanced individual liberties and freedoms.

Nevertheless, in a paradoxical way, the 1967 occupation of the West Bank and Gaza has created an increased attention among Israelis to civil and human rights, strengthening the challenge to the existing and largely deficient "rights order" in the country. While the occupation of the West Bank signaled the apex of Jewish domination and strength, it simultaneously strengthened the demands of Arabs and others for protection, rights, and eventually power.

Challenging the Existing Rights Order

The intense Israeli-Palestinian conflict is the key for Israel's political dynamics in general, and for the country's civil and human rights situation in particular. To the extent to which rights have become more important in contemporary Israel, as a political currency, the two issues—the ethnic conflict and the status of rights—largely overlap. The relationship between Arabs and Jews is the engine in the complex Israeli political system, including the issue of rights.

As argued in this essay's first section, the traditional Israeli political system was clearly collectivist, statist, and ethnic. It was created by the perceived need of the Jewish majority to marginalize the Arabs and prevent the emergence of an effective Arab challenge to the control of the land by the Jewish majority.

Several general conditions in Israel have pushed forward the "rights agenda" as a counterforce to the hegemonic power of the Israeli ethnic state. First, the prolonged military occupation itself has generated enormous awareness of human rights violations among Israelis serving in the Occupied Territories, journalists and activists who research and report on such violations, and Israel's attentive public at large. Second, the last twenty years or so have seen the expansion of Israel's middle class and a very significant increase in the standard of living of these strata of the Israeli population. The growing contacts of members of this class with the democratic West have contributed to the greater awareness of human rights within the Israeli society. The combined effect of direct occupation—accompanied by massive human rights violations—and economic growth created within Israeli society, for the first time, a critical mass for significant challenge of the existing "rights order."

The occupation of the West Bank and Gaza caught the Israeli leadership unprepared. It presented the young Israeli ethnic state with serious and to a large extent unprecedented challenges. The notion of democracy via majority rule was easier to defend with a marginalized Arab population of 15 percent within Israel proper than in the face of massive violations of human rights under prolonged occupation of a sizable Arab population. But the unplanned expansion into the West Bank raised serious questions not only over Israeli practices in the Occupied Territories but also about the fundamentals of the Israeli notion of democracy. A few years after David Grossman, one of Israel's best-known novelists, wrote about human rights violations in the Occupied Territories, he authored an equally influential book on the conditions of Israeli Arabs (Grossman 1988, 1993). The link between the Occupied Territories and pre-1967 Israel was unmistakably clear.

The Israeli occupation had direct impact in several areas. First, it affected Arab-Jewish relations within Israel. The 1970s have witnessed the intensification of an organized struggle for civil equality of the Israeli Arabs, for the first time under the leadership of a national body, the National Committee of the Heads of Arab Local Municipalities (Al-Peleg 1988; Ghanem 1993; Landau 1993). Yiftachel (1997) and Smooha (1993) believe that this political activity led to "certain moderation of governmental control" over the lives of Arabs.

The overall result of these developments was positive from the perspective of human rights, but their causes varied:

1. increasing assertiveness and higher sophistication by the Israeli Arabs in formulating demands for equal treatment;
2. growing dependence of Israeli politicians and parties on the electoral support of Israeli Arabs, resulting in increased leverage for the Arabs (Lustick 1989);
3. recognition by some Israeli leaders, especially on the left, that as part of the Oslo peace process between Israel and the PLO, there should be an equivalent reconciliation process between Arabs and Jews inside Israel.

The last factor explains the positive human rights developments that occurred during the administration of the Labor government in 1992–96 (Ozacky-Lazar and Ghanem 1995). In introducing his government to the Knesset, Prime Minister Rabin committed himself to "full equality of all citizens," stating that he was "ashamed that there is still discrimination against Arabs" (*New York Times*, July 14, 1992). He emphasized that the state of Israel is the state of all its citizens, a legal formula that most Israeli Jews have refused to accept.

Despite the growing awareness among high Israeli officials, the actual *implementation* of equality for the Arabs progressed rather slowly. While budgets to Arab localities increased in the 1990s, government ministries hired few Arabs, especially in high positions. The macro-issues of Israel's ethnic

democracy have remained unresolved both in terms of the overall character of the state as primarily a Jewish republic, and in terms of the status
of the Arabs as a minority. Although under the Barak government some
observers suggested that a *quiet revolution* in the status of Arabs has begun
(Sontag 2000), it did not prevent the major, unprecedented, and extremely
violent clashes between Israeli Palestinians and Israeli security forces in the
fall of 2000.

Arab-Jewish relations have not been the only area where challenges to
the existing system of rights have been evident. Over the last two decades,
demands for the completion of a constitution and a bill of rights have intensified. In fact, several important developments of constitutional significance have occurred, indicating a qualitative (although yet not decisive)
change in the country.

First, under the leadership of Chief Justice Aharon Barak, Israel's High
Court of Justice has emerged as a major champion of civil and human rights
of all Israelis. While the court has traditionally been inactive in protecting Palestinians in the West Bank and Gaza (Peleg 1995), it proved rather
assertive in offering leadership inside Israel Proper. Thus over the last
decade or so, the court came out against the discrimination against Arabs
in land allocations (Kedar 2000; Steinberg 2000), a common practice with
enormous political and economic consequences that has been used by all
Israeli governments for more than fifty years. The court has also become
the promoter of the rights of women deciding, for example, that they ought
to have equal access to service in public institutions (such as religious
councils); in April 2000, it ruled in favor of a group known as Women of
the Wall, endorsing their right to pray, as a group, at the Western Wall in
Jerusalem (Lahav 2000). The Court has proven equally supportive of the
rights of homosexuals. In brief, groups traditionally suffering discrimination have found support in the Israeli High Court of Justice.

In taking upon itself promoting the civil rights of Israelis, the court has
traditionally had two major obstacles: the lack of a constitution to rely on
in opposing human rights violations and the absence of judicial review in
the country's parliamentary system. Nevertheless, as early as the 1950s, the
court began to look at the Declaration of Independence as a constitutional
document, guaranteeing rights that all Israelis are entitled to (for example,
freedom of expression).

The Israeli constitutional debate (with rights at its very center) has been
intense and dramatic. In April 1992 the Knesset enacted two new basic laws
of great significance, laws that the High Court of Justice has viewed as
giving it yet another tool in promoting civil rights in Israel: the Basic Law:
Freedom of Occupation and the Basic Law: Human Dignity and Freedom.
Some analysts have described the addition of these laws to the country's
evolving legal system as "a mini-revolution" (Kretzmer 1992; Goldstein
1994). Gavison (1994, 8) believes that the 1992 Basic Laws "constitute,

structurally, the beginning of a Bill of Rights in Israel," while Chief Justice Barak (1992) saw them as a genuine "constitutional revolution."

While important areas of human rights are still uncovered in Israel, two ideas have now gained wide acceptance among Israelis: the Knesset can and should enact basic laws on human rights issues and the High Court of Justice is the legitimate interpreter of such laws. Those two developments mark a significant move toward greater commitment to civil and human rights in the country.

In terms of the overall balance of power between various Israeli governmental branches, there has clearly been an increase in the relative power of institutions sensitive to individual rights. The courts have always been among Israel's most liberal components (along with the academic and artistic community). This is particularly the case in regard to the High Court of Justice. The power of the Court has been on the ascendant over the last two decades, a positive sign for human and civil rights. In the absence of a constitution the Court has, historically, played a major role in guaranteeing and, more important, expanding the civil and human rights of Israelis. It gained a reputation as the *guardian* of human rights (Briskman 1988, 5; Bracha 1982). Goldstein maintains that Israeli judges created an extensive system of human rights despite the absence of a constitution and constitutional tradition. In fact, he argues, in Israeli law "human rights have been protected almost exclusively by judge-made law" (Goldstein 1994, 605).

Over the last few years, the High Court of Justice has been increasingly active in protecting human rights and especially freedom of speech, press, and association. Thus in the late 1980s it decided against the continuation of governmental censorship of plays. The court has shown increasing willingness to challenge governmental assertion of "security interest" as grounds for restricting human rights and did not even shy away from intervening in other branches' activities (Goldstein 1994, 613). Lower courts followed the liberal line of the High Court. Thus in the 1980s a Jerusalem justice of the peace allowed the showing of films on the Sabbath. These institutional changes, as well as the constitutional ones, indicate that the Israeli system has not only the capacity, but also the inclination to adopt liberal solutions to many, if not all, long-term problems. This process is reflective of the growth of a larger and more assertive Israeli middle class.

One area in which challenges have emerged and some changes have begun to occur is the all-important area of security. The Israeli society has always been strongly committed to, focused on, and some would say obsessed with issues of security. The long struggle with the Arabs and the British, the historical experience with anti-Semitism, and the Holocaust explain this condition.

A strong commitment to state security, in any country, is usually correlated negatively with adherence to civil and human rights, particularly when there is a large minority within the country and when that minority is assumed to be hostile to the interests of the majority. In that kind of situation, civil and human rights violations are built-in, structural, and inevitable.

And, indeed, the state of Israel has violated for years the civil and human rights of its Arab citizens and established, in general, an unfriendly human rights environment for many of its citizens. Thus while most Arabs lived under Military Government until 1966, all Israelis had to endure censorship.

Nevertheless, the last thirty years have witnessed a relative strengthening of human rights. Says Ruth Gavison: "On balance, between state security and human rights, we see in Israel consistent improvement of human rights" (1994, 144). Yet Gavison recognizes that "the situation is still far from satisfactory." Dana Briskman, who studied the High Court's attitude toward national security by comparing Israel's formative era with its more recent past, noted "a shift in the Court's approach to the issue of national security. The Court became more active both in its interpretive and its review role. The notion of security became more specific as a result, narrower than the notion of security accepted by the Court in the first period" (Briskman 1988, 123). Yet for a long time the court remained reluctant to adopt a decisive pro-human rights approach when security was involved.

In terms of Israel's overall political situation, it is important to recognize that over the last thirty years, Israel has experienced the mushrooming of human rights activity on an unprecedented level. Although it is difficult to establish direct cause-and-effect relationships between this phenomenon and the occupation, some link is self-evident and a significant link is almost surely in existence. A great number of organizations came into being specifically in response to the occupation. Some deal directly with human rights violations in the Occupied Territories (for example B'Tselem), and others with the involvement of the Israeli society in the occupation or other military activity (Dai Lakibush, The 21st Year, Women in Black, Physicians for Human Rights, and Yesh Gvul are but a few of these).

Moreover a very large number of civil and human rights organizations dedicate themselves to the fostering of understanding and tolerance between Arabs and Jews (Van Leer Institute and Givat Haviva are among the largest organizations of that type; others are Interns for Peace, Sikkuy, Beit Hagefen, the Open House, and many others). But beyond the activity of organizations dealing with various aspects of the Arab-Israeli conflict, Israel has witnessed the development of a very large number of organizations dealing with women's issues, the rights of the handicapped, gay and lesbian concerns, and so forth. Existing civil rights organizations such as the Association for Civil Rights in Israel (ACRI) intensified their activity in a rather significant way.

In entering the twenty-first century, the Israeli society faces several challenges. The most immediate, pressing challenge was and remains the country's relations with Palestinians in both the Occupied Territories and Israel proper. While a negotiated settlement with the Palestinians on the West Bank and Gaza and a termination to the occupation are expected (in the longer if not shorter run), the challenge for Arab-Jewish relations inside Israel remains as serious as ever. Despite some improvements in the situation of Arab citizens of Israel, the degree of resentment among them remains high. The Arab challenge to the Jewish republic is at least threefold: a demand for equality of all citizens as individuals, recognition of minority rights, and a redefinition of the polity as the "state of all its citizens."

A second challenge for the Israeli state is in the area of state-religion relations. The existing order in Israel accorded Israeli orthodox and ultra-orthodox unique privileges in numerous areas. Not only were their values imposed on the largely secular Israeli public in areas such as the keeping of Jewish religious laws and in regulating "personal status issues" (marriage, divorce, burial, and so forth), but the religious minority was allowed to run its own educational system, many of its members were exempted from military service (while supported generously by the state), and so forth. The combination of privileging a minority and imposing its values on the majority has been damaging from the perspective of civil rights in Israel.

There are today, in Israel, two countervailing demands in terms of the "rights order" as it relates to this area. On the one hand, the large majority of secular Jews want to terminate the special privileges accorded to the orthodox. On the other hand, the orthodox minority, led by new and assertive political forces, demands even more power than before. A resolution of this issue is not yet in sight.

The third challenge for the Israeli "rights regime" is the most general one—it goes beyond the demands of the Arab minority, women's groups, or secular-orthodox relations. It is an ongoing debate over what could be called the very essence of the Israeli polity. Will Israeli citizenship continue to be ethnically based or will it evolve into a civic citizenship? Will the state maintain its legal definition as a Jewish entity or will it become a "state of all its citizens"? Will the ethno-nationalistic order evolve, eventually, into a truly pluralist, liberal democracy? It is to these questions that the final section of this paper is dedicated.

Redefining Israel's "Rights Order"

It is clear from the analysis provided above that Israel's traditional "rights regime" has been extensively and intensively challenged over the last three decades or so. Can this established order be redefined and what forms might this redefinition assume?

To answer this question, a broader perspective on the Israeli human rights agenda is needed. The most interesting fact about this human rights agenda is that it has been thoroughly politicized since the 1967 war and that it is characterized now by a curious duality, a condition that could lead to a political explosion or, alternatively, to a quantum leap forward in terms of the Israeli "rights regime."

Traditional Israeli politics was primarily not about rights but about nation building and survival. Thus, the very first national survey of public attitudes toward civil liberties in Israel was conducted (by the Institute for Applied Social Research in Jerusalem) only in 1975. Yet over the last two decades human rights have become a "leadership resource base," a pad for the launching of a national political career. Thus several political figures in Israel succeeded through activities focusing on civil and human rights (for example, Knesset member Dedi Zucker, before him Knesset member Shulamit Aloni, and today Shinui leader Tommy Lapid). This trend is likely to continue.

Moreover some political parties in Israel have become identified with the "Rights Agenda." While in the past only Arab parties focused on civil and human rights, and almost exclusively on the concerns of the Arab minority (with the exception of the Zionist-Socialist Mapam), in the 1970s and 1980s growing numbers of "Jewish" parties became rights-driven (notably Dash, Ratz, Shinui, and eventually Meretz). Today more and more parties use "rights terminology" in their political platforms, promoting various civil and human rights causes.

In general a human rights focus in the Israeli political arena has become legitimate and even respectable. Large numbers of Israelis, especially members of the middle and upper-middle class professionals and intellectuals, are strongly committed to civil and human rights. Most important, the overall political pattern suggests that activity in one area of human rights (for example human rights violations in the Occupied Territories) is likely to spill over into other areas of human rights (for example women's issues, state-religion relations, and so forth).

Nevertheless, despite the increasing popularity of rights issues in Israel, the progress of civil and human rights in Israel has not been linear, consistent, or unambiguous. A major reason for the uneven progress is that civil and human rights are part of the much larger, murky, and conflictual political picture of the country. Only within a vacuum could one have a sudden, full-blown appearance of rights on the political scene. Such a vacuum occurred, for example, in Germany and Japan following World War II, or in France and the United States following their revolutions. When civil and human rights are the subjects of a larger political game, their development is likely to be "messy" and gradual as indeed has been the case of Israel.

Thus Simon and Landis (1990, 197–99) noted a sharp decline between 1975 and 1986–87 in the overall tolerance in Israel toward persons supporting direct talks with the PLO, the establishment of a Palestinian state, and so forth. I would venture that this seemingly anti-human rights attitude is reflective of the reign of Likud and this party's position toward these substantive issues.

Like Michal Shamir, Simon and Landis (1990, 98) report, "persons with higher education and higher incomes were more likely than less educated and poorer respondents to be tolerant of unpopular political sentiments." Moreover secular Jews were more tolerant than religious ones.

These findings are indicative (along with many other phenomena) of the evolvement of two camps, two publics, and two agendas, competing with each other for dominance within the Israeli polity:

1. The communal, ethnic, nationalist camp (associated with the Likud and several other right-wing and religious parties), which speaks the language of primordial tribalism, a language that rejects civil and human rights as nonexistent, unimportant, peripheral, or, at best, secondary.
2. The liberal, secular, Westernized public (associated with Labor, Shinui and Meretz), which increasingly uses the language of civil and human rights, not only or even mainly in regard to the Arab issues. For this camp, civil and human rights have become the central litmus test for the quality of Israel's democracy.

The split in Israeli society is reflected institutionally, where certain groups (artists, academics, jurists, journalists) are in the forefront of the movement toward greater civil and human rights. To argue that "the Israeli public is not homogeneous in its support" of civil and human rights (Simon and Landis 1990, 102) is to *understate* the case: the division is extremely deep and there is no evidence that it is about to disappear.

In terms of the larger historical picture, it seems that the traditional Israeli policy of total domination over the Arabs—inside and outside Israel—has backfired insofar as civil and human rights are concerned. It has not only galvanized Arab resistance inside Israel, but has also led to practically worldwide condemnation of Israeli human rights policy, especially in the Occupied Territories.

The debate over civil and human rights has now "spread" into a much more fundamental conflict over the very nature of the Israeli polity. The single most important question has now become the following: Can Israel be both Jewish and democratic, or, in the language of some analysts, is the notion of "ethnic democracy" oxymoronic? While there is a consensus today that the relations between Israel's Jewishness and democracy in Israel is the *key* for the country's civil and human rights status (a consensus reflected in a 1996 volume edited by Dafna Barak-Erez), there is a serious debate over the solution to that dilemma.

The Israeli case, although fascinating, is by no means unique. It is almost a "classic" in reflecting the emergence of deep awareness of rights in the contexts of majority-minority struggle. While Israel defines itself, and is often defined by others, as a Jewish state, the precise content of that "Jewishness" remains hotly debated, not only between Israeli Jews and Israeli Arabs (or Palestinians in Israel), but also between different "kinds" of Jews.

While the future of human rights in Israel remains unclear, it is reasonable to argue that the establishment of a Palestinian state in the West Bank and Gaza could have a profound impact on everything political in Israel, including the status of human rights. Nevertheless the direction of the impact is unclear. It is possible that the emergence of a Palestinian state would ease some of the Arab frustrations with the Jewish state. On the other hand, it is even more likely that a solution for the West Bank Palestinians would result in the intensification of Palestinian demand for full equality *inside* Israel. The demand for national minority rights and even a change in the character of the state would likely become more and more important. It is essential to recognize that the redefinition of the human rights agenda in Israel is not merely about individual equality; it has a complicated communal dimension that is as yet unresolved.

The reaction of Israeli Jews to the Arab challenge has already assumed a *dual* character, duality that is likely to intensify. On the one hand, the "internal" Palestinian challenge is likely to lead many Israeli Jews to the conclusion that Israel must further emphasize its "Jewishness" and reject outright the Arab demands to full individual and, especially, communal equality. If Israel adopts that line, it will follow the footsteps of other ethnicized polities such as Sri Lanka or India.

On the other hand, pro-human rights forces in Israel are likely to push the country in the direction of at least some acceptance of its inherent bi-national character. There are already numerous signs that the Israeli political establishment has begun to move, for the first time, toward the equalization of Palestinians rights, at least on an individual basis. It remains to be seen whether the "core nation" in Israel, Israeli Jews, will be capable of accepting the presence of another nation in Israel. Several countries have changed their character from uni-national entities to bi- or multinational ones (Canada in the 1960s, Spain in the 1980s, and Northern Ireland today are relevant examples). The challenge for Israel is serious. It has enormous implications for human rights in the state and for the lives of all Israelis. It requires a rethinking of the country's constitutional order.

Chapter 7
Northeast Asia: China

Edward Friedman

How China, a permanent member of the United Nations Security Council, acts on human rights is a matter of global import. A nuclear power with ambitions for regional predominance, China is home to some one-fifth of the human race. Since 1978 China has also enjoyed the world's fastest economic growth, receiving far and away the most Foreign Direct Investment (FDI) of all developing nations.

Since 1993 China has thrown its clout against the human rights movement. This chapter clarifies why China has been successful in opposing human rights and identifies political factors that might lead Beijing to support human rights. There is no cultural genetics that permanently predisposes the Chinese against human rights. In fact China's great 1989 democracy movement, larger than many in former Leninist states, fully embraced human rights.

China may well be the major government blocking continuing progress in universal human rights, a project that surged in the 1970s as a virtual global consensus developed in opposition to human rights violations in South Africa, the exclusion of Palestinians from self-rule, and Latin American military tyrannies. Supported, too, were the protections for human rights in the Soviet bloc, especially East and Central Europe.

In no small part human rights universalism opposed the United States, seen as a backer of apartheid South Africa, an oppressive Israel, and rightist regimes in Latin America. When East Europeans democratized starting in 1989, however, they imagined their victory for human rights as the West (of Europe) defeating the East (of Europe), eliding Washington's historical role in Pretoria, Jerusalem, and Santiago.

Economic reform leaders of post-Mao China, who on June 4, 1989 bloodily crushed a nationwide democracy movement centered in Tiananmen Square in Beijing, were shocked at becoming the target of human rights sanctions. They saw themselves as ending the inhumanities of the Mao era—famine, millions in slave labor, hundreds of millions prodded into vigilante campaigns of degradation, violence, and torture. Chinese were freer and richer than ever. Beijing felt itself a great success (Harding 1987), with a democratizing Russia a chaotic failure. Democracy and human rights were therefore understood as an American plot to weaken China and prevent its rise.

Ruling groups in China dismissed the American version of universal human rights as an imperialist manifestation of a hypocritical West. Patriotic Chinese long saw Christianity, supposedly the carrier of a higher civilization, as actually the foot in the Chinese door of an immoral imperialism, symbolized by the Opium War. In again opposing so-called Western values, Chinese leaders imagine themselves as standing up for Chinese independence and dignity. Patriotic Chinese conservatives view the individualistic language of human rights activism as a threat to order, unity, and national dignity. They believe that their collective values are threatened by an alien project of antisocial atomization, a cause of family, societal, and national disintegration, a decline into disorder, disunity, weakness, impoverishment, and national vulnerability.

The Singapore government has invoked a similar discourse (Bauer and Bell 1999). In like manner, seventeenth-century English reactionaries demonized constitutional liberties as a Dutch project and eighteenth-century French reactionaries scapegoated freedom as an alien English import. The Chinese dismissal of human rights as "other" is a standard political discourse for despotic regimes, East or West. Democratic Chinese see this clearly, ridiculing the former dictatorship in Indonesia's embrace of Asian values. "Suharto's public stance was . . . a screen behind which to hide his dictatorial rule" (Liu 1998, 411).

The individualist vocabulary of human rights activists is, nonetheless, strategically suicidal and ideologically mystifying. Because human rights are a political project, bad political strategy has consequences. After all, Britain's constitutional liberties, early on, were available only to English, male, mainstream Protestant, property-owning taxpayers. Groups were excluded: Irish, female, dissenting Protestants, Catholics, Jews, Muslims, propertyless workers, and the poor.

Over time, group after group was included in the political nation in Europe and North America. With almost everyone finally included, each then was protected. At that point, a language of individual human rights made sense. It would be more historically accurate, as well as politically more pragmatic, to approach China in terms of collectivities, because Beijing indeed denies rights to groups, to Buddhist Tibetans, Uyghur Muslims, Falun Gong spiritual practitioners, and politically conscious people who point out unpleasant truths.

Human rights are a project of inclusion. An individualistic language of human rights leads most Chinese to reject that discourse as an amoral source of disorder, even while the Beijing government injures the Chinese people by denying them basic human rights, such as freedom to travel to find work and live with family and choose one's children's school. Thousands of Chinese who each year protest and petition for a redress of grievances do not imagine themselves as pro-human rights. The Chinese government, seeking to curb police brutality, does not imagine itself as an inveterate violator of human rights. Democratization should be presented, as it actually is, a system conducive to inclusion, legitimacy, and stability, not as individual rights that seem to threaten basic order.

China is far from the worst violator of human rights. Some Chinese even feel that the post-Mao era is the best China has experienced since the failure of its 1911 republican revolution. There is more secure space for family members to pursue their own happiness. This real progress is acknowledged in the section on China in the annual human rights reports issued by the U.S. State Department.

Beijing does not wish to be considered a human rights violator. It issues annual reports claiming that America is worse. The Beijing government signs human rights covenants. The PRC has, when wooing international public opinion for particular benefits, such as becoming the site of the Olympics or entering the World Trade Organization (WTO), released nonviolent prisoners of conscience. Once freed, innocents argue that their suffering would have been worse if not for international human rights efforts. Beijing still runs a system of Soviet style psychiatric hospitals that mistreat prisoners of conscience (Munro 2001).

What matters most for the promotion of human rights, however, is less China's daily violations and more China's efforts against the global project of expanding human rights (Young 2002). Human rights abuses in Burma and North Korea are far worse. But Burma and North Korea have no international clout. In contrast, Beijing uses its power to block progress in human rights. What requires explanation is China's political success.

The credit for blocking progress in human rights is not solely attributable to Beijing's cleverness or clout. Two facilitating conditions make its task easier. First, nations fear loss of access to China, the world's largest emerging market, in an era when economic growth is a priority for the richer democracies. Second, Asia—southeast, east, and south—is the one region that lacks a transnational human rights organization. This precludes isolation of China as a violator of regional standards.

However, Asia is replete with NGOs concerned with human rights. The region is mainly democratic (Friedman 1994). Political freedom prospers in Mongolia, South Korea, Japan, Taiwan, the Philippines, Thailand, and India (Diamond and Plattner 1998; Morley 1999). Democratic Sri Lanka was, late in the twentieth century, plagued by ethnic violence. Indonesia in the early twenty-first century was trying to make a transition to democracy. Bangladesh, like Pakistan, has been a democracy on and off. The tyranny in Burma, to hang on to illegitimate power, had to crush a truly popular democratic movement and keep democracy leader Aung San Suu Kyi under control. Singapore and Malaysia are home both to democratic institutions and to ruling blocs that prevent those institutions from functioning in a fully democratic way.

Consequently, aside from the military despotism in Burma, the only thoroughly anti-democratic regimes in Asia are a handful of remaining Communist Party dictatorships. All Leninist systems face crises of legitimacy because market-disregarding command economies are incapable of raising a people out of poverty. Human rights are quite appealing in Asia.

Thus it is not some culturally shared opposition to human rights in general that discredits them in the region. Rather, the Chinese policy of opposing human rights progress is facilitated by contingent political factors in south, southeast, and east Asia. Politics is decisive.

South Asia

India, the predominant power in South Asia, is a flourishing democracy. Its political landscape is densely filled with human and civil rights movements. After all, all democracies are flawed. That human rights groups flourish in democracies is a fact missed in criticisms of international human rights activism. Defenders of despotism wrongly contend that democracies hypocritically preen by presenting themselves as free of human rights faults.

Indian human rights groups do not criticize China's human rights posture for diverse reasons. First, India's human rights activists have so much pressing work to do at home on issues relating to gender, caste, tribals, bonded labor, and police that they see the international arena almost as a distraction from far more crucial matters. Second, Indians are impassioned, as Kochanek's chapter details, by a potent anti-imperialist nationalism, buttressed by a Gandhian self-reliance that tends to lead Indians to see human rights as imperialist intervention to hurt developing nations. Third, India has a particular problem in Kashmir, a region in which international human rights observers find New Delhi guilty of massive human rights violations. Given an Indian nationalistic feeling that the incorporation of Muslim Kashmir is essential to a national project of India as a secular, multi-cultural nation, even patriotic Indian human rights activists resist foreigners looking into Kashmir. Some outside observers even see a trade-off in which Beijing gives India a free pass on Kashmir and New Delhi does likewise for China on Tibet.

When the Chinese compare themselves to democratic India's actual human rights performance, including sati, caste exclusions, and military rule in Kashmir, the Chinese find it unfair to single out China as a violator. Some Chinese even imagine India as a natural ally in opposing American imperialism. The government in Beijing has good conscience in rejecting criticism of its human rights performance. After all, the world's most populous democracy sides with the most populous authoritarian regime on opposing the expansion and implementation of a universal human rights agenda. Not only is there nothing in the cultures of Asia preventing eventual success for a project of democracy and human rights (Friedman 1999b, 346–59), but nations, even the Asian nondemocracies, see themselves as leaders in fostering human rights (Friedman 1999a, 56–79). There is a politics at work that helps the anti-human rights purposes of Beijing.

Southeast Asia

Similar political factors facilitating China's efforts in blocking further global progress on human rights lie in the history of ASEAN, the Association of Southeast Asian Nations. ASEAN began as a mid-1960s survival mechanism to end regional strife so that each nation could promote economic growth and prevent conquest by communist forces. Consequently a presupposition within ASEAN was not being judgmental about one's neighbors' internal affairs.

After Hanoi invaded Cambodia in 1970, Thailand saw China as a protector against Vietnam. China helped Thailand in the 1997 Asian financial crisis. Bangkok-Beijing entente limits ASEAN activism against China.

In the 1980s and 1990s, ruling groups in Malaysia, Singapore, and Indonesia legitimated violations of human rights as superior Asian values guaranteeing a harmonious social order and rapid growth. But Singapore dropped that culturally chauvinistic fiction around 1995 and Indonesia began to democratize in 1999 (D. Kim 1994, 189–94; Aung San 1991). Indeed, by 1999 the democracies within ASEAN even began to raise a couple of human rights concerns about violators. The tyranny in Burma felt pressured, as Neher's chapter points out. So while ASEAN was long silent on human rights, facilitating Chinese success in opposing international activism on human rights, ASEAN might change course, especially if Indonesia's democracy stabilizes.

Not all in ASEAN view China as benign. Vietnam, the Philippines, and Indonesia worry about a Chinese takeover of the South China Sea. Were a democratic Indonesia to lead ASEAN into democracy, Asia could foster human rights activism. A democratic South Asia led by India and a democratic East Asia led by Japan could then join a democratic ASEAN and create an Asian human rights movement. An Indian professor commented in 2000 that

The rise of China . . . is the main story of the post-Cold War era . . . the growth of a vigorous constellation of democracies . . . would clearly represent a bulwark against Chinese expansionism . . . a flourishing compact of democracies in the Asian region might . . . stoke democratic aspirations in China. (Chand 2000)

A senior Japanese analyst agrees. Pointing to partnership with India, he notes, "Japan and India together stand the best chance of countering the

influence of China" (Seki 2000, 38). The Centre for Democratic Governance founded in 2000 in New Delhi has a goal of "advancing freedom across
Asia" (Chanda 2000, 23). With an Asian human rights movement, China
would seem the odd nation out.

Easily imaginable changes in contingent factors could prod Chinese seeking Asian leadership to move China in a more democratic direction. After
the 9/11 terror attack, Beijing aligned itself with the "civilized" nations.
That tendency might lead Chinese to argue that peaceful reunification with
a democratic Taiwan requires an end to tyranny in China. In fact, after
Taiwan's 2000 presidential election during which two reform parties won
more than three-quarters of the vote on a platform of cleaning up the massive corruption in Taiwan's politics, some politically conscious Chinese,
who hate the PRC's pervasive corruption, imagined a democratic Taiwan as
useful to China. A professor of students holding such views explained,
"They saw a lot of positive aspects and think we should research Taiwan's
democracy as a model" (Forney 2000). It is therefore premature to treat
China or Asia as inherently incapable of human rights universalism.

When Beijing protested to Indonesia in 1999 about rape and pillage
against Indonesians of Chinese ancestry, Beijing did not make it a human
rights issue but rather one of blood racism. That Chinese rhetoric frightens
neighbors. Chinese know that democratic Taiwan had spoken out more
forthrightly. A democratic China could do more for the human rights of
ethnic Chinese threatened by racist violence.

In the hearts of Chinese and in their calculus, a democratizing Indonesia
that cruelly mistreats people of Chinese blood has no standing on human
rights issues. As with India, Beijing has good conscience in imagining itself,
relatively speaking as, yes, a government with problems, but in no sense of
the word a major and systematic violator of basic human rights. This is what
Chinese official documents say as they resist criticism of China's record on
human rights.

East Asia

The human rights issue on which China may be most culpable, the mistreatment of refugees and immigrants, plagues the region.[1] In the globalized new
economic era of rapid movement, aliens who cross borders to improve their
lives merit serious attention. This too is a matter of group rights. But as
badly as Thais may have treated Burmese or Malays have mistreated Indonesians, Chinese long did worse by the thousands of Koreans fleeing famine
and inhuman rule in Pyongyang. These uprooted folk have been returned
to the Democratic People's Republic of Korea (DRPK) authorities in North
Korea, where they are sentenced to forced labor or swift execution (Pomfret
2000). An apparent Chinese awareness of this human rights abuse, has led
Beijing to allow some from North Korea to reach democratic South Korea.

A democratic China would not act so cruelly and would have standing permitting a credible voice on the issue of the mistreatment of ethnic Chinese suffering racial injustice in neighboring countries. People of "Chinese blood" would be better off if China adhered to human rights. Should China democratize and become a promoter of human rights universalism regionwide, the global impact could be enormous.[2] China has clout.

Beijing's self-confident resistance to a universalist agenda of human rights is strengthened by perceived political realities in East and Northeast Asia. The major East Asian democracy, Japan, has no human rights standing in China. It is myopically seen in China as similar to Nazi Germany after the Nazi era, but unapologetic and potentially revanchist.[3] In the post-Mao era, the historical crimes of Hirohito's Showa Era Imperial Army in China have been magnified. In 2002, 65 years after the horrific Nanjing massacre, Japanese are treated by the Beijing government as more guilty than they were during the Mao era. Finding China's Communist Party dictatorship ever more powerful yet silent on its crimes against its own people and on its backing for tyrannies in North Korea, Pol Pot's Cambodia, and Burma, anti-China feelings have surged in Japan.

Chinese claims of victims from Hirohito's Japan keep rising. More Chinese are claimed to have died in the 1937–38 Nanjing massacre (340,000), than Japanese supposedly died in Hiroshima and Nagasaki combined. Similarly more Chinese are said to have died during the brutal military occupation by Hirohito's Imperial Army than apparently died in the Mao era. Whereas the Chinese death toll ascribed to Hirohito's regime in 1945 at war's end was ten to eleven million, by the end of the twentieth century the total had skyrocketed to more than forty million, a total greater than Mao's victims, conservatively taken to be more than thirty million.

To raise a human rights complaint about China is to sound like an apologist for executioners, especially Hirohito era inhumanities. To attack China on human rights is, to Chinese, to turn right and wrong upside down. Every time a right fringe politician in Japan makes an unrepentant statement, it is played up in China, proof that China is an innocent, that China's enemies are guilty (Friedman 2000b). Chinese chauvinism will not countenance the thought that another people suffered more from foreigners than the Chinese did.

Democratic Japan seldom challenges authoritarian China on human rights. Japan even forcibly repatriated democratic activists, safely in Japan after the 1989 Beijing massacre, back to China where they were treated as criminals. Because China's domestic policy assigns priority to economic growth and its foreign policy is to join with anyone and everyone against America, Beijing expresses warm appreciation to the Japanese government, which is a major source of aid, loans, investment, and import earnings for China.

This warmth toward Japan delegitimates China's party rulers, making them look to patriotic Chinese as soft on unrepentant Japanese. Democrats and super-patriots in China since 1982 have used a demand to stand up to Japan as a way of criticizing China's authoritarian regime as not standing up for China (Whiting 1989). It is conceivable, therefore, that the anti-Japanese hatred Beijing fans could come back to haunt the despots and serve the cause of democratization in China. The complication of the politics of human rights in China discredits a cultural approach to human rights universalism.

As with Japan, so with the democracy on Taiwan. Beijing imagines what is in fact a flourishing free land with no political prisoners as if it were a monstrosity. Beijing seldom discusses autonomous Taiwan as in the Mao era, a leftover item from a revolutionary civil war. The Taiwan Strait, in an era of economic openness, does not feel like a region of war. Taiwan is becoming the leading investor in China.

Taiwan has been reimagined as a throwback to colonialism, a territory stolen by Japan in 1895. As British Hong Kong in 1997 and Portuguese Macao in 1999 were returned to the motherland, so must Taiwan be. Democracy on Taiwan is imagined as "splittism," the greatest enemy of China's return to greatness. Patriots in China experience the discourse of democracy and human rights as the language of enemies who want to see China divided, weak, and in chaos.

In addition, Taiwan seems to many in China to be not a democracy, but a site for the worst violations of human rights. Even a most liberal Chinese thinker, someone far more enlightened and cosmopolitan than conservative nativists, equates Taiwan democracy with Hitler's holocaust: "Didn't a Western democracy elect Hitler? Isn't that a lesson? . . . The people thought Hitler was good and elected him. The people are sometimes simply not very clear. After they have had their emotions shaken about, they don't think rationally" (Liu Ji, interview, Lawrence 1998, 28). As Chinese increasingly identify with a racist Han chauvinism, they imagine Taiwan as bent on exterminating the Han race because Taiwanese experience themselves as members of a vibrant, pluralistic, multicultural society, enriched by diverse and mixed ethnicities—Austronesian, Hakka, Hoklo, mainlanders (recent arrivals), and so forth. That is, Taiwan would extinguish the great Han race.

As nationalists in China survey Asia, they feel that authoritarian China is in no way an inferior nation on human rights. They conclude that criticizing human rights violations in China is driven by ulterior motives such as besmirching China's good name, trying to split China, and, in general, trying to prevent a return to greatness of the pure and rising Han Chinese race. Consequently, when Beijing challenged human rights universalists attacking Chinese inhumanities, it did so both with self-confidence and popular support.

Defaulting Democracies

Chinese Communist leaders insist that their human rights record is good, while that of the United States, a racist country with an out-of-control police, is bad. Beijing is certain that democratic leaders elsewhere will not sacrifice the profits of doing business in China to advance human rights. Rulers in Beijing seek praise instead for feeding more than 20 percent of the human race, a feat purportedly staunching refugee floods in an age where refugees are already a fearsome human rights issue.

As the PRC sees it, rather than persecuting believers, as foreign detractors claim, China maintains freedom of religion, except for foreign subversive forces and destructive cultic influences. Likewise, advocates of democracy, when they attempt to destabilize the nation, are said to be imprisoned for threatening chaos as in Rwanda, Chechnya, and Bosnia. Surely, rulers in Beijing reason, any responsible government would oppose such evils. Because of the leadership of China's Communists, its leaders aver, China is doing well economically, with economic well-being the first of human rights.

While the regime actually imprisons democratic activists, its defense of China's human rights record is popular in China. Proud patriots fear that political change could destabilize society, bringing chaos and even civil strife, precursors of massive human rights violations. Chinese tend to accept the claims of rulers that foreigners have ulterior motives. They believe that human rights reports on China are lies. Even reformist intellectuals see human rights activist Harry Wu, living in California, as hateful, and interpret the balanced, nuanced, and understated annual U.S. State Department human rights report on China as full of malicious falsehoods.

Chinese believe their anti-American nationalism has little to do with government propaganda, pointing to the societal popularity of Starbucks, Bill Gates, and Hollywood movies. Preserving the CCP's hold on power, facilitating China's rise, Beijing opposed human rights diplomacy, understood as an anti-China crusade. The target of China's resistance is the United States, although other members of the OECD have often taken the lead to improve human rights conditions in China. Beijing's global campaign against international human rights activism is but one form of its multifaceted post-1992 anti-U.S. diplomacy.

The abusers of human rights in Beijing actually have long benefited from a U.S. double standard. "There had been no protest [from the democracies] at the suppression of Democracy Wall and the savage sentences on [human rights activist] Wei Jingsheng and other Chinese dissidents in 1979–1981. They attracted none of the support given by Washington and its allies to their counterparts in the Soviet Union" (Gittings 1999, 10). When American leaders went to authoritarian Moscow, they tried to meet dissidents. Not so in China.

In fact, after the 1989 Beijing massacre of democracy movement supporters, U.S. President George H. Bush resisted sanctions on China. Canada
and France, at the Paris bicentennial anniversary celebration of the French
Revolution, took the lead to pressure China to reverse its repressive policies. Bush had to be dragged into the coalition of democracies outraged at
Beijing's massacre of many hundreds—probably a couple of thousand—of
unarmed civilians. Indeed, Bush swiftly sent a secret mission to Beijing to
reassure Chinese leaders that Washington would continue a policy of engagement with China.

In comparison to the European Union, the U.S. government often has
been quite constrained on human rights. China even signed human rights
covenants resisted by Congress. Professor Samuel Kim has pointed out that
the Chinese rationalization of sovereignty as prior to human rights seems
purloined from the language of the U.S. Congress (Kim 2000). At the end
of the twentieth century, in contrast to Europe, America, prodded by uni-
lateralists in Congress, rejected both a land-mine treaty and international
court jurisdiction for war crimes and kept from even voting on equal rights
for women.

In contrast, as Newman's chapter details, Europe has been a world leader
on universalizing human rights. This seems natural because European
Union members experience themselves as a cross-border joining of peoples
committed to democracy, a process that has allowed freedom, peace, and
prosperity to flourish in Europe. European parliament members feel it
imperative to act on a human rights agenda, as do members of no other
region of the world. Yet by 1999 the French, for commercial gain, led
Europe to abandon human rights activism face-to-face with China, permitting Beijing to treat U.S. human rights gestures, feeble though they were, as
isolated acts of maliciousness.

Facilitating China's success with Europe is the latter's desire to sell to
the world's most populous surging economy. China played Europe's Airbus
against the U.S. Boeing. It punished Denmark with a loss of business for
human rights activism on China and rewarded France for leading the
European Union in opposing investigations of human rights violations by
letting billions in business contracts to French firms. At the end of the twentieth century, when China's president Jiang Zemin traveled to London and
Paris, the governments of Britain and France constrained the protests of
their own citizens. Throughout the OECD, businesses lobbied democratic
governments to neither censure nor sanction China. Even Hollywood, the
source of films depicting Beijing's inhuman practices in Tibet, supported
WTO accession for China, hoping to get more films into the China market
(Parkes 2000).

Despite lagging U.S. promotion of human rights, Beijing targets Washington as a leader of an anti-China effort. In reality President Bill Clinton,
soon after taking office, abandoned his campaign rhetoric about punishing

"the butchers of Beijing." Clinton de-linked human rights conditionality from U.S.-China trade. When he went to Beijing he "made no effort to meet any Chinese dissidents . . . and even as he was in Beijing, local dissidents were being harassed and prevented from talking to foreign journalists" (Parkes 2000, 16). Strategic concerns and economic interests were given priority. Clinton felt he had no political choice but to give priority to growing the economy. George W. Bush likewise peripheralizes human rights. Consequently rulers in China see no need to concede anything to human rights diplomacy (Friedman 1997).

Dr. Susan Shirk, outgoing deputy assistant secretary of state for East Asian and Pacific affairs, acknowledged China's defeat of the United States on human rights in February 2001. In a website statement, she reported, "we tried everything, ranging from linking human rights and trade through annual MFN reviews, to de-linking and engaging in dialogue to a lot of public shaming through speeches and resolutions in Geneva and Washington. But basically nothing has worked. And the external pressure is resented. . . . We need to realistically acknowledge the limits of our influence . . . what drives change in China are domestic demands and domestic developments."

In like manner, John Kamm, a human rights advocate who opposed the United States moving to investigate human rights abuses by China at the UN Human Rights Commission in Geneva, inquired, "I'm asking someone to explain to me how a resolution that will almost certainly fail and will not be supported by our allies, can help the human rights situation in China (Perlez 2001)." Not only did China defeat the resolution, but it also mobilized nations to temporarily drop the United States from the Human Rights Commission.

Yet Beijing continued to target Washington for *realpolitik* reasons. Beijing sees Washington as the military guarantor of Taiwan's autonomy. Discrediting the United States as an unfair aggressor on human rights is part of a Chinese policy of trying to get the U.S. military out of the Asia-Pacific region.

Beijing also wants to undermine the U.S.-Japan security treaty. Chinese nationalists see themselves as the natural leader of Asia, not Tokyo through its alliance with Washington. Beijing looks at the U.S. Seventh Fleet as an obstacle to China's full incorporation of the South China Sea, with its many billions in wealth, into Chinese territory. China has singled out the United States as the roadblock to China's predominance in Asia. All evils, including alleged human rights aggression against China, are blamed on the United States. That is the politics of human rights in China at the turn into the twenty-first century. It is not a matter of clashing cultures.

The Chinese political success against human rights universalism, which includes suppressing Tibetan Buddhists and Muslim Uyghurs, has contributed greatly to making human rights activism almost seem an impossible cause. The post-September 11 war on terrorism, with China as an ally, reinforced the factors defeating human rights universalism. China's success has been a major factor stymieing further progress in universalizing the human rights agenda.

Chinese Political Contingencies

It is important not to treat Chinese official claims about cultural relativism as facts. Sometimes people insist that a Confucian China uniquely has no tradition of human rights. This is false (de Bary and Tu 1998; Svensson 1996; Kelly and Reid 1998). The Confucian tradition was no insuperable obstacle to democratization in Japan, Taiwan, South Korea, or Hong Kong. In fact when Chinese colleges were told in the mid-1980s to teach Confucianism, with the hope that this would legitimate authoritarianism. Instead, I found when I visited Chinese universities that the Confucianism students apprehended was the Mencian tradition of "people as the root," such that the works of the Ming dynasty constitutionalist Huang Zongxi (1610–95), became popular.

Even in a PRC history of philosophy, Huang's democratic thrust stands out. He is one of the "progressive intellectuals" in "an opposition party" of advanced thinkers of the early Enlightenment. His Enlightenment ideas were directed predominantly against autocratic despotism attacking the theory of the divine rights of sovereigns. The keynote in his theorization was

that human beings were by nature self-interested. . . . [I]n. . . . antiquity . . . sovereigns were but public servants. But . . . step by step . . . sovereigns began to take the whole community as their private properties. . . . Huang . . . raised the question: "Is it that the world is destined only to favor one person . . . ?" (He 1991, 376–77)[4]

Because culture is multi-stranded and contested, politics decides the struggle between freedom and authoritarianism. Politicocultural identities change rapidly. Before the French Third Republic, many French believed their culture was uniquely hierarchical and authoritarian, incapable of democratization. Yet less than a generation later, in 1901, China's leading public intellectual, Liang Qichao, could identify France with natural rights. To Liang, Germany was the opposite of France, identified with state not human rights (Svensson 1996, 100). Since France and Germany were opposites, there was no homogeneous West. To imagine the West as democratic requires forgetting the actual history of France and Germany.

China's constructed post-Mao authoritarian identity obscures how politically self-serving are China's recent binaries of East and West. Chinese forget how modern human rights thinking first entered China. It came via Japanese commentaries on German works early in the twentieth century. Chinese saw how statist ideologues in Japan treated human rights as superstition and invoked a supposedly scientific Social Darwinism to legitimate Japanese expansionism. In contrast, "in the theory of human rights, people were born with innate rights of . . . self-rule . . . which others could not infringe " (Svensson 1996, 97). Independence was a human right, one of the group rights mentioned earlier in this chapter. Seeking freedom and opposing Japanese deniers of human rights, the Chinese embraced the cause of liberty. The UN Universal Declaration of Human Rights is infused with Confucian (Mencian) ethics, thanks to delegate P. C. Chang (Glendon 2001).

At the 1919 Versailles Conference, the democracies, led by U.S. President Woodrow Wilson, fended off an effort led by Japan, Haiti, and others to outlaw racism. Japan too is not one-dimensional. Asia has not been a laggard in promoting human rights.

Post-Mao dictators construct legitimations for authoritarianism. These self-serving efforts are not the fruit of an unchanging Chinese culture. Chinese civilization is as rich and diverse as any. The Chinese communists conflate their politics with their culture. For a while after 1991, as an independent Russia began to democratize, Chinese propaganda claimed that Russia failed because it reformed politically and practiced an economics of shock therapy, while China succeeded because it did not reform politically and acted gradually in the economic realm. Such a contention is nonsense (Friedman 1995, ch. 10). In fact, Leninist state socialist dictatorships Poland, Latvia, and Estonia, which both democratized and carried out an economic reform of shock therapy, soon grew steadily and swiftly. As with its legitimations of opposition to human rights promotion, the Chinese government has politically interpreted the world to advance ruling class interests. This is politics, not culture.

Since 1995, as China has sought Russia as a strategic partner against the United States. Beijing has changed its line on Russia, praising the strong government in Moscow for standing up to a U.S.-led NATO even while grappling with severe economic problems (Li 2000, 8–9). The Chinese media depict democratic electoral politics in Russia in a positive way. It is a reminder that Chinese interpretations of human rights could change, too, if the political balance moves that way. Nonetheless, most Chinese have been persuaded that democracy and human rights would not be good for China for the reasons sketched above. Still, public sentiment is volatile in a dictatorship.

Rulers in Beijing have pursued their policies on human rights winningly. Very quickly China defeated the sanctions regime imposed after the 1989 massacre. Also, China has marshaled its resources and its leverage over market access to defeat attempts to use the UN human rights system to probe China's systemic and massive violations of human rights. At the fifty-sixth session of the UN Commission on Human Rights in 2000, the PRC ambassador claimed that the freedoms of religion, speech, and association in China were better than ever and that the United States falsely accused China of human rights violations only because of Washington's "cold war mentality and hegemonist mindset" (*China Daily* 2000). Finally, China has played the market-oriented, prosperous democracies against each other so that virtually none will any longer risk a sustained bilateral confrontation with China on human rights. In short, authoritarian China has defeated the global effort to promote universal standards of human rights.

These victories reflect political struggles in China. The regime in 1999 brutally crushed a fledgling Democratic Party and Falun Gong, a spiritual good health movement. Beijing put out reams of propaganda to try to justify these abuses of basic human rights. Prison sentences were calibrated for deterrence at home and minimizing outrage abroad.

In 2000 China punished outspoken democrats, called liberals in China. The regime has censored the Internet. It sacks editors who run articles that expose the corrupt and brutal and polarizing reality of an unreformed Party dictatorship. Yet when a southern newspaper and its founder, Wang Yan, a successful businessman, were penalized for breaking the story of the murder in Nanjing of a German executive of Daimler Chrysler and his family, Chinese websites reported, "The removal of Mr. Wang and suspension of the *Jiangnan Times* are part of a broader campaign to restrain . . . media. Four prominent academics were criticized or sacked for outspoken opinions on economic and political reforms." A contradictory combination of loosening and constricting characterized Chinese politics entering the twenty-first century. Chauvinism and anxiety about disorder intensified. The direction of political movement "helped strengthen conservatives who argue for greater control" (Kynge 2000).

By insisting, in the traditional Leninist manner, that democracy is simply a cover for capitalist dictatorship, by portraying China as a pure race fending off pollution by germ-carrying foreigners who spread, with their democracy, spiritual and material pollution—drugs, AIDS, divorce, juvenile delinquency, prostitution, consumerism, and so forth—the systematic breach of human rights has strengthened the forces of China's new left. This group is associated with conservative communists and military hardliners in an expansive territorial project of militaristic nativism, understood as defending and reincorporating what has supposedly always been China's. This is both a coalition which can slow economic reform and one that advances a war-prone agenda, a discourse that contradicts the imperatives of deepening economic reform to ensure China's continuing economic rise.

If the reactionary nativists rein in the reform project, the Chinese economy will be badly wounded. Societal tensions will intensify in the country. Democratic India might even begin to overtake authoritarian China. It is not yet clear what the economic impact is, in an age of information technology, of China's preventing a free flow of information. There are real tensions in China between the politics of repression and the economics of growth.

China's successful politics of opposition to human rights may yet carry a high price tag. A few courageous people, reflective of a growing number of prestigious Chinese, right and left, are anxious over a surging chauvinism in China whose dynamics bode ill for the rise of a peaceful, powerful, and prosperous China. Examining the nationalist passion of victimization and opposition to alleged surrender to the so-called West, Shanghai neoconservative Xiao Gongqin sees a strengthening in China of forces favoring survivalist closed-door policies that make possible a "reenactment of the rise of twentieth century leftism in twenty-first century China," with leftism meaning the closed-door, economically stagnant, super-Stalinist chauvinism of the Mao era, something not in good repute in China. Professor Xiao fears this surging irrational nationalism will lead "the Chinese nation to lose its direction of modernization," its "opening-up, and calm rational thinking, thus leading to uncivilized irrationalism" (Xiao 2000, 97, 98).

In like manner, but from the other end of the political spectrum, the liberal Shanghai theorist Zhu Xueqin finds in China a resurgence of "leftist xenophobia," a "fanatical nationalism" that links up politically with a massive populism, facilitating a turn toward and return to the left. The liberal Zhu understates his anxieties for a China returning to self-wounding extremist ways, producing "serious chronic fits . . . bringing more burdensome historical costs" (Zhu 2000, 107, 108).

To use a more transparent political vocabulary to describe the shared concerns of the conservative Xiao and the liberal Zhu, they are worried about a rise, as in Europe in the 1920s and 1930s, of a rightist, racist, authoritarian, militarist, fascist-tending regime. They also see why such politics can be very popular in China. Even reformers in China tend to hate and condemn international human rights universalism as a plot against the rise of the great Chinese race.

Because the issue is politics, not deep culture or economic imperatives, Chinese leaders and people continue to contest these key issues. The future is uncertain. President Jiang Zemin began silencing some of these chauvinist forces after July 1, 2001. With China's subsequent entrance into the WTO, winning of the hosting of the 2008 Olympics and joining the post-9/11 coalition against terrorism, liberal voices again began to speak up.

It would be wrong to project a straight line of worsening tensions in the region leading directly to a large war, although a paranoid view of Taiwan politics could take China on a warpath. There, however, is "a small, but significant group of thinkers who take a stance that is at variance with the dominant Chinese [Communist Party] line and has much in common with liberal rights theory" (Weatherly 1999–2000, 28–33).[5] There is also a group that argues against the policy of singling out the United States as an enemy of China, claiming in opposition to the dominant line that globally there is a trend inexorably creating a pluralist world, not an international system dominated by a hegemonic United States (Chu, Wang, and Yan 1999; 2000, 190–91).

While nativists structure the debate and seem, at least on the surface, undefeatable, the logic of economic reform is also quite powerful. In 2000, when "China's dominant oil and gas producer," PetroChina, took an initial public offering, fund managers found that "charges of human rights and labor abuses" scared off investors (Lundler 2000). This increasing international human rights activism from society, not from the government, is "making it more difficult for traditional Chinese companies to float IPOs [Initial Public Offerings] in the United States" (Hiebert and Saywell 2000, 56).

It is still unclear what the outcome will be of the surging movements in rich democracies against foreign direct investment in sweatshops that repress labor rights. The impact of international human rights efforts can help make a positive Chinese politics of human rights good for the Chinese economy. With Taiwan's and Indonesia's democratization, plus India and Japan's possible changing attitudes toward international cooperation on democracy and human rights, there is much in regional and international politics potentially conducive to human rights improvements in China. This is a story about mutable politics, not about deeply rooted cultures.

One should not, however, overestimate what the U.S. government can do. Certainly it should not readily allow the democracy on Taiwan to be overwhelmed by force from the mainland of China. Certainly Washington should cooperate with Asian human rights efforts, including embracing collective human rights projects. Most important, the United States should treat China as a country that can democratize and contribute to the advancement of universally recognized human rights. There are Chinese who increasingly protest abuses in China. There are Chinese who wish to institutionalize the rights of protestors so that China can be a stable country of legal due process rather than a corrupt tyranny threatened by destabilizing explosions from below. Still as Shirk learned (quoted earlier), there is not that much that the United States can do. Politics in China will determine China's political direction. Change for the better from internal forces is not impossible. While the political success of Beijing in defeating human rights universalism does not bode well in the immediate future for the people of China or of the world, the issue continues to be contested. For world progress in human rights, a rising China is a decisive factor.

Chapter 8
South Asia

Stanley A. Kochanek

The problems of democracy, legitimacy, and human rights in South Asia are inextricably intertwined with questions of nationalism, national integration, economic development, globalization, and political, cultural, and social change. South Asia is a highly diverse, relatively self-contained geographic region that accounts for one quarter of the world's population. South Asia is divided into seven states—India, Pakistan, Bangladesh, Sri Lanka, Nepal, Bhutan, and the Maldives—that vary considerably in size, population, level of development, and power, as seen in Tables 1 and 2.[1] The population of the region is largely rural, religiously, linguistically, and ethnically diverse and is among the poorest, most illiterate, most malnourished in the world. Because of the region's ancient history and diverse traditions, religious, ethnic, linguistic, and tribal groups overlap modern territorial boundaries and have come to complicate the task of nation building and regional inter-state relations.

Although all the world's major religions are represented in South Asia and each state has its share of religious minorities, Hinduism is the dominant religion in India and Nepal, Islam is the majority religion in Pakistan, Bangladesh, and the Maldives, and Buddhists are the largest religious group in Sri Lanka and Bhutan. The overlap of religious communities in the region is compounded by the existence of some twenty linguistic and ethnic groups, many of which transcend national borders. This overlap of religion, language, and ethnicity has often transformed intrastate identity conflicts into interstate hostilities. These hostilities in turn have made the development of regional institutions and cooperation extremely difficult. They have also given rise to serious problems of human rights abuses and threats to government legitimacy.

The states of South Asia have had a complex and varied past, but they share a British colonial heritage. Since independence in the late 1940s, however, these states have followed divergent paths of political and institutional development. British colonial rule in South Asia not only had a varied impact on the traditional societies of the region, but also left behind two quite distinct governing traditions. On the one hand, British liberal democratic values, educational policy, and gradual introduction of elections and representative institutions in South Asia created a new, Western-educated, urban middle class that developed a strong commitment to British-style liberal democracy. On the other hand, the British vice-regal system of colonial rule and the paternalism of the colonial civil service created an equally strong legacy of centralized authoritarian rule.

Although the major states of South Asia began their independence as liberal democracies, some quickly succumbed to a vice-regal style authoritarian rule. The liberal democratic tradition has proven to be strongest and most enduring in India and Sri Lanka, while the vice-regal system has come to dominate Pakistan and Bangladesh. Since Nepal and Bhutan were under indirect British rule, both retained a strong indigenous tradition of

TABLE 1. South Asia: Demographic and Social Profile, 1997

Country	Area (sq. mi.)	Population (millions)	Population per sq. mile	Life expectancy	HDI rank
India	1,200,000	967.6	782	62.4	138
Pakistan	310,432	138.2	426	63.9	139
Bangladesh	55,598	125.3	2,254	58.1	144
Sri Lanka	24,962	18.8	752	73.1	91
Nepal	56,827	22.6	398	57.3	154
Bhutan	18,200	1.9	102	53.2	155
Maldives	115	0.3	2,438	—	—

HDI (human development index rank) measures the average achievement of a country in basic human capabilities, based on life expectancy at birth, educational attainment, and income. Dashes indicate information not available.
Source: John L. Allen, *Student Atlas of World Politics* (Guilford, Conn.: Pushkin-McGraw-Hill, 1998).

TABLE 2. South Asia: Economic Profile, 1997

Country	GNP per capita	PPP per capita
India	370	1,660
Pakistan	500	1,580
Bangladesh	360	1,090
Sri Lanka	800	2,460
Nepal	800	2,460
Bhutan	—	—
Maldives	—	—

PPP (purchasing power parity) measures levels of goods and services someone holding a country's money can buy locally. Dashes indicate information not available.
Source: John L. Allen, *Student Atlas of World Politics* (Guilford, Conn.: Pushkin-McGraw-Hill, 1998).

monarchy. The Maldive Islands were a British protectorate from 1867 to 1966 and were ruled by a sultan until 1968, when the islands were transformed into a republic.

The relative success or failure of British parliamentary democracy in South Asia was more than simply a result of the colonial legacy. Other factors also played an important role, including indigenous historical and cultural traditions, the character and strength of nationalist movements and parties, the quality and effectiveness of leadership, the pattern and impact of public policies, and the contrasting security compulsions of each state. Even in those states where liberal democracy began to develop roots, however, democratic systems have come under strain from increased politicization and popular mobilization, erosion of national parties and state institutions, sluggish economic growth, and the rise of identity politics based on religion, language, ethnicity, and tribe that transcended national borders and threaten the integrity of the state.

As seen in Table 3, India was the only state in South Asia ranked as politically free in the 2001–2 Freedom House Comparative Survey of Freedom. The survey ranks each country on a seven-point scale, with 1 representing most free. Bangladesh, Sri Lanka, and Nepal were ranked partly free, while Pakistan, Bhutan, and the Maldives Islands were ranked not free.

The states of South Asia face three quite distinct challenges to their authority and legitimacy that affect their ranking on the question of political freedom and human rights.[2] The challenges of secessionist movements and group conflict have led to a major expansion of police, paramilitary, and military forces in South Asia and an increasing resort to coercion and repression in dealing with these perceived threats to the authority and integrity of the state. The sharp rise in coercion and repression in dealing with insurgencies, the management of intergroup conflict, and the persistence of a colonial style police and prison system have resulted in serious human rights abuses and an erosion of governmental legitimacy. Increasingly the state in South Asia is seen as the primary instigator of violence and human rights abuses.

TABLE 3. Freedom House Freedom Index for South Asia, 2001–2

	Political rights	Civil rights	Freedom rating
India	2	3	Free
Bangladesh	3	4	Partly free
Sri Lanka	3	4	Partly free
Nepal	3	4	Partly free
Pakistan	6	5	Partly free
Bhutan	7	6	Not free
Maldives	6	5	Not free

Source: Freedom House Survey, *Freedom in the World, 2001–2002* <http://216.119.117.183/research/Freeworld/2001/Table1.htm>.

The most serious threat to state authority in South Asia has come from identity-based subnational movements. While the emergence of these movements has its own local dynamics, most originate from a perceived threat to the linguistic, ethnic, religious, or tribal identity of the group or feelings of state discrimination against the group (Kakar 1995). The development of perceived threats to group identity and discrimination tends to be fueled by social dislocation, the homogenizing impact of modernization, and contrasting historical narratives. Political, economic, and international forces that result in organized movements for autonomy or independence reinforce the emergence of these cultural identities.

Linguistic, ethnic, religious, or tribal insurgencies have come to plague each of the larger states in South Asia regardless of regime type. The longest and bitterest insurgencies have been those that overlap state boundaries and receive support from neighboring states in the region or aid from group supporters living overseas. The most devastating and only successful insurgency in the past fifty years in South Asia was the breakup of Pakistan and creation of Bangladesh in 1971.

The most important insurgencies in South Asia today are the twenty-nine-year-old struggle for independence by the Hindu, Tamil minority in Sri Lanka; the persistent rebellion in Assam and the northeast, Punjab and Kashmir in India; the periodic outbreak of revolts in the Pakistan provinces of Sind, the Northwest Frontier, Baluchistan, and the city of Karachi; and the long-standing conflict in the Chittagong Hill Tracts (CHT) between the majority Bangladeshi community and the tribal Chakmas. Almost all these insurgencies have cross-border implications. India has been deeply involved in the Sri Lanka conflict and is accused of supporting dissidence in Sind and the CHT. Pakistan has been accused of being involved in the Punjab crisis and the long dispute over Kashmir, and the People's Republic of China has been involved in the past in Assam and the northeast (Mitra and Lewis 1996; Chadda 1997).

The State and Human Rights

Although most South Asian elites claim a strong commitment to liberal democracy and human rights, many insist that Western definitions of human rights must take into account local context and basic needs and cannot be applied in the same way as in the West. Most government and nationalist elites tend to see attempts by the West to impose Western definitions of human rights on the states of the region as a challenge to their newly won sovereignty and a form of neocolonialism. State level commitment to human rights in the region varies considerably depending on formal constitutional guarantees, government interpretations of those guarantees, and state response to dissent and perceived threats to state authority.

The government of India and nationalist Indian intellectuals have developed the most comprehensive critique of Western-inspired definitions of human rights and attempts by the West to apply these values on a global scale. This Indian critique is much more sophisticated than the doctrine of a set of distinct Asian values employed by leaders in Southeast Asia. The human rights debate employed by the West is viewed as largely partisan and is used as an instrument of Western pressure, domination, and expression of superiority reminiscent of the missionary zeal of early colonialism. These definitions fail to take into account the local context, especially the critical link between development and human rights. The West tends to apply its doctrine of human rights in a highly confrontational, selective, polarizing, self-righteous, and partial way. Indians believe that the West employs a double standard and has neither the moral credentials nor the comprehensive understanding of human rights to act as the self-proclaimed champion of a global human rights agenda.

Western conceptions of human rights, Indians argue, lack historical perspective and ignore the West's own internal failings. The West conveniently ignores the racism, xenophobia, intolerance, discrimination, and marginalization of indigenous peoples and migrants within its own borders, human rights abuses in the early years of industrialization, attacks on indigenous peoples, and the era of colonialism. These attitudes, insists India, continue today in the way the West refuses to take responsibility for poverty and underdevelopment in the Third World and the human rights problems that go with it. The West confuses the symptoms of underdevelopment with human rights and glorifies anarchic individualism at the cost of social obligations. Indians see Western notions of human rights as "defective" (Shah 1997, 24–44) and use these arguments to diffuse Western criticism of their human rights record.

Indians further prefer a global human rights agenda, not through a policy of confrontation, but through the promotion of democracy, rule of law, pluralism, and development. This can be done most effectively not by self-serving criticism, insinuations of bad faith, and confrontation, but by greater support for economic development. The West should encourage the creation of national human rights institutions, human rights education programs and provide technical and advisory services. In the words of Dag Hammarskjold, notes an Indian UN representative, no individual or nation has "a monopoly on rightness, liberty, and human dignity" (Shah 1997, 44).

Liberal Democracies: India

Among the states of South Asia, India and Sri Lanka have the longest tradition of liberal democracy. Although India lacks almost all the pre-conditions that theorists insist are essential to democracy, its democratic system has proven to be quite resilient. While some critics have characterized Indian democracy as a "hollow shell" or a formal democracy tainted by authoritarian strains and not very different from that of Pakistan, most observers see India as one of the most successful democratic experiments in the Third World.

As the largest state in South Asia, India tends to set the trend for the rest of the region, yet it also invokes fears of regional dominance. The successful development of Indian democracy has been attributed to the character and development of its long and difficult nationalist struggle, the Indian elite's commitment to British liberal democratic values, the emergence of a well-organized and dominant party, strong and effective leadership, a federal constitution, and the policy of accommodation of the Nehru era.

The Indian National Congress that led the long fight for independence was founded in 1885. The Congress elite became strongly committed to the British tradition of liberal democracy and as early as 1931 endorsed the principles of fundamental rights and basic civil rights to counter British colonial repression (Chiriyankandath 1993, 248). The elite later incorporated these values into the Indian constitution in the form of fundamental rights and directive principles of state policy and established the strongest and most sustained pattern of democratic rights in the region. India has a vibrant free press, an independent judiciary, civilian control over the military, a growing civil liberties movement, and a long tradition of an internally driven human rights agenda.

But, confronted by the chaos of partition, the need to integrate some 561 princely states into the Indian union, and a war with Pakistan over the disputed region of Kashmir, the Indian elite was also preoccupied with the need to establish a strong, centralized political order capable of preserving the territorial integrity of the state and authority. It equipped the new state with a wide array of emergency powers, sweeping security statutes, and laws designed to maintain order and stability.

The Indian constitution grants the president of the republic a wide array of emergency powers. These have been supplemented by a variety of security statutes that include preventive detention. During the first two decades of independence the government of India used its enormous powers very sparingly. However, by the late 1960s the country began to experience a series of stresses that resulted in an increased resort to the state's coercive power and a temporary breakdown of the democratic order.

The systemic pressures that began to build up in the 1960s were the result of the decline of the once dominant Congress Party, a growing centralization and personalization of power, two wars, two droughts, sluggish economic growth, increased ethnic and religious challenges to central authority, intensified social conflict among an increasingly politicized and mobilized society, erosion of political institutions, and increased global tensions. Unable to cope with these challenges, the democratic framework of the state began to crack, culminating in the declaration of a national emergency in 1975. The emergency ushered in a period of authoritarian rule that lasted from 1975 to 1977. During the twenty-one-month emergency some 110,000 people were arrested and detained without trial (Hardgrave and Kochanek 2000, 261–62).

Although the Indian democratic order was restored by the defeat of Indira Gandhi and election of the Janata government in 1977, the Indian state once again came under increasing pressure in the 1980s and 1990s. These pressures were generated by the emergence of separatist forces in Punjab, Assam, and Kashmir, the rise of communalism and Hindu nationalism, and the "Mandalization" of Indian politics as increasingly conscious and politicized lower castes demanded enhanced opportunities through a system of caste-based reservations of government jobs and access to education. The state responded to these challenges by adopting a wide variety of security laws and expanded the police, paramilitary forces, and military.

Although each insurgency in India has arisen from a special set of local factors, subnational movements have also been fueled by a combination of factors that involved the rise of identity politics, heightened political consciousness, expanded participation, increased competition for scarce resources, ethnic and religious insecurities, and problems of poor political management.

The most serious challenges facing the integrity of the Indian state all involve border provinces and insurgent groups. The three most critical are Punjab, Assam, and Kashmir. All three states have been affected by the residual impact of the partition of the subcontinent in 1947 and the rise of a separatist identity movement based on language, ethnicity, tribe, or religion. The Indian state has attempted to defuse these insurgencies by a combination of formidable security statutes, negotiations, and repression. These actions have led to severe curbs on civil liberties and charges of violations of human rights.

The most important security statutes in India are the National Security Act of 1980 and its Amendment in 1984, the Terrorist Affected Areas (Special Courts) Act of 1984, the Terrorist and Disruptive Activities (Prevention) Act of 1985, and the Armed Forces (Jammu and Kashmir) Special Powers Act of 1990 (Sripati 1997, 93–136). These laws provide sweeping powers of preventive detention, in camera trials, and destruction of property, and grant the armed forces freedom from prosecution. Human rights groups have charged that these statutes have led to widespread abuses including rape, torture, beatings, disappearances, staged encounters, extrajudicial killings, and deaths in custody. The government of India challenges the validity of the allegations, claiming to have punished human rights abusers; it established a Human Rights Commission in 1993 to help maintain and deal with possible human rights violations.

A second serious challenge to the legitimacy and integrity of the state arises from the high levels of violence that result from intergroup conflict, political agitation, interest-based demands, social movements, and protest groups of all types. Protest and violence in India are so diverse that India has developed its own unique vocabulary to describe these forms of public protest (Hardgrave and Kochanek 2000, 218).

The most serious forms of intergroup conflict in India revolve around clashes between religious communities, which the Indians refer to as communalism and hostility among various castes. The bitterest communal clashes have taken place between the majority Hindu community and the large Muslim minority. It was the Hindu-Muslim division that led to the partition of India and the creation of Pakistan. The partition did not end the problem. It led to armed conflict and war among the new states and left a divided India with a large Muslim minority that today is estimated to be about 120 million, or 12 percent of the population.

Following partition, communal disturbances between Hindus and Muslims once again became a problem in India in the 1960s. They intensified in the 1970s and became rampant in the late 1980s and early 1990s. The most devastating communal riots came in December 1992 and January 1993 following the destruction of the Babri Masjid (Mosque) at Ayodhya by Hindu nationalists. The problem of communal violence has also spread to the Sikh religious community and the small Christian minority.

Despite its constitutional commitment to secularism, the Indian state has been very slow to respond to attacks against religious minorities and prevent human rights abuses (Engineer 1995, 140).

Police and Prisons

The undemocratic behavior of the Indian police in carrying out their duties and the condition of the penal system represent another human rights problem facing the Indian state. The Indian police, paramilitary forces, and military have expanded enormously over the past fifty years and have come to command a larger and larger share of the budget. The police and paramilitary forces have acted in ways that subvert the maintenance of democratic political forms. A high level of distrust and apprehension characterizes public feelings toward the police (*Seminar* 1999). The police are seen as rude, brutal, devious, dishonest, and partial. However, defenders of the police point to the fact that the Indian police work under very difficult conditions. They are poorly paid, overworked, and have severely limited physical, administrative, and social support.

Many of these problems are reflected in the Indian prison system. Indian prisoners suffer from massive overcrowding, a lack of sanitation, poor food, inadequate medical facilities, and a high degree of custodial violence. In addition corruption, torture, and deaths in custody are pervasive. The National Human Rights Commission (NHRC) has made prison reform a major issue on its agenda, but so far its impact has been minimal.

Supporters of the Human Rights Agenda

The Indian human rights agenda is largely internally driven, principally by an impressive array of indigenous forces. They include an increasingly active judiciary, a strong and independent press, one of the most active and vocal human rights movements in the Third World, and a newly created National Human Rights Commission. Among the major institutions of the state, the Indian judiciary has become one of the most important voices for human rights in the country.

Stung by the strong criticism of its passive role during the emergency, the courts underwent a major transformation in the post-emergency period. The courts have come to play a more activist role in promoting social and economic justice and human rights by expanding their interpretation of articles 14 and 21 of the constitution to include the principles of equal treatment under the law and due process. Under this reinterpretation of the constitution, the judiciary has promoted the concept of Public Interest Litigation (PIL) by inviting class action suits and writ petitions from the poor, it has begun to intervene on behalf of downtrodden groups, including bonded labor, tribals, women, the homeless, and defendants held in custody for years awaiting trial. The courts have also become an active promoter of civil liberties and human rights by curtailing abuses of power by the executive and parliament.

Strong and independent print media buttress the judiciary. Although freedom of the press was guaranteed by the constitution, the press was subject to indirect control through government allocation of newsprint and government advertising and was subject to rigid press censorship during the emergency. In the post-emergency period the Indian press has become increasingly vocal in exposing communal violence and the abuse of government power, and in protecting human rights.

In addition to an independent judiciary and a free press, India has also developed one of the most active human rights movements in Asia. The 1980s and 1990s gave rise to high levels of violence in India. This violence and the human rights abuses that accompanied it have increasingly come under the scrutiny of both international and domestic human rights organizations. Except for a very limited role in Jammu and Kashmir, local, independent human rights organizations also operate throughout most of the country, investigating abuses and issuing public findings.

Human rights organizations began to develop in India after the emergency and maintain close contact with a variety of social movements, the press, and the judiciary in an effort to place curbs on the executive and parliamentary power. The emergency made it clear to the Indian elite that government was not simply a benign force and that civil liberties needed to be actively protected, especially among the socially marginalized. Human rights groups have come to realize that many of India's laws are not enforced and are regularly ignored or violated by the state itself. They have also been confronted by the fact that communalism and caste conflict have eroded the elite consensus in favor of a democratic, secular, legal state. They have therefore attempted to use the courts to protect popular movements, civil liberties, and social and economic rights.

The explosion of nongovernmental organizations (NGOs) designed to protect the rights of the poor, women, tribals, and minorities reinforces human rights organizations in India. NGOs have come to articulate new sets of issues including the environment, women's rights, prison reform, bonded labor, alternative development models, and legal rights for the poor. They have fought for the protection of tribal populations, the rights of villagers displaced by development projects, and the rights of victims of the Bhopal gas disaster of 1984, and have pressed the government to adhere to international human rights treaties and conventions (Banerjee 1997, 23).

In an effort to ward off threats of foreign intervention in the human rights field, the government of India responded by creating a National Human Rights Commission (NHRC) in 1993. The NHRC has taken a special interest in laws that lead to violence and abuse of human rights, problems of custodial violence, and reform of the prison system.[3]

Despite all efforts to protect human rights in India, the problem remains a formidable challenge to the state and Indian liberal democracy. The state's refusal to act on the recommendations of its own inquiring commissions in cases like the anti-Sikh riots of November 1984, the post-Ayodhya violence in Bombay, and violence against religious and other minorities make the country susceptible to international criticism and external pressures on the question of human rights.

Liberal Democracies: Sri Lanka

Like India, Sri Lanka adopted a British-style liberal democracy at the time of independence in 1948. This system was based on free and fair elections, competitive political parties, mobilization across ethnic communities, and a state controlled by an elite that had diverse social and economic roots. The system became well established and functioned very effectively for the first three decades following independence.

However, a political and economic decline began to set in in the late 1970s because of modest economic growth, increased popular demands, the politicization of the lower castes, the rise of ethnic conflict, and a growing personalization of power. These factors combined to produce an acute rise in violence by the country's unemployed youth, led by the Marxist movement Janatha Vimukthi Peramuna (JVP), and an outbreak of ethnic conflict between the majority Sinhala-speaking Buddhist community and the minority Tamil-speaking Hindu community (Wilson 1993, 327–33).

Tensions between the Tamils and Sinhalese had been growing ever since

1956, when a Sinhalese-dominated party captured control of the government and amended the constitution to make Sinhala the national language of the country. By the late 1970s a growing sense of Sinhalese chauvinism was making the Tamil minority feel increasingly alienated and isolated. The Tamils feared that the majority Sinhalese community was trying to transform Sri Lanka into a Sinhala-speaking Buddhist state in which the Tamil minority would have little or no place. Growing feelings of discrimination and the belligerent response of Sinhalese leaders to these feelings led to demands for partition of the island and the creation of an independent Tamil-speaking state (Tamil Eelam).

Like Hindu nationalists in India, Sinhalese nationalists, despite their majority status, see themselves as a minority in a hostile world. They feel that the language and culture of their tiny island are threatened by the presence of a massive Tamil population just across the Palk Strait in the Indian state of Tamil Nadu. These feelings of insecurity, the fears of being submerged in a Tamil sea, and a failure to respond effectively to Tamil demands for autonomy have resulted in a threat to the very survival of the state.

The Sri Lankan civil war that began in 1983 has already claimed more than 60,000 lives and has given rise to serious charges of human rights abuses on both sides. Although the Sri Lanka constitution provides for civil liberties protections, the country has been under an almost continuous state of emergency since 1983 and the government has undermined the legal system in the name of protecting the security of the state. Under the constitution of the second republic, adopted in 1978, which transformed the Sri Lankan political system from a parliamentary to a mixed presidential-parliamentary system, the courts were prevented from striking down special security statutes. Since then the executive has introduced a whole series of new security acts. These acts combine to provide the government with special powers of arrest and detention and have led to numerous human rights abuses, including extra-judicial killings, disappearances, and arbitrary arrests.

As is the case of insurgencies in India, the Sri Lankan civil war has been complicated by the role of outside powers in the region. Following the anti-Tamil riots in July 1983, thousands of Tamil refugees took refuge in the South Indian state of Tamil Nadu. The local Indian Tamil population provided the Sri Lankan Tamil refugees with humanitarian aid and supported Tamil independence. The government of India also became involved and began to arm and train the Sri Lankan rebels and provide them with bases and staging facilities. The Indian government justified its actions as a way to placate subnational sentiments in Tamil Nadu and forestall a resurgence of Tamil separatism in the south. Indian support came to play an important role in enabling the Tamil insurgency to survive Sri Lankan government efforts to crush the rebels.

A serious crisis developed in 1987, however, when the Sri Lankan government launched a major military operation to end the rebellion. When the operation looked as if it might succeed in crushing the rebels, the government of India under Rajiv Gandhi threatened to intervene militarily on behalf of the Tamil insurgents. The result was a halt in the offensive and the signing of the Indo-Sri Lankan Accord of July 1987. In the Accord the government of Sri Lanka agreed to grant regional autonomy to the Tamils in return for an end to hostilities. The Indian government, in turn, agreed to dispatch a large peacekeeping force that at its height numbered 50,000 Indian troops to supervise the surrender of arms. The Indian military and diplomatic intervention in Sri Lanka turned into a major disaster for the Indians. The Indian Peace Keeping Force (IPKF) became embroiled in a conflict with Sri Lankan Tamils who refused to surrender and suffered heavy casualties, with 1,100 dead and 2,890 wounded (Hardgrave and Kochanek 2000, 427–28). The IPKF was finally forced to withdraw in March 1990 at the request of the Sri Lankan government.

Supporters of Human Rights

As is the case in India, the major supporters of human rights in Sri Lanka are the judiciary, the press, local human rights organizations, NGOs, and social action groups. These groups, however, suffer severe restrictions because of the wide array of emergency regulations (Udagama 1998, 269–94).

In response to international pressures, the government of Sri Lanka passed the Human Rights Commission Act in July 1996 that created a permanent Human Rights Commission (HRC). The HRC is empowered to monitor human rights practices, ensure compliance with the fundamental rights provisions of the constitution, and investigate complaints of human rights abuses. Until the civil war is ended, however, Sri Lanka will continue to pay a heavy price not only financially, but also in terms of human rights.

A Partial Democracy: Bangladesh

In December 1990 Bangladesh joined the third wave of democratization that was sweeping the post-Cold War world when General H. M. Ershad was toppled by a mass movement demanding the restoration of democracy. Ershad's overthrow ended fifteen years of military rule in the country. Since 1990 Bangladesh has held four national elections and has had two changes of government. The country, however, has a long way to go in its effort to create a liberal democracy. Democracy in Bangladesh is largely a formal affair. The country holds popular elections and has a president, prime minister, cabinet, parliament, and courts, but power is highly centralized in the hands of the executive and the country is plagued by extra-parliamentary violence, mass demonstrations, a repressive government, and an opposition determined to topple the government of the day.

Following almost a quarter of a century of authoritarian rule as a province of Pakistan and a brief but bloody civil war, Bangladesh became an independent state in December 1971. The founders of the new state sought to create a liberal democratic order free from the authoritarian practices of the past. The new constitution that came into force in 1972 guaranteed fundamental rights to all Bangladeshis and eliminated all references to preventive detention, special emergency powers, and other constitutional provisions that had been used in the past to repress political freedoms. These newfound freedoms lasted less than two years. Faced by the chaos of the liberation war, deteriorating law and order, near economic collapse, radical revolutionary movements, and threats to its monopoly on political power, the ruling Awami League amended the constitution to restore many of the emergency provisions of the Pakistan period. The amendments granted the government extensive emergency powers and enabled the Awami League to pass broad security statutes and the Special Powers Act of 1974, which provided for preventive detention, detention without trial, and detention without warrant for up to 120 days. In 1975 the constitution was amended once again to transform Bangladesh from a parliamentary democracy to a highly centralized presidential, authoritarian, one-party state. The judiciary was made subordinate to the executive, all newspapers were banned except for the four owned and managed by the state, and a new exploitation-free socialist society was proclaimed under the leadership of Bangabandhu Sheikh Mujibur Rahman. But the new order came to a crashing halt within a few months with the assassination of Mujib on August 15, 1975 by a group of disgruntled army officers.

Mujib's assassination was followed by a series of coups and counter-coups that led to the rise of General Ziaur Rahman as the dominant ruler of Bangladesh. Zia reestablished a bureaucratic-military state similar to the one created by General Ayub Khan in Pakistan from 1958 to 1969. Zia retained the presidential system, restored multiparty politics, granted a degree of independence to the judiciary, and, like Ayub, founded his own political party in an effort to civilianize his rule. Unlike Ayub's Muslim League, however, Zia's Bangladesh Nationalist Party (BNP) was a broad-based coalition of political forces opposed to the Awami League and Mujib's one-party state. The very composition of the BNP enabled the party to survive the assassination of Zia in 1981 and remain a major political force in Bangladesh. Although the BNP succeeded in electing Zia's successor following his assassination, the new regime failed to survive. In March 1982 the BNP government was toppled by a military coup led by General H. M. Ershad.

The Ershad government was a military government built on patronage and opportunism. Ershad founded his own political party, the Jatiya Party, and attempted to legitimize his rule by holding popular elections. Elections under Ershad, however, were notorious for being rigged in the government's favor and provided a very thin veil of legitimacy. A popular movement demanding the restoration of democracy in December 1990 overthrew the Ershad government. It collapsed because of Ershad's overconfidence, high levels of corruption, weakening donor support, and a withdrawal of military backing (Kochanek 1996, 704–22).

The popular movement that overthrew Ershad agreed to restore a Westminster style of parliamentary government. The restoration of democracy in Bangladesh, however, has not lived up to expectations. Politics in Bangladesh have become polarized between two major political forces that each commands the support of about one-third of the electorate. The BNP, led by Begum Khaleda Zia, the widow of General Ziaur Rahman, won the elections in 1991 and ruled until 1996, when it was forced to resign under pressure from a mass movement led by the Awami League. The Awami League, led by Sheikh Hasina Wajid, the daughter of Mujibur Rahman, won the elections of June 1996, but remained under pressure by the political opposition to resign and hold new elections. The BNP was returned to power in October 2001, but the Awami League refused to accept the results and once again took to the streets. The country's dominant political forces seem unable to reach any consensus on the basic rules of democratic governance.

The political instability that has plagued Bangladesh has had a negative effect on human rights. Although the constitution guarantees fundamental rights and the courts are pledged to sustain human rights and civil liberties, the government of Bangladesh restricts or denies most fundamental rights. Despite repeated promises by both the BNP and the Awami League when in opposition to repeal the Special Powers Act, neither has been willing to repeal the Act or other repressive "black laws" once in power. These laws are used by the government of the day to repress political opposition. Political leaders are subject to arbitrary arrests and preventive detention, the press faces intimidation and possible closure, limits are placed on freedom of association, and women, minorities, and indigenous peoples are susceptible to discrimination. Other human rights problems include poor prison conditions and the use of torture, extra-judicial killings, and deaths in police custody.

Supporters of Human Rights

As elsewhere in South Asia, support for human rights comes largely from the judiciary, the press, local human rights groups, and the NGO community. Despite the constitutional status granted to the judiciary by the 1972 constitution, successive authoritarian regimes have substantially eroded the authority of the courts in the country. The restoration of democracy in 1990, however, has reinvigorated the courts, and the judiciary has adopted a more activist stance. The status of the higher judiciary has increased considerably in recent years as supreme court judges were selected to head the Neutral Caretaker governments in 1990, 1996, and 2001 and successfully supervised free and fair elections, the chief justice of the Supreme Court was elected president in 1996, and an activist court has become more responsive to the needs of the poor through the use of public interest litigation (Hossain, Malik, and Musa 1997). These actions have helped to rehabilitate the image of the higher judiciary. Further improvement in the position of the judiciary is expected from a massive aid program financed by the World Bank to strengthen and reform the entire judicial system of the country. The courts, however, continue to have a variety of problems, including intimidation by the government, corruption in the lower courts, and refusal of political parties to honor their repeated commitments to separate the judiciary from the executive.

Although the constitution of Bangladesh provides for freedom of the press, the highly vocal and partisan print media remain intimidated by the government and the electronic media remain under government control. The one private TV channel is devoted almost entirely to entertainment. The print media in Bangladesh continue to face governmental restrictions and intimidation. The press remains governed by some twenty-five restrictive laws, including the Special Powers Act, and is subject to a variety of government pressures such as withholding newsprint supplies, withdrawal of government advertising, and closure of errant newspapers. In addition, local journalists are subject to violent attacks by the police and local thugs, are poorly paid, and work under very difficult conditions.

Since 1971 Bangladesh has developed a vibrant NGO community. In 1998 Bangladesh had roughly 30,000 registered NGOs that received $300 million in funds largely from foreign donors. Most of these NGOs are engaged in the delivery of services or are involved in development work. In recent years, however, a variety of human rights organizations have come into being. These groups produce their own annual human rights report on Bangladesh and have become an important voice in pressing for public accountability on human rights.

Return to Military Rule: Pakistan

Although Pakistan, like India, began as a parliamentary democracy, the country proved to be ill prepared by history and circumstances to operate the new governmental system. It became transformed almost immediately into a Pakistani version of a vice-regal state. Pakistan inherited a weak, factionalized dominant party that lacked a local base of support; the territory that became Pakistan was not geographically contiguous, the region was among the least politically developed on the subcontinent, and the new government was confronted by a massive refugee crisis and a war with India over Kashmir.

Since its very creation, Pakistan has suffered from political and systematic instability. The country has had at least eight constitutions since 1947, and each has failed to outlive the tenure of its founder (Maluka 1995). Over the past fifty years Pakistan has faced long periods of martial law, extended periods of military-bureaucratic rule, and short periods of weak, unstable, and ineffective civilian government. From 1985 to 1999, for example, Pakistan had four national elections and eleven civilian governments as power passed back and forth between Benazir Bhutto and her Pakistan People's Party (PPP) and Nawaz Sharif's Pakistan Muslim League (PML). Each was accused of attempting to rule Pakistan as a private fiefdom and looting the state for its own benefit and that of its friends. This pattern of unstable civilian rule was brought to a halt on October 12, 1999 by a military coup led by General Pervez Musharraf and the Pakistan army.

Despite the highly centralized character of the Pakistani state, Pakistan faces a major crisis of governance, identity, and legitimacy. The country is threatened by a breakdown in law and order, an erosion of state authority, rising ethnic and regional insurgencies, religious and sectarian violence, the growth of Islamic extremism, and external threats from its neighbors. In an attempt to deal with these challenges the state has equipped itself with a comprehensive array of security acts and ordinances, criminal statutes, anti-terrorist laws, military and Shariʿat courts, and a variety of Islamic edicts, including blasphemy laws. These draconian laws combined with a restricted judiciary, intimidation of the press, and attempts to control the activities of human rights groups and NGOs have resulted in a persistently poor human rights record for the state. International human rights reports and local human rights groups cite brutal prison conditions, suppression of women's, children's, and minority rights, bonded labor, and violation of basic rights of citizens. Both military and civilian governments have proven to be insensitive to human rights, impatient with the rule of law, and intolerant of dissent.

Because of the breakup of Pakistan in 1971, the government has become acutely conscious of the danger of ethnic and regional nationalism. It has tended to treat the rise of ethnonationalism as a law and order problem and has even made matters worse by attempting to manipulate ethnic tensions in an effort to maintain control. Major threats of armed resistance in Pakistan come from the provinces of Sind, the Northwest Frontier and Baluchistan, and the city of Karachi (K. Ahmed 1999).

The ethnic diversity of Pakistan has been further compounded by heightened religious and sectarian tensions resulting from General Zia ul Haq's Islamization policies of the 1980s and 1990s. These policies have threatened freedom of religion, led to major sectarian clashes and have resulted in severe hardships for non-Muslim religious minorities (Mahmud 1995, 83–101).

The Supporters of Human Rights

The main voices in Pakistan attempting to support human rights are the judiciary, press, human rights organizations, NGOs, and the Human Rights

Commission of Pakistan. These supporters of human rights, however, face stiff resistance from a state that is not readily amenable to criticism or challenges to its authority and is prepared to take steps to limit or suppress dissent.

Although executive pressure, inadequate resources, inefficiency, and even corruption have hampered the Pakistani judiciary, it represents one of the few official agencies capable of acting as an intermediary between society and the state. Because of repeated periods of authoritarian rule, the Superior Courts of Pakistan have been forced to walk a narrow path between a cautious quest for jurisdiction and threats to their institutional survival as Pakistani governments have repeatedly attempted to bring the courts under executive control and limit their jurisdiction (Rizvi 1999, 177–90).

The press, human rights groups, and NGOs in Pakistan all work under the same difficult conditions as the courts. Although the government-owned Press Trust of the Ayub Khan era has been liquidated, the press still faces a variety of pressures, including the possible withholding of government advertising, government control of newsprint, harassment by tax audits, and various press regulations. News reporters face intimidation, heavy surveillance, and legal action by the state. Newspapers that displease the government are threatened or closed down. Still the print media are able to enjoy some degree of freedom, primarily because of the existence of competitive politics. Radio and television in Pakistan continue to be a near government monopoly, and the government still controls the Associated Press of Pakistan, the country's main news distributor.

Despite the presence of human rights organizations, NGOs, and the Human Rights Commission of Pakistan, the basic rights of Pakistani citizens continue to be violated by the authorities. The status of women is the lowest in the region, forty-nine minors face the death penalty and several thousand minors are in jails, bonded labor is still prevalent, and NGOs are prosecuted for anti-state activities. In short, Pakistan continues to have a rather poor human rights record.

Democracy and Human Rights in South Asia

Despite differences in regime type, religious and ethnic diversity, size, and power, the states of South Asia reflect a remarkably similar human rights profile. In all the states of the region police abuse, torture, rape, extra-judicial killings, and custodial violence are pervasive, prison conditions are deplorable, and the failure of the police to protect minorities, women, children, and bonded labor is common. This human rights environment is largely a product of the extreme poverty of the region, the survival of repressive colonial statutes and traditions, a poorly paid, badly trained, under-equipped, largely illiterate, and corrupt police and paramilitary force, and a political elite determined to exercise absolute control over political institutions independent of public accountability. This pattern of state behavior is a major source of alienation and contributes to the problem of developing political legitimacy. It has also led to an internally driven human rights movement, external pressures, and public criticism by foreign governments and international human rights organizations.

The human rights record of the states of South Asia tends to be least satisfactory in those states that are facing major internal insurgencies. These insurgencies are the result of the over-centralization of power, highly personalized styles of rule, the rise of ethnic and religious chauvinism, unchecked majoritarianism, and group fears of a loss of ethnic, religious, or tribal identity. The rise of insurgencies tends to be seen by elites as a threat to the identity of the state and is dealt with primarily by repression rather than accommodation or negotiations. Insurgencies are used by regimes to justify the introduction of a variety of repressive security statutes, preventive detention laws, and special powers acts that transcend existing constitutional guarantees. These repressive acts lead to a variety of human rights abuses, including arbitrary detention, abductions, faked encounters, incommunicado detentions, custodial rape, torture, and death, and extra-judicial executions.

The problem of domestic insurgencies in South Asia is compounded by the fact that religious, ethnic, linguistic, and tribal identities overlap state boundaries. This overlap transforms these domestic insurgencies into potential interstate conflicts as neighbors offer political, economic, moral, and military support to insurgents. As a result, ethnonationalism has the potential to explode into interstate conflict in a region where boundaries and old animosities continue to be a source of international tensions.

The states of South Asia have also begun to experience the rise of religious and ethnic majoritarianism. The most acute problem of minority rights exists in Pakistan, where the rise of Islamic fundamentalism has resulted in conflict between Muslims and the Ahmadiya community, the majority Sunni community and the minority Shi'as, and the use of blasphemy laws against Christians and other religious minorities. In India the rise of Hindu nationalism has come increasingly to threaten the large minority Muslim community, the Sikhs, and even the small Christian community, which has recently come under attack from the Sangh Parivar. In Bangladesh, the issue of the Biharis and Chittagong hills tribals has plagued the country ever since its creation. The problems of Muslims in Sri Lanka, Bangladeshis in India, and minorities throughout the region continue to create a human rights crisis in South Asia.

Those who support the state and oppose Western interference in the region as a form of neocolonialism look forward to a time when rising economic growth will enable the state to resist Western pressures, sanctions, and conditional aid. They also see the rising gap between rich and poor in the West as weakening social solidarity and tolerance and creating the same kind of social conflict in the West that now exists in South Asia. This grow-ing Balkan syndrome, they argue, will gradually erode Western notions of human rights and reduce Western interference and neocolonialism in the Third World.

The groups and institutions in South Asia that see human rights in terms of a set of more universalistic values have become major supporters of a domestic human rights agenda. In all the states of South Asia the major sup-porters of human rights are the courts, the print media, the rising foreign-funded NGO community, local human rights organizations, and state-created national human rights commissions. While each of these groups and institu-tions benefits from broad-based moral and political support from the West, the groups most amenable to external nurturing are the local human rights organizations and NGOs. These are the advocacy groups that are in the best position to influence the local human rights agenda and debate, sup-port human rights principles, and strengthen the role of national human rights commissions. It is only through strong, locally based support that a human rights agenda has any hope of gaining widespread public accep-tance in South Asia.

The development of a global human rights agenda also requires the West to set a consistent example on human rights, help strengthen the rule of law, pluralism, and democracy, and provide continued support for the develop-ment of locally based human rights advocacy groups capable of monitoring developments, pressing for policy reform, and acting as a voice for human rights principles.

Chapter 9
Southeast Asia

Clark D. Neher

Human rights have become important to Southeast Asian citizens and their leaders because the Western world, in particular the United States, has argued that modern nations must adhere to certain principles. Western leaders believe that, because the world is increasingly interdependent politically and economically, universal values of human rights must be followed by nations that expect to be viewed as democratic and modern. Modern technology has shrunk the world. A global society has emerged that is led by a "world culture" that is predominantly Western. Since the end of the Cold War, for example, free enterprise has emerged as the consensus "superior" economic system, while democracy is the accepted "best" governmental system. The rights of citizens to live in freedom are viewed as obvious, even by societies formally oppressed.

The ten Southeast Asian nations have not been left out of the Western worldview. However, their responses to Western human rights values have differed from one nation to another. These notions of interdependence and convergence do not neatly fit the Southeast Asian milieu. Not only are the Southeast Asian nations not reaching consensus about human rights and democratization, but the leaders of some of these nations are also assiduously opposing their spread.

Diversity in Southeast Asia

All too often, analysts refer to Southeast Asia as if it were an identifiable entity about which one can generalize. Although the goal of political scientists is to find uniformities and patterns, generalizations across the nations of Southeast Asia confuse more than clarify. This remarkable region includes nations with fundamentally different histories, including French colonization (Vietnam, Cambodia, Laos), British colonization (Malaysia, Singapore, Burma, Brunei), Dutch colonization (Indonesia), Spanish and U.S. colonization (Philippines), and independence (Thailand). The people worship according to the traditions of Islam (Indonesia, Brunei, Malaysia), Christianity (Philippines), Hinayana Buddhism (Burma, Thailand, Laos, Cambodia), Mahayana Buddhism (Vietnam), and Taoism and Confucianism (Singapore). I have simplified a complex set of beliefs and understated the diversity of religious views in each of the countries. The nations today practice semi-democracy (Thailand, Philippines, Indonesia), "soft" authoritarianism (Singapore, Malaysia), Communist authoritarianism (Vietnam, Laos), military dictatorship (Burma), and absolute monarchy (Brunei).

Finding patterns in Southeast Asia is difficult because the region is constantly changing. In contemporary times, for example, Indonesia has been transformed from military dictatorship to semi-democratic rule. Since 1997 Thailand has moved from being the world's fastest growing economy to negative growth rates. Malaysia has moved from democracy to authoritarianism. The Communist regimes in Vietnam and Laos have opened their economies to free enterprise. Cambodia was taken over by the United Nations and had a semi-democratic government installed, which in turn evolved into a civilian dictatorship and at present a semi-democratic government. The Philippines moved from the dictatorship of Ferdinand Marcos to the democracy of Corazon Aquino, Fidel Ramos, and Joseph Estrada. The Burmese voted for democratic rule, but the military refused to give up power and denied their choice. The changes are stunning, rapid, and unpredictable.

Human Rights Diversity in Southeast Asia

Diversity also marks the way Southeast Asian nations practice human rights. Southeast Asian leaders differ markedly about the norms and rules that they believe should govern their societies. The nations differ regarding rights of individuals and groups face-to-face with the power and authority of the rulers. The standard Western definition of human rights is based on presumed universal rights: equality of rights without discrimination; protection of life, liberty, and security of all persons; protection against slavery; protection against torture and cruel and inhuman punishment; presumption of innocence; protection of privacy, family, and home; freedom of thought, conscience, and religion. Using this definition, the nations of Thailand and the Philippines have a generally positive record. At the other extreme, Burma, Vietnam, Laos, and Cambodia violate human rights. Indonesia, Brunei, Singapore, and Malaysia have mixed records at the present time. For a summary of each country's record on human rights see the 1998 *Human Rights Watch World Report.*

Westerners claim that human rights are universal, whereas many Southeast Asian leaders view their societies as sufficiently different to justify divergent normative prescriptions. Indeed, these Southeast Asian leaders believe that the West is bullying Asia to adopt Western values even though they are "inappropriate" for Asian societies. Every time the U.S. State Department issues its annual human rights report, these leaders vociferously complain that Southeast Asia does not need to follow the "distorted" human rights views of U.S. policy-makers.

From the viewpoint of Southeast Asian citizens, in contrast to the region's leaders, it is Southeast Asians themselves, not Westerners, who are most vigorously fighting for human rights and democracy in their respective countries. From their point of view, the Western powers have been only half-heartedly supportive of human rights. Western leaders offer limited rhetorical support for human rights, and only if they perceive that such support will not undermine stability or anti-Communist regimes. Hence, there is little, if any, consensus on the meaning of human rights in Southeast Asia among the region's leaders, between the leaders and their followers, and between the leaders and Western spokespersons.

According to UN documents, human rights are the claims that all human beings are justly entitled to make merely by virtue of their being human. From this perspective, human rights and democracy are intertwined: democracies require the observance of human rights, and the observance of human rights requires democracy. The universalist view is that human rights are absolute and inalienable entitlements of all people to human dignity and are not subject to limitation. As stated above these entitlements include respect for human life, and justice and equality before the law (Chew 1994, 933–34).

In Southeast Asia there is no consensus among the political elites that democracies require human rights and vice versa. Elites have pointed out that democracy and human rights adherence do not always occur together and that democratically elected leaders can violate human rights if these "so-called rights" undermine more important goals such as economic development. For example, Kishore Mahbubani, a leading scholar and diplomat in Singapore, argues that the West's human rights campaign is unlikely to benefit people who live outside the developed world. He suggests that the campaign for human rights could aggravate rather than ameliorate the difficult conditions under which the vast majority of the world's population live (Mahbubani 1993, 159). Former Prime Minister Lee Kuan Yew of Singapore, Prime Minister Mahathir bin Mohamed of Malaysia, and former President Suharto of Indonesia have stressed that each community must decide for itself which rights are appropriate. They view universalist arguments as a form of cultural imperialism. In their view nations should be allowed to interpret and implement their human rights goals according to their own circumstances, such as the level of economic development. In Bangkok in 1993, the ministers of state of the Southeast Asian nations affirmed that human rights must be considered in the context of a "dynamic and evolving process . . . bearing in mind the significance of national and regional particularities and various historical, cultural, and religious backgrounds" (Kelly and Reid 1998, 5).

This "relativist" view of human rights is called the "Asian Way," to differentiate "Asian" values from Western values such as individualism, materialism, and democracy. Mahathir has been particularly outspoken in his disdain for Western ways. He abhors the West's high rates of violent crime, divorce, drug use, and homelessness. He argues that Southeast Asians do not want to emulate such pathologies, most of which in his view are because of the West's emphasis on individual rights. Leaders who proclaim the Asian Way accept that the standard of living in the United States is superior to that of Malaysia and other Southeast Asian nations, "if standard of living means the number of square feet in one's home, or the number of channels on one's television." But, they note, if standard of living means not being afraid to go outside that large home after dark, or not worrying about what filth one's children will see on all those television channels, then Asian societies have the higher standard. From this perspective, Asian cultural values are deemed not only different from Western values, but superior to them.

Asian leaders champion the notion of an Asian Way to gain legitimacy for their regimes. They argue that liberal democratic politics are inappropriate for Asians more attuned to the ideals of harmony and consensus. They suggest that paternalistic rule is the proper role for societies that are less developed than the West. They argue that economic development must precede political liberalization and that economic rights are as important as political rights. They note that the economic success of Asian nations is attributable to the superiority of Asian values and that Japan, South Korea, and Taiwan represent the proper nations to emulate. The Asian Way is said to provide a basis for economic development without having to undergo the worst aspects of Westernization such as materialism, sexual shenanigans, racial discrimination, and high crime rates. Leaders such as Lee Kuan Yew assert that Southeast Asia will never become like America with its reputation for philandering presidents, violent street gangs, child mass murderers, and overweight couch potatoes.

Of course, to believe that Asian values are responsible for the astounding Southeast Asian economic miracle (until the Asian crisis of 1997) one would have to accept that a common core of distinctively Asian values exists and that Asian leaders have accurately portrayed these values. Neither of these assumptions is tenable. The most important characteristic of Southeast Asian societies, as noted above, is the area's great diversity. The following is an example of a "common core of distinctively Asian values" that, in reality, does little to explain economic growth—Asians are fatalistic and deferential. That characterization flies in the face of numerous examples of the people's revolts against their leaders: Filipino People Power in 1986 and 2001; the rise of civilian South Koreans against the military in 1987; the dramatic revolution of the Burmese against their oppressive dictatorship in 1988 and their subsequent remarkable vote for democracy in 1990; the unprecedented uprising of the Chinese at Tiananmen Square in 1989; the

Thai people's struggle against the military in 1992; and the mass insurrection of the Indonesians against their long-serving President Suharto in 1998. These examples undermine the notion that Asians fatalistically know their place.

While a listing of uprisings against the state is telling, the other side of the argument notes that most Thais quietly acquiesced to the 1991 military coup carried out by General Suchinda Krapayoon. The Thais accepted Suchinda's assertion that the civilian government was corrupt and had to be changed. (A short time later, they rose in wrath against Suchinda's acceptance of the position of prime minister.) The most popular recent Thai prime minister, Anand Panyarachun, was not elected. He was popular because he was effective and honest, not because he came to power by democratic means. Also revealing is that, only six years after Imelda Marcos and Eduardo Cojuangco fled the Philippines in ignominy, they obtained more combined votes in the 1992 presidential election than the winner Fidel Ramos (Kausikan 1994, 49).

The debate between universalists and Asian Way advocates intensified following the economic crisis that began in Thailand in 1997 and subsequently spread throughout the region. Universalists saw the crisis as evidence that Western ways were indeed superior and that the Asian leaders' vaunted emphasis on economic development to the exclusion of human rights was no more than a rationalization for perpetuating their power. The universalists saw corruption and lack of transparency within the Southeast Asian governments. That observation supported their view that Asian ways were inferior and that the world's democracies did not suffer from the weaknesses of the East.

The debate was further exacerbated by Southeast Asian majority attacks on ethnic minorities (in particular urban Chinese) that stemmed from the Asian economic crisis. Western human rights advocates noted that the economic crisis brought about instability and violence to such a degree that minorities were no longer safe. They also suggested that Asian values were not sufficiently adaptable to keep governments ruling effectively in times of crisis and to provide human rights protections to all citizens. For example, the crisis led to the overthrow of President Suharto in Indonesia and attacks against Chinese Indonesians. Proponents of Asian values noted that if Suharto had not been ousted he would have been able to stop the violence against minorities, whereas open government weakened the regime's capacity to resolve the crisis in an expeditious manner.

The irony is that most Southeast Asian leaders proclaim their adherence to human rights, even while violating them. The fact that even the military autocrats in Burma find it useful in their rhetoric to support the notion of human rights suggests that consensus exists about what is "right" in contemporary times. The fact that they abuse such rights willy-nilly suggests that there is a long struggle ahead. Whether or not a consensus exists, the leaders of Southeast Asia who support the Asian Way fail to understand that it is not simply Western human rights advocates who are bringing "individualism" to Southeast Asia. Instead, it may be the inexorable process of industrialization and urbanization that produces increasing individualization of society. Modernization is an irreversible process that is generally accompanied by an intensifying and broadening focus on human rights. This "world culture" is increasingly Western, like it or not.

The claim by Southeast Asian leaders such as Lee Kuan Yew, Mahathir, and Suharto that there are no universal rights suggests that Asians are somehow not ready for democracy and that they have a high tolerance for authoritarian rule. That patronizing position is insulting to Southeast Asians and underestimates their willingness to struggle for their rights. Moreover, democracy already exists in Asian countries such as India, Japan, and the Philippines, so there is no inevitability about authoritarian ways in Asian societies.

Adherence to human rights does not automatically legitimate Southeast Asian governments in the minds of the ruled. Instead, legitimacy comes primarily from a government's capacity to bring about stability and economic development and to govern moderately. In those countries where governments "cross the line" to gross corruption or dictatorial rule, the citizenry will view the regime as illegitimate if they believe the extreme nature of the regime threatens economic development and stable governance. Few Burmese, for example, view the military dictatorship as legitimate, because the leaders there have not met the needs of the people. Suharto lost legitimacy when the citizenry observed the out-of-control corruption of his immediate family and cronies and the catastrophic decline in the people's standard of living. Thais rose against Suchinda when he went against his promise, declared himself prime minister, and imperiled the rapid economic growth rates hitherto enjoyed by the people. Human rights play a role in legitimating regimes only when they are viewed as intertwined with effective governance and economic development. ASEAN's recent admittance of the three nations that most flagrantly abuse human rights—Burma, Vietnam, and Cambodia—indicates that for the security alliance human rights are peripheral when contrasted with perceived economic advantages.

The Asian financial crisis has undermined Southeast Asian governments' legitimacy far more than perceived human rights violations. The crisis led to changes or attempted changes in government in every Southeast Asian nation except Brunei (an absolute monarchy) and Singapore (soft-authoritarian). In Thailand, for example, Prime Minister Chavalit Yongchaiyudh was ousted for not dealing with the economic crisis successfully. Joseph Estrada was elected Philippine president on the basis of his populist message to Filipinos who were hurt by the crisis. The financial crisis was directly responsible for the overthrow of Suharto, who had led Indonesia for more than thirty years. A civilian government was later elected in 1999. Cambodia was forced to incorporate opposition in the government, and

Laos completed a leadership transition. Le Kha Phieu became head of the Vietnamese Communist Party Politburo, and conservatism returned to Vietnam when the traditional Vietnamese Communist Party leaders argued that the crisis proved that Western free enterprise was unstable. Even Burma's dictators felt they had to convert the State Law and Order Restoration Council (SLORC) to the State Peace and Development Council (SPDC). Fourteen members of the old SLORC were retired to "root out endemic corruption."

Thailand

The overall human rights record in Thailand has been positive, with improvements in labor laws that prohibit child labor and sex discrimination and that regulate working hours, overtime, and benefits. The role of the armed forces has diminished since 1992, and the army is increasingly professional. A variety of NGO human rights groups and a vibrant, outspoken press exist in Thailand to monitor potential violations. The rise of NGOs is a particularly striking aspect of civil society in Thailand. In January 2001, Thaksin Shinawatra became prime minister. He has shown authoritarian tendencies and has used his vast wealth (from telecommunications) and political power to oppress the media. This is disturbing to Thais, who desire to keep their open press.

Despite its positive human rights record, Thailand has serious intrasocietal conflict. The most serious human rights issue in Thailand is the government's treatment of refugees, including some thousands of Burmese, many of whom have fled into Thai territory to escape the military dictatorship in Burma. In addition to these new refugees, a half million other displaced persons reside in Thailand and are vulnerable to arrest and deportation. Thai authorities argue that Thailand is a poor nation that cannot afford the high costs of taking care of refugees. They argue that the refugees also undermine Thai relations with Burma, a nation with which it shares two thousand miles of border. In January 2000, Thais killed members of a Karen refugee group that had taken a hospital (including the doctors, nurses, and patients) hostage in Ratchaburi. Although the killing of the perpetrators appeared to be execution-style, Thais enthusiastically supported their government's policy to crack down on violence-oriented refugees, even if they were escaping from an oppressive country.

Human rights advocates have argued that although the Thai government has legitimate security concerns, those concerns do not justify acts that endanger refugees (Human Rights Watch 2000a, 1). Thai government leaders responded that they desired to reduce the number of Burmese refugees in Bangkok to preclude destabilization and to regulate more closely the movements of Burmese refugees who the Thai government believed were seriously undermining the Thai economy. Thai leaders responded mildly to the siege of the Burmese embassy in Bangkok in October 1999, but violently to the takeover by Burmese insurgents of the Ratchaburi provincial hospital several months later. The sieges were the work of small, radical organizations, but the Thai government used the incidents to justify a wider crackdown.

The Thai government has not signed the 1951 Convention Relating to the Status of Refugees, nor does it have its own domestic refugee law. The UN High Commissioner on Refugees has pressed the Thai government to accept a broader definition of persons fleeing conflict that would include forced relocations, porterage, and labor. Thus far Thailand has not based its decisions on whether the conditions that forced Burmese to flee are such that they are deserving of refugee protection.

In 2000 the Thai government was chosen by free elections within the context of civil liberties. The prime minister, Chuan Leekpai, led the Democrats, Thailand's leading political party, and fashioned a coalition that brought about his ascendancy to the top position. His most vociferous supporters have been the middle-class, educated, urban constituencies in Bangkok and persons living in the southern provinces where Chuan was born and raised. These supporters have been imbued with the notion that democracy and human rights are the hallmark of "modern" societies and that military rule and oppression are anachronistic.

Burma

Burma is particularly tragic because the nation has bountiful resources and a highly literate, industrious population. Burma is ruled by the military. Lieutenant General Khin Nyunt, Secretary-One, shares power with General Than Schwe, the official head of state. Followers of General Ne Win, Burma's leader for twenty-six years, have led Burma to isolation and economic catastrophe. The army runs every aspect of life in Burma, even taking 40 percent of the national budget. Because the economy is run by the military, the top generals have placed themselves on the boards of directors of joint venture companies, and they have direct involvement in heroin production. The military leaders are corrupt and live in luxury. The contrast between their high life and the disastrous life of the masses is staggering.

In Burma the human rights problems are far deeper than in Thailand. The authorities have arrested persons attending National League for Democracy (NLD) meetings and arrested opposition leaders such as Aung San Suu Kyi (who was lawfully elected in 1990 to head a government led by the NLD). Burmese prison conditions are dreadful, and numerous prisoners have died from abuse. The army is the chief instrument of repression, and torture is used to control society.

The SPDC does not recognize the concept of human rights in its policies, but does in its rhetoric. There is no freedom of assembly, no workers' rights (unions and strikes are illegal), no freedom of the press (the military controls newspapers, radio, internet, and television), persecution of political opponents (virtually all the winners in the 1990 elections have been executed, imprisoned, or exiled), ethnic cleansing and the deliberate creation of refugees, brutal treatment of tribal groups, and forced labor. For a thorough analysis of human rights in Burma see Marlay and Ulmer (2000, 1–14).

Extreme conditions in Burma stem from many sources. Traditional Burmese culture has emphasized the status of those in authority and the low position of commoners. Human rights abuses also come from the extraordinary isolation of the country from the rest of the world, so that outsiders have virtually no influence over domestic policy, and such policy is not well known or understood outside Burmese borders. More important, the military rulers have established a garrison state ideology that is akin to xenophobia. Any disagreement with military rulers is viewed as tantamount to treason. Army officers have carved out their own regional fiefdoms, taken over lucrative logging concessions, become involved in drug trafficking, and doubled as business executives. To give up their power would be to give up their wealth (Marlay and Ulmer 2000, 7–10).

In Burma, those fleeing to Thailand were primarily members of minority groups such as the Karen, Kachin, and Shan. The Burmese military dictatorship has engaged in systematic mass detentions of these minorities as well as extra-judicial executions, forced labor, forced relocations, and violations of freedoms such as the right to free association and expression. No indigenous human rights groups are allowed. The abuse of human rights in Burma is deeply rooted and entrenched throughout the country, but especially against minorities and their supporters. On the western side of the nation, a quarter of a million Muslim Rohingya refugees live in Bangladesh as a result of human rights abuses by the Burmese military.

Thus far no international forces have been able to mitigate Burma's atrocious human rights record. The Clinton administration argued that trade sanctions should be applied to Burma (but not to China). New U.S. investment in Burma is prohibited, but there is no evidence that this has altered Burmese policy. The U.S. State Department has indicated that sanctions will remain in effect until there is movement toward democracy and respect for human rights. Even foreign aid has been negligible. Despite these acts, Burma was admitted to the Association of Southeast Asian Nations (ASEAN) by the other Southeast Asian governments on the grounds that "engaging" the generals was the most effective way of persuading them to treat their citizens more humanely (Marlay and Ulmer 2000, 10). Again, there is no evidence that this strategy has achieved its ends.

Vietnam

Vietnam's human rights record is strikingly improved since the advent of Doi Moi (renovation) in 1986. However, the Vietnamese Communist Party

(VCP) continues to rule without formal opposition and periodically re-presses dissidents and religious leaders. All religious and cultural activity must be approved by the state. Travel is restricted, human rights NGOs are banned, press freedom curtailed, and independent associations and trade unions not allowed. There is no systematic legal system to guarantee the rights of the people. Corruption purges have been used, in part, to target party leaders advocating economic reforms while hard-line conservatives are not held accountable (Human Rights Watch 2000b, 2). Communication among dissidents is hampered by the interception of mail, telephone calls, and Internet accounts.

Despite this dismal record Vietnam has made great strides. Listening to foreign broadcast programs is no longer viewed as a security concern. Members of the overseas Vietnamese community are no longer followed and oppressed when they travel to Vietnam. The government has cracked down on corrupt officials. There is new concern about environmental problems, AIDS, prostitution, the decline of the educational system, and the huge wealth gap between cities and countryside. Newspapers are still controlled, but occasionally there are articles critical of a particular government policy. Tens of thousands of political detainees and reeducation camp prisoners have been released.

Cambodia

Cambodia has been a human rights disaster for decades, culminating in the horrendous years of the Khmer Rouge, whose genocidal policies from 1975 to 1979 physically and psychologically scarred the Cambodians up to the present. The degree of repression under the Khmer Rouge including torture, brutality, family breakdown, religious persecution, destruction of minorities, and widespread executions (perhaps two million persons), was so vast that subsequent governments, no matter how repressive, look positive in contrast. The UN intervention in 1993 helped Cambodia achieve a better human rights record. In 1998 elections were held, but they were preceded by widespread voter intimidation and largely controlled by the ruling authorities. In contrast to Burma, where human rights organizations are banned, Cambodian organizations are active.

Intra-societal abuses against minorities in Cambodia focused on the Vietnamese. Cambodian politicians, including Prime Minister Hun Sen, railed against the Vietnamese who have for centuries been considered enemies of the Cambodians. Government anti-Vietnamese raids were carried out partially as a cover for their attempts to root out the opposition. Although human rights violations were focused on opposition politicians and their supporters, minorities have suffered disproportionately from government-supported abuse.

Malaysia

Malaysia's human rights record has been relatively positive, at least compared to that in Burma, Laos, Cambodia, and Vietnam. However in 1998, Prime Minister Mahathir cracked down on dissidents and leaders he believed threatened his premier position. In September 1998 he had Deputy Prime Minister Anwar Ibrahim, his heir apparent, arrested under the Internal Security Act (ISA). Anwar was accused of corruption and sexual indiscretions. He was beaten in prison by the security forces. The Mahathir government has often used the ISA against political opponents. Malaysia's human rights record further deteriorated in 1998 with the mass deportation and use of excessive force against Indonesian detainees. Police arrested persons without trial, including a number of Anwar's allies. A government crackdown on opposition meetings restricted freedom of assembly.

Mahathir has supported restrictions on freedom of expression, quashed the nation's traditional separate judiciary, banned meetings of oppositionists, and curtailed the press, making it illegal to speak out on "sensitive" issues including the Anwar affair. The economic downturn became an official rationale for arrests of migrants. Nongovernmental organizations came under increasing criticism from government leaders who ascribed seditious motives to NGO leaders. Human rights groups remained active, despite periodic harassment from the government (Marlay and Ulmer 2000, 200). The U.S. State Department 1998 Country Report noted no reports of government sponsored extrajudicial killings or politically motivated disappearances, although there have been numerous reports of police brutality.

Singapore

Singapore does not fit the pattern that shows that a high standard of living is correlated with democracy and strong human rights. Singapore has the highest standard of living in Southeast Asia and is approaching the Western European nations and the United States in per capita income. Nevertheless, the nation has chosen "soft authoritarianism" rather than democracy. The "Singapore School" of human rights states that human dignity is best achieved by a political regime dedicated to social order and rapid economic growth. To achieve those goals, many rights such as free expression, free association, multiparty elections, and free press are sacrificed (Chew 1994, 934).

United States citizens became aware of Singapore's notion of human rights with the Michael Fay case. He received six strokes of the cane for vandalism. Singaporeans argued that the punishment was not necessarily appropriate to the crime. Instead, the punishment was designed to protect the community as a whole and to act as a deterrent (Chew 1994, 934). Lee

Kuan Yew stated that following Western style human rights policies would lead Singapore "down the drain," with people in the streets, more drugs, more crime, more delinquency, and a poorer economy. Such assertions did not keep international publications from detailing the country's violations of human rights, including the use of preventive detention, media restrictions, imprisonment without trial, restrictions on freedom of movement, union organization and speech, mistreatment of detainees, and harassment of opposition politicians. Parliamentary debates are monitored and circumscribed and the judiciary is not independent of the executive branch (Chew 1994, 942). There have been no extra-judicial killings or disappearances and no report of torture. However, the law allows arrests without warrant and detention without trial under the Internal Security Act (ISA).

The leaders of the People's Action Party (PAP) have acquiesced to Lee Kuan Yew's "Confucianist" notion of government: order, stability, and hierarchy are essential values for economic growth, and Western practices of human rights undermine these values. Prime Minister Goh Chok Tong, Lee's successor, has continued "soft authoritarianism" despite his initial promise to be a more "gentle" leader than Lee.

Indonesia

Under President Suharto, primarily domestic matters defined Indonesian stability and national security. The highest priority has been for stability, at least until Suharto's demise in 1998 and the rise of a civilian government led by President Abdurrahman Wahid. The independence struggles in East Timor, Aceh, and Irian Jaya have once again caused authorities to see stability as crucial. That priority could undermine advances made in support of human rights in Indonesia. The years 1998–99 were tumultuous as interim President B. J. Habibie released political prisoners, lifted political controls, and organized free elections. Indonesia signed important human rights treaties, allowed political parties to form, freed the media, and allowed East Timor to achieve independence. Human rights NGOs formed and flourished in the new era of openness. Extrajudicial killings and disappearances, prominent under Suharto, ended under Habibie and Abdurrahman Wahid. In the last months of 2001, Wahid was ousted as president and replaced by Megawati Sukarnoputri. It is too early to know how her presidency will affect human rights in Indonesia.

Under Suharto, human rights were peripheral to the power struggles and priorities of the nation's leaders. Human rights politics in Indonesia was clearly underdeveloped, a function more of leadership personalities and policies than a formal set of values accepted as basic to Indonesians as human beings. Human rights were considered a product of an "advanced" stage of westernization that Indonesia had not achieved. New leaders brought about new policies. President Wahid stated that Indonesia had indeed reached this stage, and the Indonesian people enthusiastically concurred. Almost miraculously, the general population fundamentally changed priorities from order to democratization and rights as soon as their new leaders allowed them to do so. How long the concurrence will last is unclear as Indonesia unravels and the people's standard of living does not appreciably improve. Human rights remain a luxury for most rural Indonesians.

Intra-societal human rights abuses have a long history in Indonesia and have been exacerbated since the economic crisis and the subsequent change in government. Violence against the ethnic Chinese has occurred for decades and was fearsome in the mid-1960s, when an estimated 500,000 Chinese were killed following Suharto's rise to power. In recent years, the Chinese were blamed for the economic crisis, forcing many to flee the country. Widespread atrocities have been reported in Aceh province, on the northern tip of Sumatra, and military authorities reportedly carried out killings in East Timor (even after East Timor had achieved an independent status). In the Malukus, Muslim citizens slaughtered several hundred Christians. President Wahid eventually declared martial law in the troubled provinces.

Principal Actors for Human Rights in Southeast Asia

Intra-societal conflict has been at the heart of human rights abuses in Southeast Asia. Targeting minorities by abusers has increased as a result of the financial crisis. Southeast Asian leaders have scapegoated minorities, in particular the indigenous Chinese, blaming them for the economic downturn. Clearly there is a close interrelationship between the state of the economy and intra-societal conflict and human rights. Fortunately nothing approaching ethnic cleansing has occurred in Southeast Asia in the past decade. There are no states so weak that ethnic cleansing can occur. It is impossible to go much beyond such an assertion for Southeast Asia because each nation of the region has handled its human rights agenda differently.

The key actors in Southeast Asian politics are the state leaders. Historically these actors have been the patrons in the ubiquitous patron-client relationships that pervade Southeast Asian societies. Patron-client ties are hierarchical, face-to-face relationships of reciprocity. These groups have formed a network of personal relations that extend throughout Southeast Asia. The network is different from one nation to another. In Thailand and Indonesia the politicians, bureaucrats, Sino-business executives, and military officers have been paramount patrons. In Burma the military has predominated. In Vietnam and Laos Communist Party officials run the network. In the Philippines landowners, politicians, and bureaucrats are the major political actors. In Singapore civilian politicians with personal ties to Lee Kuan Yew are central. In all these nations personalism is more important than institutions. For these actors human rights considerations are secondary to the more important considerations of regime and societal stability, economic development, and effective governance.

The principal actors are elites. However, human rights is an issue that most directly affects minorities, women, dissidents, and the poor. To discuss actors as elites is to approach the matter from only one perspective. To understand the issue of human rights in Southeast Asia, one has to go to the margins. Talk to Bangkok businesspersons about political legitimacy, and they will talk about stability, exchange rates, and Thailand's image abroad. Talk to a worker in Klong Toey, Bangkok's major slum, and you hear about unemployment, inflation, and corrupt politicians. From the vantage point of those at the bottom of the economic ladder, governance, economic growth, and human rights are more closely intertwined than from the point of view of the elites.

In Thailand, where human rights are flourishing, there is even consensus about the one area where free speech is limited—the role of His Majesty the King. Thais believe that *lese majesté* is appropriate. Both defenders and critics of the society endorse this constraint on freedom of expression. Oppositionists, then, must find battles where there will be less resistance and that are locally acceptable (Bauer and Bell 1999, 15). This Thai example illustrates a belief found throughout Southeast Asia that human rights are not necessarily the priority issue. Lee Kuan Yew argued that position when he stated, "his task was to lift his country out of the degradation that poverty, ignorance, and disease had wrought. All other things became secondary" (Bauer and Bell 1999, 7).

The military generals control every aspect of politics and economics in Burma. They know that, given a free election, the opposition would win another landslide victory. They have arrested, exiled, or executed much of the opposition, but they have not yet executed Aung San Suu Kyi, the leader of the National League for Democracy and the most prominent person in Burma. She has not been touched, partly because of her vast international reputation and partly because the generals are not sure about the loyalty of their underlings. If she were to be hurt, it is possible that soldiers would turn against their leaders and create a civil war.

To ensure the perpetuation of their power, the generals have closed Burma's universities (except for technical and engineering colleges where approved students can attend). Since Burma is largely rural, there is little organized demonstration for economic betterment among industrial workers. The dictators have coopted leaders of ethnic minorities and have killed dissidents. The short-term prognosis for improved human rights is bleak.

International Strategies for Human Rights

The region's preoccupation with the Asian economic crisis has kept human rights concerns on the back burner since mid-1997. Even the region's principal security alliance, the Association of Southeast Asian Nations, placed economics at the forefront of its concerns. Since the end of the war in Vietnam and the demise of the Cold War, ASEAN has not, as a group, rallied against any direct threat to the sovereignty of the member nations. Nor has ASEAN, as an organization, focused its energies on human rights issues. Burma, Vietnam, Laos, and Cambodia, the region's major violators of human rights, were all admitted to ASEAN by 1998. When Thai Foreign Minister Surin Pitsuwan proposed a change in practice that would allow member states to raise critical questions about each other's policies, a proposal called "flexible engagement," ASEAN leaders quickly rejected the proposal (Human Rights Watch 1998, 159). The ASEAN members argued that they were reluctant to become involved in the "domestic" policies of member states including human rights policies. They argued that Western isolation of Burma's State Peace and Development Council (SPDC) and Western trading sanctions were discriminatory and counterproductive (Human Rights Watch 1998, 169–70).

International organizations have not played significant roles in determining the human rights policies of Southeast Asian nations. The one arguable exception is Western policies toward Burma that have included limited sanctions and the political isolation of the SPDC, Burma's military dictatorship. The United States and other Western nations have boycotted Burma's economy. SPDC leaders were banned from visiting European Union countries. The European Commission decided in 1997 to suspend trading benefits to Burma and to exclude Burma from participation in numerous conferences. Despite these international policies, designed to place pressure on the Burmese government to improve its human rights record, European investments continued to flow into Burma. A huge gas pipeline project across Burma was completed by the French oil company Total, in partnership with the U.S. corporation Unocal. In addition, China remained Burma's main trading partner and arms supplier, so the Western boycott was not effective in changing Burma's human rights direction.

The point is that even in Burma international action for improved human rights has been ineffective. U.S. sanctions have certainly denied Burma foreign investment and loans. Nevertheless the sanctions have not kept ASEAN countries, Japan, and South Korea from conducting economic relations. Most important, China has remained close to Burma and has supported its economy. As long as the United States desires to improve its relations with China, there will be no meaningful pressure on China to end its support for the Burmese generals.

International attention on human rights problems in Cambodia has been ineffective because the global focus has remained on the nation's terrible economic conditions and on acquiescence to the existing political regime led by Hun Sen. The nation's fragility has caused international organizations to ignore the government's abuses of human rights (Human Rights

Watch 1998, 192–94). The United Nations did coordinate the deployment of observers for the 1998 elections, but the organization could not stop the widespread election fraud. The European Union contributed some $11 million for voter registration in Cambodia, then issued a resolution noting the rapidly deteriorating human rights climate in Cambodia and "called on all parties to work together" to halt the violence (Human Rights Watch 1998, 176). However, the resolution had no teeth and was generally ignored. Although the United States had suspended aid to Cambodia after Hun Sen's 1997 coup against his co-prime minister, Norodom Rannarridh, the suspension was lifted after the 1998 elections. The Cambodian government has allowed indigenous human rights NGOs, but they are viewed as ineffective in changing regime policies.

Except for the International Monetary Fund (IMF), international agencies played virtually no role in forcing out President Suharto. Instead the Asian economic crisis and domestic groups, chiefly students, were responsible for his downfall. Once he was out of office, the international community rallied to the support of East Timorese independence fighters. Under interim president B. J. Habibie, political prisoners were released and human rights treaties signed. The U.S. Pentagon suspended a joint defense program with Jakarta when evidence was presented that the Indonesian military had abused human rights, but that decision was not crucial for overthrowing Suharto.

The U.S. State Department has criticized the use of the Malaysian ISA to restrict the rights of citizens. Neighboring states, led by Indonesian President Habibie and Philippine President Estrada, both friends of sacked Deputy Prime Minister Anwar, criticized Malaysia. There is no evidence that Prime Minister Mahathir was swayed by these criticisms. He spoke against foreign meddlers who were involved, unconscionably in his view, in Malaysian politics, the implication being that he would dig his heels in rather than to accede to outside pressures for change.

Thailand has emerged in the past several years as the center of human rights activities. Numerous human rights NGOs have been established, with headquarters in Bangkok. Thailand's open press and human rights organizations raised issues throughout the region. Much of the activism centered on neighboring countries because Thailand's own human rights record was relatively satisfactory. The IMF played an important role (contributing $270 million of a $17 billion rescue package) in assisting Thailand's efforts to resolve the economic crisis, but played no role in human rights policies.

The picture in Vietnam regarding international involvement in human rights policies was considerably different from that in Thailand. The World Bank, IMF, Asian Development Bank, and UN Development Program all have supported international aid packages to Vietnam, while pressing for economic and legal reform, privatization of state-owned companies, measures to address corruption, and greater financial transparency (Human

Rights Watch 1998, 216). In the first known intervention by Japan with Hanoi in the case of a political prisoner, the Ministry of Foreign Affair's appeal on behalf of a prominent dissident, Doan Viet Hoat, helped bring about his release in 1998. Despite minor improvements in human rights policies, Vietnam continued to detain critics and suppressed all religious activity that was not state approved. Human rights NGOs have not been allowed.

Vietnam's human rights policies were influenced by international organizations because the regime was dedicated to the policy of renovation, and desired legitimacy from its own population and from other nations. Formally the Vietnamese Ministry of Foreign Affairs rejected linkage between foreign aid and human rights. Vietnam insisted that human rights are part of its own internal affairs and are inherently connected with the country's history, culture, traditions, and socioeconomic conditions (Ninh 1998, 457). When Human Rights Watch published its criticism of Vietnam's human rights record, the Vietnamese responded: "There is no violation of freedoms of speech, press, expression, or *silencing of dissent* . . . in Vietnam as mentioned in the Human Rights report. Everyone has the same legal and constitutional rights and duties and transgressors are all prosecuted according to the law" (Human Rights Watch 2000b, 2–3). Vietnam did release some prisoners, opened its economy, and even received U.S. praise for these efforts.

Conclusion

Foreign policy analysts include three distinct schools of thoughts regarding human rights in Southeast Asia. The first believes that human rights should be *the* primary issue. Numerous NGOs, many U.S. foreign policy-makers, and only a few Southeast Asian government leaders, primarily in the Philippines, hold this view. The second school believes that human rights are significant, but not primary, and subordinated to various other issues and goals. This view predominates throughout Southeast Asia even among those officials who hold that human rights are fundamental to all human beings. However when other considerations arise, such as economic development and national security, human rights become secondary. The third school argues that human rights are not relevant in Southeast Asia. No one publicly states such a position, although government leaders in Burma, for example, practice that principle.

Human rights in Southeast Asia are no longer simply domestic issues. The ten states are now affected by the international community and by the forces of globalization. This is no longer an era of national sovereignty. Indeed, there has been an erosion of national sovereignty that has given international bodies and superpowers influence over human rights policies in Southeast Asia. The problem is that sometimes the U.S. allies violate human rights that make it difficult to respond meaningfully. U.S. support for Marcos, Suharto, Diem, Sarit, and other Southeast Asian violators of human rights makes "human rights" policies appear hypocritical. Moreover many of Southeast Asia's leaders today (Mahathir, Lee Kuan Yew, Than Shwe) claim that U.S. government emphasis on human rights is arrogant and ethnocentric, especially in the face of U.S. unwillingness to weaken its own national sovereignty in human rights matters, as in the U.S. refusal to join various UN conventions. Finally, the U.S. view of human rights, emphasizing political liberties, differs from the Southeast Asian view that emphasizes economic needs.

These differences and problems are reminders that human rights issues can best be solved within Southeast Asia itself, not externally. Second, human rights cannot be thrust on a nation from outside or by an indige-nous leader and remain effective until the rights have been institutionalized through an evolutionary process. This process will take a great deal of time and require patience from human rights spokespersons who must under-stand that human rights are only one aspect of a nation's domestic and foreign policies. Southeast Asian nations must balance human rights con-siderations with many other interests. The region's officials know that their legitimacy is primarily a matter of meeting people's economic needs and retaining stability against outside aggression.

From the Western perspective, Southeast Asia can be divided into three groups based on their leaders' commitment to human rights. Those nations with a positive commitment (circa 2000) include Thailand and the Philip-pines; those with a modicum of commitment include Singapore, Malaysia, Indonesia and Cambodia (both in transition); those with severe abuses of human rights are Burma, Vietnam, Laos, and Brunei. These categories should not ignore the fact that all Southeast Asian nations have less ability to carry out human rights as new global actors wield greater influence. Global corporations have tremendous policy influence in terms of employ-ment, the environment, and in economic policy. However these corpora-tions have little incentive to enhance civil liberties because their goal is profit.

This chapter argues that generalizations about human rights in South-east Asia are difficult to state. Nevertheless some patterns hold. For exam-ple, human rights concerns have been peripheral to most of the nations' leaders. Instead, regime legitimacy has been based primarily on the crea-tion of political stability, economic development, and effective governance. Although each of the ten nations differs over what norms and rules should be invoked to govern their countries, Southeast Asian nations have adopted and adapted the notion of Asian values. These values are not based on Western ideas of human rights. Southeast Asian leaders have used the idea of a separate Asian Way to perpetuate their own power and to rationalize their autocracy.

In Thailand, the Philippines, Singapore, Malaysia, and Indonesia (post-Suharto) there are human rights organizations that play a role in keeping the human rights agenda public. In these countries human rights must be viewed within the larger power struggles and priorities of the regimes and populations. In Vietnam, Laos, Cambodia, Brunei, and Burma such organizations are not allowed and hence the human rights agenda is not a part of these countries' day-to-day power relationships. In Burma, the human rights agenda is paramount, but this is an exceptional case because of Aung San Suu Kyi's national and international renown. Hence the context of human rights politics plays out differently in each country as a consequence of the kind of political system, the domestic power holders, the outside actors, and more general historical and cultural circumstances of the individual states (including the notion of the Asian Way). In Southeast Asia the evolution of human rights politics is underdeveloped; few domestic institutions exist to enhance human rights. Finally, the world's major powers have played only a minor role is ending human rights violations in Southeast Asia. The philosophical values of the Western nations have not been sufficiently broad or articulated to protect and promote human rights in Southeast Asia.

Chapter 10
The European Union

Michael Newman

The founding treaty of the European Economic Community, signed by the original six member states in Rome in 1957, did not mention human rights. Forty years later, a new treaty agreed to by the current fifteen member states in Amsterdam, included specific clauses on the subject as conditions of membership for the European Union. And in Cologne in June 1999 they decided that it was time to establish a Charter of Fundamental Rights. The task of elaborating this charter was then entrusted to a convention, and the European Council at Nice adopted a final draft in December 2000.

The objectives of this chapter are to explain why this evolution in the EU's human rights agenda has taken place, to assess the contemporary situation, and to evaluate the prospects for change.[1] But before turning to the substantive issues, it must be noted that the European Union is not the primary European legal framework in which human rights issues have been codified and enforced. This has been the task of the European Convention on Human Rights (ECHR), the parent body of which is the Council of Europe. These institutions not only predate the European Union and its predecessors, but also remain quite separate from them. All the member states of the European Union are also members of the Council of Europe and have ratified the ECHR, but the European Union itself is not a member of the Council of Europe or a signatory of the ECHR. Nevertheless, the Council of Europe is a gatekeeper for the European Union in the sense that applicants for the latter are now expected to secure prior membership of the former. It is therefore crucial to consider the ECHR if human rights within the European Union are to be understood.

Following a brief outline of the ECHR, the chapter explores the evolution of the EU agenda in relation to human rights, considers some of the key issues in greater depth, and finally examines the possibilities for reform, with particular reference to the Charter of Fundamental Rights.

The European Convention on Human Rights

At the time of its foundation in 1949, the Council of Europe was a purely West European institution, which was largely immune from the direct influence of the Soviet bloc and the polemics between East and West that were to characterize debates over human rights in the United Nations. Signed in Rome in November 1950 (and coming into force in September 1953), the Convention for the Protection of Human Rights and Fundamental Freedoms (the formal title of the ECHR) was therefore primarily liberal in its orientation.[2]

There are several weaknesses in the practical application of the ECHR. Individuals have experienced considerable difficulties when seeking redress against their governments in terms of long delays and expenditure. The Convention's standards are sometimes minimal, so that, for example, the alleged need for security still enables Britain and France to restrict the flow of information in a way that would be unthinkable in Sweden or the United States. There are also cases where political factors have clearly influenced decisions. For example, in 1978 the European Court of Human Rights was not prepared to condemn British treatment of suspected members of the IRA as "torture" under Article 3. This may have avoided the risk of non-compliance by a signatory state, but it was almost certainly a political rather than a legal decision (Bagshaw 1994, 24) Furthermore, the "war against terrorism" in the aftermath of the attack in New York on September 11, 2001 has led to an erosion of traditional rights, with the British government seeking a derogation of Article 5 of the Convention (guaranteeing the right to no imprisonment without trial) for suspected terrorists. Yet despite its lapses and structural weaknesses, the ECHR is normally regarded as the most successful of any international regime in the world in relation to civil rights (Donnelly 1996, 213–15), and governments have complied with the judgments and changed their own laws where necessary. However, there is an important distinction in terms of legitimacy and power between the role of the ECHR in relation to its long-term and more recent members. West European liberal democracies devised a convention that substantially reflected existing domestic norms and legal codes. They have therefore tended to conform to ECHR judgments because they have attached importance to their reputations in relation to human rights and because the European Court of Human Rights generally provides reinforcement for conceptions that are already regarded as legitimate. This is not necessarily so with Turkey and some of the states of the former Soviet bloc. In these cases, the Council of Europe may be regarded as an external regime, with compliance seen as a necessary entry price into a European institution; this is particularly important for those states that also seek membership of the European Union.

The role of the Council of Europe has been much less significant in relation to social and economic rights. The limitations of the original Convention appeared to be overcome in October 1961, when the members also signed the European Social Charter, which came into effect in February 1965. However, these rights were supervised through separate and much weaker procedures. Subsequent protocols extended the scope of the Charter, but several EU countries have failed to ratify some of them and no separate European court of social rights has been introduced despite demands for this. And even though the Charter explicitly acknowledges trade union rights, the ECHR has upheld individual rather than collective rights in the cases it has judged (Sciarra 1999, 482–84). This means that the defense of the rights to strike or to organize is generally dependent on national legislation.

This leads to the more general conclusion that civil and political rights are more deeply embedded in both the signatory states and the ECHR system than are social and economic rights.

The European Union

The original purposes of West European integration had little to do with human rights, although there was an underlying assumption that integration would help stabilize liberal democracy within the member states. And although the current European Union is vastly more complex than the Community established in the 1950s, there is continuity in some of its most fundamental characteristics. First, the Treaty of Rome was essentially a contract among *states*. Despite the increasing extent of supranationalism, the governments still play a key role in the policy-making process and treaty reform requires unanimity. Second, economic goals have always been the "core" priority on which the other features of the EU have been built. The primary assumption in the original treaty was that these goals would be attained by the elimination of barriers to competition and to the free movement of goods, persons, services, and capital. This meant that the Community did not, in general, have a conception of rights beyond those that followed from the aim of removing such barriers, although the definition of their scope was enlarged as time went on. In other words, enterprises had a right not to be discriminated against in terms of competition or location, and workers had a right not to be discriminated against in terms of barriers to movement (for example, by immigration restrictions and discriminatory social security systems). The task of the European Commission was to propose legislation to attain these goals, while that of the European Court of Justice (ECJ) was to ensure that the law was enforced and to provide authoritative interpretations where there was ambiguity or in case of conflicts with domestic legislation. Why, then, has a human rights agenda evolved in the European Union? There is no simple answer, but various forces and influences can be identified.

The most significant of these has been the European Court of Justice. The progressive creation of a single market depended on the establishment of supranational law with the ECJ as the highest court of appeal. This body

secured its position through the doctrines of direct effect and legal supremacy, which meant that in cases in which the Community had competence,
the treaty was "constitutionalized." In other words, individuals could invoke
rights that were guaranteed by EC law. But were these simply "legal rights"
or were they "human rights" in some sense? Certainly, the Treaties only
granted the ECJ the power to adjudicate on matters covered by Community
law, but the Court has had an integrationist mission and by 1970 had formulated its own doctrine of the protection of fundamental rights as an
unwritten part of the Community's legal order (de Witte 1999, 863–64). It
established these principles because it believed that such a doctrine would
secure its legal supremacy against challenges from member states (particularly from the German Constitutional Court), and also because it became
clear during the 1960s that the Community had a far greater capacity to
affect such rights than was foreseen at the time of its creation. The Court's
claim was then retrospectively legitimized in the Maastricht treaty (signed
1992; effective from 1993), which stated that

The Union shall respect fundamental rights, as guaranteed by the European Convention for the Protection of Human Rights and Fundamental Freedoms . . . and as
they result from the constitutional traditions common to the Member States, as general principles of Community law. (originally Article F; now Article 6)

The ECJ also has jurisdiction on human rights issues vis-à-vis the Community institutions, and against the member states when the latter are acting "within the scope of Community law" and, with respect to this provision,
it has adjudicated in numerous cases of equality of treatment. However,
given the nature of Community law—and possibly the predilections of the
judges—the ECJ has generally privileged free market and property rights
above others (Koskenniemi 1999; Kuper 1998).

While the ECJ has clearly been a crucial force in promoting rights issues
within the European Union, social and political movements have also played
a key role. This has been particularly evident in relation to gender equality.
A commitment to gender equality was one of the very few social policy
matters given a specific legal basis in the Treaty of Rome, but this was very
limited from a human rights perspective. Women's movements then played
a key role in activating the treaty article and broadening the scope of Community policy in this field (Hoskyns 1996). Ever since the 1970s, gender
equality has therefore been a relatively high profile policy issue in the European Union and, although there are several criticisms of the EU's approach
(see below), the equality campaign demonstrates the interaction of various movements and institutions in putting human rights questions onto the
agenda. Thus women's movements, both within particular countries and
transnationally, have been able to use the fact that the Community has some
competence in this sphere to press for changes—sometimes against their
own governments. They have also been able to work within the European

Parliament to facilitate transnational networking and lobbying. This has had some impact on the policy-making bodies (the governments and the Commission) and on the ECJ.

A further actor in promoting human rights has been the European Parliament. Its subordinate role in the policy-making process and its peripheral status in relation to foreign policy and justice and home affairs have had paradoxical effects. Because the Parliament is simultaneously the only directly elected body within the European Union and an institution that has always been dissatisfied with its status, it has been very active in campaigning for democracy and human rights. For example, it has long campaigned for an EU anti-racist policy and has taken an active role in exposing abuses both in non-EU countries and within the member states themselves. Through its committees on Citizens' Freedom and Rights, Justice and Home Affairs, and Women's Rights it has carried out detailed work that is also reflected in its annual reports on human rights in the European Union. The EP has not had significant *power* in relation to human rights, but it has been an important actor in highlighting issues and sometimes embarrassing governments into taking action.

One reason for collective governmental embarrassment is that both the ways some decisions have been made at the European level and the nature of those decisions raise human rights issues. In particular, from the 1970s onward the governments of the member states undertook policy development on an intergovernmental basis in two major areas: foreign policy and internal security (including immigration and asylum policies). They did not follow the procedures of normal Community policy-making and their agreements did not lead to legislation. Instead, meetings of relevant ministers and secretive committees formulated policy, particularly in relation to internal security and immigration.

The Treaty of Maastricht regularized the position in some respects, but hardly improved the situation in relation to human rights. The European Community was now replaced by a "three-pillar" structure, collectively termed the European Union. The European Community became "pillar one" and continued to operate with the full institutional and legal procedure developed since the Treaty of Rome. There was thus a mix of supranational and intergovernmental decision-making, involving the European Commission and the European Parliament, leading to legislation over which the ECJ maintained a clear judicial status. However, the treaty also created "pillar two" for Common Foreign and Security Policy and "pillar three" for Justice and Home Affairs. These remained fundamentally intergovernmental, without significant involvement by the Commission or the EP, and their decisions took the form of rather secretive policy coordination. This also meant that this Court could not extend its general—if undefined—doctrine of fundamental rights to these areas of policy, while the ECHR only had jurisdiction for the policies of the individual member states. This led to major concerns from the European Parliament and several NGOs about existing and potential policies, particularly in the "third pillar." The human rights issues involved, and the resulting protests, led to limited concessions in the Treaty of Amsterdam (see below). However, the demand for more explicit and extensive human rights policies remained. This relates to a further key factor in the evolving human rights commitment: the EU's legitimation problems.

The original six member states constructed the European Community on the basis of the so-called "permissive consensus," which meant that their electorates and parliaments paid little attention to the integration process so long as it delivered prosperity and peace. This changed with the accession of more "Euroskeptic" states, which were less enthusiastic about European integration than the original members, the economic downturn in the 1970s, and the increasing penetration of the Community into domestic affairs. From the 1980s it became evident that the governments might not be able to move forward with the integration steps they favored unless they could secure the support of their peoples. This then led to efforts to legitimize the Community by highlighting its non-economic aspects. The creation of EU citizenship (see below) in the Treaty of Maastricht was a particularly important stage in this search for legitimation, but did not resolve the problems. This means that there is a constant need to seek greater legitimacy, which was certainly a factor in the June 1999 decision that a Charter of Fundamental Rights should be drawn up.

The final important element in the evolution of the human rights agenda has been the change in the international context. During the 1960s there was already a shift in this respect that meant that the 1962 Association agreement with Greece was suspended from 1967 to 1974 because of the military dictatorship in Athens. Sensitivity on such issues was reinforced by West European participation in the Helsinki process during the 1970s, and there was now a general consensus that none of the then Mediterranean dictatorships (Greece, Spain, and Portugal) would be allowed to join the Community until they established liberal democratic systems. But it was the end of the Cold War that really highlighted human rights for the governments. Freed from competition with the Soviet bloc in the developing countries, the European Union started inserting human rights conditions into its development aid, particularly following a Council resolution of November 1991. The prospect of Eastern enlargement then led the EU governments to try to put some flesh on the undefined assumption that member states must be democratic. This led to the so-called "Copenhagen criteria" for enlargement set by the Council in June 1993 and to subsequent significant amendments in the Treaty of Amsterdam (see below). However, human rights conditions that were introduced primarily as part of the entry conditions for new applicants may also have inescapable effects for existing Member States. Thus in February 2000 the other fourteen Member States took action against Austria—an existing member—on the grounds that the inclusion of the Freedom Party in its government posed a potential threat to democracy and human rights.[3]

The interactions between the various forces and factors that have put human rights onto the agenda in the European Union are complex, but the origins and nature of the Community remain highly relevant for an understanding of the current situation. For human rights are not central to the operation of the European Union in the way that economic integration is. And the increasingly neoliberal orientation of the 1980s and 1990s meant that socioeconomic rights (that, in any case, had a weak basis in the original treaties) have been extremely vulnerable: hence the growth of poverty, unemployment and underemployment in some of the richest countries in the world.

Specific Human Rights Issues

Gender Equality

Under Article 119 of the Treaty of Rome, women were to receive equal pay for equal work, but nothing was said about the position of those who were not in paid work or about the general rights of women in society or in the family. Once the treaty article was activated, the ECJ issued a series of judgments that led to several member states being forced either to introduce equality laws or to reform existing legislation. It also meant that Greece, Spain, and Portugal had to take on EC legislation when they joined the Community. These initial judgments coincided with the incorporation of the goal of gender equality into the Community's 1974 Social Action Program, which led to further legislation. By now the Commission recognized that the fundamental causes of gender inequality were deeply embedded in social, economic, cultural and political structures and that the formal equality legislation would have only a limited impact. Three Action Programs for equal opportunities followed, and the scope of Community policy was gradually widened. The Treaty of Amsterdam thus explicitly introduced equality between men and women as one of the tasks (Article 2) and activities (Article 3) to be undertaken by the Community. The original Article 119 has been amended significantly and, as Article 141, it extends the definition of equal pay for equal work. The legal basis for the Council to adopt equal opportunities measures was also strengthened.

Despite this activity in relation to gender equality the results are disappointing. Women still earn only 75 percent of the pay of men on average, and even in Sweden, which comes closest to equal pay, the female average is only 84 percent of that of men (Barnard 1999, 247–48). Furthermore, the inequalities tend to be greater at higher levels so that women managers and those with college educations tend to earn a smaller percentage of male earnings. The statistics on the participation of women in politics are equally striking, as are the variations among the Member States. Thus a comparative table on women in government in 1996 showed Sweden as the highest with 50 percent and Greece the lowest with 4 percent (Barnard 1999, 274). Gender equality policies are supposed to apply to the EU's own institutions, but the inequalities there are also dramatic. Fewer than 25 percent of the Members of the European Parliament elected in 1999 were women, and there are still only five women commissioners (out of twenty) and two female judges (out of fifteen) on the ECJ, with the first appointed only in October 1999. Why has the European Union been relatively unsuccessful in equalizing opportunities?

Its approach still reflects the employment-based assumptions underlying the original article in the Treaty of Rome. Although the scope of Community action and legislation has broadened very considerably—to incorporate such matters as indirect discrimination, sexual harassment, training, and provision for paternity leave—this hardly touches many of the most fundamental issues, particularly in the cultures that are the most deeply patriarchal. This means that the European Union has appeared to have very little relevance in relation to some of the women who are in the most vulnerable positions, particularly among ethnic minorities where gender inequality is often the most marked (Vaughan-Roberts 1997). It has also had comparatively little impact in harmonizing conditions among the member states. EU policy on sex equality has certainly developed, but the main weaknesses concern its scope (that is, its concentration on employment-related issues) and approach (that is, a tendency to formal rather than substantive equality). Women's groups are thus campaigning for extensive further changes (European Women's Lobby 2000).

Citizens, Non-Citizens, and the Paradoxes of Free Movement

The gradual removal of the barriers to the free movement of labor exposed particular problems for legal residents without citizenship in a member state. From a human rights perspective it would be anticipated that a legal resident in one country would also be able to move to others if the Community was eliminating its barriers. However, the opposite approach has generally been taken (Bernitz and Bernitz 1999). As approximately 65 percent of the legal residents in the European Union are from Asia, Africa, and Turkey, it is evident that the majority of those with limited movement rights are members of visible ethnic minorities from poorer countries (Newman 1996, 181). This discriminatory aspect of Community policy, which became increasingly evident from the time of the Single European Act (effective from 1987), was reinforced by other related developments.

In 1985 the Schengen Agreement was signed among a group of member states to abolish their internal frontiers in advance of the general abolition of frontiers by the Community as a whole.[4] However, any weakening of a country's own immigration controls—such as to enable freer movement for the nationals of other member states—inevitably makes the countries more dependent on each other for policing the external frontiers of the area as a whole. Thus the initial Schengen Agreement led to moves to exchange information about immigrants, including the establishment of the computerized Schengen Information System that has become increasingly sophisticated and is open to all member states. A further almost inevitable development of the diminution of border controls is a tendency to resort to a greater use of internal checks by police within countries and, once again, this is likely to be discriminatory: that is, they are more likely to ask for the identity papers of a person who belongs to a visible ethnic minority, particularly if there are weak antiracist policies within the state in question.

The category of EU citizenship introduced under a new Article 8 in the Maastricht Treaty (now Article 17 following the Treaty of Amsterdam) brought together many of the rights that already existed, while adding some new ones.[5] But the introduction of Union citizenship highlighted some of the discriminatory aspects of the existing policies. For the precondition of securing Union citizenship was citizenship in one of the member states, with EU citizenship following automatically from this. The specified rights were therefore not generally available to legal residents who were not citizens of any of the states. But this then exposed a further human rights issue: the conditions for securing citizenship were not similar in all the countries, and in some—most notably Germany until its new citizenship and nationality law came into effect in 2000—it was difficult for anyone without ancestral lineage to acquire nationality. The Maastricht Treaty thus both exposed the inequality of rights between citizens and non-citizens and the arbitrariness resulting from the differences in naturalization procedures across the member states.

A further relevant difference among the member states lay in the policies and legal provisions to tackle racism and discrimination. Apart from this leading to human rights abuses within individual countries, by the early 1990s it was an issue for the Community as a whole. If free movement for citizens of any member state was supposed to be guaranteed, a black national of one country should, in theory, be able to move to another country as easily as a white person. But in practice the differences in antidiscriminatory legislation and attitudes to racism could present barriers to movement. This, in conjunction with the increasingly restrictive policing of the external frontiers and the rise of the extreme Right, inevitably put the issue of racism on the agenda, particularly as the European Parliament and NGOs were calling for action at Community level. Nevertheless, nothing was done about this in the Maastricht Treaty. However, there has been greater impetus in recent years. The most significant breakthrough was the new Article 13 in the Treaty of Amsterdam. This included a general competence to enact measures prohibiting discrimination based on the grounds of sex, disability, age, and sexual orientation, and authorized the Council to "take appropriate action to combat discrimination based on . . . racial or ethnic origin, religion or belief." This was an encouraging step, implying that the governments were finally prepared to tackle racist discrimination in a comparable manner to discrimination against women. The European Parliament kept up the pressure, in December 1999 the Commission submitted a proposal for a fairly wide-ranging Directive, and a package of measures was adopted at the end of 2000. Governments are now transposing the Directive into legislation that should eventually mean that anyone working or traveling within the European Union would enjoy the same minimum level of protection from discrimination in all the member states. This would constitute a major advance and provide a basis for further development, as was the case with the gender equality commitment in the original treaty. However, the difference in rights between the nationals of member states and those legal residents without citizenship remains.

There are various ways in which this could be rectified, but there are obstacles to any major change. For example, one remedy would be to transform the conditions for securing citizenship of the Union so that a new category of EU citizenship would become available to all legal residents after a certain period of abode. However, all the evidence suggests that the member states would not currently be prepared to countenance such a change. An alternative would be to detach the rights of free movement from citizenship and to confer them instead on all legal residents. But this would require a positive will by the EU governments, which they do not currently possess, to end this form of discrimination. Furthermore, EU citizenship—even in its limited form—was introduced in the Maastricht Treaty in an attempt to legitimate the Union by providing a stronger sense of identity. While detaching rights of free movement from the possession of nationality is certainly justified on the grounds of universalizing human rights, it would also further denude the concept of Union citizenship. During 2001 more limited measures to provide greater comparability among the situation of long-term legal residents in the different member states were proposed by the Commission. A draft Directive was put to the Council and the Parliament in the autumn, but had not been agreed to by the end of the year.

Immigration and Asylum

These human rights issues have been exacerbated by the parallel developments in immigration and asylum policies. From the mid-1970s Community Justice and Home Affairs ministers began to meet to coordinate increasingly restrictive policies against migrants from outside the Community area. However, the attempt to control immigration has been complicated by the fact that famine, economic crises, and civil war have led to a vast increase in refugees seeking asylum. As a result, asylum policies have also become ever more stringent, with an increasing tendency to treat asylum seekers in the same way as illegal immigrants, often holding them in appalling conditions while their cases are heard. A formidable policy-making apparatus constructed by the end of the 1980s had no effective democratic control. The European Parliament had no involvement at all, and the ECJ was not in a position to adjudicate because the measures were not implemented as part of Community law. In theory, the governments were accountable to their domestic parliaments, but this was quite inadequate given the secretive and collaborative nature of the policy-making process. Populist xenophobia and its impact on government policies exacerbated the increasingly restrictive approach.

As already noted, the Maastricht Treaty formalized the apparatus that had been constructed since the 1970s by establishing Justice and Home Affairs as the so-called "third pillar" of the European Union. It thus brought asylum, external borders, and immigration policies together with such matters as crime, terrorism, and police cooperation. It is true that a new treaty article (K.2) stipulated that such matters would be dealt with in compliance with the ECHR and the 1951 UN Convention Relating to the Status of Refugees, but overall there remained a very confusing mixture of Europeanization and state autonomy in the treaty provisions. Furthermore democratic control by the European Parliament and the legal basis for ECJ involvement remained inadequate. Yet because the European Union as a whole was outside the jurisdiction of the ECHR, there was no external legal accountability for these areas of policy, which are among the most sensitive from a human rights perspective.

Under the Treaty of Amsterdam a new Title IV was established in the EC Treaty (first pillar), which meant that visa, asylum, immigration, and other policies relating to free movement would be in the form of Community legislation (Art. 249, ex. 189). Thus policy harmonization in the areas of immigration and asylum would subsequently be carried out through normal Community procedures (rather than simply by intergovernmental discussions), which would be binding on the member states. However, there were two important provisos. First, for a transitional period of five years (that is until 2004), except for decisions on visas, such policies could only be agreed to by unanimity among the governments. Second, some key measures on the protection of refugees—such as burden sharing—have been exempted from the five-year limit. Nevertheless, from a human rights perspective, these changes constitute some progress.

The Treaty of Amsterdam also instituted some important advances in relation to the policy-making process and the role of both the European Parliament and the ECJ. Nevertheless, several features in the current policies toward refugees contravened the spirit of the ECHR or 1951 Refugee Convention.[6] Furthermore, the "war against terrorism" appears likely to undermine many of the protections that had been secured.

External Policy and Enlargement

The emphasis on human rights in *external policy* developed rapidly during the last decade of the twentieth century. The Treaty on European Union (Art. J.1(2); now Art. 11(1) TEU) explicitly calls for respect for human rights and fundamental freedoms as one of the five objectives of the Common Foreign and Security Policy (CFSP), while Article 130u of the EC Treaty (now Art. 177 TEC) provided that Community policy in the area of development cooperation "shall contribute to the general objective of developing and consolidating democracy and the rule of law, and to that of respecting human rights and fundamental freedoms." Furthermore the Community has inserted specific human rights clauses in all agreements with other countries. Economic sanctions may be imposed for abuses, while unilateral trade preferences and comprehensive assistance programs may be used to encourage countries to move in a more positive direction.

There has been a kind of "structural hypocrisy" in the policy, particularly in relation to developing countries. However laudable the original motives of the founders of the Community may have been within the European continent, their external aims were to strengthen the new economic bloc in relation to the rest of the world. This was to lead, over time, to a formidable concentration of power, so that the EU countries now account for 27 percent of the world's GDP, almost one-fifth of its trade flows, and more than half the official development assistance flows to developing countries (Alston and Weiler 1998, para. 34, 33). While these statistics are misleading in the sense that they represent the aggregate of the member states, the European Union does act as a single entity in trade relations and this gives it colossal weight in negotiations with poorer countries, the majority of which were formerly victims of European colonization. The United States and the European Union may accuse one another of protectionism in the World Trade Organization (WTO), but they have been united in economic policies, which have increased the inequality between the north and the south (Randel, German, and Ewing 2000).

To accuse the European Union of "structural hypocrisy" is not to argue that it is wrong to try to enhance human rights externally, but to suggest that the general economic impact of its policies reinforce the difficulties faced by those committed to political reform within developing countries. Development assistance is simply a palliative in this context and only 2 percent of the total assistance given by the Community goes in positive measures to promote civil society (Simma, Aschenbrenner, and Schulte 1999, 573). Moreover while the European Union has in theory accepted the indivisibility of rights, it has paid much less attention to promoting social and economic rights in poorer countries than civil and political ones (Simma et al. 1999, 604–8; Alston and Weiler 1998, 57–60). When the EU's increasingly restrictive immigration and asylum policies are also recalled, it is hardly surprising that its insistence on inserting human rights clauses in cooperation and trade agreements is sometimes viewed with deep skepticism (Clapham 1999, 659).

The EU record on the external aspects of human rights is also open to more general criticism. Human rights issues are not normally perceived by governments to be as important in the determination of foreign policy as economic and strategic considerations and, if this is the case in a single state, the difficulties of finding a place for human rights in the Union as a whole are far greater. These are further compounded by the existence of NATO that continues to determine the main security policies of the member states. During the prolonged Yugoslav crises, the EU's role has been generally ineffective and inconsistent, and its response to human rights violations elsewhere has also clearly been dependent on wider interests. For example, it has been reluctant to confront China because of commercial considerations (Clapham 1999, 633–35) or Russia over Chechnya for strategic reasons. The human rights agenda has thus had a limited impact in counteracting more traditional priorities in the foreign policies of either the individual member states or the Union as a whole.

The issue of *enlargement* has had a major impact on the EU's politics on human rights. After the fall of the Berlin Wall, the majority of East Central European states sought entry into the Community, which was associated with a "return to Europe" following more than four decades of Soviet domination. Until 1993 the main thrust of Community policy was to insist that economic and legal changes would be necessary before membership could be considered and to provide some aid to facilitate the transition. This insistence on the adoption of a market economy exacerbated the difficulties in stabilizing the political systems in the area, and the new trade agreements were more beneficial to the Community than to the would-be applicants (Gowan 1996). Nevertheless, the East Central European states were so keen to secure entry that, in general, they moved in the direction sought by the West European governments. However, it was also clear that liberal democracy had not been stabilized in all the countries and that human rights abuses were evident in some of them. In June 1993 the European Council therefore stipulated that, in addition to meeting the existing conditions for membership, applicants would need stable institutions guaranteeing democracy, the rule of law, human rights, and respect for the protection of minorities. A so-called "pre-accession" strategy was agreed to the next year and the Commission indicated the progress of the various applicants in relation to the criteria and explicitly stated that Slovakia did not satisfy the political conditions (Agenda 2000 for a Stronger and Wider Union 1997). Negotiations began in 1998 with a leading group (Cyprus, Slovenia, Estonia, Czech Republic, Poland, and Hungary), but in December 1999 another seven countries (Bulgaria, Romania, Latvia, Lithuania, Slovakia, Malta, and Turkey) were added to the list. During 2002 a further decision was made to accept ten of these countries (excluding Bulgaria, Romania, and Turkey) as possible new members by 2004.

The Copenhagen criteria, which all the new applicants must satisfy, have had an obvious impact on the Union itself. Thus, following a significant amendment in the Treaty of Amsterdam, Article 6(1) of the Treaty on European Union (TEU) reads:

The Union is founded on the principles of liberty, democracy, respect for human rights and fundamental freedoms, and the rule of law, principles that are common to Member States.

Whereas it was previously stated that any European state could apply to become a member of the Union, following Amsterdam it is explicitly stated that only a European state that accepts the above principles may do so (Art. 49 TEU).[7] The Treaty also includes a new Article 7 that for the first time establishes a procedure for the suspension of rights in the case of a "serious and persistent breach by a Member State" of the principles in Article 6(1). The Treaty of Nice strengthened the procedures in a new Article 7.1. However, some obvious weaknesses remain: in particular, it is still not entirely clear what would constitute the kind of breach of principles leading to sanctions, and there is no independent or judicial role, so the Council's judgments could be subject to a political bargaining process (Nowak 1999, 692–94). Nevertheless it is a significant step that the European Union has now elaborated some of its defining principles. This means that it is no longer simply "Eurocentric" in character: its members must also maintain a commitment to liberty, democracy, and human rights. The task now is to strengthen both the theory and the practice.

Conclusion: The Future for Human Rights in the European Union

Various strategies for reform have been suggested. One approach is to stress the importance of new and improved institutions. Alston and Weiler have made a number of important proposals to overcome existing weaknesses, arguing that strong institutions provide the indispensable basis for effective policies (Alston and Weiler 1998, 107–9). This is true, but the danger is that the governments could accept the new institutions without necessarily allowing them sufficient power to make a significant impact on the problems. A second approach is to strengthen the legal basis for human rights protection and to remove the differences in ECJ jurisdiction among the three pillars of the European Union.[8] Accession to the ECHR would establish a clear hierarchy of human rights legislation, and individuals and groups would then be entitled to challenge Community acts (or the acts of member states in transposing EC law into national law) before the ECHR. It would also probably mean that the Community would take on further substantive legal obligations (Clapham 1999, 678). However, although the European Commission proposed accession as long ago as 1979, no real progress has been made on this question and no change is likely in the near future. The third approach to reform is that which was adopted in 1999–2000: the elaboration of a Charter of Fundamental Rights. This has highlighted some of the underlying tensions and contradictions in the EU stance on human rights.

A notable positive point was that the policy-making process was innovative. The normal procedure for treaty reform within the EU is by means of an intergovernmental conference, so that the governments maintain exclusive control over the process. However, the task of drawing up a draft charter was entrusted to a convention with the following composition: fifteen representatives of the heads of state or government, sixteen members of the European Parliament, thirty members of national parliaments (two from each state), and a Commissioner representing the president of the Commission. Furthermore, the working method was unusually open and there was extensive use of the Internet, so that it was possible to follow the process and to read the numerous arguments that were presented by governments, NGOs, and other interested parties. All this reflected recognition of the importance of human rights in civil society. However the final decisions were still to be taken by the European Council (that is, the heads of state and government).

The original decision in June 1999 to draw up a charter had stressed that this should make the overriding importance and relevance of fundamental rights "more visible to the Union's citizens." The minimalist interpretation of this statement was that the task was simply to *clarify* the existing rights guaranteed by the European Union because the treaties were notoriously difficult to understand. The maximalist position was that the Charter provided an opportunity to decide what rights the European Union *should* protect. There were some important differences among the governments, but they were in general agreement that the Convention should not propose new rights that went beyond the existing treaties. The need for unanimity for treaty reform also meant that it was always probable that agreement would ultimately tend toward the more minimal end of the scale, and in the event the result was a rather predictable compromise. The charter drawn up by the convention was largely a codification of existing rights, although there were some areas of ambiguity.[9] The European Council in Nice accepted it in December 2000, but a decision on its status was deferred for another intergovernmental conference to be held in 2004. The whole episode reinforces the key points that the governments of the member states remain the final decision makers and that human rights policy tends to be subordinated to other priorities in the bargaining process.

This leads to one final observation. It is evident that, with respect to both internal and external aspects of human rights, the European Union has so far placed more weight on civil and political rights than on social and economic ones. When social, economic, and collective rights are acknowledged, the tendency is to set them at a low level and to subordinate them to the economy. The argument for fundamental rights attempts to circumvent the problems by stressing their indivisibility, but still fails to confront the fact that the dominant economic interests want to limit social rights and normally succeed in persuading decision-makers that their arguments are valid. Given the slow pace of policy-making and the embedded injustices that exist, it would be utopian to anticipate any rapid transformation in the situation. However the European Union has only recently acknowledged the importance of human rights and some advances have been made. It is to be hoped that the combined pressure of relevant NGOs, parties and parliaments at both national and transnational levels will lead to more significant changes in the future.

Chapter 11
Eastern Europe:
The Russian Federation

Carol Skalnik Leff

Human rights politics play out within a complex web of domestic and transnational relationships. As Thomas Risse-Kappen (1994) says, "ideas do not float freely"; they are encapsulated in normative regimes that are incorporated into institutional structures and championed by concrete actors embedded in political networks. An examination of these actors and institutional structures is critical to explaining the outcomes of Russian human rights battles after communism; these battles have been fought in a transnational setting in which the domestic and foreign linkages must be specified.

Before tackling this task, it is sensible to ask what is meant by a human rights agenda. One can, of course, set a broad-gauged agenda that encompasses an extensive checklist of social and economic rights as well as civil and political ones. This is the format adopted in the annual U.S. State Department assessments of human rights. This generalized approach has some useful payoffs for performing summary comparative analyses across cases. However, a politically operative agenda of human rights would be defined rather differently; the very term "agenda" presupposes that relevant political actors are setting priorities within a larger possible universe of human rights concerns. The criterion for this agenda formation need not be the urgency of the issue; it may be its amenability to resolution, its salience as a focus of international concern, or the fact that it is an issue around which concerned actors are ready to mobilize. What is important is to identify which actors are engaged in issue definition, and what human rights issues are of central concern to them. Agendas vary in specificity, scope, and salience, as well as in the enforcement power able to be mobilized to pursue defined objectives. All this is relevant to outcomes in the form of human rights observance.

In this chapter, therefore, I will be looking at two clusters of actors—states, multilaterals, and nongovernmental organizations (NGOs) in the international environment and the Russian government, party system, and NGOs in the domestic environment—as well as at their agendas and the strategic context in which these actors operate. The agenda that emerges from this examination is a more limited one, with the highest profile issues, as defined by the agenda-setters, being the conduct of military operations and the treatment of conscripts; restrictions on mobility and foreign travel imposed by the survival of the Soviet-era "propiska" or residence permit in defiance of constitutional strictures and court rulings; and pathologies of the criminal justice system. In this analysis, I will first set out the basic features of Russian domestic rights politics, and then turn to the interface between this political environment and the key transnational actors engaged in monitoring, and trying to influence, the Russian human rights agenda.

The Domestic Politics of Human Rights in Russia

It is important briefly to review the human rights regime that characterized Soviet Russia. Although human rights were widely violated, there was a logic for the pattern of observance and nonobservance—a fundamentally statist logic rooted in German jurisprudence and Soviet ideology. Russian legal analyst A. Chistyakova pinpoints three defining principles of classic Soviet theory and practice: the state as "the sole source of human rights," without recourse to any higher universal principle, with concomitant government authority to define and constrain how these rights would operate in practice; the subordination of individual needs to those of the state; and the primacy of social and economic rights over civil and political ones (Bowring 1995, 89).

This legacy must be taken seriously in both negative and affirmative terms—in negative terms because of the burdensome legacies imposed by a politicized legal system, and in affirmative terms because the emphasis on social and economic rights as fundamental has persisted in public perception. Today the Russian government, public, and human rights NGOs all share, to varying degrees, a recognition of economic security as a fundamentally resonant value and human entitlement. Thus the human rights activists have joined calls to pay arrears in salaries and pensions, viewing government responsibility in this area as the manifestation of a basic human right to security.

In other respects, the rights logic of the post-communist state would appear to have changed dramatically. Article 2 of the post-Soviet Russian constitution turned the earlier statist logic on its head, touting the supremacy of individual rights and freedoms. Thirty-five articles codify specific political, civil, and socioeconomic rights that have the additional standing, in contrast with the Soviet period, of having "direct application"; that is, courts must enforce them even in the absence of enabling legislation. Indeed, the elaboration of constitutionally protected rights is quite extensive, and Western commentators are more apt to query the inclusion of socioeconomic rights in this charter—as the over-elaboration of human rights norms—than they are to lament the absence of other formal human rights guarantees.

To actualize these constitutional commitments, however, requires political mechanisms. It is here that problems arise. In the first place, rights protection requires a state whose power is both effective and bounded. State capacity is a critical factor in the implementation of any policy, and Russian state capacity is currently rather problematic.

Second, rights protection in democratic states depends on the mobilization of constituencies in support of the rights agenda. Party systems may perform that function, to the extent that parties respond to the claims of core constituencies for protection. The Russian party system, however, is not coherent in that sense. Its dominant features are the persistence of organized Communist electoral power and the "parties of power," which formed and reformed in response to Boris Yeltsin's proclivity for indulging in a "prime minister of the month" strategy for deflecting criticism. Human rights have no obvious entry point in such parties. The two other durable partisan entities have been Grigory Yavlinsky's Yabloko and Vladimir Zhirinovsky's Liberal Democrats, the latter hopeless as a human rights tribune and the former sporadically significant in certain issue areas, such as critiques of human rights abuses in the Chechen war. On the whole, however, electoral politics have not given much purchase for rights protection. Even at the margins, human rights issues are unlikely to influence electoral outcomes in states like the Russian Federation with an agenda overload of pressing economic and security issues. Where such an impact does exist, it tends to be very broad and unspecific, as when Russian voters are faced with a presidential choice between Yeltsin and communist leader Zhyughanov. Nor have top government leaders cemented a human rights emphasis. As the 1990s wore on, it is perhaps telling and certainly not heartening that Yeltsin's last three prime ministers—Yevgeny Primakov, Sergei Stepashin, and of course Vladimir Putin—were recruited from the ranks of the Soviet secret police (KGB) and its Russian successor organizations.

In most advanced industrial democracies, the community of NGOs is a source of mobilization and lobbying for rights observance. Indeed, there is an active human rights community of Russian NGOs, with roots in the international community, Soviet-era dissidence, and the informal organizations of the Gorbachev period. Most notable are the broad-spectrum rights groups, Moscow Human Rights/Helsinki Watch, the Moscow Research Center for Human Rights (with partial European Union funding), and "Memorial." They have been instrumental in providing detailed documentation of human rights violations, and they contribute heavily to the flow of information through transnational networks, information flows that both shape the perceptions of foreign actors and exert the pressure of publicity on these actors. They have certainly helped define an agenda that highlights the shortcomings of the legal process itself, from arrest and detention to trial and incarceration, a process rife with abuse, neglect, and overcrowding. The Russian branch of Amnesty International has been particularly vigilant on this issue, documenting prisoner abuse and chronic overcrowding that surpass the Soviet era. Helsinki Watch and others have also been important in drawing attention to the uneven observance of human rights in the outlying Russian regions. Perhaps the most powerful indigenous force for rights observance in a specific sector is the Committee of Soldiers' Mothers, which both pursues public campaigns against military hazing or the military death toll in Chechnya and counsels families in the intricacies of the conscription process.

The evident commitment of such groups notwithstanding, Russian NGOs function in a far less favorable context than that of established democracies. They are resource-poor in funding and in mass membership. Short of resources to mount an electoral threat, post-communist NGOs suffer additionally by lacking routinized policy access nodes (such as legislative testimony or executive consultation) for direct input to the decision process. A central problem is that Russian media, while free, is not independent, and government television news sources and even the Russian press agencies tend selectively to ignore the press conferences and released reports of NGOs,[1] just as they equally selectively report on international criticism of Russian human rights policies.

The security of human rights organizations appears to have deteriorated starting in the late 1990s. Advocacy organizations and NGOs in general have been on shaky legal ground in one important respect: the requirement that existing groups re-register in 1999. Organizations whose registration attempts were denied or delayed beyond the deadline subsequently operated in a juridical limbo—neither banned nor accredited, and accordingly vulnerable to harassment. The travails of human rights organizations are particularly striking. Prominent rights organizations such as Citizen Watch and Memorial were reportedly told during re-registration efforts that phrases alluding to protection of human rights must be deleted from their mission statements, because such protection was the function of the state (Mendelson 2000)!

In analyzing Russian compliance with human rights commitments, it is useful to distinguish different forms of human rights enforcement "problems." One form of human rights violation could be formulated as a principal-agent problem, where subordinate officials systematically deviate from official policy. Let us say, for the sake of argument, that the principal, President Putin, has no general interest in fomenting torture and mistreatment in Russian prisons, a human rights violation that has been repeatedly documented by domestic rights organizations and Amnesty International, and acknowledged by the government.[2] At issue here is not that Putin and other top leaders wish to promote horrible prison conditions, but rather that their bureaucratic agents at the enforcement level enjoy considerable slack, because monitoring compliance with a higher normative standard of behavior is not costless, and there are other priorities—such as a display of toughness on crime. For example, the presidency issued decrees in 1994 and 1996 relaxing the rules on detention, which in turn contributed to overcrowding and prisoner abuse.

A clearer example is the behavior of regional governments in human rights questions, behavior that rights activists have repeatedly reported to be considerably more objectionable than that of the central government, including the harassment and jailing of regional human rights advocates. There are a number of recorded instances in which Kremlin officials have had to intercede to win the release of rights advocates incarcerated for their activities in the Russian regions. Again, monitoring the behavior of eighty-nine federal units is not costless, and the central government has tended to intervene primarily in cases where independent reporting has pinpointed a specific abuse.

By contrast, there are situations in which the principals themselves sanction noncompliance, finding it directly or indirectly useful in maintaining power. The two Chechen wars, both heavily documented instances of systematic rights abuse, basically fall into this category. The logic of encouraging compliance may be quite different in each of these cases. Provision of resources to ameliorate prison conditions might alter the cost-benefit calculations in a direction favoring greater compliance. The incentives for compliance may be complex in cases where the central government itself benefits from noncompliance.

The compliance problem is very salient for the weakened post-communist state, where enforcement capacity on *any* policy dimension is highly circumscribed (McFaul 1995). Stephen Holmes, a leading authority on Russian law, makes a sustained argument along these lines. He links effective rights protection to state capacity, available resources, and political control over the behavior of relevant actors (Holmes 1999, 120, 122). Human rights agendas, he concludes, can only be effectively prosecuted where political institutions, such as parties, courts, and parliaments, are effective and legitimate. The implied first-order task is thus to tackle the problem of developing a favorable legal-institutional context for self-correcting domestic activity. A legal system lacking provision for class action suits or clear-cut citizen standing to sue in defense of rights is not "rights ready" (Petrova 1996). Nor is a political system that is unable to enforce its own policy mandates. Vladimir Putin's popularity has largely been due to the perception that he may be able to achieve that kind of control over a weak and corrupt state. However, a strong individual leader is emphatically not equivalent to strong state institutions. To the contrary, this situation is symptomatic of the *absence* of such institutions, and creates pathologies of its own in undermining horizontal accountability in government, as Guillermo O'Donnell (1998) has repeatedly noted.

In this transitional Russian system, political actors with clear commitments to human rights observance have in some cases found their way into positions of public responsibility, but their influence has not been pronounced. The tenuous political rootedness of human rights enforcement is illustrated in the checkered history of the Russian Human Rights Commissioner, a constitutionally mandated position. In the first place, the accountability of the office to the presidency was vigorously contested by the Duma, which began a legislative effort to arrogate the Commission to itself starting in 1994, and voted overwhelmingly to remove the incumbent, Sergei Kovalev—Soviet-era dissident and former chair of the legislative Human Rights Committee—from the office in March 1995, just over a year after his initial appointment.

While the Duma fought over the terms of a new law on the Commission, Commissioner Kovalev experienced his own frustrations; bedecked with international awards from Freedom House and other international rights organizations, he nonetheless had to battle at home even to have his reports submitted to President Yeltsin, who ignored their charges of "systematic and flagrant" human rights violations. Kovalev's outspoken criticism of human rights violations in the first Chechen war won him both *Izvestia*'s Man of the Year Award and his final marginalization by both Yeltsin and the Duma. He resigned from the position, and from Yeltsin's Presidential Council, after releasing the 1994–95 report. In January 1996, in an open letter to Yeltsin, he chastised the presidential preference for using force, increasing state secrecy, and indifference to public opinion (OMRI Daily Digest 17, January 24, 1996).[3] The majority of the commission followed his lead.

The Duma failed repeatedly to revise Human Rights Commission legislation, hobbled by partisan maneuvering over appointment power, but impelled to persist because the Council of Europe mandated such an agency for all members. New legislation was not enacted until December 1996, some two and a half years after the measure's first reading. By spring 1997, Russian human rights groups had severed relations with the official commission, demanding still further legislation in which the major rights organizations were consulted. Meanwhile the Duma floundered in naming Kovalev's successor until late spring 1998. Just in time, for President Yeltsin had designated 1998 as a "Year of Human Rights" in the Russian Federation. A more recent example is the powerlessness of Putin's special rights commissioner for Chechnya, appointed in February 2000, but devoid of a budget, reliable communications with Chechnya, or clout to gain information from the Russian military. Oleg Mironov, Putin's appointee as Human Rights Commissioner, has lamented Putin's failure to meet with him or to respond to his reports and letters.

The weakness of Russian state institutions is paralleled by inchoate public opinion on the importance of rights protections. In a society where unemployment is a new and demoralizing prospect, where workers often suffer months of wage arrears and unpaid pensions, it should not be surprising that socioeconomic rights continue to have profound resonance. A 1995 survey of human rights salience by Inga Mikhailovskaya (1995), social scientist and board member of the NGO Russian-American Human Rights Group, found that the number of Russian citizens who identified the Brezhnev era as the time when human rights were most effectively observed was more than twice that of those who chose any other historical period, including the post-communist 1990s. She regards this, correctly I feel, as evidence of the primacy of socioeconomic over political rights in Russian civic consciousness, an implication reinforced by questions about the importance of a range of specific rights. Most tellingly, when citizens were presented with a trade-off between rights and order (which is more dangerous, an unpunished guilty criminal or a wrongfully accused innocent one?), almost half those surveyed opted to assure that the guilty be punished. Her conclusions about Russian rights consciousness are thus considerably more pessimistic than those of some earlier U.S. survey researchers.

More troubling than any one weakness in the Russian political context for human rights enforcement is the fact that the general trend has been downward. The Freedom House summary index downgraded the country's overall political and civil liberties rating in the late 1990s. The rating as late as 1997 was 3.5 (Rose, Mischler, and Haerpfer 1998) on a seven-point scale in which 1 is the most free. In the surveys of 1998 and 1999, Russia rated a 4 and descended still further in the years 2000 and 2001, with both civil and political rights earning a rating of 5 (Piano and Puddington 2001). Putin's presidency has given cause for further concern, especially because key targets of restriction have been the NGOs and the media, key institutional support systems for effective rights protections.

Engagement of International Actors in Human Rights Initiatives

To analyze the capacity of external actors to affect responsiveness to human rights concerns in a target state such as Russia, it is useful to think in terms of networks of interaction that process variant forms of initiatives.[4] Figure 1 offers a simple schematic depiction of these networks, webs of interaction linking Russian governmental and societal agents discussed in the previous section with three important types of external actors: states, multilateral organizations, and NGOs. These networks are not rights-specific; they sustain interactions in many quite unrelated areas—a point that is central in two critical areas that will be discussed below. The first point is that the other policy flows in the network may have priority over human rights, blurring the resonance of those same channels when rights issues *are* being processed. Conversely, multipurpose channels can also provide opportunities for linkage of human rights agendas with economic and security issues.

On this basis I characterize four types of activity that circulate through transnational networks: normative elaborations of human rights, encoded in conventions and membership criteria; financial or technical human rights assistance; declaratory assessments (some episodic and some routinized in the form of annual reports); and conditionality incentives that link human rights performance to rewards and punishments in other areas. In the following discussion I will use these reference points to assess the dynamics of human rights interaction between Russia and the West.

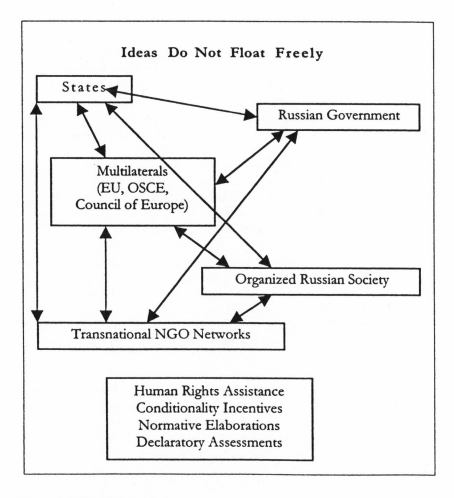

Figure 1. Webs of interaction.

State Actors

Multilateral organizations, not states, are the primary locus for defining human rights norms. Once normative regimes are formulated, however, the response of state actors is critical in assessing human rights performance, providing assistance, and imposing conditionality on target states.

The efficacy of individual states and multilateral organizations as guardians of civil liberties is constrained in several ways, above and beyond the questions of formal sanctioning power or the existing resources for providing incentives. Both states and multilaterals share common constraints, because the pressure for human rights compliance exerted by the multilateral agency is conditioned by the complex policy agendas of the states that make up its membership. For both types of entities, exerting pressure for human rights compliance is not costless, because even sanctionless criticism can strain relations with the target country. This in turn can impede progress in issue areas that have independent and often superior priority for the actors concerned. As a consequence, both the state and the multilateral organization face chronic trade-offs between aggressive pursuit of the human rights agenda, on the one hand, and priorities attached to normalized trade and security relations, on the other. Gordon Crawford (1997), in his analysis of the effectiveness of foreign assistance for promoting democracy and human rights, has severely criticized the "clear pattern of subordination of human rights and democracy to other dominant foreign concerns," even where the donor countries have increasingly and explicitly attached political conditions to that aid in the 1990s. He notes pointedly that it was the Western donors *themselves* who introduced the normative dimension to the donor-recipient relationship, and that it is therefore incumbent on *both* parties to take that emphasis seriously.

Indeed, a state targeted for human rights violations expects such tacit trade-offs between rights observance and other international interests. Convinced that the U.S.-Russian alliance against terrorism after September 11 had provided latitude for its own "anti-terrorist" crusade in Chechnya, the Russian Foreign Ministry was stung by critical passages, particularly regarding Chechnya, in the annual State Department human rights report on Russia in spring 2002.

Even when the human rights agenda itself is paramount, both individual states and multilateral organizations feel compelled to "choose their battles," subordinating the pursuit of individual rights violations to the larger project of developing an ongoing working relationship with the target state—the often debated strategy of constructive engagement. The result can be a certain amount of drift in the rigor with which external actors pursue their objectives.

The major state actors in the Russian case—key Western states—had developed official programs of democratic assistance and support for transitional countries before the collapse of the Soviet Union. These programs generally expanded their assistance "portfolios" to embrace Russia and the Soviet successor states. Key agencies were the National Endowment for Democracy and especially the U.S. Agency for International Development (USAID) in the case of the United States, for example, and the German party foundations in the case of Germany. Cold War leaders had been reluctant to complicate the superpower relationship with sustained institutionalized attention to human rights. Daniel Thomas (1995) offers an important example when he documents the establishment of the U.S. Commission on Security and Cooperation in Europe as a congressional initiative, backed by transnational networks of NGOs and communist dissidents; the Ford administration initially hesitated to burden diplomatic ties with such focused attention to Helsinki's so-called "third basket," its package of agreements on human rights. Successive presidential administrations have also preferred to retain executive initiative in deciding the relative priority of such concerns within the larger agenda.

Even following the collapse of communism, democratization assistance activities that incorporate a human rights agenda have tended to run on a lower-profile track in which aid is increasingly targeted to the development of post-communist civil society, and reportage on violations is left to annual State Department reports; sanctions, if any, are incorporated into the larger foreign policy agenda. There is thus something of a disconnect between routinized activity in support of human rights and the decidedly unroutinized imposition of conditionality to constrain rights violations (OMRI Daily Digest 57, March 1, 1997). Probably the single most important consideration that intervenes to modify Western emphasis on human rights is an overarching preoccupation with the dangers of isolating Russia and thus destabilizing it. In the absence of a clear conception of Russia's place in the post-Cold War order and the European state system, the problem of isolating it is very real and corresponds directly to Russian sensitivities about its eroding international position.

These stability concerns underline the fact that the impact of external actors on Russia's human rights practices is distinctly constrained in contrast with Eastern Europe. East European countries do have an identifiable position in the post-communist order—the prospect of "joining Europe." Despite ongoing reconfiguration of the NATO-Russia relationship, most recently in the NATO-Russia council of 2002, there is no immediate hope or expectation of Russian entry to the European Union or NATO, thereby diminishing Russia's stake in Western approval. The Russian leadership does of course have compelling interest in Western aid, trade, investment, and security cooperation. But the tight conditionality that attends East European compliance with both the EU's *acquis communitaire* and broader strictures of

Western governments and multilateral organizations set as requirements for accession to the European Union and NATO does not operate on the Russian government.

Concerns with stability may dovetail rather nicely in the long term with a project of promoting democracy and human rights as the underpinning of a broader democratic peace, but in the shorter term, states and multilaterals often tend to consider the interests of stability better served by acquiescence in the Russian policy of the moment. At times there is even a direct convergence of interest in repressive behavior, or at least a form of mental double bookkeeping, as when Western states contemplate the nightmare of Russian federation dissolution and further instability in the Caucasus and in the broader transition zone that borders the Islamic Middle East and South Asia. Likewise, Western officials gritted their teeth and refrained from calling Yeltsin to account for the violent dissolution of the Russian Supreme Soviet in 1993, or for the murky circumstances under which the new constitution was formulated and approved. If Soviet Russia threatened mightily in its strength, just how much does it now threaten in its weakness?

These considerations are compounded by the fact that Russia's international weight, even as a faded superpower, still mandates special treatment. A nuclear power with a permanent seat on the UN Security Council is in a bargaining position to repel specific external expectations. The Russian capacity to cooperate or defect from UN coalition building in security matters is but the larger sense in which the West needs Russia as a partner in global order, whatever the state of its own domestic constitution. Hence some of the general limitations of human rights activism are writ large in dealing with Russia.

Multilateral Actors

In Europe since World War II, multilateral organizations have provided the most important venue for normative elaboration of human rights protocols. (Indeed, after the collapse of communism, the proliferation of new normative rights regimes even led some analysts to worry that such organizations as the European Union, the Council of Europe and the Organization for Security and Cooperation in Europe might be getting in each other's way, as they strove to codify democratic norms in their membership requirements.) Although this multilateralism was stimulated in North America and Western Europe as an antidote to overriding state self-interest inherent in bilateral relations, it is fair to say that multilateralism is only partly successful in shaking the stigma of power politics from relations with Russia, where for both elites and the public the multilateral agency is the voice of the "West." The "West" is a construct that imputes an overriding intentionality to an abstraction, but it is nonetheless a very vivid one in Russian public discourse on power relationships. This prescription is particularly problematic in human rights assistance efforts; significant segments of both the Russian public and its leadership flirt with the conspiratorial understanding of Western aid as a plot to weaken Russia. And the Russian media are quick to pounce on evidence of double standards, as when linking the disputed U.S. presidential election of 2000 to American lectures on free elections in Russia, or in contrasting U.S. treatment of prisoners and civilians in Afghanistan with Russian behavior in Chechnya.

Even where conspiratorial thinking is absent, international initiatives play into a climate of public opinion in which external influence carries a sting. In a 1999 poll more than seven out of ten Russians felt Moscow to be over-dependent on the West (RFE/RL Newsline, May 10, 1999). Such sentiments tend to reach a crescendo when, as during the NATO Kosovo offensive in the spring of 1999, Western actors are perceived to be riding roughshod over Russian international interests.

External human rights initiatives also flow into the elite debate over the Atlanticist versus Eurasian emphasis in the post-Soviet formation of Russian identity and national interests. Eurasianist thinking—increasingly predominant since the mid-1990s—tends to view human rights advocacy as a specifically Western package imposing a new hegemonic ideology—and to assail it on that basis. Even the relatively sympathetic reformist elites with a more Atlanticist orientation show limits to their tolerance for Western intercession. Former deputy prime minister and Duma vice chair Boris Nemtsov (2000) conveys something of this resentment of Western engagement:

For a decade we have experienced humiliation after humiliation: loss of superpower status, vast and disorienting social problems, NATO's eastern expansion. No one pays any attention to Russia: not over Yugoslavia; not over decisions concerning former Soviet republics, where significant Russian populations reside. The West often claimed to be helping. Russia made a show of gratitude. But honestly speaking, nothing has been done that could not be explained by pure self interest.

Absent the conspiratorial reading, Russian officials are of course correct to understand multilateral agencies as responding to broader Western policy agendas of their member states. The impact of those considerations on multilateral activity in enforcing normative rights regimes has been pronounced, as I hope to illustrate in the cases of the engagement of the Organization for Security and Cooperation in Europe (OSCE) and the Council of Europe with Russia.

The Organization for Security and Cooperation in Europe

The OSCE had its genesis in the Helsinki process of the 1970s. Although it became more fully institutionalized in the 1990s and its agenda has evolved and expanded, some of its dynamics remain constant: the framework remains inclusive (54 European countries now belong), basically consensual in its activity, and organized as a context for deliberation and ongoing follow-up on areas of contention. It is important to emphasize the mission that the organization's title inscribes: the OSCE is not, despite the significance of its original "third basket" human rights agenda and its continuing engagement in democratic and human rights questions, *wholly* concerned with promoting such an agenda. To be sure, at the Copenhagen conference of 1990, all member states subscribed to the declaration that "pluralistic democracy and the rule of law are essential for ensuring respect for all human rights and fundamental freedoms" (Kritz 1993; Manes 1996). The value dissensus of the Cold War has given way to a convergence that enabled considerable expansion of OSCE activity (to encompass, for example, election monitoring and mediation). Nonetheless, its core concern continues to be security and conflict resolution. Like individual states, therefore, the OSCE has potentially conflicting priorities.

This point can be illustrated in its intensifying engagement in ethnic conflict prevention, a landmark in the evolution of the organizational mission and a centerpiece of the components of that mission grouped under the heading of the "human dimension." Although the treatment of minorities was mentioned tangentially in the Helsinki Final Act, there was no institutional mandate to respond to the volatile ethnonational tensions that erupted in post-communist Europe. Spurred in part by the organization's helplessness to modulate festering Yugoslav tensions, discussion of ethnonational threats to security began in earnest in 1990, when the documents of the Copenhagen meeting included a separate chapter on minority issues. This detailed listing of expectations about minority treatment, although heavily qualified by concessions to raison d'état, was underscored the following year when the expert conference on national minorities in Geneva resolved that minority issues were of "legitimate international concern" rather than "an exclusively internal affair."[5]

This normative reformulation of the limits of national sovereignty regarding minority rights outstripped in emphasis and details any other international human rights regime on national identity questions up to that time, including that of the United Nations itself. The Moscow conference in October 1991 hammered out a "mechanism" for providing experienced mediators and fact-finding missions to deal with targeted ethnic problems. An important practical step in this process was the subsequent establishment, in July 1992, of a High Commissioner of National Minorities, charged with developing an "early warning" system to identify and help defuse ethnic tensions that might escalate to regionally destabilizing levels. Koen Koch (1993, 254) emphasizes the mission of this institution as conflict prevention rather than minority rights per se. In one sense the security focus of this approach is to the good, raising the profile of minority rights problems. All the same the purpose of interventions in such cases is not to achieve a given quality of observance of human rights as such, but rather to assure that existing tensions are contained below the threshold of violence. Thus the power resources of the contentious parties—or rather their troublemaking quotients—as much as their recognized rights have motivated OSCE intervention.

Russian interest in OSCE initiatives was initially directed outward. From the early 1990s, the Russian government made the strongest and most sustained case for its augmented importance. It was attractive both for its inclusiveness (and the consequent Russian role) and for its potential utility in minority rights championship. Because of its concern over the status of Russian minorities in the Near Abroad, the Russian government was an ardent champion of elaboration of a minority rights role for the organization, and was instrumental in the accords of the early 1990s that positioned that question as one that individual countries were not entitled to regard as a purely internal issue.

Nonetheless, for Russia as well as for the broad international community, the OSCE was above all a conflict resolution forum and potentially a vehicle for a broad pan-European security framework. The crystallization of East European interest in NATO membership only intensified Russian insistence on the superior claims of the OSCE. At the organization's Budapest meeting of December 1994, Yeltsin dismissed blocs as guarantors of security (NATO was clearly indicated), and pressed for an alternative model in which the OSCE anchored the European security order (*Rossiiskaya Gazeta* 1994). This enthusiasm dampened as the NATO alternative gained clear supremacy, and the first East Central European members joined; as the OSCE proved resistant to providing an acquiescent umbrella for Russian peacekeeping missions in the Near Abroad; and as OSCE turned frequently unwelcome attention to internal Russian issues such as Chechnya.

OSCE's enlarged normative and pragmatic focus on minority rights gave it a serious role to play in the strife-ridden former Soviet Union, where OSCE missions have engaged in fact-finding, mediating, and monitoring missions (Chayes 1996); in light of Russia's own active engagement in the "near abroad," OSCE and the Russian government have frequently tripped over each other. The saga of OSCE-Russian relations on Chechnya has been particularly fraught. OSCE perceptions that their missions have been "taken for a ride" by the Russian government have pervaded both Chechen conflicts. Although the OSCE has had the backing of threatened EU trade sanctions in some of its endeavors to establish a monitoring and mediating presence in the secessionist republic, monitors have had to battle constantly for access. In its stabilization initiative, the OSCE has undoubtedly performed valuable services, both in mediation and in Chechen election monitoring in 1997, even in the face of Russian official disapprobation. However it is possible to argue that over time OSCE mediational efforts tended to undermine sharp criticism on the human rights dimension. OSCE actors often fear that such criticism could unbalance their mediation efforts; agreement becomes the paramount value. Notable in the aftermath was the absence of a sustained effort to bring Russia to account for the well-documented human rights violations that permeated the conflict, documented in many cases by OSCE monitors. There has been a pattern of criticism, engagement, and modulation of criticism in the second Chechen conflict as well. The OSCE has been a major contributor to conflict management in the post-Cold War period, but the very complexities of its mission have sometimes impeded the promotion of its own normative agenda.

Council of Europe

Russian interaction with the Council of Europe offers a further example of the complexities of the relationship between multilateral actors and target states. As central guardian of the democratic norm, the Council of Europe became an important target of affiliation for all post-communist states. States accorded membership could herald their success as a validation of at least a minimal threshold of democratic performance. In Russia's case, this consideration had some very specific relevance.

In the case of East and Central European states, Council leverage during the admissions process was enhanced by the perception of the institution as a gateway to the prized goals of affiliation with NATO and the European Union. Council membership served as a gauge of a state's satisfactory democratization quotient for other organizations, and part of the overall integration strategy. In the words of Polish law professor Krzysztof Drzewicki, "the best way to Brussels leads . . . through Strasbourg" (1991, 88). this consideration was less constraining for Russia, whose own objectives did not include immediate affiliation with the European Union or NATO; visible public exclusion from the democracy club, however, would itself be a source of stigma for Russia, and a strategic liability in dealing with the rights claims of its neighbors.

No state was compelled to submit to democratic vetting of the Council of Europe, but those who did aspire to membership prospectively mortgaged parts of their sovereignty and agenda-setting autonomy to the organization. Over the course of its history, the Council of Europe has ratified almost 150 conventions binding on its membership, and new members are expected to come into compliance with these conventions over time. Ratification of Council human rights protocols (the ECHR), for example, entitles individual citizens or groups of citizens in member states to appeal grievances to the Human Rights Committee, and to binding adjudication by the EHCR. Moreover, the Council has a highly visible and elaborate accession process, premised precisely on rights observance. Each aspirant member must agree to a specifically targeted package of policy and legal adjustments, recommendations that emerge from the pre-membership investigation and that generally carry a timetable for compliance. Facing the wave of new post-communist memberships, the Council Assembly in 1993 empowered two of its committees to monitor and regularly report on commitments made by new members (Council of Europe Assembly Order 488, 1995). The writ of the specific biannual monitoring process ran indefinitely, until relevant Council bodies attested compliance, at which point the broader commitments inscribed in the Council's multiple conventions would remain the yardstick of membership in good standing.

In practice, however, this evaluation process has been a very delicate balancing act. In the first place, it was often a close call to determine the stage of transition at which the award of Council membership would be most effective in promoting democratization: states with clear and continuing democratic deficits achieved membership in accordance with this necessarily subjective calculation. Romania's admission, despite serious questions regarding the country's human and minority rights policies, went forward on the grounds that to delay would "discourage" both the incumbent government and its opposition[6]—a slippery logic that weighed heavily in the Russian case as well.

The Russian membership effort sheds considerable light on the payoffs and limitations of multilateral engagement for human rights protection. The timing of the Russian membership bid was closely tied to the ongoing conflicts over the status of the Russian minorities in the Baltic States, and the pace and scope of Russian troop withdrawal from Baltic territory. Estonia and Latvia in particular faced continuing Russian charges of minority discrimination. Russia in turn faced the problem of exerting pressure for the protection of its co-nationals abroad in a way that did not appear coercive, to the detriment of the new state's international standing. In effect the mutual Russian and Baltic applications put the Council of Europe in the position of arbitrator of human rights norms on the treatment of minorities.

Each side regarded early admission as a way of validating its own stance. The presumption that a state could not be democratic without having achieved a satisfactory ethnonational bargain was central here. The validation of Latvian and Estonian democratic credentials by the Council would undercut the Russian bargaining position on the minority issue. Conversely, Russian officials repeatedly noted that Council membership would provide a channel to "air grievances" on the treatment of Russian-speakers in the Baltics. Hence there was a competitive race into the Council of Europe.

In receiving the Russian application, the Swiss president of the Council delineated certain key areas of concern that amounted to a customized package of membership requirements. The obstacles to membership initially set forth included the "presence of former Soviet troops in the Baltics" and the resolution of the "situation of the Russian-speaking population there." Russia, in turn, accompanied its application with a "Memorandum on Human Rights Violations in the Baltic Countries," and continued to press that issue thereafter. However, subsequent expectations surrounding Russian qualifications for membership were responsive primarily to events in *domestic* Russian politics. Cataclysms within Russia prompted continual revisions of Council expectations about what constituted an appropriate country-specific level of achievement. Russian journalists later grumbled that the Council of Europe kept raising new obstacles: troop withdrawals, democratic elections, and resolution of the Chechen conflict.

Russian complaints about the Council's monitoring and evaluation process might seem trivial in light of the sizable disruptions of normal democratic practice that occurred in the presidential-parliamentary showdown of 1993 and the turbulent interventions in Chechnya starting in 1994, but these complaints do reflect a fairly accurate picture of the Council's vetting and its focus both on large issues of democratic practice and more detailed examination of specific statutes and procedures. Russian aspirations for Council membership temporarily came to grief over the Chechnya conflict. The scheduled Russian membership vote in February 1995, about two and a half months into that conflict, resulted in a decision not merely to defer admission, but in harsher language to "freeze" all consideration. Russian journalistic commentary immediately cried foul for the perceived "double standard" operative in admitting Latvia and Estonia unconditionally to membership the previous month. Russian officials complained bitterly that this implied Western support of Baltic minority policy. Russian officials had, as we saw in the case of the OSCE, labored to develop a multilateral context for the treatment of ethnonational disputes, but in this instance failed to gain the payoff.

The Russian Federation's eventual attainment of full membership in the Council of Europe in early 1996, however, paints a different picture of the Council's strictness in exercising its gatekeeping function. The Chechen war was still in progress, although peace negotiations had begun. The Council's parliamentary committee itself acknowledged that Russia did not meet its standards, but argued "integration is better than isolation" (OMRI Daily Digest 247, December 21, 1995). Council membership, it was urged— and even Russia's human rights commissioner reluctantly concurred—would encourage progress in problem areas. In turn the Russian foreign ministry urged the Duma to ratify the membership agreement with the by-then familiar refrain that Council membership better positioned the Russian government to protect ethnic Russians living abroad.

In theory the salutary effects of Council membership for Russia were bolstered by the specific commitments that Russia undertook to implement following accession. The Council of Europe's Parliamentary Assembly recommendation for Russian membership outlined ten general areas in which Russia had promised to improve and twenty-five specific Russian pledges of action in support of those undertakings (Council of Europe Parliamentary Assembly Opinion 1996). In short, the accession process set a human rights agenda. In practice, however, the specificity of Russian commitments was not a guarantor of compliance.

The Human Rights Watch report issued in 1997 on the anniversary of Russia's accession to the Council of Europe sheds light on this question in several respects: as documentation of the Russian human rights record on an agenda set by its accession agreement; as a reflection of the limitations of multilateral monitoring of such commitments; and as an illustration of the critical role that NGOs can play in sharpening agendas. The report makes clear that Russian compliance with its membership agreement was spotty on a range of issues, including in particular the investigation of human rights violations during the Chechnya war, prison conditions, and failure to abolish the death penalty. Human Rights Watch rapporteurs attached responsibility not only to the Russian government, but also targeted the Council itself, expressing concern about its lack of persistent follow-up and about "the degree to which Council of Europe's human rights admission requirements are negotiable, rather than standardized, leaving the process vulnerable to political, security, and other considerations that can obscure human rights goals" (Human Rights Watch 1997).

Criticism of the Council's will to pursue violations of its own specifically crafted membership agreements has been widespread. The Council of Europe's dilemma in dealing with its new "pan-European vocation" of shepherding post-communist states into the democratic fold was dramatically underlined by the resignation of its Deputy Secretary General Peter Leuprecht in 1997 in protest over what he perceived as the dilution of the Council's human rights standards through the premature extension of membership to the underqualified. Leuprecht specifically named Russia (along with Croatia and Romania) as countries far removed from the requisite standards of human rights observance. Leuprecht's protest highlights the dilemma of the multilateral organization that pursues a human rights agenda under the constraints of the larger foreign policy agendas of member states. The Council's initial equivocation in calling Russia to account for its conduct of the second Chechen war received considerable media attention, much of it focused on the Russian ability to deflect embarrassing criticism through its membership on the Council parliamentary affairs committee.

In April 2000 the Council of Europe, faced with continuing reports of rights violations in Chechnya and lack of transparency in domestic investigation of those violations, finally moved to suspend Russia's voting rights in the organization. In the same period European Union representatives had generated a chastisement of Russian practices in the UN Human Rights Commission. Still the Council refrained from taking harsher measures suggested by Russian human rights advocates or from threatening expulsion, expressing the wish to send "positive signals" to the Russian government. The discipline imposed by public criticism and by suspension of voting privilege was largely symbolic; still, the sanctions themselves and the presence of Council of Europe Assembly members at Russian Duma debates about

Chechnya highlighted the human rights dimensions of future policy and in that way shaped the domestic agenda on Chechnya.

Council membership did, however, have more clearly specifiable pay-offs for human rights advocacy. One concrete step in conjunction with accession to the Council of Europe was Duma approval of the European Convention on Human Rights in February 1998; in legal terms, the Council's strongest rights protection feature is the binding jurisdiction of the European Court on Human Rights over signatory countries. Although the appeals process is cumbersome and protracted, it does provide recourse for individuals who fail to obtain redress from their own governments; hundreds of Russian complaints already awaited evaluation by the European Human Rights Commission at the time of Duma ratification.

Nongovernmental Organizations and Transnational Human Rights Networks

States and multilateral organizations are not the only important international actors. The establishment of a human rights agenda in the communist period was intimately linked with the international community by transnational ties between nascent dissident groups and the complex of existing NGOs. For dissidents the support of established human rights organizations was central to the pursuit of a human rights strategy of holding governments to public account for the non-observance of formal guarantees inscribed in state constitutions and international agreements. In the absence of domestic enforcement mechanisms, the transnational linkages helped maintain public visibility and muster at least limited pressure in several key areas of concern, not least the harassment of dissidents and political prisoners. The transmission mechanisms for implementing this strategy had a multi-stage character. In the first instance, the responsive international audience was a complex of NGOs (the writers' international PEN or Amnesty International) whose credibility in documenting abuses of civil and political rights might in turn set an agenda for Western governments.

In many respects, transnational actors were themselves agenda setters; contacts with Western-based NGOs triggered and helped to sustain efforts to document environmental and health abuses, for example. Most powerful in impact was the Helsinki process, which had particular normative political resonance because the Eastern governments had signed on to its Western rights agenda. The Helsinki Watch committees that proliferated throughout the bloc have survived to play an important role in the post-communist era, with dramatically expanded agenda and public voice.

It is important to emphasize that the effectiveness of external NGOs is a direct function of the extent to which they operate in concert with domestic actors in the target country—in short, it is the transnational network that acts to document, analyze, and then disseminate human rights assessments. It is the network that gives these initiatives their credibility, with internal actors capable of interpreting a well-known domestic environment, and the more established and prosperous international NGO lending credibility and resources to the dissemination of those insights.

External support also produced some unintended and unanticipated consequences. First of all, the human rights agendas of international actors tended to penetrate nascent post-communist civil societies, at times distorting or usurping existing agendas. It is not hard to grasp how this could happen. When external actors with money mounted the quest for domestic partners, responsive domestic actors could easily find themselves tailoring their objectives to what was fundable—thus absorbing external priorities. Domestic resources were scarce. As Valerie Sperling (1999, 228) notes, the unpopularity of fundraising and the underinstitutionalization of it magnified the lure of outside support philanthropy. Scholars have thus identified a "dependency syndrome," in which domestic actors lose incentive to build a broader base, responding instead to the most important audience—the funders—thus creating hothouse human rights activism that could not survive the withdrawal of external support. Other critics have scrutinized the credentials of local partners, noting the opening for opportunists whose nose for grant money is stronger than their principled commitments.

Organizational resources are also diverted. As Patricia Chilton (1996) observes, Western funders expect the accouterments of Western organizational activity—offices, hierarchical structures, and regular meetings—that were often alien to the prior egalitarian logic of informal personalist networks. Sperling (1999, 234–36) is among those who have raised the additional concern, based on interviews with Russian women's rights activists, that competition for limited resources from external funders has at times proved a divisive factor atomizing broader rights communities. In such competition factors that may have no bearing on a group's effectiveness, such as English language competence to fill out the inevitable grant applications, may prove critical, breeding resentment that an in-group has "captured" foreign donors.

The transnational network itself is vulnerable to challenge by domestic opponents as interlopers. This is a specific manifestation of the broader problem of political backlash against foreign standard setting on human rights. The problems that Soros-funded groups have experienced in protecting their legitimacy as domestic actors is a case in point, even though Soros programs have been, from the outset, more sensitive to fostering local initiative than many other organizations have been. Despite the contributions that NGOs have made to the development of rights consciousness in transitional settings, therefore, intervention has had distinct limitations in generating self-sustaining civil societies capable of challenging rights abuses.

Summary

In the final analysis, the Russian government itself must effectuate reliable observance of human rights, providing the specific context within which the support of the international community is useful. However, a number of sympathetic critics of general democracy assistance programs have pointed to problematic dimensions of that support. One of the most thoughtful has been Thomas Carothers (1997, 112–16, 122–24) of the Carnegie Endowment for International Peace. A central finding of his studies is that official American efforts (through the National Endowment for Democracy and the USAID) and those of other Western governments initially tended to center on what he terms "institutional modeling," in which assistance providers work from a model of Western political structures as desired endpoints, measure recipient countries by that standard, and then target aid programs to close the gaps between the idealized Western model and local practices. Lost in this exercise, he suggests, are domestic political interests that can, of course, substantially impede or reconfigure outcomes that shape democratization.

One of the judgments made by Western states, multilateral organizations, and NGOs following the collapse of communism was that civil society in post-communist states, long suppressed under communism, was too weak to effectively press for a higher quality of democracy. As Larry Diamond (1999, 10–23) recently argued, mere electoral democracy is not an adequate safeguard of the broader array of civil liberties and human rights that make democracy sustainable. The corollary judgment was that there was a compelling need for external support in jumpstarting civil society so that post-communist citizens would develop a sense of efficacy, and the resources sufficient to compel states to put these critical issues on the agenda—in other words, the goal was not just to press for human rights from without, but to foster domestic capacity to shoulder that task.

But perhaps the most important component of an effective international rights strategy is a sober assessment of Russian "rights readiness," and priority attached to the creation of a functional legal system. Hungarian law professor András Sajó (1997, 44) comments: "Although firmly convinced of the superior quality of their detergent—that is human rights—NGOs have first to discover if washing machines in the recipient nations are in working condition and even if the people there feel a need to wash their clothing." He thus warns against imposition of formal rights in an institutional vacuum: "strategies for protecting rights that assume the existence of competent and honest courts and public bureaucracies are counterproductive whenever such conditions do not exist."

Such warnings highlight the importance for human rights of indirect strategies to create institutional order and economic stability. Enhancing criminal justice system capacities is important not only because it contributes to rule of law in a general sense, but also does so in an area that strikes a strongly resonant popular nerve. Such initiatives contribute to a climate within which citizens feel they have the "luxury" of attention to human rights concerns. Ronald Inglehart (1997) has argued that rights-sensitivity grows with the establishment of socioeconomic security that creates the basis for post-material values. However one evaluates the specific features of their post-materialist credo, there is little question that citizens pressed by fears of crime and unemployment are psychologically and practically unreceptive to less tangible problems.

The prospects for Russian actualization of the extensive human rights agenda incorporated in its constitution seem critically dependent on the establishment of law and order, in the sense of routinized expectations of personal safety, government responsiveness, and economic security. It would seem important for international actors to be able to stomach a dose of in-strumental utility along with the "oughtness" of human rights norms. Western rights proponents must continue to choose their battles to challenge practices that have maximal effect on constraining human liberty, but to define those challenges in terms that put priority on abuses that are readily identified and monitored. And then mean what we say.

Chapter 12
Latin America

Howard J. Wiarda

Latin America has always fit awkwardly into the prevailing paradigms that scholars and policy officials have used to categorize the area (Martz 1966; P. Smith 1995). Try answering these questions unambiguously: Is Latin America Western or, with its large indigenous communities, non-Western? Is it developed or developing, traditional or modern, and as compared to what, the United States or Africa? Is it Third World or, with its recent impressive economic growth, First World, or must we further disaggregate by country or area? Is it authoritarian, democratic, or "illiberal democracy," in Larry Diamond's (1999a) phrase? Is it capitalist, mercantilist, or some "crazy quilt" hodgepodge of all of these?

A good place to begin is to recognize the immense diversity of Latin America and the difficulty of stuffing the countries there into a single intellectual straitjacket. Argentina is very different from Paraguay on a host of developmental measures; Mexico and Brazil are not at all the same; within a common cultural tradition, every country is different. A second preliminary point is that every country in Latin America is an incredible mix of the dichotomies noted above: Western *and* non-Western, traditional *and* modern, First *and* Third World, developed *and* developing, capitalist *and* feudal, democratic *and* authoritarian. These mixes, this hodgepodge, make the area endlessly fascinating from the specialist's point of view but consistently frustrating from the point of view of those who would prefer to categorize the region in simplistic terms.

A third point of departure, particularly relevant for this book, is to think of Latin America as *predominantly* "Western," but as the product of a special part and tradition of the West: Spain and Portugal circa 1500. For just as the United States is a "fragment" of seventeenth- and eighteenth-century English culture and Afrikaner South Africa a product of seventeenth-century Dutch-Calvinist culture, so also the politics, sociology, economics, religion, and overall culture of Latin America are products of a particular time and place: in this case, the Iberia of the Hapsburgs, the Reconquista (the reconquest of the peninsula from the Moors), the Counter-Reformation and Inquisition, the special nature of Iberian feudalism (tied to military conquest and religious crusade), and the development of Spanish and Portuguese centralized royal absolutism set against the historic rights (*fueros*) of communities, regions, and corporate groups. All these factors would have a profound impact on democracy and human rights, or the frequent absence thereof, in Latin America.

Democracy and Human Rights in the Latin American Tradition

If the United States is, following Hartz (1955), predominantly liberal and Lockean (and Madisonian, Jeffersonian, Jacksonian, Tocquevillian, Lincolnian, Wilsonian, Rooseveltian, Johnsonian, Reaganian, and Clintonian), what then is Latin America? The answer, at least historically, is Aristotelian, Augustinian, Thomistic, Hapsburgian, Suárezian, Rousseauian, Comtean, Rodóian, Rerum Novarian, Perónian, Maritanean, Vatican II-ian, and democratic, but often in a distinctively Latin American way. Obviously this shorthand list of theorists and practitioners in Latin America and the United States is vastly simplified. But it does suggest that, while Western, Latin America is the product of a quite different and particular intellectual, philosophical, and political tradition from that of the United States (Wiarda 2001). Unless we understand this historical and sociocultural background, we will not understand the difficult travail of democracy and human rights in Latin America.

Latin America was discovered or "encountered" in 1492 and all but fully conquered and settled, in terms of its political theory and institutional arrangements, by 1570, whereas the North American colonies were not settled until the seventeenth century, fully a century and more later. Between these two dates, a veritable revolution—really, a series of revolutions—had happened in world affairs that literally separated the modern from the premodern world. The United States lies on one side of that divide and Latin America on the other (Leonard 1963).

Let us use the year 1500, as do most historians, to separate the medieval from the modern period. Latin America was (and in many respects remains) a product of the pre-1500 period: feudal, authoritarian, top-down, two-class, dominated by religious orthodoxy and monism, and with its intellectual life based on revealed truth, rote memorization, and deductive reasoning. By contrast, by the time the North American colonies were founded fully a century later, the hold of feudal and medieval institutions had largely been broken, at least in northwest Europe (Holland, England). Politically, there was already a move toward limited and representative government; economically, capitalism was replacing feudalism; socially, a multiclass society had begun to grow; religiously, the Protestant Reformation was giving rise to religious and eventually political pluralism; and intellectually, the scientific revolution of Galileo and Newton produced an empirical, inductive, experiential system of reasoning. In short, the United States in the seventeenth century was "born free" in Hartz's term, without a feudal past, and already launched into modernity; whereas Latin America, launched in the pre-1500 or pre-modern period, was obliged to wear the yoke of feudalism. Once established and consolidated, these institutions remained locked in place, showing remarkable durability and persistence even into the modern era. Essentially, Latin American history, 1492 to the present, can be read as an effort to overcome and to accommodate to this powerful feudal past.

The Spanish-Portuguese and by extension Latin American tradition of political thought—and understanding of democracy and human rights—is very different from that of the Anglo-American tradition. We begin with Aristotle, keeping in mind the overall point that there is an entirely different, but nevertheless continuous stream of thought in the Iberian-Latin American tradition that runs parallel to and competes with dominant North American Lockean liberalism (Wiarda and Mott 2001).

When Aristotle looked at the world around him, he perceived a well-organized system in which the totality of being was laid out in an ascending, hierarchical order. Contrary to U.S. egalitarian precepts, the world according to Aristotle was one in which the natural inequalities (of talents, intelligence, capabilities) of beings might exist in perfect symmetry. The path to wisdom involved comprehending every order of being from the least to the greatest.

Aristotle transposed this natural order onto the political sphere. The ascending order of natural potential became the ascending order of social and political potential. Recall Aristotle accepted the idea of a "natural" slave class; in his view slaves were only capable of labor. On the next rung, artisans were capable of labor and trade. Proceeding upward, soldiers were capable of labor, trade, and warfare; philosophers were capable of labor, trade, warfare, and intellectual activities; kings were capable of *all* activities. It was assumed that those higher on the social ladder were capable of performing all the tasks beneath them, although their level of perfection required that they focus on the higher skills. Fulfilling one's potential depended on accepting and being in one's natural place in the universe. Already, in these formulations one can begin to see Latin America's class-based, top-down, hierarchical order with its rigidities locked in place (Wiarda 2001).

Government was understood as the maintenance of harmony and proportionality in accord with the laws of nature. Those who operated on the highest rung were supposed to use their powers for the benefit of the lower creatures, directing them where they needed to go. Ruling necessitated that those at the top comprehend every order of citizen from the greatest to the least. This, of course, was a formula for later feudalism or for a national patronage system based on mutual obligation; a ruler took care of his people and they, in return, owed him loyalty and service.

Aristotle's comprehensive vision of functionally diverse groups organically unified under a just and caring ruler took on spiritual dimensions in early church doctrine. Inequality in the Christian conception was also natural; indeed, it was the method of God's creation. Along with the ladder image and its social hierarchy, however, Saint Paul used the metaphor of the human body that emphasized coordination as much as hierarchy:

> For the body does not consist of one member but of many. If the foot should say, "Because I am not a hand, I do not belong to the body," that would not make it any less a part of the body. . . . But as it is, God arranged the organs in the body, each one of them, as he chose. If all were a single organ, where would the body be? (1 Corinthians 12: 14–19)

Here, as with Aristotle's inclusive hierarchy, wisdom is predicated on understanding the system as a whole. It is not enough to work on one's own perfection; one must also strive to perfect the entire body, including the body politic, in an ordered and controlled fashion. Serving the common good requires more than the fulfillment of individual lives; more important is the recognition that, without coordination of a diversity of functions— of limbs and organs, to use St. Paul's metaphor—there would be no body politic. The body image is particularly useful because it introduces the organic, corporate notion of existence and functionality in which different types of people work together in complementary fashion. It also introduces the idea of an authoritative, if not authoritarian, ruling head, an organ again naturally created to reason for the good of all the other members, but not necessarily chosen by democratic elections.

The models of both Aristotle and Paul, given man's natural inequalities, require that the law not be applied equally to all citizens. All members have equal honor and dignity, but not all function by the same principles and needs. A recognition that different groups in society require different legal measures is consistent with the natural order of things. This argument is given particular force and clarity in Thomas Aquinas, the greatest philosopher of the Christian tradition, whose hierarchy of laws (divine, eternal, natural, manmade) and elaborate construction of a God-given Christian polity, based on the wedding of Aristotelian logic and argument and Christian principles, was enormously influential in the Middle Ages, and particularly in Spain and Portugal. One can readily see how the Spanish and Portuguese custom of group rights (*fueros*) would find political legitimacy in the doctrines established by Aristotle, Paul, and Aquinas: the law is applied differently, depending on one's place in the hierarchy. Individual rights may need to be sacrificed to corporate, society, community, or group rights. One can also see how the supremacy of an emerging central monarchy—that is, the head of the body—might challenge or subordinate corporate group rights, should they threaten to destroy the central unity of the whole. And if mere man-made law (constitutions, bills of human and civil rights) should ever be in conflict with higher law, we can be certain which of these would need to be sacrificed. All these principles had a profound effect on later Latin American conceptions of human and civil rights.

Based on Aristotelian-Christian-Thomistic principles, Spain and Portugal began to emerge as centralized nation-states in the period from the twelfth through the fifteenth centuries (Post 1964; McKay 1977). In Iberia the struggle for national unity was complicated and powerfully shaped by the simultaneous Christian reconquest of the peninsula from the Moors. The reconquest strongly influenced the particular nature of Hispanic militarism, since the fighting military orders were above and prior to the existence of the state. It similarly had a lasting influence on Spanish and Portuguese feudalism, rendering it quite different from the French model because land and the right to the labor on the land were tied to military conquest—another principle that would be carried over to Latin America.

As Spain and Portugal began to develop the first modern, bureaucratic nation-states in Western Europe, four main areas of tension emerged:

1. The struggle between the centralizing monarchy and the autonomy of various regions (Catalonia, the Basque country).
2. The struggle between the centralizing monarchy and the corporate or group rights of various towns, guilds, religious orders, military orders, and so forth. When these are in balance, it historically conforms to the Iberian-Latin American definition of "rights" and "democracy."
3. The struggle between Catholic orthodoxy and greater religious pluralism, as represented by Jews, Muslims, and eventually Protestants, Freemasons, and free thinkers.
4. The struggle between mercantilism as a guiding economic philosophy of the Crown and the more enterprising barter and free market system at the grass-roots level.

Every one of these tensions was resolved not in favor of democracy but in favor of centralist, absolutist royal authority. The personification of this series of triumphs was the "Catholic monarchs," Isabella and Ferdinand, and, subsequently, the Hapsburg and Bourbon monarchies. Hence, my use of the term "Hapsburg model" to describe this absolutist, top-down, two-class, semi-feudal, mercantilist, authoritarian, rigidly orthodox, deductive system that not only dominated Spain and Portugal for most of the next five hundred years, culminating in the regimes of Franco and Salazar, but also carried over to Latin America, where it received a new lease on life.

In the New World, the Spanish and Portuguese absolutist tradition was further strengthened by local conditions. First, the colonial countries found in the Americas a ready-made "peasantry" in the form of the indigenous populations, whom they could put to work, thus enabling every Spanish and Portuguese conquistador to live like a grandee. Where the local Indians were unwilling to work or died out, the colonists imported African slaves; hence a rigid, two-class, "feudal," and sometimes slave system was further reinforced by lines of caste and race. Second, because the New World was far away and communication difficult, the Spanish and Portuguese crowns concluded they would need to be even more absolutist in the colonies than at home—even though the writ of royal authority remained often difficult of enforcement. Third, within the colonies, given the difficult terrain, vast empty spaces, and lack of associational life and "civilization," the crowns—and their oligarchic and military successors in the period after independence—concluded they would need to be even stricter in enforcing hierarchy and absolutism, using whatever force was necessary (McAlister 1984).

Independence in Latin America was unlike the paradigmatic cases of democratization in England (1680), the United States (1776), and France (1789). Whatever there was of progressive or democratic movements was quickly suppressed; in those few instances where social and racial rebellion accompanied independence (Mexico), it was immediately eliminated. New constitutions were written that privileged order more than liberty or sought to combine the two, even while giving especially strong powers to the executive and the military. Into the vacuum created by the withdrawal of the Spanish and Portuguese crowns stepped the army, the Church, and the oligarchy (Stoetzer 1982; Dealy 1968). Latin America was democratic in law and constitution, but its operating institutions and even ideals were non- or anti-democratic.

The apostle of Latin American independence and republicanism was Rousseau. Rousseau's ideas stand in marked contrast to those of Lockean liberalism in the Anglo-American tradition. Rousseau, like Locke, sought to reconcile individual preferences with collective rules, but in Rousseau's concept of the general will, corporate, group, and societal rights were privileged more than individual rights. The interests of the state, presumably acting for the "general will," could take precedence over civil and human rights. Rousseau, in contrast to Locke, is impatient with the more prosaic aspects of democracy, like elections, compromise, and give-and-take, favoring instead a "great and glorious vision" that can presumably be accomplished by a heroic leader (such as Fidel Castro and many other "men-on-horseback" in Latin American history) who gallops into the presidential palace and miraculously "saves" the country, usually riding roughshod over human rights and ignoring the truly hard work of developing grass-roots associational life and building coalitions. Rousseau was well suited to charismatic leaders and despots who claim they alone embody that will. Rousseau's own efforts to extend human freedom were thus used and in fact subverted by the realities of Latin America and the kind of leaders that the tradition here described brought to power. Rousseau's influence is a powerful and continuing one in Latin America (witness Alberto Fujimori in Peru, Hugo Chávez in Venezuela, or the Mexican PRI), but one would be hard-pressed to say that this has been good for democracy or human rights (Rosenberg 1992).

The great leader of Latin American independence was Simón Bolívar (Belaúnde 1938). Bolívar was well educated, had traveled extensively in Europe and the United States, and was an accomplished military leader. He favored democracy and individual rights in the abstract for South America, but feared that his peoples were not sufficiently prepared for it. He pointed to the lack of education, the chaotic and violent conditions, the absence of any training or preparation in self-government, the large distances and empty territories, and above all the "falta de civilización" (literally, lack of civilization, by which he meant absence of what we would now call "civil society"). Bolívar proposed some realistic solutions: a monarchy in one place, a more limited monarchy in another, and a republic with a powerful executive in a third. Nowhere in Latin America did the prudent Bolívar propose a full-scale democracy. Hence, when Venezuelan President Hugo Chávez, a former army paratrooper, sent the Congress packing, removed court justices, wrote a new constitution that enormously enhanced his own power, argued that he alone personified Venezuela, and, variously, proclaimed himself a "Bolívarian" or "Rousseauian" democrat, *we* now know exactly what he meant.

In the course of the nineteenth century, a liberal tradition emerged in Latin America alongside the conservative Thomistic one, but it remained a minority—and generally unsuccessful—current. Beginning in the 1860s, liberalism was absorbed by the prevailing positivist influence, which dominated the continent's thinking through the rest of the century and beyond, even to today, and also provides rationalization for elite, authoritarian, nondemocratic rule (Conte 1975; Woodward 1971). What passes for liberalism in Latin America has always been closer to the continental European than the U.S. tradition: as a political philosophy that never went beyond nineteenth-century rights it was viewed as conservative and had few followers, and as an old fashioned laissez faire economic philosophy, in the words of two prominent historians of the nineteenth century, it "died" around the time of World War I (Peloso and Tenenbaum 1996). Meanwhile, in the early twentieth century a number of new political philosophies, similar to Thomism and Rousseauianism in their wholism and quasi-religious orthodoxy, sprang up, including Rodóism, which incorporated cultural nationalism and anti-Yankeeism (Rodó 1988); Hispanismo, admiration for all things Spanish (Pike 1971); nationalism; corporatism; Marxism; Christian democracy; social democracy; Fidelismo; and eventually neoliberalism (Wiarda 2001).

A number of features are common to all these political ideologies that form a part of the Latin American "living museum" (Anderson 1967). First, most ideologies in Latin America have been imported, from continental

Europe more than from the United States; the main exceptions, those that are more indigenous, include Rodóism, Hispanismo, and, arguably, Fidelismo. Second, they are almost all, in accord with the tradition outlined earlier, elite philosophies, top-down, imposed from above rather than reflecting grass-roots movements from below. Third, they have almost all been cooptive philosophies, aimed at absorbing new groups into the political system, but under elite control, with little change in the fundamental structure of power, a controlled accommodation to change rather than one that, revolutionary style, gets out of hand. Fourth, what is especially striking is how continuous this particular tradition is *and* how much at variance it is with the U.S. liberal-pluralist tradition and hostile toward individual rights.

But in recent decades, building on the earlier liberal strain already mentioned, new forces have challenged the prevailing political system. First, new, more liberal and democratic institutions—parties, unions, peasant movements, and so forth—have appeared in Latin America itself, a reflection of the changing social and power structure as outlined in the next section. Second, the influence and power of the United States in Latin America in the last one hundred years, to say nothing of such agencies as the World Bank, IMF, and now myriad international human rights organizations and NGOs, have obliged Latin America to become more democratic in the Anglo-American sense than would otherwise be the case. Third, with the Cold War over, Latin America's business community and the middle class generally recognize that they must become more democratic, or at least give off the appearance of democracy, or their "water" (investment, loans) will be cut off. So in Latin America there is always a delicate balance, as well as the ever-present possibility and even likelihood and reality of conflict and national breakdown, between doing things the old way (top-down, "Hapsburgian," cooptive, corporatist, authoritarian, patrimonialist), *and* the newer pressures of democracy, pluralism, and individual human rights.

Democracy and Human Rights in the Political Process

The analysis above paints an ideal-type portrait of a Latin America shaped and governed in a continuous, virtually unbroken pattern—before and after independence—based on conservative and quasi-feudal ideas and ideologies largely imported from the mother countries, Spain and Portugal, and from the larger, mainly continental European (Rousseau, Comte) tradition. But we know that Latin America has in fact long been torn by conflict, violence, and frequent instability over precisely these issues and over the issues of democracy and authoritarianism. In this section, building on the earlier discussion, we focus on three dimensions—intra-societal, societal-state, and state-to-state—of relevant relations in Latin America, bearing on the principles of legitimacy, norms, and the workings of the political process. The discussion is shaped by four questions that cut across and help illuminate these relations.

The first is, what is the *agenda* of democratization and human rights in Latin America? Latin America has now reached a level of socioeconomic and political development where issues of democratization and human rights are very much on the front burner. Reversing the proportions of forty years ago, Latin America as a whole is 70 percent urban and 70 percent literate. It is no longer a poor, backward, quasi-feudal area; almost all the countries occupy intermediary levels on the World Bank's listing of development, and several (Argentina, Brazil, Chile, Mexico) are poised to reach the next level of "advanced industrial economies." Latin America *wants* to be considered an advanced, modern, and First World area, and democracy and human rights are a crucial part of that agenda. Democracy and human rights, therefore, are related to the larger processes of regional and national development.

Latin America has, for the most part, passed the stage where intrastate and identity conflicts are so intense that democracy and human rights issues may, more than sporadically and temporarily, be pushed to the side. But on this issue one needs to distinguish among countries. Brazil has an increasingly self-conscious Afro-Brazilian movement, and in Bolivia, Brazil, Peru, Ecuador, Colombia, Guatemala, and Mexico there are sizable indigenous rights movements that are demanding a say in the political process or even autonomy for their region (VanCott 1994). Occasionally, these groups may cause societal disruption, as with the Zapatistas in Mexico, the Sendero Luminoso movement in Peru, or Indianist movements in Bolivia or Ecuador. Tensions on these issues remain in all the countries listed and to a lesser extent in a number of the other countries, but it seems unlikely that we will see anywhere in Latin America wholesale ethnic conflict, slaughter, and genocide as in Rwanda or large-scale "ethnic cleansing" as in the former Yugoslavia. The main process at work in Latin America is still assimilation of the indigenous population into Hispanic life or civilization, although in some countries at some times there will be tension and the potential for breakdown over the degrees and speed of assimilation-autonomy issues. A possible model might be Spain and the Basque country, a conflict that has smoldered for at least a thousand years, will never be completely resolved, and yet on most days and most issues is manageable.

While it seems unlikely that any country in Latin America will break down any time soon into full scale civil war over ethnic issues, there *are* a series of problems that affect democracy and human rights situations. The Dominican Republic is regularly criticized by human rights groups for its ill treatment of Haitian cane cutters who are often abused and their rights violated. Immigrants into the "European" countries of the Southern Cone (Argentina, Chile, Uruguay) from the more "Indian" countries of Peru, Bolivia, and Paraguay regularly complain of political, cultural, and racial prejudice. Mexico treats Indian immigrants from Guatemala badly, as Costa Rica does to Panamanian and Nicaraguan immigrants. In addition, in Brazil, Guatemala, Ecuador, Colombia, Peru, Bolivia, and other countries, indigenous groups are clamoring for recognition and often raise the charge of *genocide*, which may have some degree of truth behind it and is then often picked up by international human rights groups. Some of the larger indigenous groups' calls for autonomy cross present-day national borders (for instance, in the cases of the Mayas or Incas); they thus raise complex challenges to sovereignty and nationhood and bring the armed forces, nationalists, and other defenders of the Latin American nation-states into the dispute. Some of these disputes, as in Ecuador, have the potential to destabilize or help destabilize democratic governments and to involve serious human rights violations. At present, however, it seems unlikely that they will produce complete national breakdowns as seen in Angola, Kosovo, or Sierra Leone.

A second "null hypothesis" emerges from potential state-to-state conflict. It will surprise some readers to learn that Latin America, in terms of state-state conflict, has over the last two hundred years been the most peaceful area on earth. There is frequent internal or domestic conflict and violence, but few wars among nations. I do not wish to overstate this point, because virtually every national border in Latin America, despite those definitive-looking dark purple lines on our maps, is still contested, subject to irredentist nationalist movements, and there is the potential for interstate conflict in the twenty-first century that was not present in the nineteenth or twentieth (Falcoff 1984). Nevertheless, there is at least as much arms reduction and resolution of border and other conflicts (as recently between Argentina and Chile or Ecuador and Peru) as there are continued tensions, and at this stage it is hard to imagine full-scale war breaking out between any two countries that would not immediately be presented with the offer and pressures of mediation by the OAS, the United States, and neighboring countries. Recall also that, with Argentina and Brazil mutually abandoning their nuclear development programs, Latin America has become a nuclear-free zone.

That leaves the category of state-society relations, and it is here that the greatest potential for conflict and violence may occur. Latin America's political process as described previously has historically largely been corporatist and patrimonialist: emerging groups can either be coopted into the prevailing elitist system by accepting its norms and sharing in the benefits or face repression. That is largely the way first business groups, then the middle class, next organized labor, and more recently peasants, domestics, and day laborers have been incorporated. Now it is the "turn" of indigenous groups: they can accept the "carrot" of accommodation or they face the "stick" of repression. Often the process of assimilation of a new group such as this is a long one, lasting twenty to thirty years or more, accompanied by purposeful, structured violence on both sides that may get out of hand. For many of the groups noted above, the process of accommodation is still only partial and incomplete; the renegotiation, often accompanied by violence, of these state-society pacts is virtually an everyday occurrence. So if in Latin America there are large-scale human rights abuses, or even the breakdown of democracy as occurred in Ecuador in January 2000 and Venezuela in May 2002, it may be expected to occur in this state-society arena—affecting not just indigenous movements but also workers, peasants, and other marginal groups. An insensitive or undemocratic state is likely to be the principal source of threat to the fostering of an open society and human freedoms, often provoked by clamoring and mobilized societal groups, and offering the potential in still fragile, transitional countries for chaos, fragmentation, strife, and societal breakdown.

The second question is, how does the politics of democratization and human rights in Latin America play out? What are the principal actors and what is the balance of power among them in pushing for or against democratization and human rights? First, the traditional "evil triumvirate" of power in Latin America—church, army, oligarchy—is declining in power as the society has become more pluralistic, less Catholic, less "feudal," more educated, urban, and mobilized. As the socioeconomic basis of power has changed, the conservative ideological tradition associated with the old order has also declined. Most Latin Americans no longer accept the closed, authoritarian, absolutist, elitist ideologies and political structures that were once at the core of the political culture—even though there are still important and sometimes powerful legacies of these traditions (Wiarda 2001).

In general, as Latin America has become more developed and pluralist, support for democracy and human rights has increased. This trend has particularly strengthened as the "bureaucratic authoritarianism" (O'Donnell 1973; Collier 1979) of the 1960s and 1970s proved a failure and, with the collapse of the Soviet Union, to say nothing of Cuba's deficiencies as a model and the decline-defeat of most of the area's troublesome guerrilla movements, the Marxist-Leninist alternative has similarly declined in attractiveness. We say "in general" because in many instances, peasant, labor, student, and other movements assumed to be democratic and liberal proved to be quite conservative, preferring what I have called the "corporatist compromise": cooptation into the system along with the blandishments proffered rather than confrontation and likely repression.

During the 1950s and 1960s, that was precisely the lineup of political forces: the Church, the military, and the oligarchy often opposed to democratization, labor unions, students, intellectuals, peasants, and the democratic-Left political parties in favor. This lineup led to numerous confrontations during that earlier period, the end result of which was the numerous (fourteen of twenty countries) authoritarian takeovers in the 1960s and 1970s that preceded the more recent "third wave" of democratization (Huntington

1991). The U.S. government and most of the international organizations active in Latin America (OAS, World Bank, IMF, and so forth) favored democracy through such programs as the Alliance for Progress; but, under the Cold War logic then prevailing, they were unwilling to give up their support for authoritarianism unless they could be sure the even worse outcome of a Castro-like regime could be avoided. When the U.S. government and these international organizations lined up in support of the traditional forces, the result was consistently the overthrow of democracy (Wiarda 1975).

Now all this has changed in quite dramatic ways. First, Latin America's democratic forces are stronger than they were three and four decades ago. These include political parties, interest groups, legislatures, and community associations, as well as a shift in the political culture toward democracy. Second, there is now a very large international institutional structure—elections observers, democracy offices in State and AID, the Carter Center, and so forth—that make it much harder to steal or annul an election (Carothers 1999). Third, a host of NGOs have sprung up in the last twenty years—Americas Watch, Amnesty International, the Washington Office on Latin America, and various Latin American civil-society groups—that have political influence and are adept at generating attention if democracy-human rights are attacked, violated, or overthrown. Fourth, now that the Cold War is over, the United States (and the international agencies that reflect its influence) has concluded that its interests in Latin America—primarily stability—can best be protected by democracy, not authoritarianism (Wiarda 1990; Carothers 1991).

A fifth and crucially important factor is the transformation in Latin America's own traditional forces. Since Vatican II the Catholic church has found legitimacy in democracy, not authoritarianism; the decline of religious sentiment and the rise of liberation theology and other new currents (including evangelical Protestantism) have largely neutralized the church as a political actor. Similarly, the armed forces have seen their size and budgets cut; they know that, as in Paraguay in 1996 or Ecuador in 2000, they will have their funds and assistance cut off and be internationally ostracized if they overthrow democracy. The "oligarchy" in Latin America has modernized along with the rest of society and now constitutes the "business community"; more than anyone else it recognizes that it must adapt to globalization, of which democracy, human rights, and neoliberalism are all key components. This group especially has been influential in pushing its own governments toward democracy and better human rights because that is the only way to ensure continued, essential foreign investment and loans.

The climate for democracy is much better than it was thirty to forty years ago: democratic forces in Latin America are stronger, traditional (anti-democratic) forces either have been neutralized or themselves (for their own reasons) have become pro-democratic, and the international climate is now much more propitious for democracy. The result is a contradiction.

On the one side are the authoritarian, hierarchical, top-down, non-human rights, non-democracy culture and history of Latin America; on the other are the new forces and international pressures that push Latin America toward democracy. The agenda and politics of human rights will be the product of these diverse contending forces operating within the quite varied and still only partly modernized countries of Latin America, and therefore the results of these contending forces will not be uniform, coherent, or necessarily converging throughout the hemisphere. In a fundamental sense, the politics of democratization and human rights in Latin America, in only slightly over-simplified terms, will turn on the axes of these contending forces: the inherited legacies of the past and the newer "Lockean" concerns of human rights.

The third question is, what are the prevailing strategies as well as blandishments, compensations, and coercive means invoked by rivals to get their preferred norms adopted?

The key preliminary point to make in answering this question is that, given the unacceptability and nonviability of the earlier authoritarian or Marxist-Leninist alternatives, as well as Latin America's increased integration into world markets and culture, almost no one is opposed to democracy and human rights any more. The question is the degrees, definitions, and priorities involved. Herewith some case studies.

In Peru in 1992, President Alberto Fujimori faced a vicious insurgency in the form of Sendero Luminoso and a recalcitrant Congress and political party opposition that blocked his needed economic reforms. When he then dismissed Congress, sent the Supreme Court packing, undermined the parties, suspended the Constitution, and declared a state of emergency that enabled him to rule by decree, his popularity ratings soared to an unprecedented high of over 80 percent. Despite the domestic public support for these steps, the whole weight of international public opinion—United States, Europe, OAS, World Bank, NGOs, human rights groups—came down on his head. Fujimori was forced to promise the OAS to restore "constitutional government." In Peru, as in much of Latin America, that means an often uneasy compromise between "strong government" and democracy. Fujimori was an autocrat, but he was an effective one until his fall from power over public disclosure of large-scale corruption, and until this final dénouement he was close to the mainstream of *Peruvian* public opinion.

In Guatemala in 1993, another so-called *auto golpe* ("self-coup") was launched by President Jorge Serrano, in which he sought to suspend constitutional guarantees and rule by decree. But Serrano lacked Fujimori's strength, political skills, and popularity, and in addition to the weight of "international public opinion," he faced the near universal disapproval of local Guatemalan NGOs, the business community, and civil society groups. As these domestic and international groups converged, Serrano was forced not only to restore constitutional guarantees, but to surrender the presidency as well. As evidenced by the successor right wing-populist administration of

Alfonso Portillo, however, Serrano's surrender did not mean that the tension between democracy and "strong government" has ended in Guatemala.

In Paraguay in 1996, the popular armed forces chief Lino Oviedo attempted a coup after he felt he had been unfairly prohibited by the dominant political class from participating as a candidate for president in a democratic political process. In this case it was Paraguay's fellow members in MERCOSUR, the South American Common Market (Argentina, Brazil, Uruguay) that put on the pressure, reversing the coup and restoring Paraguay to democracy (in Paraguayan form, but at least it was a fig leaf). The United States also exerted pressure behind the scenes, but preferred to let MERCOSUR take the credit. "Globalization" appeared to have triumphed: a "democratic" regime remained in place, but in Paraguay an elitist, traditional, authoritarian, narrowly based, undemocratic political culture continued to function underneath. In 2000 Oviedo attempted another coup that similarly left the line between democracy and something else extremely fuzzy.

In January 2000, Ecuador, a country faced with almost insurmountable economic problems, an ineffective government, a demand by indigenous groups for greater autonomy and power, and signs of rebellion in the lower ranks of the military itself, the armed forces staged a coup. This was not an unaccustomed event in Ecuadorian history; indeed, coups are so endemic there that they are part of the normal political process (Needler 1964; Wiarda 1979). Unwilling to recognize that fact or to live with its possible implications for the rest of Latin America, the United States acted swiftly, telling the military that it would be isolated and international investment and loans would be cut off. In the past, the Ecuadorian military would likely have laughed off this suggestion, but now, with globalization, it recognized the dangers. The armed forces stepped aside, the vice president was allowed to take power, and "constitutional government" was preserved.

There are some remarkable parallels as well as differences in all these cases. First, in all the countries there was a genuine crisis of policy or decision-making. Second, in all the cases it was the *outside* sectors—the U.S. government, World Bank, MERCOSUR, international NGOs, and human rights organizations—that led the charge either to prevent a coup from happening or to reverse it once it had happened. As for domestic forces, they were often divided, in most cases recognizing that drastic measures were necessary, but only in Guatemala operating in accord with international public opinion and NGOs.

The implications of this tendency may be troubling. If in Latin America, as a large body of literature suggests (Anderson 1967; Kling 1967), elections are but one among several routes to power, the coup is a recurrent and ordinary part of the political process, and public opinion favors both democracy *and* strong government, then the international actors that have been so preeminently forceful in these crises may be on the verge of violating and undermining the integrity and functioning of the normal, internal political process of these countries. In the name of global democracy and human rights, they may be destroying the very political processes and institutions that enable these admittedly transitional societies to bridge the gap between the authoritarian past and a democratic future that they have not quite reached yet, and on the path to which some compromises may often be necessary.

As usual, where a person stands on this issue depends on where one sits. If the goal is some vision of transcendent, globalized democracy and human rights, then one comes down hard on the coup makers, even elected presidents who launch self-coups. But if there is some respect for and understanding of the Latin American political process (not a high priority in the United States) and the capacity of Latin Americans to solve their own messy problems in their own murky ways without outside interference, then one recognizes that in transitional societies aspiring to democracy, but not fully consolidated, there are bound to be rocky patches and one had better be prepared to compromise and adjust to them realistically rather than wishfully.

Let us move from the weaker, less-developed countries of Latin America to the more-developed ones, the A, B, C countries Argentina, Brazil, and Chile. Because these countries are more developed and sophisticated, and lack the headline-generating "comic-opera" features of some of the countries previously discussed, we tend to assume that they are safely in the democratic camp. But that assumption may blind us to the turbulence and frequent uncertainty—short of revolution or coup—that plague these countries as well.

In Argentina the armed forces have gone back to the barracks, but the relations between civil and military authority are sometimes tense; there have been several (failed) coup attempts; and the question of justice versus amnesty (and how far up or down the chain of command this should go) for military or police officials involved in earlier repression-torture (called the "dirty war") is still open. In Argentina's present bankrupt and disintegrated condition, pressures for "strong government" are again rising; democracy is in grave danger.

In Chile, we have the case of former military dictator Augusto Pinochet, arrested in Britain on a human rights charge brought by a Spanish prosecutor, eventually returned to Chile on health grounds where he was subjected to new charges of violations of human rights. There are ongoing tensions between the elected social-democratic government and the armed forces, which still enjoy a controversial, specially privileged, constitutional position in the Chilean system as almost a separate, corporate, fourth branch of government.

In Brazil, although the armed forces have been reduced in size and budget, they still enjoy a special consultative, balance-wheel, or "moderating power" role in the political system; at the same time, Brazil's simmering ethnic and racial tensions and the vast income gaps (widest in the world) between rich and poor provide a climate in which violence and human rights abuses could fester.

The fourth question is, how might the power balance be changed to advance democratization and human rights? This is a very difficult question. The process requires a delicate balance of opposed and often conflicting interests. It requires not just a commitment to democracy and human rights (that is the easy part), but also sensitivity to and an understanding of the Latin American political process (the hard part). For this is a political process that most people in the United States both fail to comprehend and, given historic U.S. prejudices and feeling of superiority toward Latin America, have little sympathy for. In addition, now that the Cold War is over and there are few threats out there to focus the mind or to bring rationality to decision-making, it is driven almost exclusively by domestic political considerations and large constituency groups. In an earlier book, writing about Central America, I suggested that U.S. policy was driven 80 percent by domestic political considerations and only in a small degree by rational considerations of U.S. foreign policy interests in the area.

The question is not whether we are in favor of democracy and human rights; instead, the issue is how best to achieve the goals on which we are agreed. Do we do so by championing a universal vision of democracy and human rights and, in our zeal, running roughshod over local institutions and ways of doing things, thus often undermining the very institutions that in the long run will be essential to achieve our goal? Or do we work patiently through indigenous institutions, relying on local solutions to local problems, seeking gradually to build support and institutions for the goals sought rather than scoring a dramatic "victory" that often proves damaging to long-term aims?

My answer is that we try to do both. The goals need to be clearly and loftily set forth: democracy and human rights. The pressure to achieve those goals needs to be kept on; whether that should involve diplomacy, pressure, economic sanctions, or other strategies obviously depends on time, country, and particular circumstances. At the same time, we need to work through local practices and institutions to accomplish those goals. It ought to be worrisome, for example, that in the cases treated above, it was often the international actors, not the local ones, that were decisive. That is not a good formula. Effective policy often involves compromises with local institutions, bridge building, medium-term solutions, halfway houses between democracy and "strong government," and crazy-quilt patchwork on the way to democracy.

That is precisely what has occurred during the last twenty years. Most of the countries in Latin America are still partial democracies, limited democracies, incomplete democracies, "formal" but not "liberal" democracies. They have often arrived at these positions by fits and starts, through struggle and compromise, as a result of both outside pressures and internal socioeconomic development that gives democracy and human rights a stronger base. They are mixes and hybrids of their own changing traditions, institutions, and values, and of what the outside world, primarily the United States, pressures them to be. But even with these partial accomplishments, no one doubts that by any measure, the situation of democracy and human rights is much better now than it was two or three decades ago. Never before in history have all the twenty countries save one (Cuba) been democratic or the overall human rights record better, even with the limits and qualifications indicated.

But the limits also need to be recognized. Elections are now held regularly, but pluralism, civil society, egalitarianism, and a civic political culture are all weak. Political democracy has been established, but not social or economic democracy; indeed, Latin America is notorious for having the worst distribution of economic resources of any area in the world. And if we accept that there is some relationship between development and democracy, then the social, economic, and political disintegration during 2001–2 of Argentina, the most literate, urban, middle class, and developed country in Latin America, cannot augur well for the future of democracy elsewhere in Latin America.

Conclusion

There has been a lot of wringing of hands and gnashing of teeth in Washington about the future of democracy in Latin America (Hakim 1999–2000). In numerous countries the high hopes that were held out a decade ago seem not to have been realized; the so-called "Washington consensus" (democracy, open markets, free trade) appears to be breaking down. I believe these fears are exaggerated and somewhat overwrought. They stem from the fact that the democracy agenda was oversold and overhyped in the past decade, and now some of the disappointments of failed, but to my mind unrealistic expectations are coming home to roost. Just as democracy's prospects were exaggerated in the course of the 1980s and early 1990s, its demise or the prospect thereof is greatly exaggerated today. Latin America needs still to find *its own* equilibrium, its own definitions, and forms of democracy, its own place and position on the spectrum (not either-or) of democracy and authoritarianism.

I have addressed these issues in other writings (Wiarda 1997, 2001), but a few comments may be offered here in conclusion. First, polls are showing that, while Latin America shows little support for political parties, parliaments, and other institutions of pluralism, its support for democracy remains, in most countries, in the 60–70 percent range. Second, while Latin Americans prefer democracy in the abstract, they also prefer strong, effective government and a nationalist (anti-IMF) populist regime. Third, the definition of democracy that many Latin Americans hold is Rousseauian rather than Lockean: centralized, direct, organic, integralist, corporatist, as much based on the "general will" as personified by strong leaders (Fujimori, Chávez) as on the "will of all" (elections). Fourth, we need to distinguish among countries: those with low socioeconomic levels and weak institutions (like Ecuador, Paraguay, Bolivia, Haiti, or most of the Central American countries), versus those with strong infrastructure and strong democratic institutions (Chile, Costa Rica, Uruguay), and a number of countries in between, including important ones like Argentina, Brazil, Colombia, Mexico, Peru, and Venezuela. Policy on democracy and human rights will obviously have to be adjusted to account for these differences among countries.

There is, thus, no one single future or model for Latin America; rather, there will be several and diverse futures. Different countries in Latin America, as elsewhere, will differentially select packages of items from the globalization-democracy-human rights agenda to absorb, reject, or modify; there will be great diversity and each country will find its own balance. At the same time there is currently a certain disillusionment with democracy throughout the hemisphere, a sense that democracy has not delivered on its promises. Almost the personification of these changing values, and virtually an exact reflection of the public opinion trends cited above, is President Hugo Chávez of Venezuela, a strong personalist, populist, charismatic, nationalist, integralist leader.

Given Latin America's diversity, it seems highly unlikely that Chávez or Chávez clones represent the future of the region, but, on the other hand, if we hear and understand what Chávez is saying and doing, then we are a long way toward understanding the Latin American political process (mixed, hybrid) and the role of democracy and human rights (limited, partial) in that context. For while the agenda of democracy and human rights has undoubtedly been advanced in Latin America in the last decades, they are still subject to the contending forces (the legacies of the past versus the newer democratic precepts) that are still lodged in an often contentious political process whose outcomes will not always be consistently or pristinely democratic.

Chapter 13
Southern Africa

Robert Mattes and Anthony Leysens

The Terrain of Human Rights in Southern Africa

The sweep of democracy's "third wave" through southern Africa in the 1990s is testimony to the increasing demands for and claims to human rights made by citizens and groups across this region.[1] To be sure, we cannot account for this trend without acknowledging the role of global forces such as the end of the Cold War and the increasing emphases on open markets and good governance by international financial institutions and donors. Few of the forty transitions from authoritarian rule in sub-Saharan Africa would have even commenced, let alone succeeded, without the end of the bipolar world, the powerful exemplars of successful transitions in Central and Eastern Europe, and increasing World Bank and International Monetary Fund demands for political and economic liberalization.

Yet, as important as these developments were, the international context only provides the starting point from which increasing claims for human rights and democracy proceed, and hence the backdrop against which the struggle for them has been played out in southern Africa. International factors alone cannot explain the wide degree of variation in why some countries expanded the range of political and civil rights and held a success-ful founding democratic election, while others did not. While the regional agenda of rights and democratization received a broad push from interna-tional forces, it has largely been driven from *within* southern Africa. Under-standing this process requires us to focus on the role of ideas, but also of politics and economics, as well as forces us to grapple with the interplay of contingency and agency.

Ideas

Human rights claims have, on one hand, consisted of political demands for dignity and freedom initially from European colonialism or settler rule (itself an international force and early forerunner of globalization) and subsequently from the indigenous authoritarian post-colonial state. On the other hand, human rights claims have also consisted of economic demands to redress the exploitation and underdevelopment of colonialism and the inequalities of settler society, as well as the grinding poverty brought about by the economic mismanagement of the post-colonial state. The consequence is that popular and elite understandings of human rights are a contested terrain.

First, there is a tension between emphases on political dignity (focusing on "negative" freedoms and political procedures) versus economic dignity (focusing on "positive" freedoms and substantive outcomes). Available evidence suggests that southern Africans' understandings of human rights and democracy include significant emphases on socioeconomic rights (see Mattes, Davids, and Africa 2000).

Second, there is a tension between individual versus collective understandings of rights. The cultural norm of *ubuntu* ("I am through others") emanating from Africa's historic experience of small-scale village life lends a strong communal tint to notions of rights. Thus, while rights claims have been asserted for individual dignity and freedom, they have also been asserted for the freedom and dignity of "the nation" from foreign rule or of "the people" (defined as the indigenous population) from racial, settler domination.

Finally, there is a tension between rights claims asserted in terms of peculiarly African or southern African standards of dignity and freedom and those asserted in terms of universal standards. Such tensions crystallize in issues such as traditional leadership, customary law, property rights, women's rights, and homosexuality. These tensions often allow interested parties (in particular, desperate despots such as Zimbabwe's Robert Mugabe) to paint rights claims asserted in universalistic terms as merely self-interested attempts by the former colonizing power, the World Bank, or simply "the West" to reimpose foreign domination.

Politics

But the advancement of human rights is more than simply the unfolding of an idea whose time has come. In southern Africa, the struggle for rights has been heavily shaped by political structural factors, particularly with regard to the nature and capacity of the post-colonial state. The extent of popular protest, subsequent expansion of political rights, and occurrence of a successful founding election in the 1990s can be explained by the legacies of the previous regimes. These legacies also shape and limit the future prospects for consolidating a rights-based democratic system (Bratton and Van der Walle 1997)

Political regimes in virtually all post-colonial sub-Saharan Africa could best be characterized as "neopatrimonial." Neopatrimonialism is a hybrid

system combining forms of rational-legal institutions with many of the personalized patterns of authority characteristic of the patrimonial political
systems of pre-colonial Africa. Its main features are clientelism, the use of
state resources for political legitimation, and personalized political authority in presidents or "big men." The few exceptions to this type consisted
of the "settler regimes" of Namibia/South West Africa and South Africa
(resembling bureaucratic-authoritarian regimes) and the few multiparty
systems that already existed in Africa at the dawn of the third wave (Zimbabwe and Botswana, which themselves displayed strong neopatrimonial
tendencies; Bratton and Van der Walle 1997).

The neopatrimonial legacy has several important implications for the
struggle for human rights across the region. The first legacy is a crisis of
order and state legitimacy. The enjoyment and protection of human rights
requires a strong state with an impartial bureaucracy that can enforce the
rule of law, discourage clientelist, arbitrary and personal rule, and resist
elite attempts to rewrite political rules to suit their own interests. In contrast, neopatrimonial regimes have bequeathed bloated yet weak bureaucracies unable to collect taxes or duties, impose penalties, protect citizens
from one another, or reach impartial decisions. The very idea of a binding
social contract between the governors and the governed, where sovereign
states provide their inhabitants with a modicum of security and human
rights and are seen as legitimate by citizens who obey their rules, is a moot
point in many African societies.

At its most extreme, some states have lost their monopoly over the legitimate use of violence. Raging civil wars in Angola and Congo-Kinshasa ren-
der those states incapable of creating the order necessary for the exercise
of human rights. Less extreme, but equally important, many states across
the region lack the capacity to fight organized crime syndicates or protect
their borders (Van Creveld 1999). Even in more developed states like South
Africa, the rise of vigilante movements and the proliferation of private security providers signals that the state's monopoly over the legitimate use of
force is problematic.

Another problem of political order is the incomplete degree to which the
modern post-colonial state has totally supplanted traditional authorities
as the source of authoritative rules. Customary law and courts still apply
to many aspects of everyday life, especially in Swaziland and rural areas
of other countries, often imposing severe limitations on the civil rights of
women.

Besides the lack of capacity to ensure order, the second legacy of the
neopatrimonial state is simply the lack of political will to do so. Through the
clientelist practices of patronage networks and appointment to key parliamentary and bureaucratic positions, strong-man presidents coopted legisla-
tors and their political parties and prevented them from developing into the
type of strong organizations that could challenge their political hegemony.

Civil society is also relatively weak in neopatrimonial societies. Where protest or opposition movements did arise during the transition away from authoritarian rule, they often quickly deflated after the "popular political enemy" was removed. The fragmentation of opposition movements has often prevented a genuine completion of the transition and to subsequent consolidation of a liberal democratic regime. In short, the new democratic regimes in these states are bequeathed with strong presidents confronted by weak legislatures, weak political parties, and weak civil societies. Thus there exist few countervailing forces to compel power-monopolizing leaders like Zimbabwe's Robert Mugabe and their clients to respect the law and human or civil rights, or to ensure that others like Namibia's Sam Nujoma adhere to constitutional term limitations. The recent effective opposition of Zambian civil society to Frederick Chiluba's attempt to obtain a third term and the rise of a civil society and the trade union-based opposition to Zimbabwe's Mugabe are encouraging counter-trends.

Economics

The struggle for rights in southern Africa is also shaped by economic crisis, yet another legacy of the neo-patrimonial state. The use of state resources to pay off clients meant that neopatrimonial states regularly overspent planned revenues. Weakened bureaucracies were unable to collect taxes from citizens and businesses. This resulted is chronically poor economic performance, massive debt, and resulting dependence on foreign aid and loans from international donors. Ironically, such desperate economic situations played important roles in expanding rights and in some cases pushing states toward full democratization. The higher a country's level of foreign aid dependence and the worse its relations with foreign donors, the more likely it was to face domestic political protest, to cede greater political rights, and to engage in extensive democratization reforms (Bratton and Van der Walle 1997, 180).

But the economic situation of southern Africa also has important implications for the prospects of consolidating stable democratic regimes in those societies that did reach a successful founding election. Research on the structural economic correlates of stable democracy suggests that only South Africa, Botswana, and Namibia appear economically ready for democracy (Przeworski et al. 1996). The rest have low per capita GNPs, low rates of literacy, and small middle or professional classes, patterns that enhance neopatrimonial traditions because the state retains a privileged economic role with few countervailing sources of power. Thus they must overcome economic crises with limited resources and a weak state. If new democratic governments are popularly blamed for prevailing economic conditions, the legitimacy of the entire democratic regime may be undermined (Mattes and Thiel 1999). The global economic environment compounds such fears. The ascendant neoliberal orthodoxy of both homegrown and externally imposed structural adjustment programs limits states' ability to provide basic needs such as water, food, or shelter, let alone education or health care. Alternatively, some scholars argue that it is the very external prescription and imposition of liberalization policies by international donors that undermines the legitimacy of democratic governments, because it forecloses domestic democratic choice and therefore limits state sovereignty and autonomy, and thus reduces perceptions of legitimacy (O'Donnell 1996; Onimode 1988).

Variations Within the Neopatrimonial State

But no matter how important they may seem as explanatory factors, the political and economic consequences of neopatrimonialism are relatively *constant* factors. Thus they provide only a partial explanation of the past outcomes and future prospects of securing human rights and consolidating democratic regimes across southern Africa. To explain fully the variation in human rights and democracy between states, it is necessary to take into account three important variable factors: the *type of neopatrimonial regime* that preceded the transition, the *type of transition* pursued by a particular country, and the *length* of the transition.

With regard to regime type, the degree of competition for political office and the degree of participation institutionalized within the neopatrimonial regime were particularly important. "Plebiscitarian" one-party regimes that allowed only ritualistic elections (Angola, Mozambique, Swaziland, and the former Zaire) and "military oligarchies" that suspended all forms of elections and participation (Lesotho) were particularly unlikely to complete successful democratic transitions. While a tradition of plebiscitarian participation did create a mass constituency for protest, it did not create commitments to liberal political values or result in a sustainable movement of nongovernmental organizations or political parties. In contrast, transitions from "competitive" one-party regimes with a history of candidate competition within the party (like Malawi, Zambia, or Tanzania) were much more likely to result in free and fair founding elections (Bratton and Van der Walle 1997).

With regard to transition type, the key question was whether it produced an effective transfer of power or a long interregnum with no clear government. The greatest prospects for success tended to occur between what O'Donnell and Schmitter (1986) called "pacted" transitions (Namibia, South Africa, Angola, Mozambique). These offered non-zero sum outcomes and created precedents of bargaining and compromise that helped institutionalize at least some degree of political competition. In contrast, nonpacted transitions provided little opportunity to develop a tradition of bargaining and compromise. Winner-take-all mentalities developed, and victorious opposition parties once in government set about to punish the losers. Rather than enter into protracted negotiations, many authoritarian regimes moved quickly to elections with no intervening mechanism or forum to negotiate new rules (Malawi, Zambia, Tanzania). Others (Zaire) pursued a largely African innovation of the National Conference. However, these paths often created power vacuums that were filled by old habits with low degrees of personnel turnover from the old to the new regime. Finally, with regard to transition length, transitions that were too short tended to limit the prospects for political learning and institution-building; transitions that were too long prolonged periods of uncertainty, thus hindering economic stabilization and growth (Bratton and Van der Walle 1997).

The Politics of Human Rights in Southern Africa

We have examined the broad structural determinants of the ideational, political, and economic terrain in which the struggle for human rights in southern Africa is played out. We now turn to the significant problems on the human rights agenda and assess the choices and strategies followed by important actors to advance or retard the cause of human rights and democracy within these structural contours. In other words, we move from a discussion of structural determinants of the struggle for human rights to an analysis of the role of agency and contingency. These choices and strategies will be reviewed at the level of intra-societal relations, citizen-state relations, and regional interstate relations.[2]

The Human Rights Agenda in Southern African States

There is a wide variation in the degree to which states across this region protect or violate human rights. Table 1 summarizes indicators of the performance of each continental Southern African state with regard to human rights, democracy, and media freedom. The worst violations of rights occur in the region's two war-ridden countries, Congo-Kinshasa and Angola. There is also a serious, though much less violent problem of civil liberties and political rights in authoritarian Swaziland, the region's only remaining monarchy.

While Zambia and Zimbabwe conduct regular multi-party elections, serious limitations on political rights have led Diamond (1999) to categorize them as "pseudo-democracies." While Lesotho, Malawi, Tanzania, and Mozambique have electoral machinery that qualifies as free and fair, recent election results have been challenged. They also have limitations on individual rights sufficient to warrant only "partly free" labels from Freedom House.

Namibia is rated as a "liberal democracy" because of the relatively high quality of its young electoral machinery as well as the matrix of constitutional rights enjoyed by its citizens. Yet it imposes limitations on the news media sufficiently serious to warrant a "partly free" label in the area of press

Table 1. Governance and Democracy Indicators for Southern African States, 1998–1999, Freedom House Scores

	Average score		Political rights score		Civil liberties score		Press freedom score	
	2000–2001	Change 1998–2001	2000–2001	Change 1998–2001	2000–2001	Change 1998–2001	2000	Change 1999–2000
Liberal democracies								
South Africa	Free 1.5	—	1	—	2	—	Free 25	+3
Botswana	Free 2.0	—	2	—	2	—	Free 28	+2
Namibia	Free 2.5	—	2	—	3	—	Partly free 34	+4
Electoral democracies								
Malawi	Partly free 3.5	−1.0	4	−2	3	—	Partly free 52	−10
Mozambique	Partly free 3.5	—	3	—	4	—	Partly free 48	—
Lesotho	Partly free 4.0	—	4	—	4	—	Partly free 56	+3
Tanzania	Partly free 4.0	+0.5	4	+1	4	—	Partly free 49	+2

Pseudo-democracies								
Zambia	Partly Free 4.5	—	5	—	4	—	Not free 62	—
Zimbabwe	Not free 6.0	-1.0	6	-1	6	-1	Not free 67	-3
Angola	Not free 6.0	—	6	—	6	—	Not free 80	-6
Authoritarian regimes								
Swaziland	Not free 5.5	-0.5	6	—	5	-1	Not free 77	-2
Congo-Kinshasa	Not Free 6.0	+0.5	6	+1.0	6	—	Not free 90	—

"Liberal democracies" are rated "free" by Freedom House. "Electoral democracies" are rated "partly free." "Pseudo-democracies" are multiparty systems with competitive elections that are not free or fair by international standards.

Sources: Freedom House; Diamond (1999); Piano and Puddington (2001); Karatnycky (2002).

freedom. In Botswana and South Africa, clearly the region's best hopes for creating thriving liberal democratic states, the problems of rights are of a qualitatively different nature. While there are worries about continued dominance of political space by a single political party, the agenda focuses on the difficulties of simultaneously providing a greater space for individual rights, economic prosperity, and a more peaceful social order.

The rights situation has remained relatively stable across the region with four exceptions. Malawi qualified as a liberal democracy in 1999 but has moved downward into the electoral democracy category. Tanzania, rated as a pseudo-democracy in 1999, has now advanced into the electoral democracy category. Zimbabwe and Swaziland experienced declines in the quality of rights.

Though the number of cases in southern Africa is relatively small, some interesting patterns are observable that broadly confirm the proposition that a country's political-institutional past shapes subsequent attempts to safeguard rights and consolidate democracy.

- Both societies that were settler regimes with traditions of bureaucratic-authoritarian states now rate as "liberal democracies" (Namibia, South Africa)
- Three of the four countries that went through pacted transitions are functioning democracies (Namibia, Mozambique, South Africa).
- All three former "competitive" one-party systems are practicing some semblance of electoral politics. Two rate as electoral democracies (Malawi, Tanzania), but Zambia is classified as a pseudo-democracy.
- The one former military regime experienced an incomplete "managed transition" due to a major dispute over its second election (Lesotho).
- Three of the four societies that had "plebiscitary" one-party states are undergoing severe problems. One is still an anti-democratic monarchy (Swaziland), and two are embroiled in intractable civil war (Angola, Congo-Kinshasa).
- The sole country that had a National Conference transition has an authoritarian regime (Congo-Kinshasa).
- Of the two societies that had multi-party states before 1989, Botswana has developed into a maturing democracy. Zimbabwe, however, has moved in the opposite direction. Yet it possesses many of the things that will be necessary to create a healthy democracy if the Mugabe regime falls, such as a newly competitive party system, a relatively vibrant civil society, strong trade unions, and a relatively strong and independent court system.

Reestablishing the Basis of a Social Contract

In Congo-Kinshasa and Angola the human rights agenda in the area of citizen-state relations focuses first on establishing the basic conditions of peace that would enable a civic relationship between people and the state. It then focuses securing the most basic human rights against the state, rights such as freedom from state-sponsored violence, arbitrary arrest, and abuse, and the freedom to travel, not to mention the right to representation and the ability to change your government. In Zimbabwe, 2000–2001 saw a rapid deterioration in basic law and order as government-sponsored thugs killed around 100 political opponents, assaulted at least 3,000, and displaced an estimated 75,000 workers and their families from their homes and jobs on commercial farms (Peta 2002, 9).

Freedom of Association, Criticism, and Opposition

A basic issue of human rights across almost all southern African countries is the degree to which the state allows criticism and opposition. While the most fundamental violations take place in Congo, Angola, and Zimbabwe, serious limitations on opposition have occurred in a number of countries. In Congo-Kinshasa, Kabila's three and a half years of rule reversed the limited advances made by civil society during the blocked democratic transition of the early 1990s. Over 300 political parties initially legalized in 1990 were outlawed; NGOs survive but are often harassed. Public demonstrations are banned, and freedom of expression and assembly are limited by presidential decree. In Swaziland, pro-democracy advocates and labor leaders were detained prior to the last election. Up until the 2001, Zambia remained under a state of emergency that suspended many basic rights. State security services have used legal and illegal wiretaps against political dissidents. After a 1997 coup attempt, opposition leader, former President, and founding father of the country Kenneth Kaunda was accused of involvement and arrested, although later released.

The government of Zimbabwe continues to use emergency legislation and existing restrictive laws dating back to the Rhodesian era to stifle criticism and opposition. The right of public assembly is limited, and the police can impose arbitrary curfews. Intelligence agencies and the police are allowed to disperse assemblies and arrest participants. The government of Tanzania banned demonstrations in Dar-Es-Salaam in 1999; only officially registered parties are allowed to have rallies. Political parties that form on religious, ethnic, or regional bases, or oppose the union of Zanzibar and Tanganyika, are banned. Mozambique also bars political parties based on ethnicity or religion. Freedom of assembly is guaranteed but limited by notification and timing requirements.

Free and Fair Elections

While the electoral process is stillborn in Congo-Kinshasa and Angola, it exists in some form in every other country in Southern Africa. In Swaziland, however, low turnout elections have been neither free nor fair since the multi-party system was ended in 1973. The king controls nominations for local council elections. In the rest of the region, elections suffer from a range of problems.

The most pressing item on the human rights agendas of Tanzania, Zambia, and especially Zimbabwe may be to make their nominally democratic structures produce true democratic processes and outcomes. Since the end of the Rhodesian civil war, Zimbabwe has held regular elections nominally open to all political parties. But their freeness and fairness are seriously infringed by intimidation and violence during election campaigns and the widespread use of legislative patronage by the ruling Zimbabwe African National Union-Patriotic Front (ZANU-PF) to favor itself in the allocation of state party subsidies. The 1999 parliamentary election was the most competitive in its history, with ZANU-PF winning a narrow majority of seats further widened by the president's ability to appoint another dozen loyalists to Parliament. In the widely repudiated 2001 presidential election, opposition campaigners and candidates suffered widespread intimidation and violence.

While Zambia's 1992 election was judged to be free and fair, its 1996 elections were seriously flawed. The ruling Movement for Multi-Party Democracy (MMD) barred its most potent electoral threat, Kenneth Kaunda, from running for president, used state media and resources to support its campaign, and failed to produce an accurate voters' roll, which may have disenfranchised 2,000,000 voters. This produced a boycott by most opposition parties. The 2000 election was held on December 26, a date widely seen as an attempt to catch urban-based opposition voters on holiday in rural areas. Though Tanzania's 1995 elections were its freest since independence, the poll in Zanzibar was judged to be neither free nor fair. Significant irregularities in Zanzibar in 1999 required a nullification of the first ballot and a rerun of the vote that itself was not transparent. Malawi's second democratic elections of 1999 were conducted amid a climate of increasing civil unrest, attacks on the news media, and government attempts to manipulate media coverage through disinformation campaigns.

Elections have been judged to be free and fair in Mozambique and Lesotho, but opposition parties and supporters have balked at accepting the results. As noted earlier, RENAMO's challenges to the 1999 results were accompanied by threats of secession or partition. The results of Lesotho's 1999 elections were badly distorted by the "first-past-the-post" electoral system: opposition parties collectively won 40 percent of the popular vote yet received just one of eighty legislative seats. South Africa's 1999 election went much better than its first open election in 1994, and it undoubtedly produced a result that was free and fair. Yet new registration requirements also disenfranchised many voters, as thousands never received the identity document they applied for in order to register. In Botswana, limited access to the media for opposition parties and government critics is a continuing source of concern.

Freedom of the News Media

Freedom of the news media is a serious problem. Only two countries (South Africa and Botswana) are judged by Freedom House to have widespread press freedom. Even one of the region's "liberal democracies," Namibia, places important restrictions on press freedom.

State coercion is widely used. Over the past two years journalists have been beaten because of specific stories they have produced in at least four countries (Congo-Kinshasa, Angola, Malawi, Zimbabwe) and in Angola and Mozambique print and television journalists have died under mysterious circumstances. Arrest and official harassment and intimidation are commonplace in Congo-Kinshasa and have also occurred in Zimbabwe, Malawi, and Zambia. Legal restrictions, threats of criminal prosecution for libel or defamation, and jailing are far more widespread, occurring in Swaziland, Tanzania, Zambia, Zimbabwe, Mozambique, Malawi, and Namibia. In the run up to its 2001 presidential election, Zimbabwe's government forced legislation through criminalizing virtually all criticism of the president or negative reporting and requiring government licensing of all news media.

In many areas, media freedom is heavily constrained by government ownership. In Swaziland, Tanzania, Zimbabwe, Mozambique, Malawi, and Lesotho, the state dominates the electronic broadcast media. In Zimbabwe and Mozambique, the government also owns several newspapers. At the very least, this results in extreme self-censorship by media officials and an under-reporting of criticism and opposition voices. At the extreme, such as Zimbabwe, government officials interfere with appointments and editorial policy. In Lesotho the government demanded the resignation of all state media employees who had participated in the 1999 anti-government protests. Malawi's independent press faces periodic government threats to withdraw its advertising, thus driving the papers toward bankruptcy.

Even in Botswana, the government has floated proposals for stricter rules for registration of newspapers and journalist accreditation and filed charges (later dropped), of "spreading false rumors likely to cause alarm" against a British journalist. Illiberal laws banning sedition and ridicule of the president remain on the books, though they are rarely used. In South Africa, the South African Broadcasting Corporation is far more independent than under apartheid, yet it still suffers from self-censorship. Privately owned television and radio stations are on the increase. While the country possesses a wide number of newspapers and magazines, concentrated ownership patterns by a few large corporations raise worries of constraints on aggressive reporting of issues critical of the corporate structure.

Rights of the Accused

The final significant, widespread human rights failing of the state in southern Africa lies with the criminal justice system. In Congo-Kinshasa and Angola police and other security forces function as an arm of state political retribution and often inflict flagrant human rights violations such as beatings, torture, and arbitrary execution. Courts have little power to restrain them and opposition supporters have been jailed after trials of questionable probity.

More widely, the problem is simply that the criminal justice system does not deliver due process or guarantee equality before the law. In the past three years, there have been reports of police torture (Zambia, Zimbabwe), arbitrary arrest (Tanzania, Zimbabwe), police brutality (Malawi, Mozambique, Swaziland, Zimbabwe), and illegal search and seizure (Zimbabwe). Because of overburdened and under-resourced court systems suspects are often held for years in pre-trial detention in Congo-Kinshasa, Angola and Zambia. Long periods of detention are quite legal in Swaziland, Mozambique, and Lesotho. Pre-trial detainees in Congo-Kinshasa, Zambia and Mozambique confront especially poor, overcrowded conditions with inadequate food or medical care.

The Human Rights Agenda in Southern African Societies

Post-colonial states in southern Africa, indeed throughout the continent, comprise plural societies that often do not make historical, cultural, or geographical sense. A key human rights question then centers on the rights individuals and groups have against their fellow citizens and whether they are able to claim protection of those rights from the state.

Violent Sectional Conflict over the State

Sectional rivalries with strong ethnoregional alignments and conflict over control of the state in Congo-Kinshasa and Angola are so intense that they have resulted in prolonged civil war and prevented the functioning of an effective state. Thus the human rights agenda comes to focus on the most basic and fundamental of rights such as freedom from ethnically based persecution, or from arbitrary security force violence. In Congo-Kinshasa, the power base of President Laurent Kabila (assassinated in January 2001) increasingly relied on people from Katanga Province, a trend that triggered the violence of the preceding few years. Increasingly the country witnessed the types of incitements to ethnic hatred and cleansing characteristic of the former Yugoslavia, Rwanda, and Burundi. While the death of rebel leader Jonas Savimbi in February 2002 may shift fortunes, Angola has not known peace for at least a quarter of a century. The twenty-five-year-old civil war between the governing Movement for the Popular Liberation of Angola (MPLA) and opposition Union for the Total Independence of Angola (UNITA) has claimed over 1,000,000 lives.

Ethnic Dominance of the State

In other plural societies in the region, the key problem is the less extreme but no less important one of trying to reflect yet contain this pluralism within a democratic state. In Zimbabwe, the two main liberation organizations that fought the Rhodesian settler state originated in two separate ethnoregional bases. The ruling ZANU-PF is dominated by the majority Shona-speaking language group. After losing the 1980 election, the minority Ndebele-speaking group and its Zimbabwe African People's Union (ZAPU) suffered widespread repression and atrocities at the hands of ZANU-PF's North Korean trained Fifth Brigade, who were sent into Matabeleland to neutralize it. However, the recent development of broad based popular support for the opposition Movement for Democratic Change (MDC), which appears to cut across these cleavages, is an encouraging countertrend.

In Mozambique, the legacy of almost two decades of civil war is a politically divided society also with ethnoregional bases. Following 1999's disputed and geographically cleaved election results, the opposition National Resistance of Mozambique (RENAMO), which still keeps a small armed force in its northern stronghold, threatened to return to civil war or set up a parallel government in the northern provinces where it has majority support. In Namibia, the political base of the ruling South West Africa People's Organization (SWAPO) among the Ovambo of the far north brings complaints of government discrimination from other groups, notably Herero, Damara, and Nama. This was evidenced at its most extreme in 1999 when the Carprivi Liberation Army started an armed insurrection aimed at secession of the country's far northeastern panhandle. Government security forces sent into the region to quell the rebellion were accused of human rights violations by NGOs and the news media.

Low intensity conflict in rural sections of South Africa's KwaZulu-Natal Province between supporters of the rural-Zulu based Inkatha Freedom Party and other Zulu-speaking supporters of the ruling ANC remains an ongoing problem. Though at far lower levels of political violence than in 1994, the 1999 election was marred by several high profile assassinations, and more widespread political violence threatened to erupt right up until the start of the actual campaign. Tanzania is troubled by cleavages between the largely Christian mainland and the mostly Muslim federated semi-autonomous offshore island archipelago of Zanzibar. Even in apparently homogeneous Botswana the Baswara (Bushmen) are an important exception: 50,000 of them have been relocated (some reportedly by force) from their traditional lands in order to make way for farms and wildlife reserves.

Racial Divisions

Ethnic pluralism is only one element of the complexity of Southern Africa. The legacies of significant European settlement in British and Portuguese colonies and the impact of apartheid in South Africa and Namibia all underscore the particular role of race in this region.

In Zimbabwe, Namibia, and especially South Africa, white minorities control disproportionately large shares of the economy. In South Africa, blacks constitute three-quarters of the population, yet share less than one-third of national wealth (though there have been significant advances in black corporate ownership and investment and the growth of the black middle class). Racial inequality and discrimination is especially evident in these countries' farming sectors. White farmers, in turn, become targets of resentment. In South Africa, several hundred farmers and their families have been killed in violent attacks or robberies over the past five years.

President Robert Mugabe has traditionally used Zimbabwe's white farmers as scapegoats. Beginning in November 1999, self-styled ZANU-PF supporting "war veterans" occupied over 1,000 white-owned commercial farms with the police, attorney general, and president steadfastly refusing to enforce successive court orders ending the illegal occupations. Since the defeat of his draft constitution in a national referendum and ZANU-PF's narrow escape in the 2000 parliamentary elections from the unprecedented challenge of the opposition MDC, Mugabe's tactics shifted to a legislative assault on property rights, and political intimidation of any judges who found these laws unconstitutional. Approximately 3,600 of the country's 4,000 white commercial farmers were evicted or otherwise intimidated from their farms in 2002 (Peta 2002, 3).

Owing to its apartheid past and its highly diverse population, South Africa faces daunting challenges in creating a civil society. The array of legislation and new policies designed to redress past inequalities have increased fears among white, colored, and Indian minorities of political, social, and economic marginalization. The past three years have seen substantial conflict over school integration, generally revolving around language policy, but easily becoming conflated with issues of race. Accusations of white dominance of the public agenda through ownership of the print media have recently been leveled in hearings of the state's Human Rights Commission, raising concerns over press freedom.

Women's Rights and Minority Rights

A major problem is de facto and in many rural areas de jure discrimination against women. While women's rights are often protected by constitutional stricture or ordinary legislation, they enjoy fewer employment and educational opportunities, and generally receive unequal pay for the same work.

In almost every country customary law and traditional values discriminate against women. Customary law discriminates against them in a range of ways, such as the ability to enter into economic contracts, own property, secure loans, and receive inheritances. The king of Swaziland has been challenged in court by the mother of an eighteen-year-old girl whom he selected as a wife and who was then abducted by representatives of the royal household. Forced marriages still exist in Tanzania. Violence against women is common. Domestic violence and wife beating are widespread and rarely prosecuted. South Africa currently has one of the highest levels of rape in the world.

The rights of minority groups are also under threat. First, while apartheid South Africa always received large amounts of migrants from neighboring countries to feed its large mining industry, there has been a significant increase of African migration into a relatively prosperous democratic South Africa following 1994. This has led to increasing xenophobic, violent reactions from South Africans who see African migrants as a threat to jobs and public health. In Zimbabwe, Zambia, and Namibia, homosexuals face not only societal intolerance but also official intolerance from the President and ruling party. In contrast, the South African state has committed itself to uphold gay and lesbian rights.

Human Rights and Regional Relations

These human rights problems persist in spite of three facts. First, Southern Africa is a region dominated by democratizing states. Second, the regional organization created by these states, the Southern African Development Community (SADC), has a professed commitment to protecting human rights. And third, its most powerful member state, South Africa, possesses an impressive amount of moral political capital on the international stage. Why?

The first part of the answer is that SADC has failed to elevate the universal values of human rights and democracy over the national sovereignty of its member states. Second, member states have been unable to come to any operational consensus about how the organization should intervene in order to resolve domestic conflict or enforce human rights. Not only has the SADC been unable to end the enduring conflicts in Angola and Congo-Kinshasa, but the competing "national security interests" shaped and colored by the clientelist interests of member states' governments have turned these domestic conflicts into wider interstate conflicts.

Third, South Africa, the one member state that might have the greatest rhetorical and practical impact in promoting a more aggressive regional approach toward member state violations, has been ineffective in pursuing its human rights agenda even though it dominates the region economically. It has shown little desire to take up the mantle of moral leadership in its own region that it so much likes to assume in other continent-wide or international forums such as the Non-Aligned Movement. Three years of attempts to broker a peaceful solution in Congo-Kinshasa have come to naught, and two years of "constructive engagement" with Zimbabwe failed to bring any compliance with Mugabe's repeated assurances to South African President Thabo Mbeki. And in the only moment when it has taken more drastic action—to support the elected government of Lesotho against civil unrest—it did it so badly that Lesotho and its democratic government were left in a much worse situation than when the crisis began. Much of this failure is due to problems inherent in South Africa's new government and a military force in transition. However, a great deal has to do with the fact that South Africa's advocacy of human rights and democracy co-occurs with its advocacy of liberal market reforms and regional free trade.

Universal Values Versus National Sovereignty

Both SADC and South Africa subscribe to a regional agenda in which order, welfare, human rights, and democracy are placed high on the list of priorities as values and as policy goals. The SADC Treaty emphasizes the rule of law, sustainable development, human rights, and democracy, and calls for the evolution of "common political values, systems, and institutions" based on these principles. The basic framing documents of the democratic South Africa's new post-1994 foreign policy also emphasize human rights and democracy as "cornerstones" and keys to guaranteeing the peace and security of member states, and thus the growth and development of the entire region. Yet there is an uneasy tension with the organization, as well as within South Africa, between advancing universal values on one hand and advancing national interest and protecting sovereignty on the other. The SADC combines a vigilance of state sovereignty with a rhetorical commitment to universalizing values. Even as it lists the rule of law, human rights, and democratization, the SADC Treaty also commits the organization to principles such as equity, balance, mutual benefit, and the equality of all member states. These values not only reflect a jealousy of state sovereignty, but also reveal a deep-seated suspicion of South African hegemony. While South Africa's foreign policy has come to embody the principles of human rights and democracy it has also undergone significant reprioritization increasingly emphasizing its own national interest.

Normative Rhetorical Commitment

Related to the first problem, SADC has yet to develop any regional consensus on *how* to enforce its normative commitments in practice, let alone the ability to do so. Congo offers a useful illustration. First, the very fact that Laurent Kabila's request to join the organization was approved, even though he was making every effort to stall or discontinue the transition to democracy, flew in the face of the organization's objectives and principles. Second, there have been serious differences, particularly between Zimbabwe and South Africa, over how to use SADC's collective defense arm, the Organ on Politics, Defense, and Security (OPDS). As set out in a 1996 Heads of State Summit communique, the creation of the OPDS was supposed to, among other things, help achieve "the development of democratic institutions and practices within member states" and encourage "the observance of universal human rights" (Cilliers 1999, 20, 77). Zimbabwe's Mugabe insisted that the OPDS, which he chaired, should operate independently of the SADC summit, while South Africa wanted it to function under the summit. The initial decision to intervene in Congo-Kinshasa was made by a 1998 Harare meeting of SADC defense ministers and subsequently upheld by Mugabe, who called it a "unanimous" decision of all SADC member states (Malan 1998, 6). But South Africa initially condemned the intervention and called for a cease-fire and peaceful resolution of the conflict. Yet its apparently principled position was quickly undercut by its own subsequent military intervention in Lesotho under SADC auspices. The failure of SADC to make any significant comment, let alone condemnation or sanction of Zimbabwe's moves toward dictatorship, only confirms these problems.

SADC's inability to develop an operational consensus on dealing with internal conflict and member states' human rights violations not only allows these domestic conflicts to continue, but also leads to increased conflict among member states. In the Angolan conflict, rebel UNITA forces and civilian refugees fleeing government forces crossed borders east into Zambia and south into Namibia. This led to increasing border tensions, with Angola accusing Zambia of acting as a conduit for UNITA arms supplies and a route for UNITA's illegal diamond exports. UNITA forces also spilled over the Namibian border, killing a number of civilians; Angolan troops were subsequently allowed to operate inside Namibia. Congo-Kinshasa's unresolved internal conflict eventually led to the armed involvement of Angola, Namibia, and Zimbabwe (in support of the Kabila government) and the East African states Rwanda and Uganda (in support of the two main rebel movements). Ugandan troops in northeastern Congo were subsequently accused by Congo-based human rights organizations of involvement in clashes between two domestic ethnic groups that UN agencies estimated killed 5,000 to 7,000 civilians and displaced 150,000 people.

The peculiar "twist" placed on the concept of national interest or national security by neopatrimonial governments is an important factor behind foreign involvement in these clashes. In places like Zimbabwe, the concept of national interest often means no more than the economic interests of a restricted set of people with familial and clientelist ties to the leadership of the ruling party and military. The parties involved in the Congo and Angolan conflicts have much to gain from access to the vast mineral wealth of both countries (diamond and oil in Angola, and diamonds and other minerals in Congo-Kinshasa). Zimbabwe's government made no secret of the material advantages of its involvement in Congo. Large tracts of Congo farmland were allocated to the Zimbabwe Agricultural and Rural Development Authority, and consignments of copper began to arrive in Zimbabwe for processing. Both Kabila's and Zimbabwe's armed forces reportedly set up companies dealing in gold and diamonds. In July 1999, Belgian customs officials reported that Zimbabwe, Rwanda, and Uganda, none of which produce diamonds, were all exporting diamonds. In Angola, the governing MPLA has financed its war efforts with the proceeds gained from rich offshore oil fields and UNITA has funded its war machine through the illegal sale of diamonds on the world market.

The Pursuit of Welfare and the Defense of Human Rights

We have already alluded to the suspicions of South Africa's neighbors as a potential factor preventing that country from exploiting its considerable international moral political capital in an aggressive defense of human rights. For many, these suspicions were borne out by South Africa's advocacy of regional trade liberalization and its subsequent economic advances across the region beginning in 1996, when the ANC government abandoned its Reconstruction and Development Program (RDP) and shifted to a neoliberal Growth, Employment, and Redistribution Plan (GEAR), a self-imposed structural adjustment program. South Africa did not confine its newfound faith in free and open markets to its domestic economy, but began proselytizing the benefits of reduced trade barriers (along with human rights and democracy) to its neighbors.

As late as 1994, many analysts entertained hopes that a democratic South Africa would act as an engine of regional growth and an economic gateway to the region from the rest of the world. But South Africa's economy has been marked by sluggish growth and widespread unemployment. However it has been able to exploit its substantial comparative material advantages vis-à-vis its neighbors. South African exports increased by 30 percent in the first four years after apartheid, almost all of which was accounted for by growth in manufactured exports to southern Africa (Leysens 1998). Southern Africa is now South Africa's most competitive market, taking nearly 30 percent of South Africa's manufactured products. Compared to its trade deficit with the north (−23.2 billion Rand) it has a very favorable trade surplus within the region (+19.5 billion Rand) (Ahwireng-Obeng and McGowan 1998, 1–12, 68). Industries in several countries, particularly Zimbabwe's textile and tire manufacturers have suffered declining profits and job losses due to increased South African competition. South African businesses in the supermarket, hotel, foodstuff, beer, and construction sectors have moved aggressively into neighboring states, putting local businesses under increased pressure. A number of these companies, such as the supermarket chain Shoprite, have been accused of failing to buy local produce or appoint local personnel to management positions. The takeover of local stalwart Zambia Breweries by South African Breweries fuels local resentment further.

Thus South Africa is now suspected by its neighbors of doing on a regional scale what the United States or the "West" is often accused of doing on an international scale. That is advocating self-interested versions of welfare in the form of open markets and free trade and, correspondingly, self-interested versions of human rights and democracy in the guise of mutual benefit and universal values (Lieberman 1997; Abrahamsson 1997).

Securing Greater Protection for Human Rights in Southern Africa

While the extent of human rights and democracy in Southern Africa is at its highest point since independence, we have seen a stagnation and even reversal in several countries. Even in the most democratic states, there is significant room for improvement. A brief review of the possible ways to improve the state of human rights can be most usefully expressed in terms of the three key concepts with which we began this chapter: ideas, power, and welfare. With regard to the role of ideas, the domestic protests and subsequent reforms of the 1990s certainly helped entrench the legitimacy of the larger ideas of human rights and democracy. But human rights and democracy advocates need to broaden the societal consensus around specific elements of these larger concepts, especially the legitimacy of criticism and dissent, opposition, the right of disliked social groups to participate in the political process, the rights of unpopular minorities such as homosexuals, and women's rights.

Yet greater societal consensus around the legitimacy of human rights will carry us only so far. Advancing the human rights agenda in Southern African also requires a radical restructuring of the balance of political power. First, to deal with the problems posed by the pluralism and diversity of Southern African democratic states, governments need to become more broadly representative of the societies they attempt to govern. The literature on constitutional engineering sets forth a fairly well-known set of tools with which to do this, such as proportional representation electoral systems, power-sharing in the executive branch of government, and federalism (Lijphart 1996; Horowitz 1996). Other avenues would include constitutionally entrenched respect for diverse cultural rights. However few of these have been seriously entertained outside Namibia and South Africa.

Second, while neopatrimonialism and power-maximizing "big men" will not simply disappear, reforms need to focus on ways to strengthen and institutionalize countervailing forces and actors able to check them. This means constitutional reforms and capacity building efforts aimed at revitalizing legislatures and expanding their role in law-making and oversight (especially with regard to the budget process), creating independent Ombudsman, Auditor Generals or other independent watchdog commissions, building political party organizations, strengthening court systems, and strengthening independent media.

However, prescriptions calling for constitutional and other structural reforms beg the point that is the very state itself which must ultimately make these reforms. This means that we need to look for key windows of opportunity that provide the potential for structural reform. One such window could be new transitions that might take place in Congo-Kinshasa or Angola following an end to those conflicts. Another may be the emerging balance in strength between governing and opposition parties in Zimbabwe, Zambia, and Mozambique. A final window could be "mini-transitions" from pseudo-democratic to democratic practice (such as might now be occurring in Zimbabwe).

Across all these initiatives, organized civil society appears to be the best placed actor in the region to play a proactive role in this process. While it may be relatively weak compared to other areas of the world, Southern Africa's civil society organizations offer one of the few areas of real countervailing pressure against power-monopolizing states. With a few exceptions, relatively few legal limitations have been placed on civil society across the region. Civil society organizations increasingly are monitoring various areas of state performance, publicizing human rights violations or other policy failures, and helping victims use the political system to defend their rights.

Trade unions are also an important source of potential guardians of rights. Even where governments have acted against free speech and political assembly, they rarely have tried to limit trade union activities. The legitimacy of their voices enables them to point out violations of basic human rights as well as workers' rights, and place demands on government to observe and respect them. However, the political significance of unions is probably restricted to the region's few industrialized or semi-industrialized states, South Africa, Zimbabwe, Zambia, and Namibia. A final source of civil society that enjoys popular legitimacy in Southern Africa are the churches. In the past few years church organizations in Zimbabwe, Zambia, and Namibia have put pressure on governments to stem corruption and injustice and end human rights violations by the military. In South Africa revitalized church voices are beginning to play an important role in stimulating a growing backlash against President Thabo Mbeki's eccentric views on the cause of AIDS and his government's refusal to provide anti-retroviral drugs to pregnant women.

In concert with churches and trade unions, other civil society organizations can mobilize public protest in order to pressure government toward necessary reform. They can play important roles in constitutional advocacy, putting reform initiatives on the public agenda. Nonpartisan organizations with no clear alignment can play key roles as "honest brokers" in providing forums and resources to debate and develop potential reforms. They can also play a vital capacity-building role assisting nascent independent actors like legislatures, independent commissions, courts, or media. Finally, civil society organizations are well placed to provide critical civic education that helps to build popular awareness and consensus around the legitimacy of human rights. But we need to be clear: civil society cannot provide or enforce human rights. Beyond the most basic matters such as disaster relief, they are not a viable substitute for states or governments.

Because of the state of the economy and often-restrictive legislation, few civil society organizations can rely on internal sources for financial sustainability through charitable giving or membership dues. Most are dependent on external sources. Yet support from foreign donors is always a double-edged sword. It can easily undercut their domestic legitimacy and become their greatest deficiency when they enter into a conflict with a national government. Where governments are not seriously interested in political reform, international "democracy and governance" funds have little place to go except to civil society, thus ensuring that this delicately balanced but necessary partnership will continue.

Beyond fostering the capacity of civil society and other sources of countervailing political power, the other key area of power politics to which human rights advocates must look is organizational reform of the SADC. The most important would be its Organ on Politics, Defense, and Security (OPDS) and developing processes to deal to deal with human rights violations by member states. Yet it is difficult to see how the organization can adopt serious reforms if "repeat offender" member states like Congo-Kinshasa or Zimbabwe have to ratify them. It will be important to take advantage of key windows of opportunity to press through reforms when recalcitrant autocratic regimes are preoccupied with domestic crises. In the meantime the other best hope is a more vigorous and effective defense of human rights within the region by South Africa and Botswana the region's two liberal democracies that also possess significant military and economic resources.

Finally, with regard to welfare, the benefits of economic liberalization need to be spread more equitably across the region or else the losers of the regional economic game will conclude that advocacy of open markets is simply the self-interested claims of economic victors. South Africa needs to understand that its advancement of human rights and democracy will not be understood independently of its international economic policies. It needs to understand that its values are not readily shared and that the strategies that secured its own peaceful transition to democracy will not be readily accepted nor always relevant to every instance of conflict across the region (Cilliers 1999, 5–6).

Chapter 14
West Africa: Nigeria

I. William Zartman

The thesis of this chapter is that Africa has undergone—and presumably continues to do so—waves of democratization for its own reasons, perhaps related but not dependent on the putative waves on a global scale (Huntington 1997). In that process, a key state such as Nigeria has an influential role. But that role is part of the wave effect, not its motor. The causes lie elsewhere, in the nature of the waves themselves within African events and within the logic of their own effects. The essay will explore and develop these assertions.

The term *democratization* has been used in preference to *democracy*, on the assumption that democracy is a process, not an ever fully attained goal. Indeed the assumption that it is a goal that can be attained is not only a false but an undermining idea, since it engenders complacency and leads, in the hands of fallible human beings, to the neglect and destruction of the very goal it seeks to embody. Even the most deeply rooted democracies can slip into nondemocratic moments, from Chicago to Watergate, and are brought back on track only by vigilant efforts to continue democratization. New *democracies*, even more than others, are really only democratizing, and their efforts can be better assayed, assessed and assisted on the basis of that understanding.

Democratization here is used to refer to the process of enforcing accountability of the government to the governed and the participation of the governed in the periodic selection of their governors. Benchmarks in that process are the regular holding of free and fair elections involving meaningful choice (several parties and candidates), freedom of the judiciary from political control, accountability before the law, freedom of the media and of public discussion and association, and bill of rights protection in general. Such measures will not all be enacted at once and when enacted may take some time to become rooted in the popular and legal culture. The first elections may be more or less free and fair, somewhat regular, with a dominant party that has not yet split or become seriously challenged, and so on.

Democratization and human rights are related. While it may be possible to have either without the other, that situation would not be likely to last very long. But more deeply, the two are indissociably linked philosophically: Both say, "Don't torture your citizens, because they are your masters," emphasizing different elements of the statement. Torture is cited as an extreme element in an enlarging number of rights in the evolution of the politics of human rights as a global process. In its operational sense as regular, free and fair elections, democratization may be somewhat easier to install and control than a broad and more subtle human rights schedule of measures. But in a broad as well as a deep sense, advances in human rights foster advances in democratization and vice versa. This chapter focuses on the democratization aspect, but within that understanding.

Waves of Democratization

The independence movement was for Africa the first wave of democratization (Zartman 1997). Like any national liberation movement, it was a struggle for national self-determination, in which the nation, in the African cases, referred to the colonial territory. Subterritorial nations were not legitimate, both in and of themselves, because they were an infringement on the notion of indivisible territorial sovereignty by definition, and by extension, because they were associated with delayed decolonization practicing divide and rule. Defeat in the early 1960s of the French attempts at separating the Sahara from (coastal) Algeria and of the Belgian attempts to support Katangan secession were the marking events in the definition of legitimacy, formalized by the territorial integrity principle in the 1963 charter of the Organization of African Unity (OAU), article 7, and the 1964 OAU Cairo resolution on boundaries and then operationalized by the OAU position in the Biafran War.

But this first wave was truncated. National self-determination referred to self-rule only negatively, as rule not by others, and not as any operational system of governance. It was Isaiah Berlin's (1958) negative self-determination, the freedom from external interference, without internal content. Focusing on the defense of the nation, it did not indicate how the nation was to govern itself. Practice rapidly filled the void, as it does, determining that the nation would govern itself through its organizational expression, the nationalist movement turned single party, led by its historic paramount chief, the nationalist leader turned president. These two elements claimed to incarnate the nation and to be in no need of confirmation; opposition to them was antinationalist, hence pro-colonialist, and thus treasonous; the needs of the nation were known and consensual; and elections were therefore useful at most only for acclamatory purposes. Thus, democratization was stopped short at its definitional and negative implementation, as the national self turned over governance to those who claimed to know, lead, and incarnate it.

This system of national self-determination had its internal flaws, however, that led to its undoing. The national paramount chief was in general apt at leading the attack on the colonial government at best, but less so (or not at all) at leading the newly independent government. Yet the system contained no mechanism for his retirement and succession, since opposition was illegitimate. The military coup became the mechanism of succession, in the absence of elections. The new military regime soon found that it needed a means of organizing the population and so revived the single party from the top down. There was no need for an organization functioning from the bottom up, since rising expectations and overwhelming demands in the aftermath of independence were one of the causes of the previous government's incapacity. Instead, the new single party and military regime worked to squeeze politics out of the system, and restrict its domain only to the bureaucratic and factional infighting of the junta. The process of emptying the first wave of democratization of its content was thereby completed.

Along with it, human rights were weakened as well. While the record of the colonial regime in human rights was scarcely exemplary, the nationalist regime had some obligations toward the nation it purported to incarnate. Enemies of the nation were beyond the pale, however, and their category was liberally interpreted with widely illiberal consequences in many countries, from Ghana to Mozambique. The government killed, cowed, and tortured its citizens, showing them that they were not its masters. The disestablishment of self-government in the military regimes removed any ethos of human rights and any effective agent for their representation.

This evolution did not pass unnoticed. Aided by external events, support, and pressures, African civil society became increasingly aware of the unfulfilled promise of national self-determination in its current status, and moved to reclaim the rest of its inheritance. Probably the most significant aspect of this action lies in the resilience of civil society under the conditions of neglect and repression that it rose to change. Doubtless the repression itself strengthened the demand, although it also weakened it, which explains both the second wave of democratization and human rights and its shortcomings.

Civil society was not only rising as an inexperienced and only inchoately organized force, suffering under repression and vulnerable against government control. It was also fighting against an ethos rooted for three decades (nearly two generations) in the minds of both the rulers and the ruled. The rulers tended to feel (with a few exceptions) that the system worked fine for their benefit, with the main opposition coming from those outside who felt they should be in but who did not challenge the system itself, only its incumbents. The ruled tended to lose faith in the possibility of change, seeing how power was so firmly held. It was not as if those who sought to revive and complete democratization found solid support from cheering crowds; any positive support they received when opportunities appeared quickly vanished under stress, as the riposte of the repressors merely confirmed the impossibility of change. Happily, this fickleness has not been universal, but it must be noted to understand why the second wave of democratization has been as incomplete as the first.

Finally, the relationship between ruler and ruled was also part of the reigning ethos. Instead of regarding government as the servant and representative of society and the manager of conflict, each side regarded the other as the adversary and source of conflict, and this image of government did not change even when representative governments were elected. Government sees the people as the hostile source of unwelcome demands, without providing corresponding supports (allegiance, identification, tax revenues) for its activities, whereas the population regards government as the rapacious source on controls (repression, prices, exactions), without providing the corresponding supplies (Zartman 1997). In these views, both sides revert to the images of ruler and ruled held before independence and nurtured by the anti-colonial struggle.

The second wave of democratization called for the completion of the first through the installation of democratic regimes, with regular, free, and fair elections producing accountable, revocable governments through a process of open pluralistic competition.

It also expected that this new system would produce substantive improvements—an end to corruption, better welfare for the population, reinvigoration of development, an end to Africa's marginalization on the global level. It is similar to Berlin's (1958) positive liberty, the freedom to be self-governing and self-directed, a liberty with content even if a liberty with constraints. The procedural change rests on a number of difficult preconditions—the presence of strong alternatives in elections, responsible participation by the electorate, open and informed election campaigns, and an autonomous and responsible institutional base in the judiciary and the media, all in circular relationship to democratization itself. The substantive change is even more elusive, since it is well known (but not widely recognized) that democracy does not guarantee the achievement of good results in the short run, only the correction of bad results in the longer run. Thus, the nature of the challenge also helps explain the shortfalls, to date, in the second wave of democratization.

If the agents of the first wave were essentially the nationalist movements operating within a propitious global context, the agents of the second wave have been more numerous, but also benefitted from global changes. First have been the NGOs and elements of civil society which grew under cover during the authoritarian rule. Human rights organizations, pro-democracy groups, parts of the labor organizations, religious groups, universities, and student groups, among others, called for a return of governance to the hands of the people, even when subject to government attempts to make them state and party auxiliaries.

Beneath them lay the popular reaction to the substantive insufficiencies of the authoritarian system. Authoritarian government had simply not produced results, a shortfall made all the more glaring for the ideological claims the rulers had produced instead. The deficiencies in welfare in turn created deficiencies in legitimacy, both for African socialism and other ideologies the rulers extolled and for the rulers themselves for having preached insufficiency. The collapse of welfare and legitimacy in its turn produced a collapse in order, as the repressive structures of the state revealed their clay feet, even if only momentarily.

Third came the loss of heart on the part of the rulers. Just as in the collapse of the colonial order, where the colonizers themselves suffered a loss of legitimacy for their enterprise, so the authoritarian rulers frequently lost heart, in part from fatigue from decades at the job. This effect was less widespread than the others, and it often was only momentary, but it gave the forces of democratization an opportunity.

Before leaving the domestic arena of agents of the second wave of democratization, it is worth noting that the list does not include political parties, the heirs of the agents of the first wave. Although political theory would indicate that parties, beneficiaries of democratization, should be its agents, under the state-party system in Africa parties were either compromised by their position in the old system or inexperienced because of their position outside it. Voters were faced with a choice, posed awkwardly by the new political competitors, between experienced (but of course reformed) politicians from the party-state and inexperienced (but of course pure) politicians from the new wave. Frequently the former won and the parties of both groups were the beneficiaries but not the motors of the democratization wave.

Fourth was the international context, an enabling factor that helped but could not have had its impact without the agents on the ground. The contextual change came from the free world victory in the Cold War, not just as a strategic rivalry in the global system but also as a triumph of values (which is, after all, why the Cold War was fought). In analytical terms, welfare and order became open, pluralized, and privatized; on the strategic level, the communist bloc forces that had hitherto protected and legitimized closed, centralist, statist systems were no longer in a position to do so (not even at home, for that matter).

"Open" means that transparency became an accepted value and the public had a right to know about public servants who served themselves first from the meager public plates. For U.S. business, it is illegal to pay bribes directly or indirectly to foreign government officials, an extraordinary deviation from African mores (Miles 1991; Nelton 1996). "Pluralized" means that the party-state is no longer the sole and single source of political power

and economic resources, but that these means are up for continual competition. Legitimacy in the political and economic systems depends on the
existence of competing forces that are assumed to be oppositional, albeit
loyal. "Privatized" means that political power and economic resources were
not only divided and subject to competition within the political system, but
that they also existed in strength outside the political system. Civil society
was to be recognized as an important source of functions previously reserved
for the party-state, including supplies and demands, supports and controls,
and conflict management itself, while economic activity was opened to the
private sector. (What was often forgotten was that political and economic
resources had long been privatized, as rulers took power and wealth as personal commodities; they had just not been pluralized and open.)

Clearly, the enunciation of these agents and characteristics says nothing
about their success. The contextual values, like any of their kind, have only
been ideals, at best approximated by reality. In addition, they and the domestic agents have been contested by the entrenched forces of the incumbent
system, residues of the first wave of democratization turned sour. The second wave is scarcely a decade old, having arisen at the end of the 1980s and
only had its impact in the first half of the following decade.

One of the most important series of events in this democratization wave,
and a bellwether for its evolution, has been the Sovereign National Conference (CNS from its name in French), an extraordinary event in the political chronicles of any continent at any time. Invented in Benin in 1990, the
CNS occurred when civil society took sovereignty in its own hands and away
from the authoritarian ruler of the party-state, convened a conference that
set up a new political system, wrote a new constitution, held (rather free and
fair) competitive elections, and set government off on a new track. CNSs
were held in a dozen countries in West and Central Africa, most of then
French-speaking, over the first half of the 1990s. Significantly, half of them
were overturned by skillful politicians of the old system by the end of the
decade (Ottaway 1997). Those where the new system endured followed their
own courses of democratization, joined by a slowly growing number of other
states, some of which joined the path of democratization by other doors,
including a restorative military coup. One of these was Nigeria.

The Key State of Nigeria

Nigeria could scarcely help being a key state in the region, and in a more
attenuated sense in the continent. One out of every four sub-Saharan Africans, and one out of every five Africans, is Nigerian. Its British colonial
history and its hallmark federal status put it in structural conflict with
the states of its own and the neighboring regions, most of which had been
part of French West and Equatorial Africa and French trusteeships, whose
smaller populations across a larger territory had been divided into fourteen

independent states in 1960, the same year as Nigeria received its independence. Three years later, Nigeria was one of the founding OAU members
who determined the basic form of African international relations. Because
of its size and federal status, Nigeria has been an "international relations
system" of its own and its style in relations with other African countries has
been restrained and not overtly hegemonial. Only during the 1970s, when
the Biafran attempt at secession was defeated, did its military regime throw
its weight around in dealing within the continent and outside.

As a key state, Nigeria exemplifies the waves of democratization, incarnat-
ing them in its own way within its own specific system, rather than being
at the cutting edge or a leader in the waves. Nigeria has sometimes been
treated as a *pivotal state* or a *hegemon* in subregional or regional affairs, and
its weight and influence are undeniable (Chase, Hill, and Kennedy 1996).
But the full implications of either term are overblown. The whole pivotal
state idea is a misleading caricature, as if the world were divided into states
that mattered and those that did not, and it grew out of the sense of a
need for triage in dealing with the growing world population of states. Nigeria is neither a representative, nor a subcontractor, nor a surrogate for its
(sub)region. It is a very important state that has played a variety of roles
in its neighborhood, from a major leader to a major problem, but has at
times been overshadowed or at least rivaled by others such as Ghana, Ivory
Coast, Senegal, and possibly Cameroun. Nigeria's position as a regional
hegemon is similarly attenuated, depending on the situation (Myers 1991).
As such it is an important part of the waves of democratization, but not their
motor.

Nigeria's unique status as a federation reinforces the notion of its position as part but not leader of the wave. Democratization has been an issue
in Nigeria on the two levels of its governance institutions—among the
people within each of the federal states and among the federal states on the
national level. Thus, while it can be claimed to be doubly concerned about
democratization, at the same time some of its problems are not those of the
other African states. On the other hand, as a prominent case in the swing
between military and civilian regimes, Nigeria shared difficulties with human
rights as well as democratization that were common to the continent.

Although the above discussion of the waves of democratization is generalized for Africa, it could have been written specifically for Nigeria without
changing a word. Nigeria began its independent life in the First Republic in
1960 as a showcase of federal democracy, with a multiparty parliamentary
system. In reality, however, each of the three regions was a dominant-party
state, engaged at the national level in an unstable coalition game for control. The Hausa-Fulani North, with the Northern Peoples Congress (NPC),
had the largest population. The south was composed of the Yoruba Western
Region with the Action Group (AG). The Igbo Eastern region with the
National Council of Nigerian and the [Northern] Cameroons (NCNC) was

the third key region with the largest number of educated people and possessing oil resources. With independence,

the compromises (in revenue allocation formulas and political representation) that sustained the amalgam of the North and the South now gave way to pursuit of narrow regional interests. As a result of increasing unwillingness to compromise, no methods were too bad to employ in the quest of political power, especially of the [federal] center. The 1959 election, the last before independence, was the beginning of a new era when the basic rules of conflict management changed dramatically. A constitutional conference ceased to be an adequate mechanism for reaching a consensus on basic demands. An election [such as the next federal elections in 1964] became threatening, rather than enabling, to the three ethnic giants. The new strategy for regional participants was, in the long run, to achieve unilateral hegemony. Military intervention in 1966 was the ultimate move in the gradually escalating use of physical violence to settle political conflicts. (Gboyega 1997, 158–59, 164)

Two coups in 1966, a pogrom against Igbos living in the north and the secessionist struggle of Biafra in 1967–70, led to federal government weakness and to a third coup by activist reform-minded officers led by General Murtala Muhammed and then, after his assassination, by General Olusegun Obasanjo. In addition to strengthening the federal structure, Obasanjo's regime prepared the country for a return to elected civilian government in 1979. But democratization meant merely a return to the same regional rivalry and single-party maneuvering, accompanied by growing corruption fueled by the gushing oil revenues. The National Party of Nigeria (NPN) was the reincarnated party of the north, with some eastern allies; the Nigerian People's Party (NPP) was the Igbo party of the middle belt; and the Unity Party of Nigeria (UPN) was the party of the Yorubas in the west. The NPN again dominated the political system, playing on internal divisions with the other regions and their parties, with officials and politicians at all levels enriching themselves at public expense (Zartman 1982). The reelection of President Alhaji Shehu Shagari in 1983 was scarcely free and fair, and the Second Republic ended at the end of the same year with another military coup, by General Muhammadu Buhari.

Although the Buhari regime sought to remove the sources of Nigeria's decline—corruption, disorder, inefficiency, regional infighting—these problems proved to be more deeply entrenched than the efforts to correct them, and the regime turned repressive, unpopular, and ineffective. It was removed in August 1985 by General Ibrahim Babangida, with a stronger hold on the political process. Over the next eight years, his government pursued a political program of preparation for democratic rule that would restructure the political system and remove the corrupt politicians and regional roots of rivalry that had destroyed the first two republics. In this, it mirrored the evolution throughout the continent borne by the second wave of democratization. A thorough study commission report in 1987 recommended a restoration of constitutional government maintaining the federal system but with separation of powers and a competitive two-party system; two years later, when an invitation to political organization produced more replicas of the old party structures, Babangida decreed two new organizations—a conservative National Republican Convention (NRC) and a Social Democratic Party (SDP)—with stringent requirements for balanced slates and distributed majorities among the states to obtain election, although in practice the initial letter in each party came to symbolize the part of the country where its center of gravity lay. A careful and gradual process produced two broadly (and specifically, to the junta) acceptable presidential candidates and an election in June 1993 that was widely acclaimed as national (trans-regional) in its participation and free and fair in its practice, electing Chief Moshood Abiola of the SDP as president. For reasons still unclear, Babangida declared the results unacceptable, annulled the elections, and retired from office in favor of a civilian appointee two months later. The new government, weak in legitimacy, was overthrown in three months by the core figure behind the previous two military regimes, General Sani Abacha (Lewis 1994, 1996).

The coup was a blow to the democratization process followed up to that point, however flawed, and an arresting example to the rest of Africa struggling with the effects of the second wave. Abacha's regime over the next five years was the lowest point in Nigeria's fall from democratization and respect for human rights (Osaghae 1998). Repressive, corrupt, authoritarian, the regime became the target of sanctions by the Commonwealth, the European Union, and the United States. Regional and ethnic tensions rose, popular resentment increased, and human rights activists and major political figures—including General Obasanjo—were imprisoned and some executed or assassinated. Abiola's stature rose correspondingly in popular esteem, although as a political leader he was a rather weak figure. It was only the hand of Providence that removed Abacha, and then Abiola, in sudden heart attacks, leaving the country in the hands of the senior officer, General Abdessalam Abubakr, whose sole political ambition was to return the country to civilian rule and place his country, somewhat belatedly, into the second wave of democratization. Careful preparations throughout 1998 produced somewhat free and fair elections in February 1999 that brought the NRC candidate, General Obasanjo, back to the presidency on a platform of democratization, human rights, and a cleanup of corruption, regional discrimination, and economic inefficiencies. While results will take a while, his stature in the country and the army, his past record, and his program made his regime the best chance for a return of Nigeria to the path of democratization and human rights.

Nigeria illustrates well the effects of the two waves of democratization in Africa, tempered in their details by the particular conditions of the country, its own federal political system, and its attempts at democratic restoration and military reform. Nigeria was in the forefront of truncated democratization as the three nationalist-movements-turned-single-party dominated the politics of the three major regions. Their excesses brought in the military and then spun off into a civil war over a secessionist movement; the military intervention continued the sequence of coups begun in Togo in 1963 and was emulated a month later in Ghana and then in a number of states in the region. Nigeria sought to return to democratization earlier than the others but that return was merely a restoration of the old truncated system of self-rule, bringing back the military again. The second wave of democratization crashed up against the military in Nigeria and only increased their obduracy, but it animated the populace and finally converted the military leaders. In the second wave, Nigeria was a follower rather than a leader of the continent, but Nigerian events have still been part of the pattern. Much more of a leadership position was shown within Nigerian civil society by domestic efforts to promote civil rights and democratization, but also by a movement to spread its values across the continent, led as well by General Obasanjo.

An African Regime for Democratization and Human Rights

While the discussion of democratization generally focuses on the domestic political system of individual states, the formal state rules and institutions are fragile if they do not rest on a firm foundation in civil society. By the same token, state practices are more firmly held in place when they are nested, along with the practices of other states, within an international regime that sets standards, rules, and expectations. The first wave of democratization met these requirements in part. The national liberation movements grew out of voluntary associations and emerged from a sequence of activities that went through a stage of reform groups before uniting in nationalist movements (Hodgkin 1962; Brown 1964; Wallerstein 1966). The rules of self-determination were codified in UN law, such as UN General Assembly Resolution 1514 (XV) of 1960 on colonial liberation, and then written into the OAU Charter among the norms of the African international political system. However, the international regime thus established was as clear in its limitations as it was in its prescriptions, faithfully translating the truncation nature of self-determination. Alongside the right of the new states to be free of foreign rule was also the right of new states to be free of interference in their internal affairs and the absence of any commitment to practice self-rule democratically. Only two decades later, in 1983, did the OAU adopt a Charter on Human and Group Rights, adopting the Universal Declaration to its own African form in principle and in operation.

As the second wave drew near, Africans in civil society realized the insufficiency of their own official practices on the state level. While discussions on democratization and human rights had continued since independence, if not before, they became more urgent, more widespread, and more coordinated under the impact of the flagrant denial of their values, as noted in the discussion of developments within the states. One particularly prestigious figure of civil society, Olusegun Obasanjo, then a chicken farmer, eventually named a member of former President Jimmy Carter's group of former elected heads of state and government, founded a group for the discussion of continental concerns in 1989, the African Leadership Forum (ALF) (Deng and Zartman 2002). Moved by the domestic conditions on the continent and its international marginalization as the Cold War drew to an end, he began a series of consultations across Africa and in Europe to determine the feasibility of drawing up a document of standards in the political, economic, and social fields that would emulate for Africa the 1975 Helsinki Declaration on Security and Cooperation in Europe. The efforts led to a meeting in Kampala in 1991 of some 500 delegates, mainly from African civil society but including some heads of state and other government representatives, producing a Declaration on Security, Stability, Development, and Cooperation in Africa and calling for an official drafting conference (CSSDCA) on the same subject (Obasanjo 1991).

The Kampala Declaration enunciates a series of goals and standards for African countries in regard to interstate relations (security), domestic governance (stability), economic and social conditions (development), and cooperation within Africa and in the larger world arena. The focus in regard to security is on the management of conflict, the consideration of sovereignty as responsibility rather than as protection, and the association between individual and state security. The aim of the stability provisions is to endorse responsible, responsive governance based on regular free and fair elections, accountability, participation, transparency, and human rights. Development is to be rooted in open, competitive economic practices, cooperation between private and public sectors, social concerns including education, and improved use of local resources. The Declaration is a most statesmanlike document, clear, comprehensive and penetrating in its implications for improving order, welfare, and legitimacy in Africa.

The Declaration and its accompanying call for a conference were submitted to the OAU meeting in Abuja in 1991; both the chair, General Ibrahim Babangida, and the OAU Secretary-General, Salim Ahmed Salim, had relations of personal rivalry with Obasanjo. The proposal was sent to the OAU Council of Ministers and then the 1992 OAU Summit in Dakar for further study, where it was opposed by some of the member states whose regimes were particularly threatened by its provisions and then tabled by the inaction of the majority of states who were uncertain of its implications and unwilling to challenge their threatened colleagues. The African Leadership Forum continued to publicize the Declaration and its principles within the context of the second wave, until 1995, when General Abacha arrested and incarcerated Obasanjo and put an end to his activities.

The ALF continued the work, planning to focus its attentions on civil society organizations in African states and on subregional organizations.

Obasanjo's release in 1998 and his election to the Nigerian presidency the following year brought CSSDCA and the Kampala Declaration into Nigerian foreign policy as a major plank. The project was accepted at the 1999 Algiers summit as a statement of the OAU's purposes, and a working group was charged with the preparation of the conference. At the 2000 Lome meeting of the OAU, however, a vague and ambitious plan was adopted for orienting the Organization in a different direction, as the African Union. At the same time, with its adoption as a foreign policy goal by one of the OAU member states, the Kampala movement gained official status but lost its roots in civil society. The ALF became an arm of the Nigerian government, the Kampala principles became absorbed into the official diplomacy of the African states they were to control, and the democratization and human rights regime became a verbal appendage to the organizational politics of the OAU, as it transformed itself into the African Union (AU). But many of the Kampala principles found their way into the AU's new sister organization, the New Economic Partnership for African Development (NEPAD).

Like the second wave of democratization on the state level, the attempt to institute a continent-wide regime has known its steps back and forward, and the shuffle is not over. Efforts to revive civil society support are not ended, and attempts to gain more meaningful engagement by subregional organizations continue. Even if CSSDCA has not yet been scheduled, the Kampala principles are still alive. But, like any wave, their force diminishes as it reaches higher ground and rolls on in time, until new waves of energy renew their drive. The backflow of the initial wave can undermine the thrust of new waves in the same direction, yet the fuller the retreat of the initial wave when spent, the more powerful the rush of energy in the next round.

Explanations and Conclusions

The recurrent pressure for human rights and democratization rises from many levels of causes in the African experience. It is first of all a basic part of that experience, deeply ingrained in the precolonial as well as the anticolonial history of Africa. Individual rights are an integral part of the group rights that constitute African society; the South African saying, "Umuntu ngumuntu ngabantu" (I am because we are) is a statement not merely of the communitarian soul of Africa but also of the place of the individual within the collectivity, also translatable as "Because we are, I am" (Masina 2000). The formative political experience of modern Africa was the national liberation struggle, political in its form in most of Africa and violent only in selected, obdurate colonies. As a struggle for national self-determination, it has lain at the base of longings for democratization.

Second, the shortcomings of both heritages in achieving their realization in contemporary practice have only heightened the pressure. African political attitudes are formed by negative socialization, a longing for the form of government one does not have. As this longing becomes an idealization, it tends to make its own realization more difficult but it also reinforces the images of democracy and human rights. If the shortfall goes on too long, populations can become alienated from government in general and cynical about achieving any change, falling into the pattern of considering government of any form as the opponent—another inheritance of the anticolonial struggle—and unable to recognize the offspring of one's desires when it finally does appear. But the longings remain, and to date have been able to add energy to the successive waves of pressure for democratization and human—both group and individual—rights.

Third, in the long run, repression has simply failed, although it has left its effects. Neither Abacha in Nigeria nor Mobutu in Zaire-Congo nor Siad Barre in Somalia have been able to destroy civil society in its various manifestations and the inherent desire for participatory self-rule and respect for human dignity. Mobutu's vacuum left local initiatives and organizations to thrive, Abacha's repression trained civil society to operate under pressure, and Siad Barre's ruthlessness left strong feelings of democratization and dignity within the clans even if not always between them. It is true that it took the intervention of Providence to call Abacha and Mobutu from the spoils of this world, but the fact remains that even their Time at the Trough only sharpened African longings for civic values.

But the other face of the same coin is that Mobutu left a vacuum and an ethos of politics that allowed Laurent Kabila to come in as a leftist version of his predecessor's rightist model; Abacha left a military and party structure for politics that continues to pose a serious obstacle for even a charismatic reformer such as Obasanjo; Siad Barre carried the state with him to his grave and left the clans unable to unite in a national political system over a decade later. Examples could be multiplied from around the continent, too. Lesser disciples of the most egregious despots still thrive: Denis Sassou-Nguesso in Congo-Brazzaville wrapped his 1997 coup in a constitutional legitimacy that gives him thirty-one years of monopolized power; Robert Mugabe in Zimbabwe was reelected unfreely and unfairly in 2002 to thirty-five years of rule over a repressed and starving country; Gnassingbe Eyadema's election in Togo in 2001 assures him of four decades in power. Democracy and human rights still remain values and aspirations pitted against state power in many countries, no matter how strong those ultimate aspirations may be.

A fourth point, more debatable in its ramifications, is that authoritarian, repressive systems supply only private goods and therefore pass with their beneficiary, at least in their specific form. Democracy and human rights systems endure across individual incumbents, but dictators cannot be cloned.

There is an opportunity for deep change in every succession, even if author-itarian systems offer that opportunity only at longer intervals than do democracies. The attraction of private goods in a situation of poverty where any goods are in limited supply is of course enormous, and so is the occur-rence of the Time at the Trough ethos—the officers' feeling of entitlement to political power for personal gain—that perpetuates authoritarianism and repressiveness (Zartman 1997). Even worse than the incidental effects can be the perpetuation of negative political socialization, as described, to the point where any governance system is rejected as short of the ideal. If society as a whole loses hope and concurs that government only supplies pri-vate goods, whatever it may be supposed to do in the unattainable ideal, future waves of democratization and human rights in Africa are in danger of not occurring or of not occurring with the necessary strength.

In the end, however, it is the innate nature of human rights and partici-patory self-rule that provides the strongest guarantee for the recurrence of pressure for their attainment. The very quality of human rights and democ-racy as internally contested notions and values and human rights and self-rule as both social values and social power mean that they will be an inevitable part of the discourse in debate and practice both among their adherent and between their adherents and their opponents, a necessary part of the agenda. And that means that the developing polities of Africa, in quest of themselves, cannot avoid recurrent pressures to find their legit-imacy in the procedures of democracy and the substance of human dignity.

Part III
Retrospect
and Prospects

Chapter 15
Whither Human Rights?

Edward A. Kolodziej

Some brief stocktaking is useful at this point to sum up where we are. Based largely (but not exclusively) on the findings of this volume, I first hazard some observations about where the power, politics, and promise of human rights are today. This will not be easy. The scope of the discussion and the richness, depth, and complexity of the preceding chapters caution against sweeping generalizations that fail to account for different and contradictory patterns of human rights struggles across the regions of the world. This brief survey is viewed from an imaginary point in conceptual space that plots how far the ideational claims of human rights have been able to command the mobilized will and material resources of the world's populations and where the promise of human rights has succeeded or fallen short of its potential power to shape and shove human societies.

The second section outlines some practical steps for further progress that partisans of human rights might pursue to enlarge their scope.

A *Force Profonde*: The Power, Politics, and Promise of Human Rights

How do we know that human rights, as a potentially detectable, empirically verifiable *force profonde*, exist? Emile Durkheim argued that deeply held social values, though invisible, were indissoluble bonds binding self-defined groups together. These could still be demonstrated as powerful determinants of human thought, decisions, and action by reference to the religious practices, communal ceremonies, and tribal rituals through which they were mediated and confirmed by the members of the group. They could be "seen," too, in the institutions and systems of law created to reflect, sanctify, and protect what humans cared about most.[1] To his evidentiary base can be added the strivings of millions of anonymous individuals who have been engaged in costly struggles—reckoned in untold pain, anguish, torment, material losses, imprisonment, torture, and death—to win human rights for themselves and others.

Human rights must certainly be conceived as universal ideals defining the rights and obligations of states, international bodies, groups, and individuals to each other. Chapters on Western and Islamic perspectives on human rights affirm and underscore this moral and legal understanding of human rights. These competing claims and the issues they join tell us much, but not nearly as much as we need to know about how rights are seeded, germinate, mutate, grow, and flourish or, conversely, how they wither and die. These matters can only be addressed by linking human rights to the material resources—force, technology, and wealth—and, accordingly, to the social power needed to realize them. Making those links explicit across cultures, regions, and states are central aims of this volume as preconditions to better understand and explain the evolution of human rights as a prerequisite to use this knowledge to advance them.

If human rights are a *force profonde*, working their way through human societies and history, as this volume contends, they find specific and discernible expression in countless local and regional struggles for power. These are embedded in a myriad centers of conflict of enlarging and thickening networks, forming an emerging world society. Viewed through these multiple power lenses, human rights are protean. They both shape and are informed by the socioeconomic and political power structures in which they are suspended and alternately supported or suppressed. They assume many forms and advance or retract at variable rates of social speed. Viewed across centuries, the movement has certainly been forward, if seldom in a straight line or necessarily assured or a fait accompli in many regions of the world. As the chapters in this volume show, even today, human rights have also been dealt significant and devastating blows in every continent of the globe, including Europe and North America.

What we are witnessing today, as observers *and* participants, is the gradual recognition by increasingly larger numbers of peoples from different and often contesting national, ethnic, and cultural identities that they are also members of a human race to which rights, as universally applicable properties, can be ascribed simply by being human (Searle 1995). These are "social facts," as Max Weber might have noted. While human rights, as a systemic force affecting people and states in unequal measure, is detectable, as this volume exposes, convergence on a single, simple, coherent notion of human rights is not likely any time soon. Nor is such a result necessarily inevitable, given the refracting societal prisms of power through which this *force profonde* works its will in *and* on the contesting values and contrasting identities of individuals and groups around the globe. Nor is congruence necessarily desirable, if debilitating conflicts are to be avoided over the precise content of human rights when viewed through the blurred lenses of rival cultural, religious, and ideological perspectives. Immanuel Kant reached a similar conclusion in rejecting world government as a solution to war. He put his faith in a coalition of republics, each animated by its own set of values but resting on popular consent, as a formula for "perpetual peace" rather than on what he concluded was an unattainable unified, cosmopolitan world government (Kant 1970).

The regional chapters repeatedly underscore the point that human rights do not float freely in conceptual space. Their reality arises in their practice, supported by the social power structures protecting and animating them. They depend for their realization on the enabling and constraining power attributed to them by the diverse and divided peoples comprising the multiple societies composing an increasingly interconnected, if not integrated, world society. Members of this emerging world society are concerned not only with human rights, but with a lot more. These competing interests pose serious opportunity costs. Hard choices have to be made between lending their power and support to human rights and to a host of other compelling interests. Social power is neither infinite nor inexhaustible. Human rights compete for support with strivings for security, material betterment, and countless other aims. These are pursued by a bewildering array of actors, only some of which are directly concerned with human rights. The pursuit of human rights is embedded in a larger global politics. This volume has attempted to abstract the actors and factors driving the global politics of human rights within the local, state, and regional contexts in which it is suspended. The agents concerned with human rights extend to states, international organizations, multinational corporations, domestic and transnational associations and empowered individuals. In their continuing and enlarging transactions, these agents form a distinct and discernible structure and process of international politics, dedicated to the power and promise (or denial) of human rights.

The global politics of human rights is more aptly understood as a process and not as a product or end point. There is no definitive end in sight. If for no other reason than human freedom and the seemingly limitless capacity of humans to redefine themselves, pronouncing closure on what it means to be human, what human rights are, and how they are realized is premature (Fukuyama 1992). Human rights are unquestionably a *force profonde* today, but that scarcely guarantees that this force will not be arrested and gradually disappear from human consciousness and eventually be selected out of evolution as a value and institution, if its social supports—human and material—gradually dwindle, decline, and disappear.

As a window on this process of reinvention, this volume has attempted to enlarge and deepen our knowledge of the scope of the international politics of human rights by focusing sharply on the many faces and contesting forms of human rights as manifestations of a singular but many-faceted *force profonde*. As a process of human self-discovery against the backdrop of a radically differentiated linguistic, cultural, socioeconomic, and moral evolution of human societies, this complex process can hardly be expected to be internally coherent, unified, or ultimately even convergent. We need better conceptual and causal maps than we have now to explain and understand why human rights have progressively evolved in one region and stalled or eroded in another. How are human rights agendas built and modified? Who are the key actors in advancing or retarding their spread? What resources do these actors dispose and what strategies are best suited to advance their progress? Which strategies have effectively blocked or distorted their development? Do different and contending value systems pose the puzzling possibility that conflicting social practices may meet a test of human rights? What may constitute sacred religious practices in one society may well be rejected as barbarous and uncivil in another. This volume provides some initial, provisional maps of these vast and enormously entangled processes. What success it may have in achieving these aims may inspire others to improve on its design and findings.

What are real about human rights, paradoxically, are their fundamentally insubstantial and subjective properties as social facts. Their power and the powerful impact they exert are evident in the multiple and continuing struggles recounted in these chapters within and across cultures, regions, and states. These are the external and discernible manifestations of the values driving contesting actors to foster or frustrate human rights. The power of human rights is registered as a social fact and force less by their enjoyment, often taken for granted by those untutored in the politics and power determinants that produced them, than by the costly efforts of innumerable peoples willing to resist those who would abuse or deny them. This *force profonde* is known more by way of its deprivation than by its free expression.

These clashes over rights, a subjective value of groups and individuals, are not reducible to, however much they may be integral to, conflicts over national and international security or over the production and distribution of material wealth. The demand for human rights constitutes an autonomous domain of human moral and political expression and power of equal importance to these order and welfare concerns. No less than the imperatives of order and welfare, they provide critical tests for the legitimacy of national and international governance. The quest for human rights is part and parcel of the process of constructing and governing what has emerged as a world society, for the first time in the evolution of the human species since its diaspora out of Africa a million years ago. This is not to say that the imperatives of order—that is, controlling violence—and of welfare—producing and distributing wealth—do not set limits for human rights and the democratizing practices with which they are associated. Those in possession of material elements of power are quite ready and able, as these chapters document, to use force and coercive threats, economic incentives, and technological know-how to prevail over human rights claims. Setbacks notwithstanding, there is still ample evidence to conclude that a line tracking the evolution of the human rights movement would clearly be upward and positive, if jagged and wavering when viewed between any two points over what Fernand Braudel (1980) calls "the longue dureé of history."

Changing, too, are the elements composing the human rights movement. In the wake of World War II, when the movement began to gather increasing steam, the claim of self-determination by the subjugated populations of Europe's empires appeared an overriding concern. The Vietnamese struggle for independence from French and American rule exemplifies the capacity of human rights to galvanize human will, even when self-determination leads unexpectedly to the denial of these rights. The principle of national self-determination, spawned by the French and American revolutions, returned with vengeance to direct the military defeat of France and the United States. All the West's empires were swept away by these forces. Dutch control over Indonesia was relinquished shortly after World War II. The Suez War in 1956 sounded the death knell of British imperial power. The French followed suit, induced to relinquish their remaining holdings in West and North Africa by 1962. The Portuguese empire fell a decade later before these same forces. With the end of white rule in South Africa in the early 1990s, the last vestiges of European dominance of the African continent were swept away. Viewed against the background of the punctuated evolutionary dissolution of European empires, it is not surprising that the Soviet Union should also succumb to the demands of its national peoples for self-determination.

Today the global agenda for human rights, while still animated by strivings for national independence and autonomy—witness Tibet and East Timor— has increasingly devolved, as the chapters in this volume reveal, to group and individual claims for human rights *within* state boundaries, either against the state or in pursuit of its material powers to defend against the depredations of rival groups. These struggles play out at several mutually interdependent levels. The most prominent are still those between the state and ruling elites in control of the government and citizens—individuals and groups—pressing for more open, democratically organized societies and respect for their civil and human rights.

Examples of these struggles, drawn from every region of the globe including the United States, can be multiplied at will. The record is hardly positive across the board. Vietnam's struggle for independence gives way to pressures to open its economy to the West and to extend greater freedoms by the Communist regime to its citizens. In Myanmar a clique of generals holds the Burmese population hostage. The efforts of Aung San Suu Kyi to create a viable democracy have been largely blocked at every turn since the overthrow of her freely elected government in 1990. The international isolation of Myanmar, North Korea, Libya, and similar oppressive regimes around the globe may have induced some to relax their hold on their respective populations, but their grip still remains firm and constraining. As Marvin Weinbaum details, Iran is in incipient civil war over what kind of Islamic republic will be created: one based on a rule of law affording its citizens wider personal liberties or another subject to the will of self-appointed clerics in league with kept courts, elements of the police and military, and covert groups organized to enforce conservative Mullah rule. Chinese suppression of the Falun Gong and of regime dissidents provides additional illustration of the shift in group and individual human rights concerns from the colonial struggles of the past for national independence and statehood to the fight for democracy and human rights within states across the world.

What makes understanding these complex struggles particularly difficult is that claims of human rights are often made by those who, on capturing state power, suppress or limit the scope of an open society to which they putatively subscribe and rely on through elections to assume power. The ceaseless civil war in Algeria, as Arfi recounts, pits two groups against each other, neither of which is a friend of democracy or human rights. Ethnic conflicts in South and Southeast Asia, as the chapters by Kochanek and Neher tell, raise many of these same problems. Hindu extremists enjoy the freedom to organize within an open society, but are bent on trampling on the religious beliefs of their Muslim neighbors and on reducing them to second-class citizenship within India. Pakistani militants similarly claim to be freeing their co-religious from Indian rule in Kashmir, but evidence little inclination to enlarge the civil liberties or human rights either of Kashmiris or of their fellow citizens in Pakistan if they accede to power. In seeking greater group freedoms, neither the Tamil Tigers nor the Palestinians have given much indication of their commitment to developing an open society if granted greater autonomy or their own state. Distinguishing between genuine and disingenuous defenders of human rights is not easy if the self-justifications of these contesting groups are simply taken at face value. The key litmus test is how they use their power: whether to foster or to frustrate human rights.

These examples illustrate but hardly exhaust the dilemmas posed in creating a civil society and a rule of law to which the state and its agents—bureaucrats, police, and military—must defer if human rights are to be observed. If the state continues to pose the principal threat to human rights, its coercive and persuasive powers also have to be enlisted, absent working and effective international institutions and bodies—as is essentially the case today—to ensure that groups do not perversely use civil freedoms to oppress others. Discrimination and oppression appear in many guises. The mere institutionalization of majority rule does not ensure the protection of civil liberties or human rights.

The threat of majority rule to minority and personal rights was well articulated two centuries ago in Federalist No. 10 by James Madison. How can a popular government be created powerful enough to arbitrate the incessant conflicts of civil society and provide for its security yet not so powerful a regime that it might become the principal threat to human freedom? This dilemma lies at the heart of states rent by ethnic, religious, or class warfare.

The state's coercive apparatus is a key stake in civil strife, driven by these divisions. Rivals have every incentive to seize and control the state's coercive powers to impose their preferences on others. In torn societies, where there exists no agreement on the rules of political struggle for power, a majority test poses, rather than resolves, the problem of internal group rivalry. If the state's power is indispensable to prevent group conflict and to protect civil liberties and human rights, it is equally true that these freedoms depend for their exercise on a rule of law backed by coercive sanctions. No regime—democratic or nondemocratic—can escape this dilemma. Both democratic theorists and their skeptical opponents can agree that to be successfully engaged either in promoting or suppressing human rights requires what Hobbes advised—awesome violence to get one's way (Mansbridge 1996; Maine 1886).

Western-styled or Western-aspiring societies, which claim to be models of democratic and human rights practices, are scarcely spared conflicts over the proper boundaries of the state's authority and coercive power and the scope of the freedoms available to its citizens.[2] The European Union struggles to define a common European citizenship consistent with the diverse meanings and practices associated with national citizenship. Disputes over the rights of women in the workplace and those of immigrants illustrate this issue. The Turkish secular state depends for its survival on an undemocratic military while beset by ethnic conflict and religious pressures to theocratize the state. The Russian Federation, as Leff describes, falls short of a test of democracy, notably in the limits placed by the state on a free press. The Israeli democracy also suffers from internal contradictions, as Peleg observes. Its secular political institutions and open electoral processes cloak an underlying principle of ethnic identity at odds with a pure liberal conception of popular government. The Israeli state rests on an ethnic and an incipient religious identity. This poses a fundamental dilemma for its survival, since it implies the permanent subordination of its Arab minority and precludes the possibility of an Arab or Muslim majority that might capture the Israeli state. The suppression of the Palestinian Intifada, the spread of Israeli settlements into the occupied territories, and continued rule over this area deepen the identity divide between the ideal image of the Israeli state and people and its conformity to liberal principles and practices and the imperatives of survival of the Israeli state in what may well be a permanently hostile environment (Barnett 1996; Peleg this volume).

A few final words may also be in order about the Western project that started the human rights movement and its status as a social fact commanding both ideational and material power both within the West and among the Rest. This volume lends credence to Michael Ignatieff's keen observation that the human rights movement has come of age in the sense that increasing numbers of otherwise contesting peoples recognize "that we live in a plural world of cultures that have a right to equal consideration in the argument about what we can and cannot, should and should not, do to human beings" (Ignatieff 2001, 94). If that is an accurate rendering of the current status of the ideational-power balance worldwide, and many would contest whether we have progressed so far (Huntington 1996), it follows that the origin of a human rights claim is not as relevant, if at all, as its intrinsic capacity to command allegiance and authority and to become the vehicle for mobilizing human will and material resources for its protection, promotion, and extension. The Western project cannot logically be dismissed by opponents simply because it is Western. Nor can its attraction for vast numbers of non-Western peoples, as Chou En-lai allows, be fully explained as simply a function of Western material power or power politics parading under the guise of human rights.

Nor, conversely, should the Western project, which by no means is internally coherent and consistent, as Newman's chapter relates (Ignatieff 2001, 92–95), be identified exclusively either with the global process or with the diverse products of the human rights movement. In principle, as Ignatieff observes, everyone has an equal say (if not equal power) in defining the content of human rights and in mobilizing the world's social power to realize their particular formulations of these rights. This poses a serious challenge to any Western exclusionary claims to be the sole global model for the human rights movement. The priority accorded by the West to procedural over substantive rights (notwithstanding the creation of welfare states in all of the Western nations) rings hollow among the peoples of the developing world. The Western project's formula of global markets, driven by scientific discovery and ceaseless technological innovation, as the appropriate and overriding solution to the demands of populations everywhere for "more now" is—at best—a necessary but hardly a sufficient answer for the vast majority of humans to their economic plight. How can they adopt these solutions when they lack the resources and skills needed to play by Western global market rules?

This converging line of attack on the West by the developing world across otherwise divergent and divided peoples is echoed repeatedly throughout this volume. The economic gap between the West and the Rest will continue to be a central bone of contention between North and South throughout this century *as a human rights issue.* This flaw in the ideational content of the West's project weakens its global pull. For the West, the expansion of democratization and the extension of procedural human rights is supposed to foster and accelerate economic development; conversely, the adaptation of developing states to the discipline of global market rules, prescribed as hard medicine by the West, is expected ultimately to increase both their wealth and welfare *and* their civil liberties and human rights. For most of the non-Western peoples, they are confronted by the glaring fact of an ever-widening imbalance between the rich and poor and a yawning digital divide between themselves and their Western counterparts. They also witness the declining disposition of Western democratic majorities and the international economic institutions they control to close these gaps. Democratic rule, paradoxically, hinders the spread of substantive human rights when viewed from the perspective of the deprived and underprivileged. Autocrats of all stripes can deflect opposition and criticism by blaming the West for their society's ills or, as in the case of the Chinese regime, Beijing's leaders can strike an implicit social bargain with the populace, trading economic development for political control and the forfeiture of human freedoms.

Whither Human Rights?

Some prudential policy lessons can provisionally be drawn from the preceding discussion. These are neither mutually exclusive nor fully compatible, given the divergent and contradictory socioeconomic, political, and moral forces at work in different social settings within which human rights claims are posed or disposed. They still provide some promise of progress in advancing human rights.

First, and following from the exposed flaw in the Western project, the economic needs of the world's populations must be seriously and systematically addressed if the human rights not only of non-Western societies but also of the West are to be preserved and promoted. Under the conditions of globalization—the increased connectedness and interdependence of human societies around the world—the notions of irremediable poverty and insurmountable subsistence limits on economic development and growth are no longer defensible. Populations everywhere now know that they can choose how to organize and govern their societies to vault what, until the modern period, appeared to be permanent obstacles to their material betterment. In light of a half century of experience with foreign aid, simply throwing resources at this problem will not relax or eliminate local social, political, moral, and religious impediments to economic growth. These bedeviled the West for half a millennium after the breakup of medieval Europe, and as transaction cost economic theory explains (Coase 1937; Coase 1960; North 1990), market imperfections still abound to frustrate efficient and effective economic practices.

Absent an increasing net transfer of effective technological knowhow and economic resources from North to South and the multiplication of socioeconomic safety nets in the developing world to reinforce those already instituted in the West, an increasing number of peoples will neither be drawn into the world's market economy nor have incentive or interest to support an economic system that fails to address their needs and demands. Threatened then are the other elements of the Western project. At risk will be the social facts of the autonomy and integrity of the individual, the realization of human freedom and equality as the foundation stones for human rights, free, fair, open democratic practices, and the toleration of divergent cultural and religious values. The stock of the Western project as a model for emulation is tied to the promise of human rights. It will rise or fall as a whole as a function of its capacity to respond to the material concerns of billions in the developing world. Many forget that it was precisely this line of reasoning that convinced a majority in the United States to support the Marshall Plan to rehabilitate Europe, including former adversaries, to ensure not only their democratic rule and economic growth but also, by that token, to secure these benefits for the U.S. people (Graebner 1964, 730–32).

Second, in moving human rights forward in Western or non-Western modes, no one strategy alone will work. It all depends on the social context in which rights claims are introduced and pressed. A precondition for effective and efficient choice by relevant actors to enhance human rights practices is knowledge of the actors contesting to advance or arrest human rights progress. To meet this condition, analysts and decision-makers must first identify who are the actors engaged in a human rights struggle, the material, psychological, and ideational resources they possess, and the effectiveness of the strategies they are pursuing to get their way. Content and timing are crucial. What may well be sensible and viable in one setting—say equal pay for equal work in pursuit of gender rights in the West—may be irrelevant as a priority of gender rights in preindustrial economies. This volume stresses the need for better theory and more detailed empirical verification of actor behavior and their ability to foster or to frustrate human rights in a particular state or region. It is an installment and, hopefully, a stimulus to others to conduct the needed theorizing and detailed empirical research to develop appropriate models adaptive to local constraints and opportunities, not only to explain and understand human rights successes and failures but also to apply this knowledge to fashion winning strategies to enlarge the chances of their extension. With better theory and more case studies as tests, policymakers engaged in human rights efforts would then be in a better position to identify those combinations of actors, resources, and strategies best calculated to be most effective in widely differing societal settings to support human rights which are at risk or ripe for expansion.

Third, outside help is almost always needed for local success. The ascendancy of the Western liberal states in the Cold War has in principle given a fillip to human rights. No longer confronting an immediate clear and present danger to their survival, a coalition of politically open, market states, dedicated to democratic practices and human rights, can now, if they choose, induce or consensually elicit increased support for human rights observance. In selected areas, these states have effectively acted to enlarge the number of the members of the liberal democratic market club. Admission to the European Union, NATO, the Council of Europe and, presumptively, the Organization of Security and Cooperation in Europe depends on states and regimes meeting these tests. Turkey, a secular state but a Muslim society, is put on notice that its violations of human rights and shaky democratic institutions seriously weaken its bid to enter the European Union. NATO has imposed the same conditions on the former members of the Warsaw Pact. Poland, the Czech Republic, and Hungary were admitted because they had progressed sufficiently along a democratic and human rights path.

Fourth, and conversely, simply applying Western-favored human rights tests or coercive sanctions will not always work. They may well backfire and unwittingly impede progress toward greater democratization and human rights unless the dilemmas of conflicting values and hard strategic choices are fully understood by all relevant actors. The examples of Indonesia and China are pertinent. Indonesia's collapse was more attributable to the unwillingness of foreign investors, notably those in Japan, to continue to support the corruption and crony capitalism of the Suharto regime than to the intervention of the Western liberal states on behalf of human rights. On the one hand, when Western-dominated international organizations like the International Monetary Fund and the World Bank intervened, ostensibly to help Indonesia (and other Asian states) through this financial crisis, the ill-designed conditions attached to their loans and grants deepened the crisis and destabilized a fledgling Indonesian democracy while inciting ethnic conflict throughout the islands.[3]

China is a more difficult problem yet. It is a crisis waiting to happen viewed through the refracted lens of contested human rights values at stake. Take, first of all, the universally proclaimed right of self-determination. Since the Opium Wars almost two centuries ago, China has confronted two challenges: to rid itself of foreign domination and to establish a unified regime for all Chinese. The Communist victory in 1949 appeared to have done both. In defeating the Nationalist forces of Chang Kai-shek, supported by U.S. military assistance, the Communist party unified the mainland under its rule and also appeared to have eliminated foreign influence in China's domestic affairs. From Beijing's viewpoint, the escape of the Nationalists to Taiwan and U.S. military intervention in the Korean War continued this twin struggle. For Beijing, Taiwan's subjugation to its rule is widely understood as the completion of China's quest for self-determination.

Taiwan has adopted an entirely different view of self-determination. It adds the condition of popular consent to whatever regime rules China. Under this aspect, the legitimate application of the principle of self-determination depends not on party dicta but on fair and free referendum and elections. The U.S. tilt to the Taiwanese interpretation of self-determination, reflected in the progressive democratization of the Taiwanese regime, poses a direct threat to Beijing. It is no less a threat to the regime than the Tiananmen Square uprising. In many ways it is more formidable because it is backed by superior U.S. military power. From the mainland's perspective the twin challenges posed initially by Western intervention in the first half of the nineteenth century are disguised as ideological commitments to democratic rule, civil liberties, Western notions of the rule of law, and human rights.[4]

Also joined are profound Chinese and Western differences over substantive and procedural as well as group and individual rights. Even as China adapts to a Western-dominated global market system by joining the World Trade Organization, the Beijing regime defends its authoritarian rule by trumpeting its record in improving the material lot of the Chinese people, who represent a quarter of the human race. Western democratic practices are portrayed as a formula for disrupting internal order and economic development. The Soviet experience is cited as proof. Western democratization is vilified as a vehicle for introducing the West's corrupting influence into Chinese social practices and mores, much as Britain forced the sale of drugs on the Chinese empire. Echoes of these charges—that the West means drugs, crime, prostitution, loose morals, disparities in wealth, and class conflict—are found across all Asia's authoritarian governments. Note the rationales of the Singapore and Malaysian regimes to justify their brand of authoritarian rule. Western support for religious freedom or for the Falun Gong are viewed by Beijing as tantamount to attacks on its very survival and its capacity to control or eliminate all real or potential opponents.

Disentangling these competing rights claims while ensuring domestic order and welfare both for the Chinese people and for the world are delicate and demanding tasks. Whose notion of self-determination should prevail? And by what tests can self-determination be authoritatively determined? How, too, can it be reconciled with the principle of state sovereignty, no less a universal value and a crucial ingredient of global order based, for good or ill as the United Nations Charter affirms, on a decentralized system of nation-states? If big power conflicts get out of hand, they threaten the progress that has already been made. In no small way, preserving big power peace is a precondition for the realization of human rights. One can also ask whether the introduction of greater but conceivably flawed democratic practices, following Russia's failed experiment, actually increase the freedoms of average Chinese citizens and their material lot. These competing human rights concerns are neither internally coherent and self-revealing nor self-executing, nor do they float freely and independently of countervailing power concerns of national and international groups contesting to have their say and to impress their preference on their rivals.

Fifth, wherever possible, the promotion of a rule of law and an independent judiciary in applying domestic law should be high priority for partisans of human rights in and outside the boundaries of a state. Kochanek makes this point in his examination of the exercise of police power in India, a democratic state. Unless the state and its officials can be held accountable for their exercise of the state's monopoly of violence, they cannot be constrained from violating civil and human rights or obliged to intervene to prevent societal discrimination and depredations. The existence of a rule of law and courts to protect those laws and citizen rights are prerequisites for the creation of an open society. It is precisely the existence of free, civil space and access to outside nongovernmental assistance that affords domestic groups the opportunity to expand group and individual rights. This political setting permits transnational groups, like Amnesty International or Human Rights Watch, to bolster domestic allies in their human rights struggles. These nongovernmental organizations, often in league with interested states and a growing number of International Governmental Organizations—now numbering more than 1,000—have played crucial roles in advancing human rights in particular locales, states, and regions. No theory of human rights or the likelihood of continued progress on the many fronts of human rights struggles is possible without the support of these outside actors.

Sixth, despite institutions like the United Nations, the European Union, the Council of Europe, and NATO, global governance is still largely under-institutionalized in its capacity to protect and promote human rights. While any attempt to specify all of the reasons for these weaknesses well exceeds the scope of this discussion, prominent among them, ironically, is the very success of the Western liberal states in ascending to their presently dominant position in the post-Cold War world. Why should democratic populations risk blood and treasure to influence and intervene in the affairs of other states and peoples to ensure human rights? NATO's belated intervention to stop ethnic cleansing in Bosnia and Kosovo can be explained as motivated as much by threats to Western economic and security interests as by genuine commitment to humanitarian purpose. Note, too, the failure of the Western states and, notably, the United States to end the Rwandan genocide in 1994 or to empower the United Nations to assume forceful and effective measures to restore basic order in the Great Lakes region where a Hobbesian end game still plays out (Evans 1997; Kolodziej 2000). The same recoil action can be seen in the rapid U.S. pullout from Somalia in the early 1990s when eighteen marines were ambushed while implementing a United Nations peacekeeping mission.

The disincentives for intervention, arising from narrow conceptions of national self-interest, must be squarely faced if the resistance of the Western states and their populations to intervening to relieve the plight of disadvantaged peoples in the developing world is to be surmounted. What is required, and it will be a long time getting there—if ever—is the recognition that to be human constitutes a moral entity to which rights can be ascribed simply because those possessing this property are human and that the defense of these moral qualities imposes an equally universal obligation on all for their protection (Searle 1995). This broad conception of self-interest has yet to be constructed and universally acknowledged in the same way, as before, notions of national unity had to be created for peoples in one region of a state—say Bretons in France or Texans in the United States—to rally to the support of their fellow citizens. But in the absence of this broader conception of self-interest, fused with the human species as a whole, there will be weak and ineffective support for mobilizing the power of the liberal democracies to human rights concerns beyond their boundaries. Had not the events of 9/11 exposed the threat of terrorism to the U.S. vulnerable population centers, there is ample room to doubt that the United States would have cobbled together a coalition of states to overthrow the Taliban regime in Kabul for having harbored the Al Qaeda terrorist organization.

The risks and hazards of armed intervention to establish the political foundations for democratization and the gradual enlargement of human rights are difficult to overestimate. On the one hand, force and the expenditure of vast human and material resources account in no small measure for the spread of human rights. Western military might, led by the United States, decisively defeated the Taliban regime and opened the way for the possibility of a popularly supported regime in Afghanistan capable of ending decades of civil war. The same can be said for democratization and human rights in NATO's intervention in Kosovo. Going further afield, the ascendancy of the Western liberal states, as a consequence of their victories over a century of hot and cold wars, was achieved at the cost of millions of lives. The regimes of Nazi Germany and imperial Japan were not transformed into democracies by persuasion.

On the other hand, intervention, as the Western experience during its imperialist phase reveals, may herald the opening of a new round of foreign rule under the aegis of democratization and human rights, self-determination, or humanitarian assistance. Or, however justified armed intervention on moral grounds may be, there may not be any amount of armed force capable of achieving these estimable objectives. Worse, as Immanuel Kant foresaw, more conflict than cooperation may be the unwitting result of well-meaning but misguided attempts to install by force a system of rule on the Western model. The liberal's dilemma remains at the center of the problem of extending human rights to deprived millions around the globe: how to use force, violence, and threats to achieve freedom without losing freedom in the bargain, at home and abroad. Under the pressure of globalization, the domestic solutions to democratization and human rights, raising the prospect of using force in their defense and extension, are now central challenges of global governance.

Finally, it is important to remember that human rights are today and for a long time to come fundamentally contested notions. No one culture, religion, or ideology has a monopoly in defining their properties, their proper practices, or appropriate strategies for their protection and promotion. Quite apart from their opponents, differences naturally arise among their partisans along the dimensions of substantive vs. procedural rights, of group versus individual rights, and of universal versus relative rights. Our lights as humans are still too dim to reconcile these contradictions. The conflicting secular and religious solutions to these value clashes caution against hasty assertions of what are the intrinsic properties of human rights applicable to all peoples. Historical circumstance and massive differences of culture, language, social custom, and tradition admit to multiple and not always coherent and compatible definitions of what humans are, what they ought to be, and what rights they can legitimately claim. These contested notions, moreover, are not frozen in time. They evolve, as anyone can readily see from even a glance at changing meanings attached by societies to the role and centrality of gender in defining their identities or at the long and tortuous, but largely successful, process of eliminating slavery as a social evil.

If past is prologue, the *force profonde* of human rights will continue to work its will through the ideas, values, and self-realization of groups and individuals around the globe. That should not suggest that its ultimate triumph is assured or that its ascendancy can be predicted with certainty. Certainly the forms that human rights will assume cannot be fully anticipated, since increasing numbers of people from diverse and divergent cultural and historical circumstances insist on a say about them. Human rights are mediated through the power structures of these particular human groupings and societies. These comprise the bewildering mosaic of an emerging global society. At once this society is both at sixes and sevens yet increasingly conscious among its disputing members that they are, however reluctantly, as William McNeill (1992, x–xi) allows, subordinate to and participants in a global system. That system is mediated through the politics of human rights being played out simultaneously on innumerable battlefields at local, national, and regional levels. Since the frustration of King Leopold's depredations in Africa over a century ago, the point of departure of this volume, human rights have come a long way. Even when viewed from the narrow band of time since the end of the Cold War, progress is discernible and palpable on many fronts, even as resourceful and determined opponents marshal their forces and band together in unholy alliances to foil their spread.

Whither human rights? It's too early to tell.

Notes

Chapter 1. A *Force Profonde*: The Power, Politics, and Promise of Human Rights

1. This was notably the case in Central Asia, where, before the creation of the Soviet Union, little or no sense of nationhood prevailed.

2. It should be evident by now that the use of "pure" models to assess the advance of human rights and to compare their progress across regions owes much to Max Weber (1958a, 1968). For a trenchant discussion of Weber's methodological use of pure or ideal types, consult Mommsen (1989, 121–68).

3. The literature, polemic and empirical, exposing the growing gaps between have and have-not nations warrants separate discussion (Hirst 1996; Sen 1992; Stiglitz 2002).

4. Ayoob (1995) makes the same point in dispelling the fear that there exists a coherent and cohesive Muslim movement capable of overwhelming all states with Muslim majorities. Different regimes with different populations and history will, ipso facto, pursue different human rights agendas.

5. That is William McNeill's (1992, x–xi) message.

6. Axelrod's later work (1997) is partially sensitive to this problem.

7. This is not the place to rehearse realist theory. Rather, the point here is to acknowledge that its insights are relevant to the development of a theory of human rights (Morgenthau 1985; Waltz 1979), its shortcomings notwithstanding.

8. There have been attempts to enlarge liberal institutionalist theory to incorporate ideas and values, but these have not wandered far from utilitarian reductionist dismissal of their independent social force (J. Goldstein 1993; Ruggie 1998).

9. Anthony Giddens (1979, 1984) makes the point throughout his numerous publications that social power structures enable humans to act but their survival, replication, mutation, and transformation depend no less on whether they are sustained and affirmed by human choice at each decision and action point of human conduct. So it is with human rights. Resisting regimes and obstructing social power, the material circumstances under which history is made, are subject to this process of human reservation, demurrers, and withdrawal.

10. Timur Kuran (1991, 1995) is clear on the linkage between human values and notions of legitimacy and their consequences for economic behavior and political rule.

Chapter 2. Western Perspectives

1. I defend the claims in this paragraph in Donnelly (2002a, ch. 4).

2. These rights are treated as "indivisible and interdependent and interrelated" (World Conference on Human Rights, Vienna Declaration and Plan of Action, paragraph 5). The United States is the exception that proves the rule: as of November 16, 2000, the United States was one of only eight states that were party to just one of the two covenants, in contrast to the 137 that were party to both; see <www.unhchr.ch/pdf/report.pdf>. It is easy, however, to exaggerate American reticence toward economic and social rights. For all its failings, the American welfare state is alive, thriving, and growing.

3. By editorial design, I treat "the West" less as a geographical region or cultural unit than as a political model or regime type. Michael Newman's chapter on the European Union provides a largely complementary account that documents some of the significant gaps between theory and practice.

4. Kolodziej presents order, welfare, and legitimacy as forms of power, thereby emphasizing the processes and resources that enable different social actors to exert differential control over "political" outcomes broadly understood. I am more concerned with structures, with dominant frames of reference that establish standard operating procedures and privilege certain visions of what is possible and desirable over others. Although the distinction is more analytical than substantive—my structures obviously shape, and are shaped by, Kolodziej's power—it may produce subtle but significant differences in our accounts.

5. A more subtle version of this argument, which still is often encountered, presents three "generations" of human rights—civil and political, economic and social, and collective—which are at least loosely associated with the West, socialism, and the Third World (Flinterman 1990; Marks 1981; Vasak 1984, 1991). I develop an extended historical and theoretical critique of this conceptualization in Donnelly (1993).

6. In contemporary discourse, especially in the United States, "liberal" is used in reference to (1) the non-Marxist left (antonym: "conservative"); (2) supporters of economic markets (usually "conservatives"); and (3) supporters of rights-based political systems (across the political spectrum). I use "liberal" here only in this last sense.

7. The six leading treaties (on civil and political rights, economic, social, and cultural rights, torture, racial discrimination, discrimination against women, and the rights of the child) averaged 154 parties at the end of 2000; <www.unhchr.ch/pdf/report.pdf>.

8. See Donnelly (1998b, ch. 4) and Forsythe (2000, ch. 3) for brief overviews. See also Hannum (1999), Alston (1995), and especially Alston and Crawford (2001), which will likely remain the authoritative scholarly source for a number of years.

9. The system was extensively reorganized in 1998 and 1999. The new European Court of Human Rights has an excellent Web site <www.echr.coe.int/default.htm> that includes a searchable database with full text of all judgments.

10. See, for example, Lipschutz (1996) and Falk (2000).

11. Note that "liberal" here has a very different sense from that in "liberal democratic," as I have used that term. See note 6 above.

12. I develop such an argument more fully in Donnelly (1998a), fully aware of the uncomfortable overtones of abusive paternalism in this language. See also Donnelly (2002b, ch. 14).

13. For a good overview of the conflict and the international response, see Independent International Commission on Kosovo (2000).

14. The international campaign against apartheid in South Africa of the 1960s, 1970s, and especially 1980s provides an earlier analogy.

15. This is probably an exaggeration, but a useful one. The Haiti intervention was earlier, but it remains anomalous because genocide was not the provocation. Few states have argued that intervention elsewhere is justifiable in the face of comparable "ordinary," nongenocidal human rights violations. The Iraq action is a problematic example because it is embedded in a settlement after an aggressive attack on a neighbor was successfully repelled. The Somalia intervention took place in the context of the collapse of central authority, rather than a direct abuse of power by the government. The Bosnian intervention was usually characterized as taking place in the special context of an internationalized civil war. And in Rwanda international action came only after most of the killing had concluded.

Chapter 5. North Africa

1. In Libya, the Qadhafi regime is still chanting the old rhetoric of popular sovereignty while in practice endeavoring to entrench an extremely absolutist state.

2. King Mohammed VI of Morocco lacks his father's clout. This as well as his ambiguous approach to politics has reopened the symbolic-religious space for appropriation, as huge demonstrations in 2000–2001 organized by the Islamists illustrate.

3. Abdessalam Yassine, the leader of the main Islamist current, who had been under house arrest for about a decade and was recently released, has called on Mohammed VI to use the royal inheritance estimated to be between $30–40 billion to improve the socioeconomic conditions of the country.

4. Similar dynamics also drive two other important issues—the role of women in societal and political life and the fate of minority ethnic-secessionist groups and movements such as the Kabyle problem in Algeria and the Western Saharan issue in Morocco. I do not, however, develop these issues in this chapter for lack of space.

5. For example, a Moroccan student group became active in the 1980s—the Association de Défense des Droits de l'Homme au Maroc (ASDHM)—worked very closely with the Moroccan exile group Association des Droits de l'Homme au Maroc (ADHM) (Sanguinetti 1991).

6. The case of Pinochet in Chile is a precedent that international human rights organizations will surely exploit in the near future.

Chapter 7. Northeast Asia: China

1. Within Europe, it is not only in Austria that a racist right rose (Stephens 2000).

2. To follow the human rights situation in China, see the journals *China Rights Forum* and *China Study Journal* as well as the U.S. State Department annual Country Reports and the papers published by human rights groups such as Amnesty International and Human Rights Watch.

3. On Beijing's views of Tokyo, see E. Friedman (2000a).

4. I have put the translation into more grammatical English.

5. Also see the references cited in Weatherly (1999; 1999–2000).

Chapter 8. South Asia

1. Given space limitations, this discussion covers only India, Sri Lanka, Bangladesh, and Pakistan.

2. For a detailed summary of the status of human rights in the states of South Asia see the U.S. State Department annual Country Reports.

3. For a review of prison conditions in India see *Prisons and Punishment, Seminar* 440 (1996).

Chapter 10. The European Union

I am very grateful for the comments of Joanne Scott, Simon Bagshaw, Hannah Newman, and Ed Kolodziej on an earlier draft of this chapter.

1. The position taken here is that the European Union is a legal, economic, and political actor that has implications for human rights over and above those arising from the actions of its individual members. The focus will therefore be on the collective body rather than its individual parts. There are also important differences between the European *Community* and the European *Union*, which will be outlined below.

2. Nevertheless, over time distinctions from the characteristic U.S. concept of rights have developed. Thus the 6th Protocol (1983), which proscribed the death penalty and abolished capital punishment, is now a condition for membership of the Council of Europe—a position that has also been adopted by the European Union under the Treaty of Amsterdam (signed in 1997; effective from 1999). There is also nothing in the ECHR that compares with Article II of the U.S. Bill of Rights upholding the right to bear arms, and this would not generally be accepted in Europe. There is also a difference over free speech, with many European countries having proscribed incitement to racial hatred without infringing the ECHR, while the United States appears to regard the right to free speech as almost absolute.

3. The European Council did not invoke the Amsterdam Treaty provisions, and technically there was no EU action against Austria. The governments suspended bilateral relations with the Austrian government; in theory, this did not affect the operation of the EU institutions.

4. This has always caused problems, with ratification constantly delayed. It was only in 1997 that a much larger group of states, which had subsequently joined the agreement, eliminated the controls. Even though the Schengen Agreement has now been incorporated into the Treaty of Amsterdam (with only Ireland and Britain maintaining frontier controls), there are still difficulties implementing it.

5. The most important of these was that a national of one member state living in another EU country was now granted the right to vote in local and European elections there.

6. Measures preventing access to asylum (for example, visa requirements), sanctions against carriers, posting immigration officers abroad, exit control by third countries that disregard human rights criteria, a refusal to adopt fair burden sharing measures, the definition of "manifestly unfounded" applications, the minimum standards on reception, and the interests of rejected asylum-seekers in relation to voluntary return, detention decisions, conditions of detention, and the use of force during removal (Noll and Vedsted-Hansen 1999, 381–409).

7. While the Copenhagen criteria mentioned the protection of minorities and Agenda 2000 paid particular attention to this issue, it is notable that Article 6(1) did not explicitly mention this as a principle. Some existing member states have not ratified the 1995 European Framework Convention for the protection of national minorities and would not want any such principle to form part of the Treaty.

8. The distinction is that the accession of the EC would mean that the ECHR would apply only to first pillar policies, while accession of the European Union would mean that the ECHR also applied to the Common Foreign and Security Policy and Justice and Home Affairs.

9. It is divided into seven chapters: Dignity, Freedoms, Equality, Solidarity, Citizens' Rights, Justice, and General Provisions. Some articles are taken directly from the ECHR, while others refer to the institutions and procedures of the European Union itself. The chapter on solidarity includes some social rights implicit in previous Community legislation and also mentions health care, environmental protection, and consumer protection. Because the drafting was not always very precise and the legal remedies are not specified, the extent of the rights envisaged is sometimes unclear.

Chapter 11. The Russian Federation

1. Amnesty International's (1997) documentation of torturous prison conditions is a case in point. Neither official press agency covered Amnesty's release of a major report on law enforcement in 1997.

2. Prison conditions were argued to be, if anything, worse than in the Soviet period because of increased overcrowding. The U.S. State Department 1997 Country Report cites Russian human rights group estimates of 10,000 to 20,000 prison deaths annually from abuse, overcrowding, disease, and inadequate medical care.

3. See T. Smith (1994) for an analysis of the Commission's report.

4. See Gurowitz (1999) for a discussion of how transnational influence enters domestic politics.

5. This proposition became a formal CSCE decision at the Moscow Meeting of the CSCE Commission on the Human Dimension in October 1991 (Korey 1994; Huber 1993).

6. Statement made by Council of Europe Secretary-General Catherine Lalumière (RFE/RL Daily Digest, 185, September 27, 1993). Doubts about this logic were reflected in an unprecedented twenty abstentions in the Council of Europe Parliamentary Assembly vote on the issue.

Chapter 13. Southern Africa

1. To limit the scope of our analysis, we use a definition of "southern Africa" that coincides with continental membership in the Southern African Development Community (SADC): Angola, Botswana, Congo-Kinshasa, Lesotho, Malawi, Mozambique, Namibia, South Africa, Swaziland, Tanzania, Zambia, and Zimbabwe. It excludes Seychelles, Madagascar, and Mauritius.

2. Unless otherwise noted, all information in this section was obtained from the specific 1999 country pages of the Freedom House website <www.freedomhouse.org/survey99/>.

Chapter 15. Whither Human Rights?

1. This methodological and evidentiary approach is suggested (Durkheim 1915, 1984, 1993). Note, too, there is reliance on a parallel form of argument in Timor Kuran's explanation for the abrupt and unanticipated collapse of the Soviet empire. The withdrawal of support for Communist regimes was not discernible during much of the Cold War, largely because of the negative material costs of opposition. Once these constraints appeared weak and enfeebled the underlying de-legitimation of Communist rule could manifest itself (Kuran 1991, 1995). Ruggie (1998) provides

an additional analysis of the power of "social facts" of subjectively constructed values on human behavior and societies.

2. Fukuyama (1992) would have us believe otherwise.

3. These criticisms are extended in Stiglitz (2002).

4. Christopher Hughes (1995) argues that Chinese reformers were more influenced by the material power of the West than by its liberal code, the latter being viewed as a cover for imperialism.

References Cited

Abrahamsson, Hans. 1997. *Seizing the Opportunity: Power and Powerlessness in a Changing World Order*. Gothenburg: Padrigu.

European Commission. 1997. *Agenda 2000*. (Com 97). Brussels: European Commission.

Agenda of the Comité des Sages. 1998. In *Leading by Example: A Human Rights Agenda for the European Union for the Year 2000*. Florence: European University Institute.

Ahmed, Feroz. 1999. *Ethnicity and Politics in Pakistan*. Karachi: Oxford University Press.

Ahmed, Leila. 1992. *Women and Gender in Islam: Historical Roots of a Modern Debate*. New Haven, Conn.: Yale University Press.

Ahwireng-Obeng, Fred and Patrick McGowan. 1998. "Partnership or Hegemon? South Africa in Africa: Part One." *Journal of Contemporary African Studies* 16 (December/January).

Al-Peleg, Zvi. 1988. In *Arabs' Rights* (in Hebrew), ed. Ann Swersky. Tel Aviv: ACRI. 94–108.

Alston, Philip, ed. 1995. *The United Nations and Human Rights: A Critical Appraisal*. Oxford: Clarendon Press.

Alston, Philip with Mara Bustelo and James Heenan, eds. 1999. *The EU and Human Rights*. Oxford: Oxford University Press.

Alston, Philip and James Crawford, eds. 2000. *The Future of UN Human Rights Treaty Monitoring*. Cambridge: Cambridge University Press.

Alston, Philip and J. H. H. Weiler. 1998. "The European Union and Human Rights." In *Leading by Example: A Human Rights Agenda for the European Union for the Year 2000*. Florence: European University Institute.

Amnesty International. 1997. "Torture in Russia: 'This Man Made Hell'." AI Index 46/04/97, April.

Anderson, Charles W. 1967. *Politics and Economic Change in Latin America: The Governing of Restless Nations*. Princeton, N.J.: Van Nostrand.

Aung San, Suu Kyi. 1991. *Freedom from Fear*. New York: Penguin.

Axelrod, Robert M. 1984. *The Evolution of Cooperation*. New York: Basic Books.

———. 1997. *The Complexity of Cooperation: Agent-Based Models of Competition and Cooperation*. Princeton, N.J.: Princeton University Press.

Ayoob, Mohammed. 1995. *The Third World Security Predicament: State Making, Regional Conflict, and the International System*. Boulder, Colo.: Lynne Rienner.

Ayubi, Nazih N. 1991. *Political Islam: Religion and Politics in the Arab World*. London: Routledge.

Aziz, Beziou. 1993. "On Ethnic Political Mobilization: The Case of the Berber Move-ment in Algeria." Dissertation, International Studies, University of Denver.

Bagshaw, S. 1994. *The Protection of Human Rights in Europe: The Role of the European Convention on Human Rights.* London: University of North London Press.

al-Bahi, Muhammad. 1979. *Al-Islam wa ittijah al-mar'a'l-muslima'l-mu'asira* (Islam and the Orientation of the Contemporary Muslim Woman). Cairo: no publisher listed.

Baldwin, David A., ed. 1993. *Neorealism and Neoliberalism: The Contemporary Debate.* New York: Columbia University Press.

Banerjee, Sumanta. 1997. "Development Projects and Human Rights." *Democracy and Development, Seminar* 451 (March): 23–26.

Barak, Aharon. 1992. "The Constitutional Revolution: Protected Rights." *Mishpat and Mimshal,* 9–35.

Barak-Erez, Dafna, ed. 1996. *A Jewish and Democratic State* (in Hebrew). Tel Aviv: Tel Aviv University School of Law.

Barber, Benjamin R. 1995. *Jihad vs. McWorld.* New York: Ballantine.

Barnard, Catherine. 1999. *Gender Equality in the EU: A Balance Sheet.* Oxford: Oxford University Press.

Barnes, Barry. 1988. *The Nature of Power.* Urbana: University of Illinois Press.

Barnett, Michael. 1996. Identity and Alliances in the Middle East. In *The Culture of National Security,* ed. Peter J. Katzenstein. New York: Columbia University Press. 400–446.

Bashkar, Roy. 1998. *The Possibility of Naturalism.* London: Routledge.

Basri, Driss, Michel Roussot, and Georges Vedel, eds. 1994. *Le Maroc et les droits de l'homme: positions, réalisations et perspectives.* Paris: L'Harmattan.

Bauer, Joanne R. and Daniel A. Bell, eds. 1999. *The East Asian Challenge for Human Rights.* Cambridge: Cambridge University Press.

Bendix, Reinhard. 1978. *Kings or People: Power and the Mandate to Rule.* Berkeley: Uni-versity of California Press.

Bensbia, Najib. 1996. *Pouvoir et politique au Maroc du rejet à l'alternance.* Rabat: Edi-tions Média Stratégie.

Berlin, Isaiah. 1958. *Two Concepts of Liberty: An Inaugural Lecture Delivered Before the University of Oxford on 31 October 1958.* Oxford: Clarendon Press.

Bernitz, Ulf and Hedvig Lokrantz Bernitz. 1999. "Human Rights and European Identity." In *The EU and Human Rights,* ed. Philip Alston with Mara Bustelo and James Heenan. Oxford: Oxford University Press.

Bosworth, C. E. 1999. "Musawat." *Encyclopaedia of Islam.* CD-ROM Edition v. 1.0. Lei-den: Koninklijke Brill NV.

Bowring, Bill. 1995. "Human Rights in Russia: Discourse of Emancipation or Only a Mirage?" In *Human Rights in Eastern Europe,* ed. Istvan Pogany. Aldershot: Edward Elgar.

Bracha, Baruch. 1982. "The Protection of Human Rights in Israel." *Israel Yearbook of Human Rights* 12, 2.

Bratton, Michael and Nicolas Van der Walle. 1997. *Democratic Experiments in Africa: Regime Transitions in Comparative Perspective.* Cambridge: Cambridge University Press.

Braudel, Fernand. 1980. *On History.* Trans. Sarah Matthews. Chicago: University of Chicago Press.

Briskman, Dana. 1988. "National Security vs. Human Rights." Thesis, Harvard Law School.

Brown, L. Carl. 1964. "Tunisian Nationalism." In Charles A. Micaud with L. Carl Brown and Clement Henry Moore, *Tunisia: The Politics of Modernization.* New York: Praeger.

Brubaker, Rogers. 1996. *Nationalism Reframed: Nationhood and the National Question in the New Europe.* Cambridge: Cambridge University Press.

Bull, Hedley. 1977. *The Anarchical Society: A Study of Order in World Politics.* New York: Columbia University Press.

Burgat, François and William Dowell. 1993. *The Islamic Movement in North Africa.* Austin: Center for Middle Eastern Studies, University of Texas.

Burke, Edmund. 1909. *Reflections on the French Revolution.* New York: Collier.

Canevi, Yavuz. 1994. "Turkey." In *The Political Economy of Reform,* ed. John Williamson. Washington, D.C.: Institute for International Economics. 188.

Carothers, Thomas C. 1991. *Aiding Democracy Abroad: The Learning Curve.* Washington, D.C.: Carnegie Endowment for International Peace.

———. 1997. "Democracy Assistance: The Question of Strategy." *Democratization* 4: 3.

Cavelli-Sforza, Luigi Luca. 1994. *The History and Geography of Genes.* Princeton, N.J.: Princeton University Press.

Cavalli-Sforza, Luigi Luca and Francesco Cavalli-Sforza. 1995. *The Great Human Diasporas: The History of Diversity and Evolution.* Reading, Mass.: Addison-Wesley.

Chadda, Maya. 1997. *Ethnicity, Security, and Separation in India.* New York: Columbia University Press.

Chand, Victor Khub. 2000. "Building a New Indo-U.S. Alliance." *Asian Wall Street Journal Weekly* (March 27–April 2).

Chanda, Nayan. 2000. "Coming in from the Cold." *Far Eastern Economic Review* (March 30): 23.

Charef, Abed. 1994. *Algérie: le grand dérapage.* Paris: Editions de l'Aube.

Chase, Robert, Emily Hill, and Paul Kennedy. 1996. "Pivotal States and U.S. Strategy." *Foreign Affairs* 75 (January).

Chayes, Abram. 1996. In *Preventing Conflict in the Post-Communist World: Mobilizing International and Regional Organizations,* ed. Abram Chayes and Antonia Chayes. Washington, D.C.: Brookings Institution.

Cheru, Fantu. 1989. *The Silent Revolution in Africa.* London: Zed Books.

Chew, Melanie. 1994. "Human Rights in Singapore." *Asian Survey* 34 (November).

Chilton, Patricia. 1996. "Mechanics of Change: Social Movements, Transnational Coalitions, and the Transformational Process in Eastern Europe." In *Bringing Transnational Relations Back In,* ed. Thomas Risse-Kappen. Cambridge: Cambridge University Press. 189–226.

China Daily. 2000. "Facts Speak Louder Than Rhetoric." April 1.

Chiriyankandath, James. 1993. "Human Rights in India: Concepts and Context." *Contemporary South Asia* 2, 3: 248.

Chu, Shulong, Zaibang Wang, and Xuetong Yan. 1999. Articles in *Xiandai Guoji Guanxi* (Modern International Relations), September. Summarized in *Foreign Policy* (Spring 2000): 190–91.

Cilliers, Jakkie. 1999. *Building Security in Southern Africa: An Update on the Evolving Architecture.* ISS Monograph Series 43. Cape Town: Institute for Security Studies, November.

Clapham, Andrew. 1999. "Where Is the EU's Human Rights Common Foreign Policy, and How Is It Manifested in Multilateral Fora?" In *The EU and Human Rights,* ed. Philip Alston with Mara Bustelo and James Heenan. Oxford: Oxford University Press.

Coase, Ronald H. 1937. "The Nature of the Firm." *Economica* 4: 386–405.

———. 1960. "The Problem of Social Cost." *Journal of Law and Economics* 3: 1–44.

Cohen, Erik. 1991. "Israel as a Post-Zionist Society." In *The Shaping of Israeli Identity: Myth, Memory, and Trauma,* ed. Robert Wistrich and David Ohana. London: Frank Cass. 203–14.

Collier, David, ed. 1979. *The New Authoritarianism in Latin America.* Princeton, N.J.: Princeton University Press.

Conte, Auguste. 1975. *August Conte and Positivism: The Essential Writings.* Ed. Gertrude Lenzer. New York: Norton.

Council of European Municipalities and Regions. 1999. *Men and Women in European Municipalities.* Paris: CEMR.

Crawford, Gordon. 1997. "Foreign and Political Conditionality." *Democratization* 4 (Autumn): 69–108.

Damis, John. 1992. "Sources of Political Stability in Modernizing Regimes: Jordan and Morocco." In *Civilian Rule in the Developing World: Democracy on the March?* ed. Constantine P. Danoupoulos. Boulder, Colo.: Westview Press. 23–51.

Date-Bah, Eugenia. 1996. "Appropriate Policy for Gender Equality in Employment, 2." *International Journal of Discrimination Law* 7.

De Bary, William Theodore and Weiming Tu, eds. 1998. *Confucianism and Human Rights.* New York: Columbia University Press.

de Witte, Bruno. 1999. "The Past and Future Role of the European Court of Justice in the Protection of Human Rights." In *The EU and Human Rights,* ed. Philip Alston with Mara Bustelo and James Heenan. Oxford: Oxford University Press.

Dealy, Glen. 1968. "Prolegomena on the Spanish-American Political Tradition." *Hispanic American Historical Review* 48, 1 (February).

Deegan, Heather. 1994. *The Middle East and Problems of Democracy.* Boulder, Colo.: Lynn Rienner.

Deng, Francis and I. William Zartman. 2002. *A Strategic Vision for Africa: The Kampala Movement.* Washington, D.C.: Brookings Institution Press.

Diamond, Jared. 1992. *The Third Chimpanzee: The Evolution and Future of the Human Animal.* New York: HarperPerennial.

Diamond, Larry. 1999a. *Developing Democracy: Toward Consolidation.* Baltimore: Johns Hopkins University Press.

———. 1999b. "Introduction." In *Democratization in Africa,* ed. Larry Diamond and Marc F. Plattner. Baltimore: Johns Hopkins University Press.

Diamond, Larry and Marc F. Plattner, eds. 1998. *Democracy in East Asia.* Baltimore: Johns Hopkins University Press.

Dogan, Melih. 1997. "What Does Refah Mean for Business?" *Turkish Times,* July 1.

Donnelly, Jack. 1984. *The Concept of Human Rights.* London: Croom Helm.

———. 1989, 1996. *Universal Human Rights in Theory and Practice.* Ithaca, N.Y.: Cornell University Press.

———. 1993. "Third Generation Rights." In *Peoples and Minorities in International Law,* ed. Catherine Brölmann, René Lefeber, and Marjoleine Zieck. The Hague: Kluwer.

———. 1998a. Human Rights: A New Standard of Civilization? *International Affairs* 74: 1–24.

———. 1998b. *International Human Rights.* Boulder, Colo.: Westview Press.

———. 2002a. *Universal Human Rights in Theory and Practice.* 2nd ed. Ithaca, N.Y.: Cornell University Press.

———. 2002b. "Genocide and Humanitarian Intervention." *Journal of Human Rights* 1 (March): 93–109.

Don-Yehiya, Eliezer. 1989. "Mamlachtiut and Judaism in Ben-Burion's Thought and Policy." *Ha'Zionut* 14: 51–88.

Dowty, Alan. 1995. "Israel's First Decade: Building a Civic State." In *Israel: The First Decade of Independence,* ed. S. Ilan Troen and Noah Lucas. SUNY Series in Israeli Studies. Albany: State University of New York Press. 31–50.

Drzewicki, Krzysztof. 1991. "Institutional Arrangements for Pan-European Human

Rights Protection." In *All-European Human Rights Yearbook: Perspectives of an All-European System of Human Rights Protection*, ed. Zdizlaw Kedzia, Anna Korula, and Manfred Nowak. Proceedings and Recommendations of an International Conference, Poznán, Poland, October 8–11, 1990. Strasbourg: N.P. Engel.

Dunn, Michael Collins. 1992. "Revivalist Islam and Democracy: Thinking About the Algerian Quandary." *Middle East Policy* 1, 2.

Durkheim, Emile. 1915. *The Elementary Forms of the Religious Life*. New York: Free Press.

———. 1984. *The Division of Labor in Society*. New York: Free Press.

———. 1993. *Ethics and the Sociology of Morals*. Buffalo, N.Y.: Prometheus Books.

Dwyer, Kevin. 1991. *Arab Voices: The Human Rights Debate in the Middle East*. London: Routledge.

Engineer, Asghar Ali. 1995. *Communalism in India: A Historical and Empirical Study*. New Delhi: Vikas.

Entelis, John P. 1989. *Culture and Counterculture in Moroccan Politics*. Boulder, Colo.: Westview Press.

Esposito, John L. 1982. *Women in Muslim Family Law*. Syracuse, N.Y.: Syracuse University Press.

Esposito, John L. and John O. Voll. 1996. *Islam and Democracy*. New York: Oxford University Press.

Europa Publications. 1995. *The Middle East and North Africa, 1995*. 41st ed. London: Europa Publications.

European Women's Lobby. 2000. Contribution from the EWL to the Drafting of a EU Charter on Fundamental Rights.

Evans, Glynne. 1997. *Responding to Crises in the African Great Lakes*. London: International Institute of Strategic Studies.

Ezrahi, Yaron. 1993. "Democratic Politics and Culture in Modern Israel: Recent Trends." In *Israeli Democracy Under Stress*, ed. Ehud Sprinzak and Larry Diamond. Boulder, Colo.: Lynne Rienner.

Falk, Richard A. 2000. *Human Rights Horizons: The Pursuit of Justice in a Globalizing World*. New York: Routledge.

The Federalist (Alexander Hamilton, John Jay, and James Madison). New York: Modern Library, 1937, 2001.

Filali-Ansari, Abdou. 1998. "Can Modern Rationality Shape a New Religiosity? Mohamed Abed Jabri and the Paradox of Islam and Modernity." In *Islam and Modernity: Muslim Intellectuals Respond*, ed. John Cooper, Ronald L. Nettler, and Mohamed Mahmoud. London: I.B. Tauris.

Flinterman, Cees. 1990. "Three Generations of Human Rights." In *Human Rights in a Pluralist World: Individuals and Collectivities*, ed. Jan Berting et al. Westport, N.Y.: Meckler.

Forney, Matt. 2000. "Secretly in Awe of Democracy, China Worries About Example Set by Taiwan." *Asian Wall Street Journal Weekly* (March 27–April 2).

Forsythe, David P. 2000. *Human Rights in International Relations*. Cambridge: Cambridge University Press.

Foucault, Michel. 1977. *Power/Knowledge: Selected Interviews & Other Writings, 1972–1977*. New York: Pantheon.

Friedman, Edward. 1994. *The Politics of Democratization: Generalizing East Asian Experiences*. Boulder, Colo.: Westview Press.

———. 1995. "Is China a Model of Reform Success?" In *National Identity and Democratic Prospects in Socialist China*, chap. 10. Armonk, N.Y.: M.E. Sharpe.

———. 1997. The Challenge of a Rising China. In *Eagle Adrift: American Foreign Policy at the End of the Century*, ed. Robert J. Leiber. New York: Longman. 215–45.

——. 1999a. "Asia as a Fount of Universal Human Rights." In *Debating Human Rights: Critical Essays from the United States and Asia*, ed. Peter Van Ness. New York: Routledge. 56–79.

——. 1999b. "Does China Have the Cultural Preconditions for Democracy?" *Philosophy East and West* 49, 3 (July): 346–59.

——. 2000a. "Preventing War Between China and Japan." In *What if China Does Not Democratize? Implications for War and Peace*, ed. Edward Friedman and Barrett McCormick, chap. 4. Armonk, N.Y.: M.E. Sharpe.

——. 2000b. "Still Building the State: Origins of China's Patriotic Fervor." In *Chinese Political Culture*, ed. Hua Shiping. Armonk, N.Y.: M.E. Sharpe.

Friedman, Thomas L. 2000. *The Lexus and the Olive Tree.* New York: Anchor Books.

Fukuyama, Francis. 1992. *The End of History and the Last Man.* New York: Free Press.

Garon, Lise. 1994. *North African Political Communication in Transition: The Case of Tunisia.* Berlin: International Political Science Association.

——. 1995a. *L'Islam dans l'agenda des droits de l'homme.* Paris: Mediaspouvoirs.

——. 1995b. The Press and Democratic Transition in Arab Societies. In *Political Liberalization and Democratization in the Arab World*, vol. 1, *Theoretical Perspectives*, ed. Rex Brynen, Bahgat Korany, and Paul Noble. Boulder, Colo.: Lynne Rienner. 149–66.

Gavison, Ruth. 1994. *Human Rights in Israel* (in Hebrew). Tel Aviv: Ministry of Defense.

Gboyega, Alex. 1997. "Nigeria." In *Governance as Conflict Management*, ed. I. William Zartman. Washington, D.C.: Brookings Institution.

Ghanem, Asad. 1993. *Israeli Arabs Toward the Twenty-First Century* (in Hebrew). Givat Haviva: Institute for the Study of Peace.

Ghannoushi, Rashid. 1998. Interview: With Tunisian Sheikh Rached Ghannoushi. *Muslim Students Association News.* <msanews.mynet.net/intra2.html>.

Gibb, H. A. R. 1953. *Mohammedanism: An Historical Survey.* 2nd ed. London: Oxford University Press.

Giddens, Anthony. 1979. *Central Problems of Social Theory.* Berkeley: University of California Press.

——. 1984. *The Constitution of Society.* Berkeley: University of California Press.

Gittings, John. 1999. *China Through the Sliding Door: Reporting Three Decades of Change.* London: Touchstone.

Glendon, Mary Ann. 2001. *A World Made New: Eleanor Roosevelt and the Declaration of Human Rights.* New York: Random House.

Goertz, Gary. 1994. *Contexts of International Politics.* New York: Cambridge University Press.

Goldstein, Judith and Robert O. Keohane, eds. 1993. *Ideas and Foreign Policy: Beliefs, Institutions, and Political Change.* Ithaca, N.Y.: Cornell University Press.

Goldstein, Stephen. 1994. "Protection of Human Rights by Judges: The Israeli Experience." *St. Louis University Law Review* 38 (Spring): 605–18.

Gong, Gerrit W. 1984. *The Standard of "Civilisation" in International Society.* Oxford: Clarendon Press.

Goodin, Robert E., Bruce Headley, Ruud Muffels, and Henk-Jan Dirven. 1999. *The Real Worlds of Welfare Capitalism.* Cambridge: Cambridge University Press.

Goumeziane, Smail. 1994. *Le mal algérien: économie politique d'une transition inachevée, 1962–1994.* Paris: Fayard.

Gowan, Peter. 1996. *EU Policy Toward the Visegrad States.* London: University of North London Press.

Graebner, Norman A., ed. 1964. *Ideas and Diplomacy: Readings in the Intellectual Tradition of American Foreign Policy.* Oxford: Oxford University Press.

Grossman, David. 1988. *The Yellow Wind.* Trans. Haim Watzman. New York: Farrar, Straus, Giroux.

——. 1993. *Sleeping on a Wire: Conversations with Palestinians in Israel.* Trans. Haim Watzman. New York: Farrar, Straus, Giroux.

Gurowitz, Amy. 1999. "Mobilizing International Norms." *World Politics* 51 (April): 413.

Haas, Ernst B. 1964. *Beyond the Nation State: Functionalism and International Organization.* Stanford, Calif.: Stanford University Press.

Haeri, Shahla. 1993. "Obedience Versus Autonomy: Women and Fundamentalism in Iran and Pakistan." In *Fundamentalisms and Society: Reclaiming the Sciences, the Family, and Education,* ed. Martin E. Marty and R. Scott Appleby. Chicago: University of Chicago Press.

Hakim, Peter. "1999–2000. Is Latin America Doomed to Failure?" *Foreign Policy* 117 (Winter): 104–13.

Hamidi, Mohammed al-Hashimi. 1998. *The Politicization of Islam: A Case Study of Tunisia.* Boulder, Colo.: Westview Press.

Hannum, Hurst. 1999. *Guide to International Human Rights Practice.* 3rd ed. Ardsley, N.Y.: Transnational.

Hardgrave, Robert L., Jr. and Stanley A. Kochanek. 2000. *India: Government and Politics in a Developing Nation.* Fort Worth, Tex.: Harcourt Brace.

Harding, Harry. 1987. *China's Second Revolution: Reform After Mao.* Washington, D.C.: Brookings Institution.

Hartz, Louis. 1955. *The Liberal Tradition in America.* New York: Harcourt, Brace.

He, Zhaowu and others. 1991. *An Intellectual History of China.* Beijing: Foreign Languages Press.

Henry, Clement M. 1996. *The Mediterranean Debt Crescent: Money and Power in Algeria, Egypt, Morocco, Tunisia, and Turkey.* Gainesville: University Press of Florida.

Hidouci, Ghazi. 1995. *Algérie, la libération inachevée.* Paris: La Découverte.

Hiebert, Murray and Trish Saywell. 2000. Market Morality. *Far Eastern Economic Review* 6 (April): 56.

Hirst, Paul and Grahame Thompson. 1996. *Globalization in Question: The International Economy and the Politics of Governance.* Cambridge: Polity Press.

Hobbes, Thomas. 1950. *Leviathan.* New York: E.P. Dutton.

Hochschild, Adam. 1999. *King Leopold's Ghost: A Story of Greed, Terrorism, and Heroism in Colonial Africa.* Boston: Houghton Mifflin.

Hodgkin, Thomas. 1962. *African Political Parties: An Introductory Guide.* New York: Penguin.

Hoffman-Ladd, Valerie J. 1987. "Polemics on the Modesty and Segregation of Women in Contemporary Egypt." *International Journal of Middle East Studies* 19, 1: 23–50.

——. 1995. "Muslim Fundamentalists: Psychosocial Profiles." In *Fundamentalisms Comprehended,* ed. Martin E. Marty and R. Scott Appleby. Chicago: University of Chicago Press.

Holmes, Stephen. 1999. "Constitutionalism, Democracy, and State Decay." In *Deliberative Democracy and Human Rights,* ed. Harold Hongju Koh and Ronald C. Slye. New Haven, Conn.: Yale University Press.

Horowitz, Dan and Moshe Lissak. 1990. *Trouble in Utopia: The Overburdened Polity of Israel* (Hebrew version). Tel Aviv: Am Oved.

Horowitz, Donald. 1996. "Comparing Democratic Systems." In *The Global Resurgence of Democracy,* ed. Larry Diamond and Marc F. Plattner. Baltimore: Johns Hopkins University Press.

Hoskyns, Catherine. 1996. *Integrating Gender: Women, Law and Politics in the European Union.* London: Verso.

Hossain, Sara, Shahdeen Malik, and Bushra Musa, eds. 1997. *Public Interest Litigation in South Asia: Rights in Search of Remedies.* Dhaka: University Press Ltd.

Huber, Konrad C. 1993. "The CSCE and Ethnic Conflict in the East." *RFE/RL Research Report* 2, 31: 30–36.

Hughes, Christopher. 1995. China and Liberalism Globalised. *Millennium* 24: 425–45.

Human Rights Watch. 1997. *Russian Federation: A Review of the Compliance of the Russian Federation with Council of Europe Commitments and Other Human Rights.* Human Rights Watch/Helsinki Report 9 (3) D. New York: Human Rights Watch.

———. 1998. *Human Rights Watch World Report 1998.* New York: Human Rights Watch.

———. 2000a. *Burmese Refugees in Thailand at Risk* <hrwatchnyc@igc.org>, May 8.

———. 2000b. *Silencing of Dissent* <hrwatchnyc@igc.org> May 3.

Huntington, Samuel P. 1991. *The Third Wave: Democratization in the Late Twentieth Century.* Norman: University of Oklahoma Press.

———. 1994. "Democracy and/or Economic Reform." In *The Bold Experiment: South Africa's New Democracy,* ed. Hermann Buhr Giliomee, Lawrence Schlemmer, and Sarita Hauptfleisch. Halfway House: Southern Book Publishers.

———. 1996. *The Clash of Civilizations and the Remaking of World Order.* New York: Simon and Schuster.

Hurrell, Andrew and Ngaire Woods. 1995. "Globalisation and Inequality." *Millennium* 24: 447–70.

Ibrahim, Saad Eddin. 1996. "Political Culture and Development in Modern Egypt." In *Development in the Age of Liberalism: Egypt and Mexico,* ed. Don Tschirgi. Cairo: American University in Cairo Press.

Ignatieff, Michael. 2001. *Human Rights as Politics and Idolatry.* Princeton, N.J.: Princeton University Press.

Independent International Commission on Kosovo. 2000. *The Kosovo Report: Conflict, International Response, Lessons Learned.* New York: Oxford University Press.

Inglehart, Ronald. 1997. *Modernization and Postmodernization: Cultural, Economic, and Political Change in 43 Societies.* Princeton, N.J.: Princeton University Press.

International Commission on Intervention and State Sovereignty. 2001. *The Responsibility to Protect.* <www.iciss-ciise.gc.ca/report-e.asp>.

Jiryia, Sabri. 1969. *The Arabs of Israel.* Beirut: Institute of Palestine Studies.

Kabemba, Claude. 1999. "Whither the DRC? Causes of the Conflict in the Democratic Republic of the Congo." *Policy: Issues and Actors* 12, 1.

Kabir, Humayun. 1998. "Minorities in a Democracy." In *Liberal Islam: A Sourcebook,* ed. Charles Kurzman. New York: Oxford University Press.

Kaiser, Robert J. 1994. *The Geography of Nationalism in Russia and the USSR.* Princeton, N.J.: Princeton University Press.

Kakar, Sudhir. 1995. *The Colours of Violence.* New Delhi: Penguin.

Kant, Immanuel. 1970. "Perpetual Peace: A Philosophical Essay." In *The Theory of International Relations,* ed. M. G. Forsyth and others. New York: Atherton. 200–244.

———. 1983. *Perpetual Peace and Other Essays.* Indianapolis: Hackett.

Kaplan, Robert D. 2000. *The Coming Anarchy: Shattering the Dreams of the Post Cold War.* New York: Random House.

Karatnycky, Adrian. 2002. "The 2001 Freedom House Survey." *Journal of Democracy* 13 (January).

Kausikan, Bilihari. 1994. "Human Rights: Asia's Different Standard." *Media Asia* 21, 1 (Singapore): 49.

Keck, Margaret E. and Kathryn Sikkink. 1998. *Activists Beyond Borders: Advocacy Networks in International Politics.* Ithaca, N.Y.: Cornell University Press.

Kedar, Alexandre. 2000. "A First Step in a Difficult and Sensitive Road." *Israel Studies Bulletin* 16, 1: 3–11.

Kelly, David and Anthony Reid, eds. 1998. *Asian Freedoms: The Idea of Freedom in East and Southeast Asia.* New York: Cambridge University Press.

Keohane, Robert O. and Lisa L. Martin. 1995. "The Promise of Institutionalist Theory." *International Security* 20: 39–51.

Kim, Dae Jung. 1994. "A Response to Lee Kuan Yew: Is Culture Destiny? The Myth of Asia's Anti-Democratic Values." *Foreign Affairs* (November–December): 189–94.

Kim, Samuel. 2000. In *What If China Does Not Democratize? Implications for War and Peace,* ed. Edward Friedman and Barrett McCormick. Armonk, N.Y.: M.E. Sharpe.

Kimmerling, Baruch. 1994. "Religion, Nationalism, and Democracy in Israel." *Zmaniun* 50–51, 116–31.

King, Gary, Robert O. Keohane, and Sidney Verba. 1994. *Designing Social Inquiry.* Princeton, N.J.: Princeton University Press.

Kling, Merle. 1967. "Violence and Politics in Latin America." *Sociological Review* 2: 119–32.

Koch, Koen. 1993. "The International Community and Forms of Intervention in the Field of Minority Rights Protection." In *Minorities: The New Europe's Old Issue,* ed. Ian Cuthbertson and Jane Leibowitz. Prague: Institute for East-West Studies.

Kochanek, Stanley A. 1996. "The Rise of Interest Politics in Bangladesh." *Asian Survey* 36 (July): 704–22.

Kolodziej, Edward A. 2000. "The Great Powers and Genocide: Lessons from Rwanda." *Pacifica Review* 12 (June): 121–45.

Korey, William. 1994. "Minority Rights After Helsinki." *Ethics and International Affairs* 8: 119–41.

Kornai, János. 1992. *The Socialist System: The Political Economy of Communism.* Princeton, N.J.: Princeton University Press.

Koskenniemi, Martti. 1999. "The Effect of Rights on Political Culture." In *The EU and Human Rights,* ed. Philip Alston with Mara Bustelo and James Heenan. Oxford: Oxford University Press.

Kretzmer, David. 1990. *The Legal Status of the Arabs in Israel.* Boulder, Colo.: Westview Press.

———. 1992. "The New Basic Laws on Human Rights: A Mini Revolution in Israeli Constitutional Law?" *Israel Law Review* 26.

Kritz, Michael. 1993. "The CSCE in the New Era." *Journal of Democracy* 4 (July): 19.

Kuper, Richard. 1998. *The Politics of the European Court of Justice.* London: Kogan Page.

Kuran, Timur. 1991. "Now Out of Never: The Element of Surprise in the East European Revolution of 1989." *World Politics* 44: 7–48.

———. 1995. *Private Truths, Public Lies: The Social Consequences of Preference Falsification.* Cambridge, Mass.: Harvard University Press.

Kymlicka, Will. 1995. *Multicultural Citizenship: A Liberal Theory of Minority Rights.* Oxford: Clarendon Press.

Kynge, James. 2000. "Nervous Beijing Gags Increasingly Vocal Media." *Financial Times,* April 8–9.

Laberge, Pierre. 1995. "Humanitarian Intervention: Three Ethical Positions." *Ethics and International Affairs* 9: 15–35.

Lahav, Pnina. 2000. "Up Against the Wall." *Israel Studies Bulletin* 16, 1: 19–22.

Landau, Jacob. 1993. *The Arab Minority in Israel, 1967–1991* (in Hebrew). Tel Aviv: Am Oved.

Lawrence, Susan. 1998. "False Dawn." Interview with Liu Ji. *Far Eastern Economic Review* (October 1): 28.

Leben, Charles. 1999. "Is There a European Approach to Human Rights?" In *The*

EU and Human Rights, ed. Philip Alston with Mara Bustelo and James Heenan. Oxford: Oxford University Press.

Leonard, Irving A. 1963. "Science, Technology, and Hispanic America." *Michigan Quarterly Review* 2 (October): 237–45.

Lewis, Peter. 1994. "Endgame in Nigeria." *African Affairs* 93.

———. 1996. "From Prebendalism to Predation." *Journal of Modern African Studies* 34, 1.

Leysens, Anthony. 1998. "The Political Economy of SADC: Challenges and Problems." Paper Presented to Conference on Society, Politics, and Economics in Africa, April 20–21, Catholic University of Argentina, Buenos Aires.

Li, Bian. 2000. "How Is Russia After Yeltsin?" *Beijing Review* (January 17): 8–9.

Lieberman, Evan. 1997. "Organizational Cloaking in Southern Africa." *Transformation* 34.

Lijphart, Arend. 1996. "Constitutional Choices for New Democracies." In *The Global Resurgence of Democracy*, ed. Larry Diamond and Marc F. Plattner. Baltimore: Johns Hopkins University Press.

Lipschutz, Ronnie D. 1996. *Global Civil Society and Global Environmental Governance: The Politics of Nature from Place to Planet*. Albany: State University of New York Press.

Liu, Junning. 1998. "What Are Asian Values?" In *The Chinese Human Rights Reader*, ed. Stephen Angle and Marina Svensson. Armonk, N.Y.: M.E. Sharpe.

Lundler, Mark. 2000. "Stakes in China Suddenly Seem Less Appealing." *New York Times*, March 31, B1, B4.

Lustick, Ian. 1979. "Stability in Deeply Divided Societies." *World Politics* 31 (April): 325–44.

———. 1980. *Arabs in the Jewish State: Israel's Control of a National Minority*. Austin: University of Texas Press.

———. 1989. "The Political Road to Binationalism." In *The Emergence of a Binational Israel*, ed. Ilan Peleg and Ofira Seliktar. Boulder, Colo.: Westview Press. 97–123.

Mahbubani, Kishore. 1993. "An Asian Perspective on Human Rights and Freedom of the Press." *Asian Mass Communication Quarterly* 20, 3 (Singapore): 159.

Mahmoud, Mohamed. 1998. "Mahmud Muhammad Taha's Second Message of Islam and his Modernist Project." In *Islam and Modernity: Muslim Intellectuals Respond*, ed. John Cooper, Ronald L. Nettler, and Mohamed Mahmoud. London: I.B. Tauris.

Mahmud, Tayyab. 1995. "Protecting Religious Minorities: The Courts' Abdication." In *Pakistan 1995*, ed. Charles H. Kennedy and Rasu Bakhsh Rais. Boulder, Colo.: Westview Press. 83–101.

Maine, Sir Henry S. 1886. *Popular Government*. New York: Henry Holt.

Malan, Mark. 1998. Regional Power Politics Under Cover of SADC: Running Amok with a Mythical Organ. ISS Paper 35. Halfway House: Institute for Security Studies, October.

Maluka, Zulfikar Khalid. 1995. *The Myth of Constitutionalism in Pakistan*. Karachi: Oxford University Press.

Manes, Jean E. 1996. "The Council of Europe's Democracy Ideal." In *Preventing Conflict in the Post-Communist World: Mobilizing International and Regional Organizations*, ed. Abram Chayes and Antonia Chayes. Washington, D.C.: Brookings Institution Press. 125–27.

Mansbridge, Jane. 1996. "Using Power/Fighting Power: The Polity." In *Democracy and Difference: Contesting the Boundaries of the Political*, ed. Seyla Benhabib. Princeton, N.J.: Princeton University Press. 46–66.

Marks, Stephen P. 1981. "Emerging Human Rights: A New Generation for the 1980s?" *Rutgers Law Review* 33: 435–52.

Marlay, Ross and Bryan Ulmer. 2000. "Human Rights in Burma." Association for Asian Studies Conference Paper, San Diego, California, March 10.

Martz, John. 1966. "The Place of Latin America in the Study of Comparative Politics." *Journal of Politics* 28 (February): 57–80.

Marx, Karl. 1970. *A Contribution to the Critique of Political Economy.* Moscow: Progress.

Masina, Nomonde. 2000. "Xhosa Practices of Ubuntu in South Africa." In *Traditional Cures for Modern Conflicts: African Conflict "Medicine"*, ed. I. William Zartman. Boulder, Colo.: Lynne Rienner.

Mattes, Robert and Hermann Thiel. 1999. "Public Opinion and Consolidation in South Africa." In *Democratization in Africa*, ed. Larry Diamond and Marc F. Plattner. Baltimore: Johns Hopkins University Press. 123–39.

Mattes, Robert, Yul Derek Davids, and Cherrel Africa. 2000. *Views of Democracy in South Africa and the Region.* Afrobarometer Series 2. Cape Town: Idasa; East Lansing: Michigan State University Department of Political Science.

Mayall, James. 1990. *Nationalism and International Society.* Cambridge: Cambridge University Press.

——. 1992. "Nationalism and International Security After the Cold War." *Survival* 34: 19–35.

Mayer, Ann Elizabeth. 1991. *Islam and Human Rights: Tradition and Politics.* Boulder, Colo.: Westview Press.

——. 1995. "Rhetorical Strategies and Official Policies on Women's Rights: The Merits and Drawbacks of the New World Hypocrisy." In *Faith and Freedom: Women's Human Rights in the Muslim World*, ed. Mahnaz Afkhami. Syracuse, N.Y.: Syracuse University Press.

McAlister, Lyle W. 1984. *Spain and Portugal in the New World, 1492–1700.* Minneapolis: University of Minnesota Press.

McFaul, Michael. 1995. "State Power, Institutional Change, and the Politics of Privatization in Russia." *World Politics* 47, 2: 210–43.

McKay, Angus. 1977. *Spain in the Middle Ages: From Frontier to Empire, 1000–1500.* London: Macmillan.

McNeill, William H. 1992. *The Global Condition: Conquerors, Catastrophes, and Community.* Princeton, N.J.: Princeton University Press.

Medding, Peter. 1990. *The Founding of Israeli Democracy, 1949–1967.* Oxford: Oxford University Press.

Mendelson, Sarah E. 2000. "The Putin Path: Civil Liberties and Human Rights in Retreat." *Problems of Post-Communism* 47, 5: 3–12.

Mernissi, Fatima. 1991. *The Veil and the Male Elite: A Feminist Interpretation of Women's Rights in Islam.* Trans. Mary Jo Lakeland. Reading, Mass.: Addison-Wesley.

Mihailovskaia, Inga B. 1995. "Constitutional Rights in Russian Public Opinion." *East European Constitutional Review* 4, 1: 70–76.

Miles, G. L. 1995. "Crime, Corruption, and Multinational Business." *International Business* (July): 34–45.

Mir-Hosseini, Ziba. 1993. *Marriage on Trial: A Study of Islamic Family Law—Iran and Morocco Compared.* London: I.B. Tauris.

Mitra, Subrata K. and R. Alison Lewis, eds. 1996. *Subnational Moments in South Asia.* Boulder, Colo.: Westview Press.

Mommsen, Wolfgang J. 1989. *The Political and Social Theory of Max Weber.* Chicago: University of Chicago Press.

Morgenthau, Hans J. 1985. *Politics Among Nations: The Struggle for Power and Peace.* New York: Alfred A. Knopf.

Morley, James, ed. 1999. *Driven by Growth: Political Change in the Asia-Pacific Region.* Armonk, N.Y.: M.E. Sharpe.

Morse, Richard M. 1964. "The Heritage of Latin America." In *The Founding of New Societies: Studies in the History of the United States, Latin America, South Africa, Canada, and Australia*, ed. Louis Hartz. New York: Harcourt, Brace.

Mott, Margaret MacLeish. 2000. "The Divine Rights of the People: Democracy in the Catholic South." In *Comparative Democracy and Democratization*, ed. Howard J. Wiarda. Fort Worth, Tex.: Harcourt Brace.

Munro, Robin. 2001. "China's Judicial Psychiatry." *Asian Wall Street Journal*, February 19.

Myers, David J., ed. 1991. *Regional Hegemons: Threat Perception and Strategic Response*. Boulder, Colo.: Westview Press.

Nardin, Terry. 1983. *Law, Morality, and the Relations of States*. Princeton, N.J.: Princeton University Press.

Needler, Martin C. 1964. *Anatomy of a Coup d'État: Ecuador, 1963*. Washington, D.C.: Institute for the Comparative Study of Political Systems.

Negbi, Moshe. 1987. *Above the Law: The Crisis of the Role of Law in Israel* (in Hebrew). Tel Aviv: Am Oved.

Nelton, Sharon. 1996. "Promoting a World Ethical Standard." *Nation's Business* 84, 4: 12.

Nemtsov, Boris. 2000. "The Right to Democratic Self-Defense." *The Day*, no. 8, March 14.

Nettler, Ronald L. 1998. "Mohamed Talbi's Ideas on Islam and Politics." In *Islam and Modernity: Muslim Intellectuals Respond*, ed. John Cooper, Ronald L. Nettler, and Mohamed Mahmoud. London: I.B. Tauris.

Newman, Michael. 1996. *Democracy, Sovereignty, and the European Union*. London: Hurst.

Ninh, Kim. 1998. "Vietnam." In *Asian Security Practice: Material and Ideational Influences*, ed. Muthiah Alagappa. Stanford, Calif.: Stanford University Press.

Noll, Gregor and Jens Vedsted-Hansen. 1999. "Non-Communitarians: Refugee and Asylum Policies." In *The EU and Human Rights*, ed. Philip Alston with Mara Bustelo and James Heenan. Oxford: Oxford University Press.

North, Douglass C. 1990. *Institutions, Institutional Change, and Economic Performance*. Cambridge: Cambridge University Press.

Nowak, Manfred. 1999. "Human Rights 'Conditionality' in Relation to Entry to, and Full Participation in, the EU." In *The EU and Human Rights*, ed. Philip Alston with Mara Bustelo and James Heenan. Oxford: Oxford University Press.

Obasanjo, Olusegun and Akin Mabogunje, eds. 1991. *Elements of Development*. The Kampala Conference. Ogun: Africa Leadership Forum Publications.

O'Donnell, Guillermo. 1973. *Modernization and Bureaucratic Authoritarianism*. Berkeley: Institute of International Studies, University of California.

———. 1996. "Do Economists Know Best?" In *The Global Resurgence of Democracy*, ed. Larry Diamond and Marc F. Plattner. Baltimore: Johns Hopkins University Press.

———. 1998. "Horizontal Accountability in New Democracies." *Journal of Democracy* 5, 1: 122–26.

O'Donnell, Guillermo and Philippe C. Schmitter. 1986. *Tentative Conclusions About Uncertain Democracies*. Vol. 4 of *Transitions from Authoritarian Rule*, ed. Guillermo O'Donnell, Philippe C. Schmitter, and Laurence Whitehead. Baltimore: Johns Hopkins University Press.

Olson, Mancur. 1982. *The Rise and Decline of Nations: Economic Growth, Stagflation, and Social Rigidities*. New Haven, Conn.: Yale University Press.

Onimode, Bade. 1988. *The Political Economy of the African Crisis*. London: Zed Books.

Osaghae, Eghosa E. 1998. *Crippled Giant: Nigeria Since Independence*. Bloomington: Indiana University Press.

Ottaway, Marina, ed. 1997. *Democracy in Africa: The Hard Road Ahead.* Boulder, Colo.: Lynne Rienner.

Ozacky-Lazar, Sarah and Asad Ghanem. 1995. *Between Peace and Equality* (in Hebrew). Givet Haviva: Institute for the Study of Peace, January.

Parkes, Christopher. 2000. "Hollywood Changes Task and Gets in on the China Act." *Financial Times,* March 28.

Peled, Yoav. 1992 "Ethnic Democracy and the Legal Construction of Citizenship: Arab Citizens of the Jewish State." *American Political Science Review* 86 (June): 432–43.

Peleg, Ilan. 1994a. "Otherness and Israel's Arab Dilemma." In *The Other in Jewish Thought and History,* ed. Laurence J. Silberstein and Robert L. Cohn. New York: New York University Press. Chap. 11, 258–80.

——. 1994b. "The Arab-Israeli Conflict and the Victory of Otherness." In *Critical Essays on Israeli Social Issues and Scholars,* ed. Russell A. Stone and Walter P. Zenner. Books on Israel 3. Albany: State University of New York Press. 227–43.

——. 1995. *Human Rights in the West Bank Gaza: Legacy and Politics.* Syracuse, N.Y.: Syracuse University Press.

——. 1998. "Israel's Constitutional Order and Kulturkampf: The Role of Ben-Gurion." *Israel Studies* 3, 1: 237–61.

——. 2001. "Culture, Ethnicity and Human Rights in Contemporary Biethnic Democracies." In *Negotiating Culture and Human Rights,* ed. Lynda Bell, Andrew Nathan, and Ilan Peleg. New York: Columbia University Press. 303–33.

Peloso, Vincent C. and Barbara A. Tenenbaum, eds. 1996. *Liberals, Politics, and Power: State Formation in Nineteenth-Century Latin America.* Athens: University of Georgia Press.

Perlez, Jane. 2001. "U.S. Is Set to Assail China on Rights at U.N." *New York Times,* February 17.

Perrault, Gilles. 1990. *Notre ami, le roi.* Paris: Gallimard.

Peta, Basiblou. 2002. "Reform Plan in Tatters as Farms Re-Seized." *Sunday Independent* (Johannesburg), October 27.

Petrova, Dimitrina. 1996. "Political and Legal Obstacles to the Development of Public Interest Law." *East European Constitutional Review* 5, 4: 62–72.

Piano, Aili and Arch Puddington. 2001. "The 2000 Freedom House Survey." *Journal of Democracy* 12, 1 (January).

Pike, Frederick. 1971. *Hispanismo, 1898–1936: Spanish Conservatives and Liberals and Their Relation with Latin America.* Notre Dame, Ind.: University of Notre Dame Press.

Pollis, Adamantia and Peter Schwab. 1979. "Introduction." In *Human Rights: Cultural and Ideological Perspectives,* ed. Adamantia Pollis and Peter Schwab. New York: Praeger.

Pomfret, John. 2000. "N. Korean Refugees Insecure in China." *Washington Post,* February 19.

Post, Gaines. 1964. *Studies in Medieval Legal Thought.* Princeton, N.J.: Princeton University Press.

Przeworski, Adam, Michael Alvarez, Jose Antonio Cheibub, and Fernando Limongi. 1996. "What Makes Democracies Endure?" *Journal of Democracy* 7 (January).

Rahman, Fazlur. 1982. *Islam and Modernity: Transformation of an Intellectual Tradition.* Chicago: University of Chicago Press.

Randel, Judith, Tony German, and Deborah Ewing. 2000. *The Reality of Aid, 2000: An Independent Review of Poverty Reduction and Development Assistance.* London: Earthscan.

Rawls, John. 1971. *A Theory of Justice.* Cambridge, Mass.: Harvard University Press.

Risse-Kappen, Thomas. 1994. "Ideas Do Not Float Freely: Transnational Coalitions, Domestic Structures, and the End of the Cold War." *International Organization* 48: 185–214.

Rizvi, Hasan-Askari. 1999. "Pakistan in 1998: The Polity Under Pressure." *Asian Survey* 39 (January–February): 177–90.

Roberts, Hugh. 1995. "Algeria's Ruinous Impasse and the Honourable Way Out." *International Affairs* 71: 247–67.

Robertson, Roland. 1992. *Globalization: Social Theory and Global Culture.* London: Sage.

Rodó, José Enrique. 1988. *Ariel.* Austin: University of Texas Press.

Roling, B. V. A. 1960. *International Law in an Expanded World.* Amsterdam: Djambatan.

Rose, Richard, William Mischler, and Christian Haerpfer. 1998. *Democracy and Its Alternatives: Understanding Post-Communist Societies.* Baltimore: Johns Hopkins University Press.

Rosenberg, Tina. 1992. "Latin America's Magical Liberalism." *Washington Quarterly*: 58–74.

Rossiiskaya Gazeta. 1994. December, 7, 6. *Current Digest of the Post-Soviet Press* 46 (January 4, 1995): 8–9.

Rouhana, Nadim. 1999. *Palestinian Citizens in an Ethnic Jewish State.* New Haven, Conn.: Yale University Press.

Ruggie, John Gerard. 1998. "What Makes the World Hang Together? Neo-Utilitarianism and the Social Constructivist Challenge." *International Organization* 52: 855–85.

Sajó, András. 1997. "Universal Rights, Missionaries, Converts, and 'Local Savages.'" *East European Constitutional Review* 6 (Winter).

Sanguinetti, Antoine. 1991. *Le livre blanc sur les droits de l'homme au Maroc.* Paris: Etudes et Documentation Internationales.

Schwarzenberger, Georg. 1955. "The Standard of Civilization in International Law." *Current Legal Problems* 17: 212–34.

Sciarra, Silvana. 1999. "From Strasbourg to Amsterdam: Prospects for the Convergence of European Social Rights Policy." In *The EU and Human Rights*, ed. Philip Alston with Mara Bustelo and James Heenan. Oxford: Oxford University Press.

Searle, John R. 1995. *The Construction of Social Reality.* New York: Free Press.

Seddon, David. 1989. "Riot and Rebellion in North Africa: Political Responses to Economic Crisis in Tunisia." In *Power and Stability in the Middle East*, ed. Berch Berberoglu. London: Zed Books. 114–35.

Seki, Tomoda. 2000. "A Japan-India Front." *Far Eastern Economic Review* (May 25): 38.

Seminar 439. 1996. *Prisons and Punishment* (March).

Seminar 483. 1999. *Policespeak* (November).

Sen, Amartya Kumar. 1992. *Inequality Reexamined.* Cambridge, Mass.: Harvard University Press.

Shah, Prakash. 1997. "International Human Rights: A Perspective from India." *Fordham International Law Journal* 21 (November).

Shamir, Michal. 1988. "Political Tolerance and Leadership in the Israeli Society" (in Hebrew). In *Arabs' Rights* (in Hebrew), ed. Ann Swersky. Tel Aviv: ACRI. 94–108.

Shamir, Michal and John Sullivan. 1983. "The Political Context of Tolerance: The U.S. and Israel." *American Political Science Review* 73: 92–106.

Shapiro, Yonathan. 1996a. *Politicians as a Hegemonic Class: The Case of Israel* (in Hebrew). Tel Aviv.

———. 1996b. "Where Has Liberalism Disappeared in Israel?" *Zmanim* (Winter): 91–104.

Simma, Bruno, J. B. Aschenbrenner, and Constanze Schulte. 1999. *Human Rights*

Considerations in Development Cooperation Activities of the EC. Oxford: Oxford University Press.

Simon, Rita J. and Jean M. Landis. 1990. "Trends in Public Support for Civil Liberties and Due Process in Israeli Society." *Social Science Quarterly* 71 (Spring): 93–104.

Smith, Peter H., ed. 1995. *Latin America in Comparative Politics: New Approaches to Methods and Analysis.* Boulder, Colo.: Westview Press.

Smith, Tanya. 1994. "The Violation of Basic Rights in Russia." *East European Constitutional Review* (Fall): 42–47.

Smooha, Sami. 1990. "Minority Status in an Ethnic Democracy." *Ethnic and Racial Studies* 13, 3: 389–413.

———. 1993. "National, Ethnic and Class Cleavages, and Israel's Democracy." In *The Israeli Society: Critical Perspectives* (in Hebrew), ed. Uri Ram. Tel Aviv: Breirot.

Sontag, Deborah. 2000. "Israel Is Slowly Shedding Harsh Treatment of Arabs." *New York Times*, April 7, A1, A12.

Souhaili, Mohammed. 1986. *Les damnés du royaume: le drame des libertés au Maroc.* Paris: Etudes et Documentation Internationales.

Spencer, Claire. 1994. "Algeria in Crisis." *Survival* 36: 149–63.

Sperling, Valerie. 1999. *Organizing Women in Contemporary Russia: Engendering Transition.* Cambridge: Cambridge University Press.

Sripati, Vijayashri. 1997. "Human Rights in India: Fifty Years After Independence." *Denver Journal of International Law and Policy* 26, 1 (Fall): 93–136.

Steinberg, Gerald M. 2000. "The Poor in Your Own City Shall Have Precedence." *Israel Studies Bulletin* 16, 1: 12–18.

Stephens, Philip. 2000. "Tony Blair's Intolerant Island." *Financial Times*, April 7.

Sternhell, Zeev. 1995. *Nation Building or Model Society* (in Hebrew). Tel Aviv.

Stiglitz, Joseph E. 2002. *Globalization and Its Discontents.* New York: Norton.

Stoetzer, Carlos O. 1982. *The Scholastic Roots of the Spanish-American Revolution.* New York: Fordham University Press.

Strum, Philippa. 1995. "The Road Not Taken: Constitutional Non-Decision Making in 1948–1950." In *Israel: The First Decade of Independence*, ed. S. Ilan Troen and Noah Lucas. SUNY Series in Israeli Studies. Albany: State University of New York Press. 83–104.

Svensson, Marina. 1996. "The Chinese Conception of Human Rights: The Debate on Human Rights in China, 1898–1949." Dissertation, Department of East Asian Languages, Lund University.

Talbi, Mohamed. 1998. "Religious Liberty." In *Liberal Islam: A Sourcebook*, ed. Charles Kurzman. New York: Oxford University Press.

Thomas, Daniel C. 1995. "Engaging Influence: The Transnational Helsinki Network and the Rise of Human Rights in U.S. Policy Toward Eastern Europe, 1975–1979." Paper presented at the annual meeting of the American Political Science Association, Chicago, September.

Tibi, Bassam. 1998. *The Challenge of Fundamentalism: Political Islam and the New World Disorder.* Berkeley: University of California Press.

Tönnies, Ferdinand. 1957. *Community and Society.* New York: Harper.

Toumi, Mohsen. 1989. *La Tunisie de Bourguiba à Ben Ali.* Paris: PUF.

Tyan, E. 1999. "Bay'a." *Encyclopaedia of Islam.* CD-ROM edition v. 1.0. Leiden: Koninklijke Brill NV.

Udagama, Deepika. 1998. "Taming of the Beast: Judicial Responses to State Violence in Sri Lanka." *Harvard Human Rights Journal* 11 (Spring): 269–94.

Van Cott, Donna Lee, ed. 1994. *Indigenous Peoples and Democracy in Latin America.* New York: St. Martin's Press.

Van Creveld, Martin. 1999. *The Rise and Decline of the State.* Cambridge: Cambridge University Press.

Vandewalle, Dirk J. 1998. *Libya Since Independence: Oil and State-Building.* Ithaca, N.Y.: Cornell University Press.

Vasak, Karel. 1984. "Pour une troisième génération des droits de l'homme." In *Studies and Essays on International Humanitarian Law and Red Cross Principles in Honour of Jean Pictet*, ed. Christophe Swinarski. The Hague: Martinus Nijhoff.

———. 1991. "Les différentes catégories des droits de l'homme." In *Les dimensions universelles des droits de l'homme*, ed. A. Lapeyre, F. de Tinguy, and Karel Vasak. Bruxelles: Émile Bruylant.

Vaughan-Roberts, S. 1997. *Women, Citizenship, and the EU: Knocking on Europe's Door.* London: University of North London Press.

Vernon, Raymond. 1971. *Sovereignty at Bay: The Multinational Spread of U.S. Enterprises.* New York: Basic Books.

Wallerstein, Immanuel. 1966. *Africa: The Politics of Unity.* New York: Random House.

Waltz, Kenneth N. 1979. *Theory of International Politics.* Reading, Mass.: Addison-Wesley.

Waltz, Susan E. 1995. *Human Rights and Reform: Changing the Face of North African Politics.* Berkeley: University of California Press.

Waters, Malcolm. 1995. *Globalisation.* London: Routledge.

Weatherly, Robert. 1999. *The Discourse of Human Rights in China.* New York: Macmillan.

———. 1999–2000. "Challenging State Orthodoxy: New Academic Thinking on Human Rights." *China Rights Forum* (Winter): 28–33.

Weber, Max. 1949. *On the Methodology of the Social Sciences.* Glencoe, Ill.: Free Press.

———. 1958a. *From Max Weber: Essays in Sociology.* New York: Galaxy Books.

———. 1958b. *The Protestant Ethic and the Spirit of Capitalism.* New York: Scribner.

———. 1968. *Economy and Society.* Berkeley: University of California Press.

Wendt, Alexander. 1992. "Anarchy Is What States Make Out of It: The Social Construction of Power Politics." *International Organization* 46: 391–425.

Wheeler, Nick. 2000. *Saving Strangers: Humanitarian Intervention in International Society.* Oxford: Oxford University Press.

Whiting, Allen S. 1989. *China Eyes Japan.* Berkeley: University of California Press.

Wiarda, Howard J. 1979. *Critical Elections and Critical Coups: State, Society, and the Military in the Processes of Latin American Development.* Athens: Ohio University Center for International Studies.

———. 1990. *The Democratic Revolution in Latin America: History, Politics, and U.S. Policy.* New York: Holmes and Meier for the Twentieth Century Fund.

———. 1996. *American Foreign Policy: Actors and Processes.* New York: HarperCollins.

———. 1997. *Cracks in the Consensus: Debating the Democracy Agenda in U.S. Foreign Policy.* Westport, Conn.: Praeger.

———. 2001. *The Soul of Latin America: The Cultural and Political Tradition.* New Haven, Conn.: Yale University Press.

Wiarda, Howard J. and Harvey F. Kline. 2002. *Latin American Politics and Development.* 5th ed. Boulder, Colo.: Westview Press.

Wiarda, Howard J. and Margaret MacLeish Mott. 2000. *Catholic Roots and Democratic Flowers: The Political Systems of Spain and Portugal.* Westport, Conn.: Greenwood Press.

Wight, Martin. 1992. *International Theory: The Three Traditions.* New York: Holmes and Meier for the Royal Institute of International Affairs.

Wilkinson, John C. 1987. *The Imamate Tradition of Oman.* Cambridge: Cambridge University Press.

Wilson, A. Jeyaratnam. 1993. "The Politics of Ethnicity and Ethno-Nationalism in South Asia." *Contemporary South Asia* 2, 3: 327–33.

Woodward, Ralph Lee, Jr., ed. 1971. *Positivism in Latin America, 1850–1900.* Lexington, Mass.: D.C. Heath.

Xiao, Gongqin. 2000. "Nationalism and Ideological Polarization at the Turn of the Century." *China Affairs* 1, 1 (Spring): 97, 98.

Yanai, Nathan. 1989. "Ben-Gurion's Concept of Mamlachtiut." *Jewish Political Studies Review* 1, 1–2.

Yiftachel, Oren. 1992. "The Ethnic Democracy Model." *Ethnic and Racial Studies* 15: 125–37.

———. 1997. *Watching over the Vineyard* (in Hebrew). Ra'anana: Institute for Israeli Arab Studies.

———. 1998. "Democracy of Ethnocracy?" *Middle East Report* (Summer): 8–13.

Young, Stephen. 2000. "China Holds the Indochina Key." *Far Eastern Economic Review* (June 6): 24.

Zakaria, Fareed. 1997. "The Rise of Illiberal Democracy." *Foreign Affairs* 76 (November–December): 22–43.

Zartman, I. William. 1982. *The Political Economy of Nigeria.* New York: Praeger.

———, ed. 1997. *Governance as Conflict Management.* Washington, D.C.: Brookings Institution

Zhong, Shukong. 2000. "NATO a Human Rights Violator." *China Daily,* March 30.

Zhu, Xueqin. "Two Spiritual 'Foci of Infection' Since the May Fourth Movement." *China Affairs* 1, 1 (Spring): 107, 108.

Contributors

Badredine Arfi is a visiting assistant professor at the University of Illinois at Urbana-Champaign. He received a Ph.D. in theoretical physics from the University of Illinois in 1988 and a Ph.D. in political science with specialties in the fields of international relations, international security, and comparative politics also from the University of Illinois in 1996.

Jack Donnelly is Andrew W. Mellon Professor with the Graduate School of International Studies at the University of Denver. He has published six books and nearly fifty journal articles and book chapters, most dealing with the theory and practice of internationally recognized human rights.

Edward Friedman is Professor of Political Science at the University of Wisconsin at Madison. His book *Chinese Village, Socialist State China* received the Association for Asian Studies Prize for best book on modern China.

Valerie J. Hoffman is Associate Professor of Religion at the University of Illinois at Urbana-Champaign. She is the author of *Sufism, Mystics, and Saints in Modern Egypt* and numerous articles.

Stanley A. Kochanek is Professor Emeritus of Political Science at Pennsylvania State University. He specializes in comparative politics, international relations, and South Asian political systems. His latest volume is *India: Government and Politics in a Developing Nation* with Robert L. Hardgrave, Jr.

Edward A. Kolodziej is Research Professor Emeritus of Political Science and Director of the Office of Global Studies at the University of Illinois at Urbana-Champaign. He has written or edited thirteen books on security and foreign policy. He has also contributed more than 100 articles to professional journals.

Carol Skalnik Leff is Associate Professor of Political Science at the University of Illinois at Urbana-Champaign. She is the author of two books on Czechoslovakia, *National Conflict in Czechoslovakia: The Making and Remaking of a State, 1918–1987* and *The Czech and Slovak Republics: Nation vs. State*, as well as numerous articles on Russian and East European politics.

Anthony Leysens is a lecturer with the International Studies Program in the Department of Political Science at the University of Stellenbosch, South Africa. He is the editor of the *Political Economy of South Africa's Relations with the International Monetary Fund and the World Bank.*

Robert Mattes is Associate Professor in the Department of Political Studies at the University of Cape Town. He studies the evolution of democratic institutions in southern Africa.

Clark D. Neher is Professor of Political Science and Director of the Center for Southeast Asian Studies at Northern Illinois University. His books include *Democracy and Development in Southeast Asia* and *Patriots and Tyrants: Ten Asian Leaders,* both with Ross Marlay.

Michael Newman is Professor of Politics and Jean Monnet Professor of European Integration Studies and Director of the London European Research Centre at London Metropolitan University. He is the author of *Democracy, Sovereignty, and the European Union.*

Ilan Peleg is Charles A. Dana Professor of Government and Law at Lafayette College. His book *Human Rights in the West Bank and Gaza: Legacy and Politics* received the Choice Award.

Marvin G. Weinbaum is Professor Emeritus of Political Science at the University of Illinois at Urbana-Champaign and is currently a research analyst in the U.S. Department of State, specializing in Northern Tier and South Asian politics.

Howard J. Wiarda is a senior associate at the Center for Strategic and International Studies (CSIS) in Washington, D.C. and Leonard J. Horwitz Professor of Iberian and Latin American Studies at the University of Massachusetts at Amherst. His most recent books include *Non-Western Theories of Development* and *Corporatism and Comparative Politics.*

I. William Zartman is Jacob Blaustein Professor of International Organization and Conflict Resolution and Director of African Studies at the Johns Hopkins University School of Advanced International Studies in Washington, D.C. He has also written extensively on African politics and relations. His latest works are *Ripe for Resolution: Conflict and Intervention in Africa* and *The Politics of Trade Negotiations Between Africa and the European Economic Community.*

Index

Acknowledgments

This volume owes much to many people. Substantial financial support was received from the Ford Foundation, through a grant for interdisciplinary global studies, and from three units at the University of Illinois: International Programs and Studies, the College of Liberal Arts and Sciences, and the Department of Political Science. The editor and authors express their gratitude, respectively, to the heads of these units—Associate Provost Earl D. Kellogg, Dean Jesse G. Delia, and Professor Peter F. Nardulli.

The authors also deserve special thanks. Experts from different fields of study, some of whom had never met or interacted before, were asked to focus their knowledge on the global problem of human rights—some for the first time. All were required to subordinate their contributions to the success of the volume as a whole. That is much to ask of anyone, and they all responded to the challenge. Each of the chapters stands on its own, but each also adds to a whole greater than the sum of the parts. As the editor, I am in their debt for their patience and cooperation in meeting my many demands to shape their contributions in ways to enhance the volume's overall quality and impact. The authors were especially helpful in the eleventh hour by cutting their manuscripts to conform to the tight word limits set by the press, no easy demand to make, nor one easily executed given the high quality of the original papers in their full-blown form and the competing pull of other projects that needed attention.

All the contributors wish to express their appreciation to the press, notably Peter Agree, Alison A. Anderson, and their talented editorial staff, for perfecting the manuscript over the long and exacting review process. Two anonymous reviewers engaged by the press also helped immeasurably to improve the volume. We hope they agree that the final product was strengthened by their suggestions, although neither the editor nor the authors always followed their thoughtful advice.

Merrily Shaw was indispensable in editing and preparing the manuscript for publication through its several revisions. Mary Anderson made an equally significant contribution in typing seemingly endless chapter drafts and in consolidating the bibliography. Delinda Swanson provided timely help throughout the editing process in meeting deadlines. The Program in Arms Control, Disarmament, and International Security (ACDIS) provided valuable logistical support. The encouragement of Clifford Singer, the director, and the availability of ACDIS facilities and staff are deeply appreciated. Ms. Sheila Roberts was flawless in keeping track of the books and financial reports. Barbara Cohen, as she has on several previous occasions of collaboration, produced a reader friendly index. My wife Antje's careful editing spared the manuscript scores of mindless errors.

And last, but scarcely least, we thank our families and significant others for their support throughout this process.